CHILTON'S
REPAIR & TUNE-UP GUIDE
CHEVY S-10
GMC S-15
PICK-UPS   Deleted
1982-85

All two and four wheel drive models,
Gasoline and Diesel engines

Deleted

President LAWRENCE A. FORNASIERI
Vice President and General Manager JOHN P. KUSHNERICK
Executive Editor KERRY A. FREEMAN, S.A.E.
Senior Editor RICHARD J. RIVELE, S.A.E.
Editor TONY MOLLA, S.A.E.

CHILTON BOOK COMPANY
Radnor, Pennsylvania
19089

SAFETY NOTICE

Proper service and repair procedures are vital to the safe, reliable operation of all motor vehicles, as well as the personal safety of those performing repairs. This book outlines procedures for servicing and repairing vehicles using safe, effective methods. The procedures contain many NOTES, CAUTIONS and WARNINGS which should be followed along with standard safety procedures to eliminate the possibility of personal injury or improper service which could damage the vehicle or compromise its safety.

It is important to note that repair procedures and techniques, tools and parts for servicing motor vehicles, as well as the skill and experience of the individual performing the work vary widely. It is not possible to anticipate all of the conceivable ways or conditions under which vehicles may be serviced, or to provide cautions as to all of the possible hazards that may result. Standard and accepted safety precautions and equipment should be used when handling toxic or flammable fluids, and safety goggles or other protection should be used during cutting, grinding, chiseling, prying, or any other process that can cause material removal or projectiles.

Some procedures require the use of tools specially designed for a specific purpose. Before substituting another tool or procedure, you must be completely satisfied that neither your personal safety, nor the performance of the vehicle will be endangered.

Although information in this guide is based on industry sources and is as complete as possible at the time of publication, the possibility exists that the manufacturer made later changes which could not be included here. While striving for total accuracy, Chilton Book Company cannot assume responsibility for any errors, changes, or omissions that may occur in the compilation of this data.

PART NUMBERS

Part numbers listed in this reference are not recommendations by Chilton for any product by brand name. They are references that can be used with interchange manuals and aftermarket supplier catalogs to locate each brand supplier's discrete part number.

SPECIAL TOOLS

Special tools are recommended by the vehicle manufacturer to perform their specific job. Use has been kept to a minimum, but where absolutely necessary, are they referred to in the text by the part number of the tool manufacturer. These tools can be purchased, under the appropriate part number, from Kent-Moore Corp. Service Tool Division, or an equivalent tool can be purchased locally from a tool supplier or parts outlet. Before substituting any tool for the one recommended, read the SAFETY NOTICE at the top of this page.

ACKNOWLEDGMENTS

Chilton Book Company expresses appreciation to the Chevrolet Motor Division, General Motors Corporation, Detroit, Michigan 48202; and GMC Truck and Coach Division, General Motors Corporation, Pontiac, Michigan 48053 for their generous assistance.

Chilton's Repair & Tune-Up Guide: Chevy S-10 and GMC S-15 Pick-Ups 1982–85
ISBN 0-8019-7564-6 pbk.
Library of Congress Catalog Card No. 84-45486

CONTENTS

Quick Reference
Specifications For Your Vehicle

Fill in this chart with the most commonly used specifications for your vehicle. Specifications can be found in Chapters 1 through 3 or on the tune-up decal under the hood of the vehicle.

 ## Tune-Up

Firing Order_____

Spark Plugs:

    Type_____

    Gap (in.)_____

Torque (ft. lbs.)_____

Idle Speed (rpm)_____

Ignition Timing (°)_____

Vacuum or Electric Advance (Connected/Disconnected)_____

Valve Clearance (in.)

    Intake_____   **Exhaust**_____

Capacities

Engine Oil Type (API Rating)_____

    With Filter Change (qts)_____

    Without Filter Change (qts)_____

Cooling System (qts)_____

Manual Transmission (pts)_____

    Type_____

Automatic Transmission (pts)_____

    Type_____

Front Differential (pts)_____

    Type_____

Rear Differential (pts)_____

    Type_____

Transfer Case (pts)_____

    Type_____

FREQUENTLY REPLACED PARTS
Use these spaces to record the part numbers of frequently replaced parts.

PCV VALVE	**OIL FILTER**	**AIR FILTER**	**FUEL FILTER**
Type_____	Type_____	Type_____	Type_____
Part No._____	Part No._____	Part No._____	Part No._____

General Information and Maintenance

HOW TO USE THIS BOOK

This book is intended to serve as a guide for the tune-up, repair and maintenance of your truck. All of the operations apply to both Chevrolet and GMC trucks unless specified otherwise.

To use this book properly, each operation should be approached logically and the recommended procedures read thoroughly before beginning the work. Before attempting any repair operation, be sure that you understand exactly what is involved. Naturally, it is considerably easier if you have the necessary tools on hand and a clean place to work.

When reference is made in this book to the "right side" or "left side" of the truck, it should be understood that these positions are to be viewed from the front seat. Thus, the left side of the truck is always the driver's side, even when one is facing the truck, as when working on the engine.

Information in this book is based on factory sources. Special factory tools have been eliminated from repair procedures wherever possible, in order to substitute more readily available tools.

TOOLS AND EQUIPMENT

It would be impossible to catalog each tool that you would need to perform each or any operation in this book. It would also not be wise for the amateur to rush out and buy an expensive set of tools on the theory that he may need one of them at some time. The best approach is to proceed slowly, gathering together a good quality set of those tools that are used most frequently. Don't be misled by the low cost of bargain tools. Forged wrenches, 12 point sockets and fine tooth ratchets are by far preferable to their less expensive counterparts. As any good mechanic can tell you, there are few worse experiences than trying to work on your truck with bad tools. Your monetary savings will be far outweighed by frustration and mangled knuckles.

Begin accumulating those tools that are used most frequently. In addition to a basic assortment of screwdrivers and a pair of pliers, you will need the following tools for routine maintenance and tune-up jobs:
- Wrenches in inch and Metric sizes— sockets and combination open end/box wrenches, up to 1 inch
- A spark plug gap gauge/bending tool
- Feeler gauges
- Tachometer/dwell meter
- Timing light
- Grease gun
- Oil filter wrench

For some suspension and engine work, a torque wrench measuring in foot pounds will also be necessary.

Special Tools

Although a basic collection of hand tools is sufficient for the majority of service procedures in this guide, in a few cases special tools are necessary. Factory-approved tools are available from your dealer, or from:

Service Tool Division
Kent-Moore Corporation
1501 South Jackson Street
Jackson, Michigan 49203

SERVICING YOUR TRUCK SAFELY

It is virtually impossible to anticipate all of the hazards involved with automotive maintenance and service, but care and common sense will prevent most accidents.

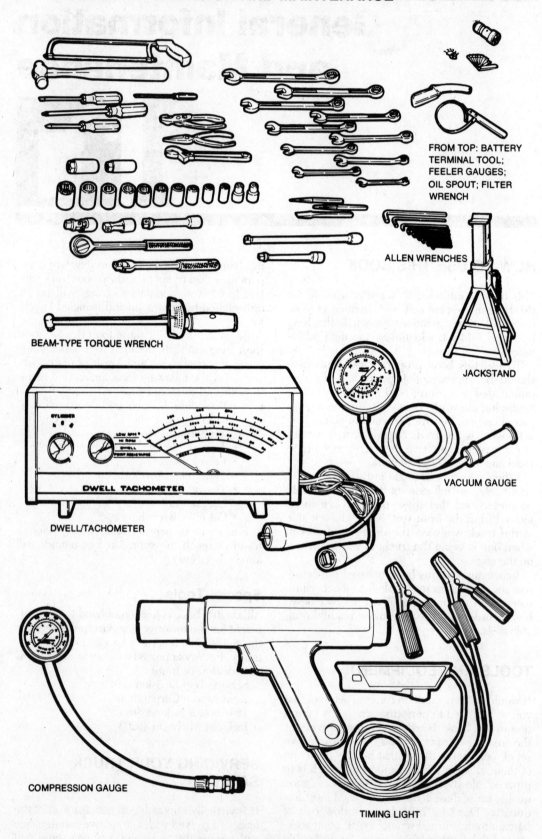

FROM TOP: BATTERY TERMINAL TOOL; FEELER GAUGES; OIL SPOUT; FILTER WRENCH

ALLEN WRENCHES

JACKSTAND

BEAM-TYPE TORQUE WRENCH

DWELL TACHOMETER

DWELL/TACHOMETER

VACUUM GAUGE

COMPRESSION GAUGE

TIMING LIGHT

You need only a basic assortment of hand tools and test instruments for most maintenance and repair jobs

The rules of safety for mechanics range from "don't smoke around gasoline," to "use the proper tool for the job." The trick to avoiding injuries is to develop safe work habits and take every possible precaution.

Dos

• Do keep a fire extinguisher and first aid kit within easy reach.

• Do wear safety glasses or goggles when cutting, drilling, grinding or prying. If you wear glasses for the sake of vision, they should be made of hardened glass that can serve also as safety glasses, or wear safety goggles over your regular glasses.

• Do shield your eyes whenever you work around the battery. Batteries contain sulphuric acid. In case of contact with the eyes or skin, flush the area with water or a mixture of water and baking soda and get medical attention immediately.

• Do use jack stands for any undercar service. Jacks are for raising vehicles; jack stands are for making sure the vehicle stays raised until you want it to come down. Whenever the truck is raised, block the wheels remaining on the ground and set the parking brake.

• Do use adequate ventilation when working with any chemicals or hazardous materials.

• Do disconnect the negative battery cable when working on the electrical system. The secondary ignition system can contain up to 40,000 volts.

• Do follow manufacturer's directions whenever working with potentially hazardous materials. Both brake fluid and antifreeze are poisonous if taken internally.

• Do properly maintain your tools. Loose hammerheads, mushroomed punches and chisels, frayed or poorly grounded electrical cords, excessively worn screwdrivers, spread wrenches, cracked sockets, slipping ratchets, or faulty droplight sockets can cause accidents.

Always use jackstands when working under the truck

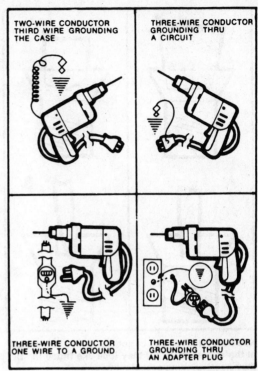

When using electrical tools, make sure they are properly grounded

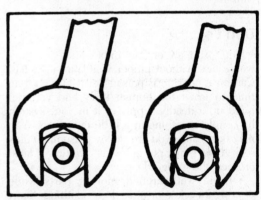

When using an open end wrench, make sure it is the correct size

• Do use the proper size and type of tool for the job being done.

• Do when possible, pull on a wrench handle rather than push on it, and adjust your stance to prevent a fall.

• Do be sure that adjustable wrenches are tightly closed on the nut or bolt and pulled so that the face is on the side of the fixed jaw.

• Do select a wrench or socket that fits the nut or bolt. The wrench or socket should sit straight, not cocked.

• Do strike squarely with a hammer; avoid glancing blows.

• Do set the parking brake and block the

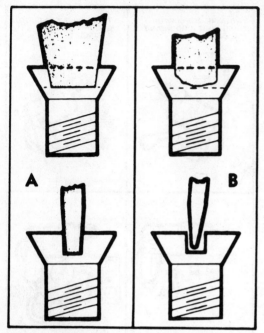

Keep screwdriver tips in good shape. They should fit the slot as in "A". If they look like those in "B", they need grinding or replacing

drive wheels if the work requires the engine running.

Don't's

• Don't run an engine in a garage or anywhere else without proper ventilation—EVER! Carbon monoxide is poisonous; it takes a long time to leave the human body and you can build up a deadly supply of it in your system by simply breathing in a little every day. You may not realize you are slowly poisoning yourself. Always use power vents, windows, fans, or open the garage doors.

• Don't work around moving parts while wearing a necktie or other loose clothing. Short sleeves are much safer than long, loose sleeves; hard-toed shoes with neoprene soles protect your toes and give a better grip on slippery surfaces. Jewelry such as rings, watches, fancy belt buckles, beads or body adornment of any kind is not safe working around a truck. Long hair should be hidden under a hat or cap.

• Don't use pockets for toolboxes. A fall or bump can drive a screwdriver deep into your body. Even a wiping cloth hanging from the back pocket can wrap around a spinning shaft or fan.

• Don't smoke when working around gasoline, cleaning solvent or other flammable material.

• Don't use compressed air to blow off brake dust, which is composed of asbestos. Breath-

ing asbestos particles is probably more dangerous than smoking around gasoline.

• Don't smoke when working around the battery. When the battery is being charged, it gives off explosive hydrogen gas.

• Don't use gasoline or kerosene to wash your hands; there are excellent soaps available. Gasoline may contain lead, and lead can enter the body through a cut, accumulating in the body until you are very ill. Gasoline also removes all the natural oils from the skin so that bone dry hands will suck up oil and grease.

• Don't service the air conditioning system unless you are equipped with the necessary tools and training. The refrigerant, R-12, is extremely cold when compressed, and when released into the air will instantly freeze any surface it contacts, including your eyes. Although the refrigerant is normally non-toxic, R-12 becomes a deadly poisonous gas in the presence of an open flame. One good whiff of the vapors from burning refrigerant can be fatal.

SERIAL NUMBER IDENTIFICATION

Vehicle

The Vehicle Identification Number (V.I.N.) is on a plate attached to the left hand top of the instrument panel, visible through the windshield. The gross vehicle weight (GVW), or maximum safe total weight of the truck, cargo, and passengers, is also given on the plate.

Engine
1950CC AND 2238CC DIESEL

The engine identification number is on a machined flat surface, on the lower left side of the block, near the flywheel end.

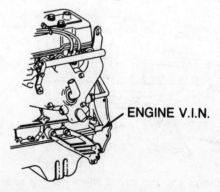

ENGINE V.I.N.

1950cc 4-cylinder engine and 2238cc diesel engine

1GCBS14A5D0123456

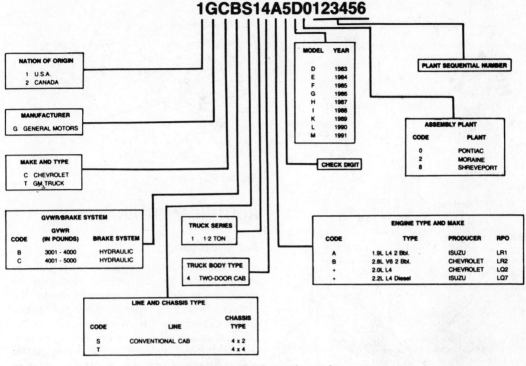

NATION OF ORIGIN

| 1 | U.S.A. |
| 2 | CANADA |

MANUFACTURER

| G | GENERAL MOTORS |

MAKE AND TYPE

| C | CHEVROLET |
| T | GM TRUCK |

GVWR/BRAKE SYSTEM

CODE	GVWR (IN POUNDS)	BRAKE SYSTEM
B	3001 - 4000	HYDRAULIC
C	4001 - 5000	HYDRAULIC

TRUCK SERIES

| 1 | 1/2 TON |

TRUCK BODY TYPE

| 4 | TWO-DOOR CAB |

LINE AND CHASSIS TYPE

CODE	LINE	CHASSIS TYPE
S	CONVENTIONAL CAB	4 x 2
T		4 x 4

MODEL YEAR

D	1983
E	1984
F	1985
G	1986
H	1987
K	1988
K	1989
L	1990
M	1991

CHECK DIGIT

PLANT SEQUENTIAL NUMBER

ASSEMBLY PLANT

CODE	PLANT
0	PONTIAC
2	MORAINE
8	SHREVEPORT

ENGINE TYPE AND MAKE

CODE	TYPE	PRODUCER	RPO
A	1.9L L4 2 Bbl.	ISUZU	LR1
B	2.8L V6 2 Bbl.	CHEVROLET	LR2
*	2.0L L4	CHEVROLET	LQ2
*	2.2L L4 Diesel	ISUZU	LQ7

Vehicle identification code numbers

Engine Identification Chart

No. of Cylinders Displacement in cc (Cu. in.)	Engine Manufacturer	Fuel System	Code
4-1950 (118.9)	Isuzu	2-bbl	A
4-2000 (121)	Chevrolet	2-bbl	Y
4-2238 (136.6)	Isuzu	Diesel	S
6-2800 (173)	Chevrolet	2-bbl	B

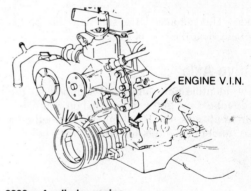

ENGINE V.I.N.

2200cc 4 cylinder engine

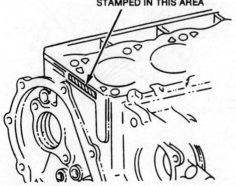

ENGINE IDENTIFICATION TO BE STAMPED IN THIS AREA

2000cc 4-cylinder engine

2000CC ENGINE

The engine identification number is stamped on a flat, machined surface, facing upward, on the left front of the engine block, just below the head.

2800CC ENGINE

The engine identification code is stamped on an upward facing, machined surface on the right front of the block, just below the head and above the water pump.

Transmission

The transmission identification number is stamped on the side of the case, usually the left

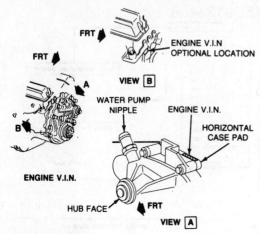

2800cc V6 engine

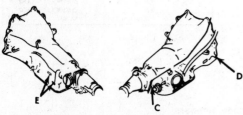

Typical transmission ID number locations

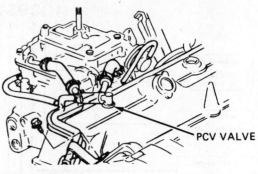

Typical PCV valve

side. The automatic transmission number is usually near the rear of the case.

Drive Axle

The identification number is stamped on the axle tube, next to the differential on rear axles. On front axles, the ID number is tamped on a tag, under one of the differential cover bolts.

ROUTINE MAINTENANCE

Air Cleaner

All engines utilize a replaceable, paper cartridge type air cleaner element. Remove the top of the air cleaner. Remove and discard the element. Install the new element and replace the air cleaner top. Chevrolet recommends that the element on all engines be checked at least once a year and replaced, at least every 30,000 miles. Frequent use in heavy traffic or under dusty conditions will require more frequent replacement intervals.

PCV Valve

The valve is located in the valve cover, connected to the intake manifold by a hose. At least every 15,000 miles, visually inspect the valve. Check for obvious signs of clogging or deposits. Shake the valve. It should rattle. With the valve removed from the valve cover, but still in the hose, start the engine. Place a finger over the

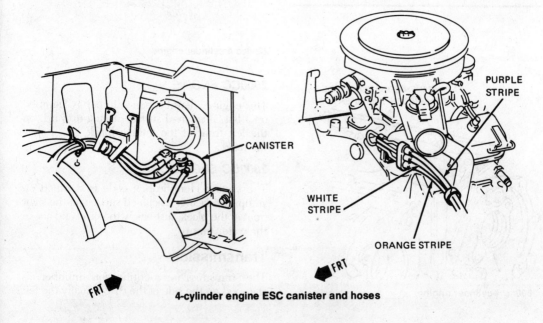

4-cylinder engine ESC canister and hoses

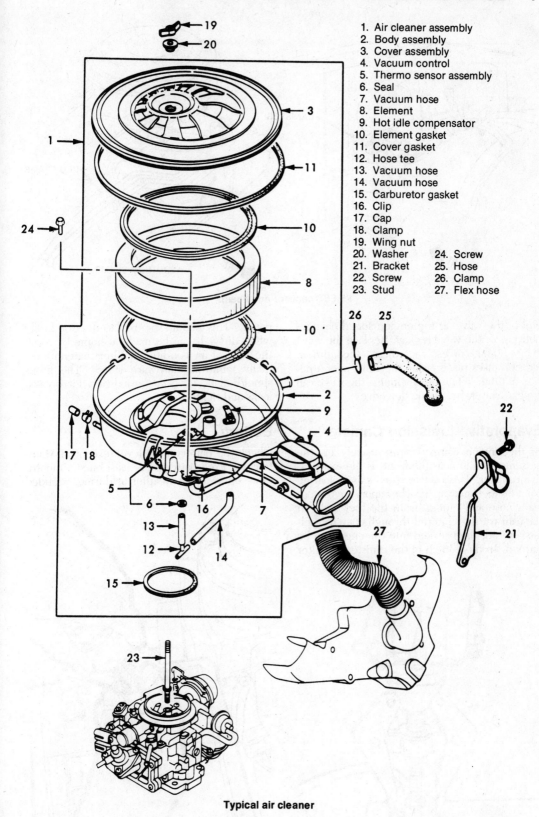

1. Air cleaner assembly
2. Body assembly
3. Cover assembly
4. Vacuum control
5. Thermo sensor assembly
6. Seal
7. Vacuum hose
8. Element
9. Hot idle compensator
10. Element gasket
11. Cover gasket
12. Hose tee
13. Vacuum hose
14. Vacuum hose
15. Carburetor gasket
16. Clip
17. Cap
18. Clamp
19. Wing nut
20. Washer
21. Bracket
22. Screw
23. Stud
24. Screw
25. Hose
26. Clamp
27. Flex hose

Typical air cleaner

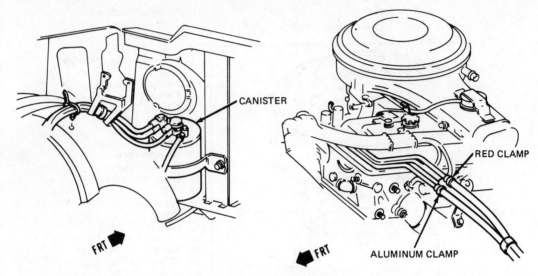

CANISTER

RED CLAMP

ALUMINUM CLAMP

FRT

FRT

V6 ESC canister and hoses

end of the valve. If the engine speed changes noticeably, the valve is okay. Replace the valve every 30,000 miles, regardless of condition. Erosion takes place inside the valve over a period of time. When this happens, the valve can appear okay, while being defective.

Evaporative Emission Canister

In the engine compartment, usually on the passenger's side near the front, is the evaporative canister. This canister serves as a clearing point for fuel tank vapors. The vapors are routed, via a hose and piping, from the fuel tank. In the canister they filtered through charcoal pellets, stored, then sucked into the engine to be burned. In the bottom of the canister is a filter

paper. This should be replaced periodically when dirty. It can be made at home by using the type of air conditioner filter material normally found in hardware stores. The hoses should all be checked periodically for breaks, leaks and tightness.

Battery

Check the battery fluid level (except in Maintenance Free batteries) at least once a month, more often in hot weather or during extended

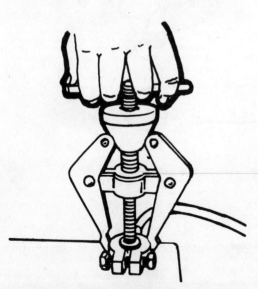

Using a small puller to remove the battery cables

Cleaning the inside of the cable end

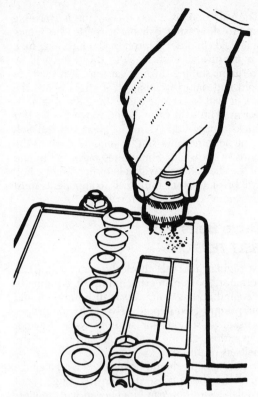

Cleaning the battery terminal

Battery State of Charge at Room Temperature

Specific Gravity Reading	Charged Condition
1.260–1.280	Fully charged
1.230–1.250	¾ Charged
1.200–1.220	½ Charged
1.170–1.190	¼ Charged
1.140–1.160	Almost no Charge
1.110–1.130	No Charge

periods of travel. The electrolyte level should be up to the bottom of the split ring in each cell. All batteries on Chevrolet and GMC trucks are equipped with an "eye" in the cap of one cell. If the "eye" glows or has an amber color to it, this means that the level is low and only distilled water should be added. Do not add anything else to the battery. If the "eye" has a dark appearance the battery electrolyte level is high enough. It is wise to also check each cell individually.

At least once a year, check the specific gravity of the battery. It should be between 1.20–1.26. Clean and tighten the clamps and apply a thin coat of petroleum jelly to the terminals. This will help to retard corrosion. The terminals can be cleaned with a stiff wire brush or with an inexpensive terminal cleaner designed for this purpose.

If water is added during freezing weather, the truck should be driven several miles to allow the electrolyte and water to mix. Otherwise the battery could freeze.

If the battery becomes corroded, a solution of baking soda and water will neutralize the corrosion. This should be washed off after making sure that the caps are securely in place. Rinse the solution off with cold water.

Some batteries were equipped with a felt terminal washer. This should be saturated with engine oil approximately every 6,000 miles. This will also help to retard corrosion.

If a "fast" charger is used while the battery is in the truck, disconnect the battery before connecting the charger.

NOTE: *Keep flame or sparks away from the battery; it gives off explosive hydrogen gas.*

TESTING THE MAINTENANCE–FREE BATTERY

All later model trucks are equipped with maintenance-free batteries, which do not require normal attention as far as fluid level checks are concerned. However, the terminals require periodic cleaning, which should be performed at least once a year.

The sealed-top battery cannot be checked for charge in the normal manner, since there is no provision for access to the electrolyte. To check the condition of the battery:

1. If the indicator eye on top of the battery is dark, the battery has enough fluid. If the eye is light, the electrolyte fluid is too low and the battery must be replaced.

2. If a green dot appears in the middle of the eye, the battery is sufficiently charged. Proceed to Step 4. If no green dot is visible, charge the battery as in Step 3.

3. Charge the battery at this rate:

Charging Rate Amps	Time
75	40 min
50	1 hr
25	2 hr
10	5 hr

CAUTION: *Do not charge the battery for more than 50 amp-hours. If the green dot appears, or if electrolyte squirts out of the vent hole, stop the charge and proceed to Step 4.*

It may be necessary to tip the battery from side to side to get the green dot to appear after charging.

4. Connect a battery load tester and a voltmeter across the battery terminals (the battery

cables should be disconnected from the battery). Apply a 300 amp load to the battery for 15 seconds to remove the surface charge. Remove the load.

5. Wait 15 seconds to allow the battery to recover. Apply the appropriate test load, as specified in the following chart:

Battery	Test Load
Y85-4	130 amps
R85-5	170 amps
R87-5	210 amps
R89-5	230 amps

Apply the load for 15 seconds while reading the voltage. Disconnect the load.

6. Check the results against the following chart. If the battery voltage is at or above the specified voltage for the temperature listed, the battery is good. If the voltage falls below what's listed, the battery should be replaced.

NOTE: *Never disconnect the battery with the ignition key ON or the engine running.*

Temperature (°F)	Minimum Voltage
70 or above	9.6
60	9.5
50	9.4
40	9.3
30	9.1
20	8.9
10	8.7
0	8.5

Heat Riser

The heat riser is a thermostatically or vacuum operated valve in the exhaust manifold. Not all engines have one. Heat riser-equipped V6s have only one valve, located in the right manifold.

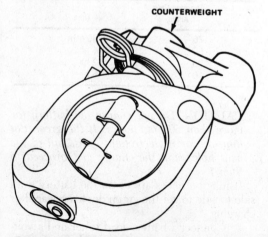

COUNTERWEIGHT

Typical exhaust manifold heat riser

The valve opens when the engine is warming up, to direct hot exhaust gases to the intake manifold, in order to preheat the incoming fuel-air mixture. If it sticks shut, the result will be frequent stalling during warmup, especially in cold and damp weather. If it sticks open, the result will be a rough idle after the engine is warm. The heat riser should move freely. If it sticks, apply GM Manifold Heat Control Solvent or something similar (engine cool) to the ends of the shaft. Sometimes rapping the end of the shaft sharply with a hammer (engine hot) will break it loose. If this fails, components must be removed for further repairs.

Drive Belts

BELT TENSION

At regular intervals check the water pump, alternator, power steering pump (if equipped), air conditioning compressor (if equipped) and air pump (if equipped) drive belts for proper tension. Also look for signs of wear, fraying, separation, glazing, and so on, and replace the belts as required.

Belt tension should be checked with a gauge made for the purpose. If a tension gauge is not available, tension can be checked with moderate thumb pressure applied to the belt at its longest span midway between pulleys. If the belt has a free span less than twelve inches, it should deflect approximately 1/8–1/4 inch. If the span is longer than twelve inches, deflection can range between 1/8 and 3/8 inches.

To adjust or replace belts:

1. Loosen the driven accessory's pivot and mounting bolts.

2. Move the accessory toward or away from the engine until the tension is correct. You can use a wooden hammer handle, or broomstick, as a lever, but do not use anything metallic, such as a prybar.

3. Tighten the bolts and recheck the tension. If new belts have been installed, run the engine for a few minutes, then recheck and readjust as necessary.

It is better to have belts too loose than too tight, because overtight belts will lead to bearing failure, particularly in the water pump and alternator. However, loose belts place an extremely high impact load on the driven component due to the whipping action of the belt.

Air Conditioning

Regular maintenance for the air conditioning system includes periodic checks of the compressor drive belt tension, covered in the previous section. In addition, the system should be operated for at least five minutes every

HOW TO SPOT WORN V-BELTS

V-Belts are vital to efficient engine operation—they drive the fan, water pump and other accessories. They require little maintenance (occasional tightening) but they will not last forever. Slipping or failure of the V-belt will lead to overheating. If your V-belt looks like any of these, it should be replaced.

Cracking or weathering

This belt has deep cracks, which cause it to flex. Too much flexing leads to heat build-up and premature failure. These cracks can be caused by using the belt on a pulley that is too small. Notched belts are available for small diameter pulleys.

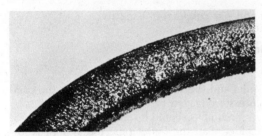

Softening (grease and oil)

Oil and grease on a belt can cause the belt's rubber compounds to soften and separate from the reinforcing cords that hold the belt together. The belt will first slip, then finally fail altogether.

Glazing

Glazing is caused by a belt that is slipping. A slipping belt can cause a run-down battery, erratic power steering, overheating or poor accessory performance. The more the belt slips, the more glazing will be built up on the surface of the belt. The more the belt is glazed, the more it will slip. If the glazing is light, tighten the belt.

Worn cover

The cover of this belt is worn off and is peeling away. The reinforcing cords will begin to wear and the belt will shortly break. When the belt cover wears in spots or has a rough jagged appearance, check the pulley grooves for roughness.

Separation

This belt is on the verge of breaking and leaving you stranded. The layers of the belt are separating and the reinforcing cords are exposed. It's just a matter of time before it breaks completely.

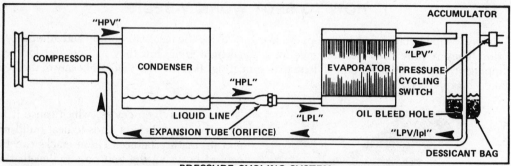

PRESSURE CYCLING SYSTEM

"HPV" — HIGH PRESSURE VAPOR LEAVING COMPRESSOR.

"HPL" — VAPOR IS COOLED DOWN BY CONDENSER AIR FLOW AND LEAVES AS HIGH PRESSURE LIQUID.

"LPL" — ORIFICE METERS THE LIQUID R-12, INTO EVAPORATOR, REDUCING ITS PRESSURE, AND WARM BLOWER AIR ACROSS EVAPORATOR CORE CAUSES BOILING OFF OF LIQUID INTO VAPOR.

"LPV" — LEAVES EVAPORATOR AS LOW PRESSURE VAPOR AND RETURNS WITH THE SMALL AMOUNT OF . . .

"lpl" — . . . LOW PRESSURE LIQUID THAT DIDN'T BOIL OFF COMPLETELY BACK TO THE COMPRESSOR TO BE COMPRESSED AGAIN.

Typical air conditioning system layout

month. This ensures an adequate supply of lubricant to the bearings, and helps prevent the seals and hoses from drying out. To do this comfortably in winter, set the air conditioning lever to "Norm," the temperature lever to "Hot," and turn on the blower. This will engage the compressor, circulating lubricating oils within the system, but prevent the discharge of cold air.

The system can be checked for proper refrigerant charge using the appropriate procedure given below. Note that these procedures apply only to the factory-installed systems. If your truck has an aftermarket unit, you should consult the manufacturer of the unit for system checks.

If the system does not seem to be properly charged, take the truck to a trained professional for service. Do *not* attempt to charge the air conditioning system yourself unless you are thoroughly familiar with its operation and the hazards involved. Escaping refrigerant evaporates at subzero temperatures, and is cold enough to freeze any surface it contacts, including your skin and eyes. These air conditioning systems have no sight glass for checking.

1. Warm the engine to normal operating temperature.

2. Open the hood and doors.

3. Set the selector lever at A/C.

4. Set the temperature lever at the first detent to the right of COLD (outside air).

5. Set the blower on HI.

6. Idle the engine at 1,000 rpm.

7. Feel the temperature of the evaporator inlet and the accumulator outlet with the compressor engaged.

Both lines should be cold. If the inlet pipe is colder than the outlet pipe the system is low on charge.

Do not attempt to charge the system yourself.

Tires and Wheels

The tires should be rotated as specified in the "Maintenance Intervals" chart. Refer to the accompanying illustrations for the recommended rotation patterns.

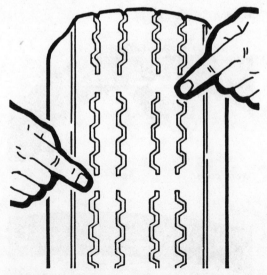

Tread wear indicators appear when the tire is worn out

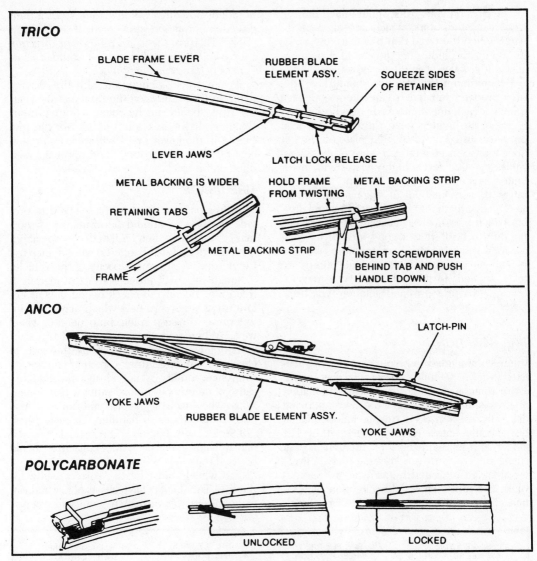

TRICO

BLADE FRAME LEVER

RUBBER BLADE
ELEMENT ASSY.

SQUEEZE SIDES
OF RETAINER

LEVER JAWS

LATCH LOCK RELEASE

METAL BACKING IS WIDER

HOLD FRAME
FROM TWISTING

METAL BACKING STRIP

RETAINING TABS

METAL BACKING STRIP

FRAME

INSERT SCREWDRIVER
BEHIND TAB AND PUSH
HANDLE DOWN.

ANCO

LATCH-PIN

YOKE JAWS

RUBBER BLADE ELEMENT ASSY.

YOKE JAWS

POLYCARBONATE

UNLOCKED

LOCKED

Three different types of wiper blades

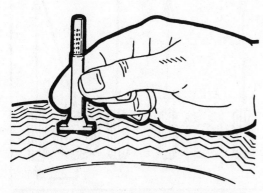

Tread depth can be checked with an inexpensive gauge

If all of Lincoln's head is visible in two or more adjacent grooves, the tire should be replaced

The tires on your truck should have built-in tread wear indicators, which appear as ½ in. bands when the tread depth gets as low as 1/16 in. When the indicators appear in 2 or more adjacent grooves, it's time for new tires.

For optimum tire life, you should keep the tires properly inflated, rotate them and have the wheel alignment checked periodically.

Some late models have the maximum load pressures listed on the V.I.N. plate on the left door frame. In general, pressure of 28–32 psi would be suitable for highway use with moderate loads and passenger car type tires (load range B, non-flotation) of original equipment size. Pressure should be checked before driving, since pressure can increase as much as 6 psi due to heat. It is a good idea to have an accurate gauge and to check pressures weekly. Not all gauges on service station air pumps are to be trusted. In general, truck-type tires require higher pressures and flotation-type tires, lower pressures.

TIRE ROTATION

It is recommended that you have the tires rotated every 6,000 miles. There is no way to give a tire rotation diagram for every combination of tires and vehicles, but the accompanying diagrams are a general rule to follow. Radial tires should not be cross-switched; they last longer if their direction of rotation is not changed. Truck tires sometimes have directional tread, indicated by arrows on the sidewalls; the arrow shows the direction of rotation. They will wear very rapidly if reversed.

Studded snow tires will lose their studs if their direction of rotation is reversed.

NOTE: *Mark the wheel position or direction of rotation on radial tires or studded snow tires before removing them.*

If your truck is equipped with tires having different load ratings on the front and the rear, the tires should not be rotated front to rear. Rotating these tires could affect tire life (the tires with the lower rating will wear faster, and could become overloaded), and upset the handling of the truck.

TIRE USAGE

The tires on your truck were selected to provide the best all-around performance for normal operation when inflated as specified. Oversize tires (Load Range D) will not increase the maximum carrying capacity of the vehicle, although they will provide an extra margin of tread life. Be sure to check overall height before using larger size tires which may cause interference with suspension components or wheel wells. When replacing conventional tire sizes with other tire size designations, be sure to check the manufacturer's recommendations. Interchangeability is not always possible because of differences in load ratings, tire dimensions, wheel well clearances, and rim size. Also due to differences in handling characteristics, "70 Series" and "60 Series" tires should be used only in pairs on the same axle; radial tires should be used only in sets of four.

The wheels must be the correct width for the tire. Tire dealers have charts of tire and rim compatibility. A mismatch can cause sloppy

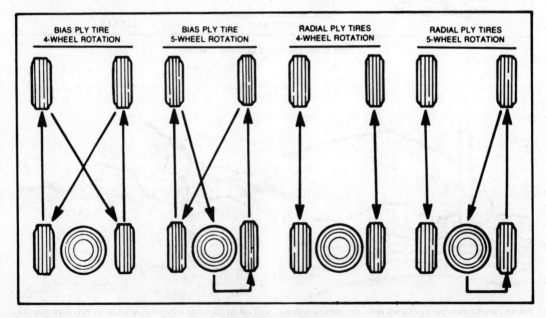

Tire rotation patterns

handling and rapid tread wear. The old rule of thumb is that the tread width should match the rim width (inside bead to inside bead) within an inch. For radial tires, the rim width should be 80% or less of the tire (not tread) width.

The height (mounted diameter) of the new tires can greatly change speedometer accuracy, engine speed at a given road speed, fuel mileage, acceleration, and ground clearance. Tire manufacturers furnish full measurement specifications. Speedometer drive gears are available for correction.

NOTE: *Dimensions of tires marked the same size may vary significantly, even among tires from the same manufacturer.*

The spare tire should be usable, at least for low speed operation, with the new tires.

TIRE TYPES

For maximum satisfaction, tires should be used in sets of five. Mixing of different types (radial, bias-belted, fiberglass belted) should be avoided. Conventional bias tires are constructed so that the cords run bead-to-bead at an angle. Alternate plies run at an opposite angle. This type of construction gives rigidity to both tread and sidewall. Bias-belted tires are similar in construction to conventional bias ply tires. Belts run at an angle and also at a 90° angle to the bead, as in the radial tire. Tread life is improved considerably over the conventional bias tire. The radial tire differs in construction, but instead of the carcass plies running at an angle of 90° to each other, they run at an angle of 90° to the bead. This gives the tread a great deal of rigidity and the sidewall a great deal of flexibility and accounts for the characteristic bulge associated with radial tires.

Chevrolet and GMC trucks are capable of using radial tires and they are recommended. If they are used, tire sizes and wheel diameters should be selected to maintain ground clearance and tire load capacity equivalent to the minimum specified tire. Radial tires should always be used in sets of five, but in an emergency radial tires can be used with caution on the rear axle only. If this is done, both tires on the rear should be of radial design.

NOTE: *Radial tires should never be used on only the front axle.*

Snow tires should not be operated at sustained speeds over 70 mph.

On four wheel drive trucks, all tires must be of the same size, type, and tread pattern, to provide even traction on loose surfaces, to prevent driveline bind when conventional four wheel drive is used, and to prevent excessive wear on the center differential with full time four wheel drive.

Fuel Filter

GASOLINE ENGINES

The fuel filter should be serviced every 15,000 miles. Two types of fuel filters are used, a bronze type and a paper element type. Inline fuel filters may be used on some engines which should be changed at the same time as the filter in the carburetor body. Filter replacement should be attempted only when the engine is cold. Additionally, it is a good idea to place some absorbent rags under the fuel fittings to catch the gasoline which will spill out when the lines are loosened. To replace the filter found in the carburetor body:

1. Remove the air cleaner assembly and clean the area around the filter connection. Carburetor cleaner works very well.
2. Disconnect the fuel line connection at the intake fuel filter nut. Plug the opening to prevent loss of fuel.
3. Remove the intake fuel filter nut from the carburetor with a 1 in. wrench.
4. Remove the filter element and spring.
5. Check the element for restrictions by blowing on the cone end. Air should pass freely. Clean or replace the element, as necessary.
6. Install the element spring, then the filter element in the carburetor. Bronze filters should have the small section of the cone facing out.
7. Install a new gasket on the intake fuel nut. Install the nut in the carburetor body and tighten securely.
8. Install the fuel line and tighten the connector. Do not overtighten. Check for leaks.

Some trucks may have an inline filter. This is a can-shaped device located in the fuel line between the pump and the carburetor. It may be made of either plastic or metal. To replace the filter:

1. Place some absorbent rags under the filter; remember, it will be full of gasoline when removed.
2. Use a pair of pliers to expand the clamp on one end of the filter, then slide the clamp down past the point to which the filter pipe extends in the rubber hose. Do the same with the other clamp.
3. Gently twist and pull the hoses free of the filter pipes. Remove and discard the old filter. Check the hoses for cracks.

NOTE: *Most replacement filters come with new hoses that should be installed with the new filter. New clamps are a good idea too.*

4. Install the new filter into the hoses, slide the clamps back into place, and check for leaks with the engine idling.

DIESEL ENGINES

Filter Element Replacement

1. Disconnect the negative battery cable.

2. Disconnect the water sensor wire connector from the filter assembly.

3. Disconnect the water sensor-to-main body hose.

4. Remove the fuel filter element by turning the cartridge counterclockwise, using a suitable filter band wrench, while being careful not to spill diesel fuel from the element.

5. Drain the fuel from the element into a suitable container and discard. Take precautions to avoid the risk of fire during replacement procedures.

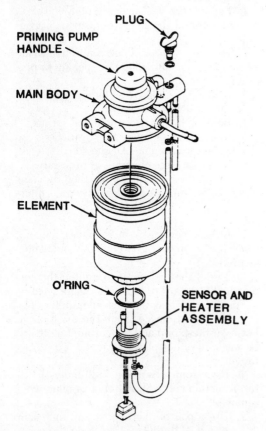

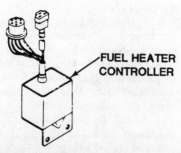

Exploded view of diesel fuel filter assembly

6. Remove the water and heater sensor from the bottom of the used filter element.

7. Apply a thin coat of diesel fuel to the water sensor O-ring, then install the water and heater sensor on the bottom of the replacement filter element and tighten.

8. Wipe all filter sealing surfaces clean before installing the new filter and apply a thin coat of diesel fuel to the gasket on the new fuel filter element.

9. Install the new filter element by turning it clockwise until the gasket contacts the sealing surfaces on the main filter body. Hand-tighten another ⅔ of a turn after the gasket contacts the sealing surface. Do not over-tighten.

10. Reconnect the water sensor wiring connector, then disconnect the fuel outlet hose from the injection pump and place the end in a clean container.

11. Operate the priming pump handle on the injection pump several times to fill the new filter with fuel, until fuel flows from the outlet hose. Reconnect the outlet hose to the injection pump when priming is complete.

12. Start the engine and check for leaks.

NOTE: *It is very important to prime the new filter element before starting the engine, as the shock of the diesel engine's high operating fuel pressure hiting a dry element can tear small pieces of debris away and allow them to pass into the injection pump and injectors, possibly causing injection pump or injector damage.*

Filter Assembly Replacement

1. Disconnect the negative battery cable.

2. Disconnect the water sensor wiring connector.

3. Disconnect the fuel hoses at the filter assembly.

4. Remove the mounting screws securing the filter assembly to the bracket and remove the

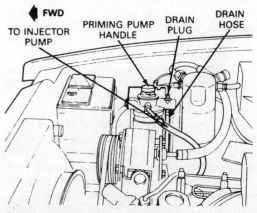

Typical diesel fuel filter assembly

filter main body, element and sensors as an asembly.

5. Installation is the reverse of removal. Follow the instructions on priming the fuel system given above.

Draining the Water Separator

1. Turn the engine off and allow it to cool.

2. Open the hood and place a two quart container under the end of the drain hose attached to the separator.

3. Turn the wing nut about four turns counterclockwise to open the drain plug, then operate the priming pump lever until all water is drained and only clean diesel fuel flows from the water separator.

4. Tighten the drain plug wing nut clockwise until securely closed. Do not overtighten. Again operate the priming pump handle until resistance is felt, indicating that the fuel filter is properly primed.

5. Start the engine and check for fuel leaks from the separator and fuel lines. Make sure the "Water In Fuel" light is off; if the light remains on, the fuel tank must be purged of water with a suitable siphon hose and hand pump fed into the tank through the fuel filler.

CAUTION: *DO NOT attempt to siphon any fuel tank contents by using mouth suction to start the siphon effect. Diesel fuel is poisonous and is by far the worst tasting stuff you can imagine. Use a hand siphon pump or power drill attachment to pull the water from the fuel tank.*

FLUIDS AND LUBRICANTS

Fuel Recommendations

GASOLINE ENGINES

The catalytic converter is a muffler-shaped device installed in the exhaust system. It contains platinum and palladium coated pellets which, through catalytic (heat-producing) action, oxidize hydrocarbon and carbon monoxide gases into hydrogen, oxygen, and carbon dioxide.

The design of the converter requires the exclusive use of unleaded fuel. Leaded fuel renders the converter inoperative, raising exhaust emissions to illegal levels. In addition, the lead in the gasoline coats the pellets in the converter, blocking the flow of exhaust gases. This raises exhaust back pressure and severely reduces engine performance. In extreme cases, the exhaust system becomes so blocked that the engine will not run.

Converter-equipped trucks are delivered with the label "Unleaded Fuel Only" placed next to the fuel gauge on the instrument panel and next to the gas tank filler opening. In general, any unleaded fuel is suitable for use in these trucks as long as the gas has an octane rating of 87 or more. Octane ratings are posted on the gas pumps. However, in some cases, knocking may occur even though the recommended fuel is being used. The only practical solution for this is to switch to a slightly higher grade of unleaded fuel, or to switch brands of unleaded gasoline.

NOTE: *The use of some types of fuel additives (especially octane boosters) can damage catalytic converters. Read the manufacturer's label before adding anything to the fuel system.*

DIESEL ENGINES

Diesel-engined pick-ups require the use of diesel fuel. Two grades of diesel fuel are manufactured, #1 and #2, although #2 grade is generally the only grade available. Better fuel economy results from the use of #2 grade fuel. In some northern parts of the U.S., and in most parts of Canada, #1 grade fuel is available in winter, or a winterized blend of #2 grade is supplied in winter months. If #1 grade is available, it should be used whenever temperatures fall below 20°F (−7°C). Winterized #2 grade may also be used at these temperatures. However, unwinterized #2 grade should *not* be used below 20°F (−7°C). Cold temperatures cause unwinterized #2 grade to thicken (it actually gels), blocking the fuel lines and preventing the engine from running.

Do not use home heating oil or gasoline in the diesel pick-up. Do not attempt to "thin" unwinterized #2 diesel fuel with gasoline. Gasoline or home heating oil will damage the engine and void the manufacturer's warranty.

CAUTION: *The mixture of gasoline and diesel fuel produces an extremely potent explosive that is more volatile than gasoline alone.*

Engine

OIL RECOMMENDATIONS

The SAE grade number indicates the viscosity of the engine oil, or its ability to lubricate under a given temperature. The lower the SAE grade number, the lighter the oil; the lower the viscosity, the easier it is to crank the engine in cold weather.

The API (American Petroleum Institute) designation indicates the calssification of engine oil for use under given operating conditions. Only oils designated for "Service SF" should be used. These oils provide maximum engine protection. Both the SAE grade number and the API designation can be found on the top of a can of oil.

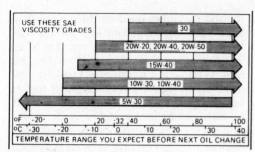

Gasoline engine oil selection chart

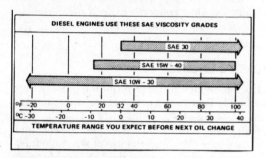

Diesel engine oil selection chart

NOTE: *Non-detergent should not be used.*

Oil viscosities should be chosen from those oils recommended for the lowest anticipated temperatures during the oil change interval.

The multi-viscosity oils offer the important advantage of being adaptable to temperature extremes. They allow easy starting at low temperatures, yet give good protection at high speeds and engine temperatures. This is a decided advantage in changeable climates or in long distance driving.

Diesel engines also require SF engine oil. In addition, the oil must qualify for a CC rating. The API has a number of different diesel engine ratings, including CB, CC, and CD.

The diesel engine in the Chevrolet and GMC pick-ups requires SF/CC rated oil. DO NOT use an oil if the designation CD appears anywhere on the oil can. Use SF/CC engine oil only. Do not use an oil labeled only SF or only CC. Both designations must appear.

For recommended oil viscosities, refer to the chart. 10W-30 grade oils are not recommended for sustained high speed driving.

Single viscosity oil (SAE 30) is recommended for sustained high speed driving.

OIL LEVEL CHECK

The engine oil should be checked on a regular basis, ideally at each fuel stop. If the truck is used for trailer towing or for heavy-duty use, it would be safer to check it more often.

When checking the oil level it is best that the oil be at operating temperature, although checking the level immediately after stopping

will give a false reading because all of the oil will not yet have drained back into the crankcase. Be sure that the truck is resting on a level surface, allowing time for the oil to drain back into the crankcase.

1. Open the hood and locate the dipstick. Remove it from the tube. The oil dipstick is located on the driver's side.

2. Wipe the dipstick with a clean rag.

3. Insert the dipstick fully into the tube, and remove it again. Hold the dipstick horizontally and read the oil level. The level should be between the FULL and ADD OIL marks. If the oil level is at or below the ADD OIL mark, oil should be added as necessary. Oil is added through the capped opening on the valve cover(s) on gasoline engines. Diesel engines have a capped oil fill tube at the front of the engine. See "Oil and Fuel Recommendations" for the proper viscosity oil to use.

4. Replace the dipstick and check the level after adding oil. Be careful not to overfill the crankcase. Approximately one quart of oil will raise the level from ADD to FULL.

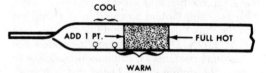

Automatic transmission fluid dipstick

CHANGING THE OIL AND FILTER

Engine oil should be changed every 6,000 miles on gasoline engines and every 3,000 miles on diesel engines. The oil change and filter replacement interval should be cut in half under conditions such as:

  • Driving in dusty conditions,
  • Continuous trailer pulling or RV use,
  • Extensive or prolonged idling,
  • Extensive short trip operation in freezing temperatures (when the engine is not thoroughly warmed-up),
  • Frequent long runs at high speeds and high ambient temperatures, and
  • Stop-and-go service such as delivery trucks.

Operation of the engine in severe conditions such as a dust storm may require an immediate oil and filter change.

Chevrolet and GMC recommend changing both the oil and filter during the first oil change and the filter every other oil change thereafter. For the small price of an oil filter, it's cheap insurance to replace the filter at every oil change. One of the larger filter manufacturers points out in its advertisements that not changing the filter leaves one quart of dirty oil in the

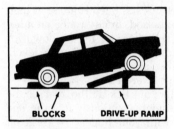

1. Warm the car up before changing your oil. Raise the front end of the car and support it on drive-on ramps or jackstands.

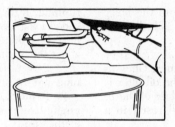

2. Locate the drain plug on the bottom of the oil pan and slide a low flat pan of sufficient capacity under the engine to catch the oil. Loosen the plug with a wrench and turn it out the last few turns by hand. Keep a steady inward pressure on the plug to avoid hot oil from running down your arm.

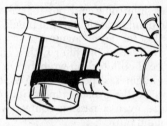

3. Remove the oil filter with a filter wrench. The filter can hold more than a quart of oil, which will be hot. Be sure the gasket comes off with the filter and clean the mounting base on the engine.

4. Lubricate the gasket on the new filter with clean engine oil. A dry gasket may not make a good seal and will allow the filter to leak.

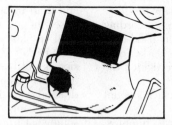

5. Position a new filter on the mounting base and spin it on by hand. Do not use a wrench. When the gasket contacts the engine, tighten it another ½–1 turn by hand.

6. Using a rag, clean the drain plug and the area around the drain hole in the oil pan.

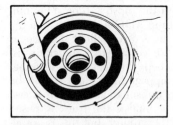

7. Install the drain plug and tighten it finger-tight. If you feel resistance, stop and be sure you are not cross-threading the plug. Finally, tighten the plug with a wrench.

8. Locate the oil cap on the valve cover. An oil spout is the easiest way to add oil, but a funnel will do just as well.

9. Start the engine and check for leaks. The oil pressure warning light will remain on for a few seconds; when it goes out, stop the engine and check the level on the dipstick.

engine. This claim is true and should be kept in mind when changing your oil.

NOTE: *The oil filter on the diesel engine must be changed every oil change.*

To change the oil, the truck should be on a level surface, and the engine should be at operating temperature. This is to ensure that the foreign matter will be drained away along with the oil, and not left in the engine to form sludge. You should have available a container that will hold a minimum of 8 quarts of liquid, a wrench to fit the old drain plug, a spout for pouring in new oil, and a rag or two, which you will always need. If the filter is being replaced, you will also need a band wrench or filter wrench to fit the end of the filter.

NOTE: *If the engine is equipped with an oil*

cooler, this will also have to be drained, using the drain plug. Be sure to add enough oil to fill the cooler in addition to the engine.

1. Position the truck on a level surface and set the parking brake or block the wheels. Slide a drain pan under the oil drain plug.

2. From under the truck, loosen, but do not remove the oil drain plug. Cover your hand with a rag or glove and slowly unscrew the drain plug.

CAUTION: *The engine oil will be HOT. Keep your arms, face and hands clear of the oil as it drains out.*

3. Remove the plug and let the oil drain into the pan. Do not drop the plug into the drain pan.

4. When all of the oil has drained, clean off

the drain plug and put it back into the hole. Remember to tighten the plug to 20 ft. lbs. (30 ft. lbs. for diesel engines).

5. Loosen the filter with a band wrench or special oil filter cap wrench. On most Chevrolet engines, especially the V6s, the oil filter is next to the exhaust pipes. Stay clear of these, since even a passing contact will result in a painful burn.

NOTE: *On trucks equipped with catalytic converters stay clear of the converter. The outside temperature of a hot catalytic converter can approach 1200°F.*

6. Cover your hand with a rag, and spin the filter off by hand. Turn it slowly.

7. Coat the rubber gasket on a new filter with a light film of clean engine oil. Screw the filter onto the mounting stud and tighten according to the directions on the filter (usually hand-tight one turn past the point where the gasket contacts the mounting base). Don't overtighten the filter.

8. Refill the engine with the specified amount of clean engine oil.

9. Run the engine for several minutes, checking for leaks. Check the level of the oil and add oil if necessary.

When you have finished this job, you will notice that you now possess four or five quarts of dirty oil. The best thing to do with it is to pour it into plastic jugs, such as milk or antifreeze containers. Then, if you are on good terms with your gas station man, he might let you pour it into his used oil container for recycling. Otherwise, the only thing to do with it is to put the containers into the trash.

NOTE: *Pouring used motor oil into a storm drain not only pollutes the environment, it violates Federal law. Dispose of waste oil properly.*

Manual Transmission

No fluid change is recommended. However, if the truck is driven in deep water, it is a good idea to replace the fluid. Every year, it's a good idea to check the fluid level. To do so, remove the filler plug from the side of the case and insert your finger straight in. The level should be up to the filler plug opening. If not, fill the case to the opening. All manual transmissions in these trucks use Dexron II automatic transmission fluid.

Automatic Transmission

FLUID CHECKING

Check the level of the fluid at the specified interval. The fluid level should be checked with the engine at normal operating temperature and

running. If the truck has been running at high speed for a long period, in city traffic on a hot day, or pulling a trailer, let it cool down for about thirty minutes before checking the level.

1. Park on the level with the engine running and the shift lever in Park.

2. Remove the dipstick at the rear of the engine compartment. Cautiously feel the end of the dipstick with your fingers. Wipe it off and replace it, then pull it again and check the level of the fluid on the dipstick.

3. If the fluid felt cool, the level should be between the two dimples below ADD. If it was too hot to hold, the level should be between the ADD and FULL marks.

4. If the fluid is at or below the ADD mark, add fluid through the dipstick tube. One pint raises the level from ADD to FULL when the fluid is hot. The correct fluid to use is DEXRON® II. Be certain that the transmission is not overfilled; this will cause foaming, fluid loss, and slippage. The fluid should be drained with the transmission warm. It is easier to change the fluid if the truck is raised somewhat from the ground, but this is not always easy without a lift. The transmission must be level for it to drain properly.

DRAIN AND REFILL

1. Place a shallow pan underneath to catch the transmission fluid (about 5 pints). On earlier models, the transmission pan has a drain plug. Remove this and drain the fluid. For later models, loosen all the pan bolts, then pull one corner down to drain most of the fluid. If it sticks, VERY CAREFULLY pry the pan loose. You can buy aftermarket drain plug kits that make this operation a bit less messy, once installed.

NOTE: *If the fluid removed smells burnt (like varnish), serious transmission troubles, probably due to overheating, should be suspected.*

2. Remove the pan bolts and empty out the

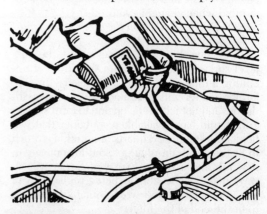

Adding automatic transmission fluid

pan. On some models, there may not be much room to get at the screws at the front of the pan.

3. Clean the pan with solvent and allow it to air dry. If you use a rag to wipe it out, you risk leaving bits of lint and threads in the transmission.

4. Remove the filter or strainer retaining bolts. A reusable strainer may be found on some models. The strainer may be cleaned in solvent and air dried thoroughly. The filter and gasket must be replaced.

5. Install a new gasket and filter. Do not use a hardening sealer.

6. Install a new gasket on the pan, and tighten the bolts evenly to 12 ft. lbs. in a criss-cross pattern.

7. Add DEXRON® or DEXRON® II transmission fluid through the dipstick tube. The correct amount is in the Capacities Chart. Do not overfill.

8. With the gearshift lever in PARK, start the engine and let it idle. Do not race the engine.

9. Move the gearshift lever through each position, holding the brakes. Return the lever to PARK, and check the fluid level with the engine idling. The level should be between the two dimples on the dipstick, about ¼ in. below the ADD mark. Add fluid, if necessary.

10. Check the fluid level after the truck has been driven enough to thoroughly warm up the transmission. Details are given under Fluid Level Checks. If the transmission is overfilled, the excess must be drained off. Overfilling causes aerated fluid, resulting in transmission slippage and probable damage. Use a suction gun and thin hose in the dipstick tube.

Axles

No intervals are specified for changing axle lubricant, but it is a good idea, especially if you have driven in water over the axle vents.

1. Park the vehicle on the level with the axles at normal operating temperature.

2. Place a pan of at least 6 pints capacity under the differential housing.

3. Remove the filler plug.

4. If you have a drain plug, remove it. If not, unbolt and remove the differential cover.

5. Replace the drain plug, or differential cover. Use a new gasket if the differential cover has been removed.

6. Lubricant may be added with a suction gun or squeeze bulb. Front axles use SAE 80W-90, GL-5 Gear Lubricant. Fill front axle to ½ in. below the filler plug opening. Rear axles use SAE 80W-90 gear oil. Positraction® axles must use special lubricant available from dealers. If the special fluid is not used, noise, uneven operation, and damage will result. There is also a Positraction® additive used to cure noise and slippage. Positraction axles have an identifying tag, as well as a warning sticker near the jack or on the rear wheel well. Rear axle lubricant level should be up to the bottom of the filler plug opening.

Transfer Case
CASE OIL CHANGE

1. Raise the vehicle and support it safely.

2. Position drain pan under transfer case.

3. Remove drain and fill plugs and drain lubricant.

4. Install drain plug. Tighten plug.

5. Remove drain pan.

6. Fill transfer case to edge of fill plug opening with Dexron® II.

7. Install fill plug. Tighten plug.

8. Lower vehicle.

Brake Master Cylinder

Chevrolet and GMC trucks are equipped with a dual braking system, allowing a vehicle to be brought to a safe stop in the event of failure in either the front or rear brakes. The dual master cylinder has two entirely separate reservoirs, one connected to the front brakes and the other connected to the rear brakes. In the event of failure in either portion, the remaining part is not affected.

1. Clean all of the dirt from around the cover of the master cylinder.

2. Be sure that the vehicle is resting on a level surface.

3. Carefully pry the clip from the top of the master cylinder to release the cover.

4. The fluid level should be approximately ¼ in. from the top of the master cylinder. If

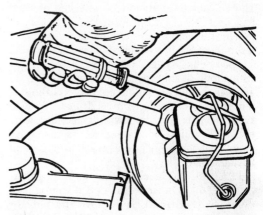

Prying the retaining clip from the master cylinder cap

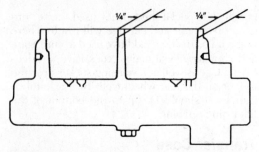

Fluid level should be within ¼ in. of the top of the reservoir

not, add fluid until the level is correct. Only high quality brake fluids, such as General Motors Supreme No. 11 Hydraulic Brake Fluid, or fluids meeting DOT 3 specifications should be used.

NOTE: *It is normal for the fluid level to fall slightly as the disc brake pads wear. However, if the level drops significantly between fluid level checks, or if the level is chronically low, the system should be examined for leakage.*

5. Install the cover of the master cylinder. On most models there is a rubber gasket under the cover, which fits into two slots on the cover. Be sure that this is seated properly.

6. Push the clip back into place and be sure that it seats in the groove on the top of the cover.

CAUTION: *Brake fluid damages paint. It also absorbs moisture from the air; never leave a container or the master cylinder uncovered any longer than necessary. All parts in contact with the brake fluid (i.e. master cylinder, and its lid, hoses, plunger assemblies, etc.) must be kept clean, since any contamination of the brake fluid will adversely affect braking performance.*

Coolant Service

The coolant level should be checked at each fuel stop, ideally, to prevent the possibility of overheating and serious engine damage. If not, it should at least be checked once each month.

The cooling system was filled at the factory with a high quality coolant solution that is good for year around operation and protects the system from freezing down to $-20°F$. ($-32°F$ in Canada). It is good for two full calendar years or 24,000 miles, whichever occurs first, provided that the proper concentration of coolant is maintained.

1. Check the level on the see-through expansion tank. On earlier models it will be necessary to CAREFULLY remove the radiator cap.

CAUTION: *The radiator coolant is under*

pressure when hot. To avoid the danger of physical harm, coolant level should be checked or replenished only when the engine is cold. To remove the radiator cap when the engine is hot, first cover the cap with a thick rag, or wear a heavy glove for protection. Press down on the cap slightly and slowly turn it counterclockwise until it reaches the first stop. Allow all the pressure to vent (indicated when the hissing sound stops). When the pressure is released, press down on the cap and continue to rotate it counterclockwise. Some radiator caps have a lever for venting the pressure; lifting the lever will release the pressure, but you should still exercise extreme caution when removing the cap.

2. Check the level and, if necessary, add coolant to the proper level. Use a 50/50 mix of ethylene glycol antifreeze and water. Alcohol or methanol base coolants are not recommended. Anti-freeze solutions should be used, even in summer, to prevent rust and to take advantage of the solution's higher boiling point compared to plain water. This is imperative on air conditioned trucks; the heater core can freeze if it isn't protected. Coolant should be added through the coolant recovery tank, not the radiator filler neck.

CAUTION: *Never add large quantities of cold coolant to a hot engine. A cracked engine block may result.*

3. Replace the cap.

Each year the cooling system should be serviced as follows:

- Wash the radiator cap and filler neck with clean water. Check the cap gasket.
- Check the coolant for proper level and freeze protection.
- Have the system pressure tested (15 psi). If a replacement cap is installed, be sure that it conforms to the original specifications.
- Tighten the hose clamps and inspect all hoses. Replace hoses that are swollen, cracked or otherwise deteriorated.
- Clean the frontal area of the radiator core and the air conditioning condenser, if so equipped.

Every 2 years or 24,000 miles, which ever occurs first, the system should be drained and filled as follows:

- Run the engine with the cap removed and the heater on until operating temperature is reached (indicated by heat in the upper radiator hose).
- With the engine stopped, open the radiator drain cock located at the bottom of the radiator, and (to speed the draining) the engine block drains, if any. 4

HOW TO SPOT BAD HOSES

Both the upper and lower radiator hoses are called upon to perform difficult jobs in an inhospitable environment. They are subject to nearly 18 psi at under hood temperatures often over 280°F., and must circulate nearly 7500 gallons of coolant an hour—3 good reasons to have good hoses.

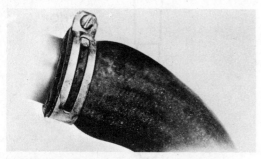

Swollen hose

A good test for any hose is to feel it for soft or spongy spots. Frequently these will appear as swollen areas of the hose. The most likely cause is oil soaking. This hose could burst at any time, when hot or under pressure.

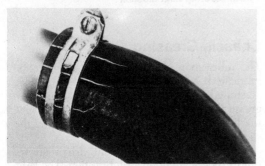

Cracked hose

Cracked hoses can usually be seen but feel the hoses to be sure they have not hardened; a prime cause of cracking. This hose has cracked down to the reinforcing cords and could split at any of the cracks.

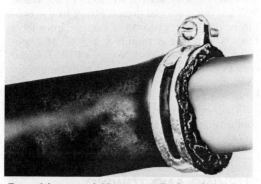

Frayed hose end (due to weak clamp)

Weakened clamps frequently are the cause of hose and cooling system failure. The connection between the pipe and hose has deteriorated enough to allow coolant to escape when the engine is hot.

Debris in cooling system

Debris, rust and scale in the cooling system can cause the inside of a hose to weaken. This can usually be felt on the outside of the hose as soft or thinner areas.

cylinder engines have a coolant drain plug on the left side of the engine block; V6s have one on each side. Some trucks are not equipped with a radiator drain. These radiators can be emptied by siphoning, or by removing the lower radiator hose.

NOTE: *Do not attempt to siphon coolant by sucking on the end of a hose. The coolant is poisonous and can cause death or serious illness if swallowed.*

- Completely drain the coolant, and close the drain cocks.
- Add sufficient clean water to fill the system. Run the engine and drain and refill the system as often as necessary until the drained water is nearly colorless.
- Add sufficient ethylene glycol coolant to provide the required freezing and corrosion protection (at least a 44% solution protecting to $-20°F$). Fill the radiator to the cold level. Run the engine with the cap removed until normal operating temperature is reached.
- Check the hot level.
- Install the cap.

For problems with engine overheating, see Chapter 3.

Steering Gear

MANUAL STEERING

The steering gear is factory-filled with a lubricant which does not require seasonal change. The housing should not be drained; no lubrication is required for the life of the gear.

The gear should be inspected for seal leakage when specified in the "Maintenance" chart. Look for solid grease, not an oily film. If a seal is replaced or the gear overhauled, it should be filled with Part No. 1051052, which meets GM Specification GM 4673M, or its equivalent. Do not use EP Chassis Lube to lubricate the gear and do not overfill.

POWER STEERING

1. Wipe off the cap and surrounding area, after stopping the engine with the wheels straight.
2. Remove the cap and attached dipstick.
3. Wipe the dipstick off with a clean, lint-free rag, replace the cap, and take a reading. If the fluid is hot, the level should be between HOT and COLD; if it is cold, it should be between COLD and ADD.
4. Either GM Power Steering Fluid or DEXRON® II Automatic Transmission Fluid may be used.

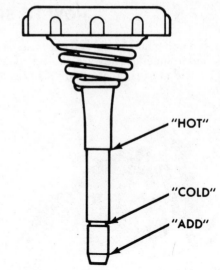

"HOT"

"COLD"

"ADD"

Power steering fluid dipstick

Chassis Greasing

The lubrication charts show the points to be lubricated. Not all vehicles have all the fittings illustrated. For example, most trucks don't have grease fittings on the driveshaft universal joints; the fittings on the shafts are for lubricating the sliding splines.

The four wheel drive front driveshaft requires special attention for lubrication. The large constant velocity joint at the front of the transfer case has a special grease fitting in the centering ball; a special needle nose adapter for a flush type fitting is required, as well as a special lubricant, GM part No. 1050679. You can only get at this fitting when it is facing up toward the floorboards, so you need a flexible hose, too.

Water resistant EP chassis lubricant (grease) conforming to GM specification 6031-M should be used for all chassis grease points.

PUSHING AND TOWING

Pushing

Chevrolet and GMC trucks with manual transmissions can be push started.

To push start, make sure that both bumpers are in reasonable alignment. Turn the ignition key to ON and engage High gear. Depress the clutch pedal. When a speed of about 10 mph is reached, slightly depress the gas pedal and slowly release the clutch. The engine should start.

NOTE: *Automatic transmission equipped trucks cannot be started by pushing.*

Capacities

Engine Displacement cc (cu in.)	Crankcase (qts)	Transmission (pts)			Transfer Case (pts)	Rear Drive Axle (pts)	Front Drive Axle (pts)	Gas Tank (gal)	Cooling System (qts)	
		4 sp	5 sp	Auto					Manual	Auto
1950 (118.9)	4.0	3.0	3.0	7.0 ②	5.2	3.5	1.7	13.0 ①	9.6	9.6
2000 (121)	4.0	3.0	3.0	7.0 ②	5.2	3.5	1.7	13.0 ①	9.6	9.6
2238 (136.6)	5.0	3.0	3.0	7.0 ②	5.2	3.5	1.7	13.0 ①	10.0	10.0
2800 (173)	4.0	3.0	3.0	7.0 ②	5.2	3.5	1.7	13.0 ①	12.4	12.4

① optional: 20.0 gal.
② figure shown is for pan removal only. Total overhaul capacity is 19.0 pts.

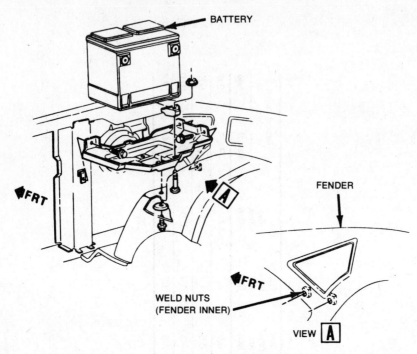

Typical battery tray installation

Towing

Chevrolet and GMC trucks can be towed on all four wheels (flat towed) at speeds of less than 35 mph for distances less than 50 miles, providing that the axle, driveline and engine/transmission are operable. The transmission should be in Neutral, the engine should be off, the steering column unlocked, and the parking brake released.

Do not attach chains to the bumpers or bracketing. All attachments must be made to the structural members. Safety chains should be used. It should also be remembered that power steering and brake assists will not be working with the engine off.

The rear wheels must be raised off the ground or the driveshaft disconnected when the transmission is not operating properly, or when speeds of over 35 mph will be used or when towing more than 50 miles.

CAUTION: *If a truck is towed on its front wheels only, the steering wheel must be secured with the wheels in a straight ahead position.*

JUMP STARTING

The following procedure is recommended by the manufacturer. Be sure that the booster battery is 12 volt with negative ground. Follow this procedure exactly to avoid possible damage to the electrical system, especially on models equipped with computerized engine controls.

CAUTION: *Do not attempt this procedure on a frozen battery; it will probably explode. Do not attempt it on a sealed Delco Freedom battery showing a light color in the charge indicator. Be certain to observe correct polarity connections. Failure to do so will result in almost immediate computer, alternator and regulator destruction. Never allow the jumper cable ends to touch each other.*

1. Position the vehicles so that they are not touching. Set the parking brake and place automatic transmissions in Park and manual transmissions in Neutral. Turn off the lights, heater and other electrical loads. Turn both ignition keys OFF.

2. Remove the vent caps from both the booster and discharged battery. Lay a cloth over the open vent cells of each battery. This isn't necessary on batteries equipped with sponge type flame arrestor caps, and it isn't possible on sealed batteries.

3. Attach one cable to the positive terminal of the booster battery and the other end to the positive terminal of the discharged battery. If you are attempting to start a Chevrolet or GMC pick-up with the diesel engine, it is suggested that this connection be made to the battery on the driver's side of the truck, because this battery is closer to the starter, and thus the resistance of the electrical cables is lower. From this point on, ignore the other battery in the truck.

JUMP STARTING A DEAD BATTERY

The chemical reaction in a battery produces explosive hydrogen gas. This is the safe way to jump start a dead battery, reducing the chances of an accidental spark that could cause an explosion.

Jump Starting Precautions

1. Be sure both batteries are of the same voltage.
2. Be sure both batteries are of the same polarity (have the same grounded terminal).
3. Be sure the vehicles are not touching.
4. Be sure the vent cap holes are not obstructed.
5. Do not smoke or allow sparks around the battery.
6. In cold weather, check for frozen electrolyte in the battery.
7. Do not allow electrolyte on your skin or clothing.
8. Be sure the electrolyte is not frozen.

Jump Starting Procedure

1. Determine voltages of the two batteries; they must be the same.
2. Bring the starting vehicle close (they must not touch) so that the batteries can be reached easily.
3. Turn off all accessories and both engines. Put both cars in Neutral or Park and set the handbrake.
4. Cover the cell caps with a rag—do not cover terminals.
5. If the terminals on the run-down battery are heavily corroded, clean them.
6. Identify the positive and negative posts on both batteries and connect the cables in the order shown.
7. Start the engine of the starting vehicle and run it at fast idle. Try to start the car with the dead battery. Crank it for no more than 10 seconds at a time and let it cool off for 20 seconds in between tries.
8. If it doesn't start in 3 tries, there is something else wrong.
9. Disconnect the cables in the reverse order.
10. Replace the cell covers and dispose of the rags.

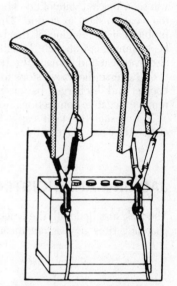

Side terminal batteries occasionally pose a problem when connecting jumper cables. There frequently isn't enough room to clamp the cables without touching sheet metal. Side terminal adaptors are available to alleviate this problem and should be removed after use.

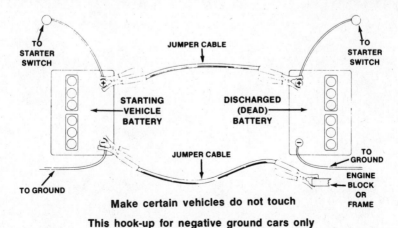

TO STARTER SWITCH

JUMPER CABLE

TO STARTER SWITCH

STARTING VEHICLE BATTERY

DISCHARGED (DEAD) BATTERY

JUMPER CABLE

TO GROUND

TO GROUND

ENGINE BLOCK OR FRAME

Make certain vehicles do not touch

This hook-up for negative ground cars only

CAUTION: *Do not attempt to jump start the truck with a 24 volt power source.*

4. Attach one end of the remaining cable to the negative terminal of the booster battery and the other end to a good ground. Do not attach to the negative terminal of discharged batteries. Do not lean over the battery when making this last connection.

5. Start the engine of the truck with the booster battery. Start the engine of the truck with the discharged battery. If the engine will not start, disconnect the batteries as soon as possible. If this is not done, the two batteries will soon reach a state of equilibrium, with both too weak to start an engine. This will not be a problem if the engine of the booster truck is kept running fast enough. Lengthy cranking can also overheat and damage the starter.

6. Reverse the above steps to disconnect the booster and discharged batteries. Be certain to remove negative connections first.

7. Reinstall the vent caps. Dispose of the cloths; they may have battery acid on them.

JACKING AND HOISTING

The jack supplied with the truck was meant for changing tires. It was not meant to support a truck while you crawl under it and work. Whenever it is necessary to get under a truck to perform service operations, always be sure that it is adequately supported, by jackstands at the proper points. Always block the wheels when changing tires.

If your truck is equipped with a Positraction rear axle, do not run the engine for any reason with one rear wheel off the ground. Power will be transmitted through the rear wheel remaining on the ground, possibly causing the vehicle to drive itself off the jack.

Some of the service operations in this book require that one or both ends of the truck be raised and supported safely. The best arrangement for this, of course, is a grease pit or a vehicle lift, but these items are seldom found in the home garage. However, small hydraulic, screw, or scissors jacks are satisfactory for raising the truck.

Jackstands should be used to support the truck while it is being worked on. Drive-on ramps, are also a handy and a safe way to raise the truck, assuming their capacity is adequate. These can be purchased from your local auto parts store.

CAUTION: *Concrete blocks are not recommended. They may crumble if the load is not evenly distributed. Boxes and milk crates of any description must not be used.*

Tune-Up and Performance Maintenance

2

TUNE-UP PROCEDURES

Neither tune-up nor troubleshooting can be considered independently since each has a direct relationship with the other.

It is advisable to follow a definite and thorough tune-up procedure. Tune-up consists of three separate steps: Analysis, the process of determining whether normal wear is responsible for performance loss, and whether parts require replacement or service; parts replacement or service; and adjustment, where engine adjustments are performed.

The manufacturer's recommended interval for tune-ups is every 22,500 miles or 18 months. These intervals should be shortened if the truck is subjected to severe operating conditions such as trailer pulling or off-road driving, or if starting and running problems are noticed. It is assumed that the routine maintenance described in Chapter 1 has been kept up, as this will have an effect on the results of the tune-up. All the applicable tune-up steps should be followed, as each adjustment complements the effects of the others. If the tune-up (emission control) sticker in the engine compartment disagrees with the information presented in the "Tuneup Specifications" chart in this chapter, the sticker figures must be followed. The sticker information reflects running changes made by the manufacturer during production. The light duty sticker is usually found on the underhood sheet metal above the grille. The heavy duty sticker is usually on top of the air cleaner.

NOTE: *Diesel engines do not require tune-ups per se, as there is no ignition system.*

Troubleshooting is a logical sequence of procedures designed to locate a particular cause of trouble. The "Troubleshooting" chapter of this book is general in nature (applicable to most vehicles), yet specific enough to locate the problem.

It is advisable to read the entire chapter before beginning a tune-up, although those who are more familiar with tune-up procedures may wish to go directly to the instructions.

Spark Plugs

Rough idle, hard starting, frequent engine miss at high speeds and physical deterioration are all indications that the plugs should be replaced.

The electrode end of a spark plug is a good indicator of the internal condition of your engine. If a spark plug is fouled, causing the engine to misfire, the problem will have to be found and corrected. Often, "reading" the plugs will lead you to the cause of the problem. Spark plug conditions and probable causes are listed in the "Troubleshooting" chapter.

NOTE: *A small amount of light tan or rust red colored deposits at the electrode end of the plug is normal. These plugs need not be renewed unless they are severely worn.*

Heat range is a term used to describe the cooling characteristics of spark plugs. Plugs with longer nosed insulators take a longer time to dissipate heat than plugs with shorter nosed insulators. These are termed "hot" or "cold" plugs, respectively. It is generally advisable to use the factory recommended plugs. However, in conditions of extremely hard use (cross-country driving in summer) going to the next cooler heat range may be advisable. If most driving is done in the city or over short distances, go to the next hotter heat range plug to eliminate fouling. If in doubt concerning the substitution of spark plugs, consult your Chevrolet or GMC dealer.

Spark plugs should be gapped when they are checked or newly installed. Never assume that new plugs are correctly gapped.

1. Before removing the spark plugs, number the plug wires so that the correct wire goes

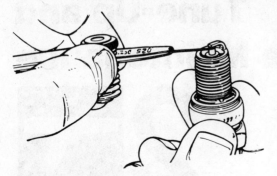

Checking spark plug gap

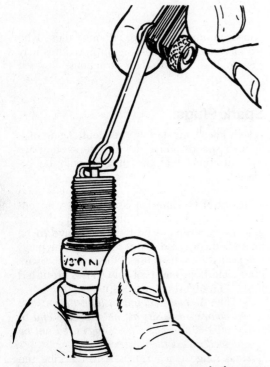

Bending the side electrode to adjust spark plug gap

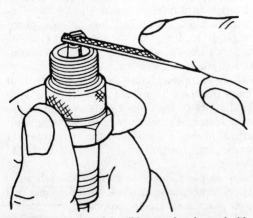

Plugs that are in good condition can be cleaned with a file and reused

on the plug when replaced. This can be done with pieces of adhesive tape.

2. Next, clean the area around the plugs by brushing or blowing with compressed air. You can also loosen the plugs a few turns and crank the engine to blow the dirt away.

3. Disconnect the plug wires by twisting and pulling on the rubber cap, not on the wire. On H.E.I. systems, twist the plug caps ½ turn in either direction to break the seal before removing the wire. Never remove the wires from H.E.I. systems when the engine is running. Severe shock could result.

4. Remove each plug with a rubber-insert spark plug socket, ⅝ in. for tapered seat plugs (designated with a letter T), 13/16 in. for the rest. Make sure that the socket is all the way down on the plug to prevent it from slipping and cracking the procelain insulator. On some V6s the plugs are more accessible from under the truck.

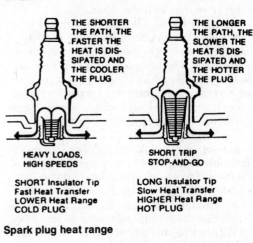

THE SHORTER THE PATH, THE FASTER THE HEAT IS DISSIPATED AND THE COOLER THE PLUG

THE LONGER THE PATH, THE SLOWER THE HEAT IS DISSIPATED AND THE HOTTER THE PLUG

HEAVY LOADS, HIGH SPEEDS

SHORT TRIP STOP-AND-GO

SHORT Insulator Tip
Fast Heat Transfer
LOWER Heat Range
COLD PLUG

LONG Insulator Tip
Slow Heat Transfer
HIGHER Heat Range
HOT PLUG

Spark plug heat range

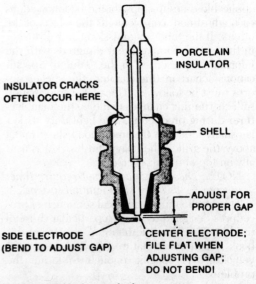

PORCELAIN INSULATOR

INSULATOR CRACKS OFTEN OCCUR HERE

SHELL

ADJUST FOR PROPER GAP

SIDE ELECTRODE (BEND TO ADJUST GAP)

CENTER ELECTRODE; FILE FLAT WHEN ADJUSTING GAP; DO NOT BEND!

Cross-section of a spark plug

Gasoline Engine Tune-Up Specifications

Engine No. Cylinders Displacement cc (cu. in.)	Spark Plugs		Distributor Type	Ignition Timing Deg.		Intake Valve Opens (deg.)	Fuel Pump Pressure (psi)	Idle Speed (rpm)		Valve Clearance (in.)	
	Type	Gap (in.)		MT	AT			MT	AT	Intake	Exhaust
4-1950 (118.9)	R42XLS	.040	HEI	6B	6B	21B	3.0	800	900	.006C	.010C
4-2000 (121)	R42CTS	.035	HEI	12B	12B	30B	5.0	750	700	Hyd.	Hyd.
6-2800 (173)	R-42TS	.041	HEI①	6B	10B	7B	7.0	1000	750	Hyd.	Hyd.

NOTE: The underhood specifications sticker often reflects tune-up specification changes made in production. Sticker figures must be used if they disagree with those in this chart.
① HEI-EST on California models

Diesel Engine Tune-Up Specifications

Injector Opening Pressure (psi)	Injection Timing (deg.)	Intake Valve Opens (deg.)	Low Idle (rpm)	Compression Pressure (psi)	Valve Clearance (in.)		Firing Order
					Intake	Exhaust	
1493	15B	16B	750	441①	.016C	.016C	1-3-4-2

NOTE: The underhood specifications sticker often reflects tune-up specification changes made in production. Sticker figures must be used if they disagree with those in this chart.
① @ 200 rpm

5. After removing each plug, evaluate its condition. A spark plug's useful life is about 12,000 miles (optimistically 22,500 with H.E.I.). Thus, it would make sense to replace a plug if it has been in service that long. If the plug is to be replaced, refer to the "Tune-up Specifications" chart for the proper spark plug type.

The letter codes on the General Motors original equipment type plugs are read this way:
- R resistor
- S extended tip
- T tapered seat
- X wide gap

The numbers indicate heat range; hotter running plugs have higher numbers.

6. If the plugs are to be reused, file the center and side electrodes flat with a fine, flat points file. Heavy or baked on deposits can be carefully scraped off with a small knife blade or the scraper tool on a combination spark plug tool. Check the gap between the electrodes with a round wire spark plug gapping gauge. Do not use a flat feeler gauge; it will give an inaccurate reading. If the gap is not as specified, use the bending tool on the spark plug gap gauge to bend the outside electrode. Be careful not to bend the electrode too far or too often, because excessive bending may cause the electrode to break off and fall into the combustion chamber. This would require removing the cylinder head to reach the broken piece, and could also result in cylinder wall, piston ring, or valve damage.

CAUTION: *Never bend the center electrode of the spark plug. This will break the insulator.*

7. Clean the plug threads with a wire brush. Lubricate the threads with a drop of oil.

8. Screw the plugs in finger tight, and then tighten them with the spark plug socket. Be very careful not to overtighten them. Just snug them in. If a torque wrench is available, torque them to 15 ft. lbs. for plug designations with a T, 25 ft. lbs. for all the rest.

9. Reinstall the wires. If, by chance, you have forgotten to number the plug wires, refer to the "Firing Order" illustrations.

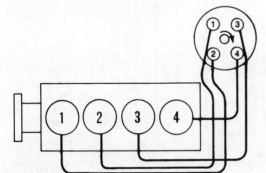

4-2000 firing order

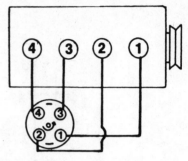

4-1950 firing order

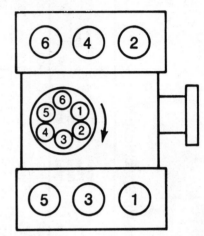

6-2800 firing order

High Energy Ignition (HEI) System

The General Motors HEI system is a pulse-triggered, transistor-controlled, inductive discharge ignition system. The entire HEI system is contained within the distributor cap.

The distributor, in addition to housing the mechanical and vacuum advance mechanisms, contains the ignition coil (except on some in-line six engines), the electronic control module, and the magnetic triggering device. The magnetic pick-up assembly contains a permanent magnet, a pole piece with internal "teeth," and a pick-up coil (not to be confused with the ignition coil).

In the HEI system, as in other electronic ignition systems, the breaker points have been replaced with an electronic switch—a transistor—which is located *within* the control module. This switching transistor performs the same function the points did in a conventional ignition system; it simply turns coil primary current on and off at the correct time. Essentially then, electronic and conventional ignition systems operate on the same principle.

The module which houses the switching transistor is controlled (turned on and off) by a magnetically generated impulse induced in the

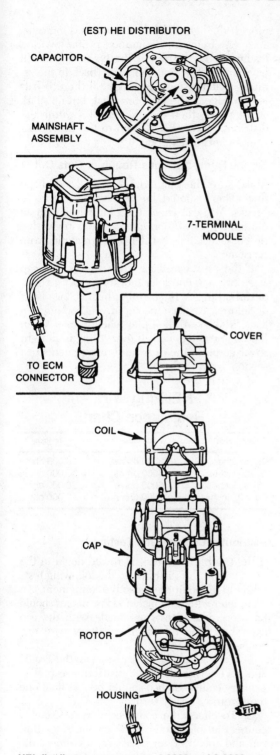

HEI distributor components, 4-2000 and 6-2800

pick-up coil. When the teeth of the rotating timer align with the teeth of the pole piece, the induced voltage in the pick-up coil signals the elctronic module to open the coil primary circuit. The primary current then decreases, and a high voltage is induced in the ignition coil secondary windings which is then directed through the rotor and spark plug wires to fire the spark plugs.

In essence then, the pick-up coil module system simply replaces the conventional breaker points and condenser. The condenser found within the distributor is for radio suppression purposes only and has nothing to do with the ignition process. The module automatically controls the dwell period, increasing it with increasing engine speed. Since dwell is automatically controlled, it cannot be adjusted. The module itself is non-adjustable and non-repairable and must be replaced if found defective.

HEI SYSTEM PRECAUTIONS

Before going on to troubleshooting, it might be a good idea to take note of the following precautions:

Timing Light Use

Inductive pick-up timing lights are the best kind to use with HEI. Timing lights which connect between the spark plug and the spark plug wire occasionally (not always) give false readings.

Spark Plug Wires

The plug wires used with HEI systems are of a different construction than conventional wires. When replacing them, make sure you get the correct wires, since conventional wires won't carry the voltage. Also handle them carefully to avoid cracking or splitting them and *never* pierce them.

Tachometer Use

Not all tachometers will operate or indicate correctly when used on a HEI system. While some tachometers may give a reading, this does not necessarily mean the reading is correct. In addition, some tachometers hook up differently from others. If you can't figure out whether or not your tachometer will work on your truck, check with the tachometer manufacturer. Dwell readings have no significance at all.

HEI System Testers

Instruments designed specifically for testing HEI systems are available from several tool manufacturers. Some of these will even test the module itself. However, the test given in the following section will require only an ohmmeter and a voltmeter.

CAUTION: *Dangerously high voltages are present in any electronic ignition system. Never attempt to connect or disconnect test leads or wires with the ignition key ON.*

TROUBLESHOOTING THE HEI SYSTEM

The symptoms of a defective component within the HEI system are exactly the same as those you would encounter in a conventional system. Some of these symptoms are:

- Hard or no Starting
- Rough Idle
- Poor Fuel Economy
- Engine misses under load or while accelerating

If you suspect a problem in the ignition system, there are certain preliminary checks which you should carry out before you begin to check the electronic portions of the system. First, it is extremely important to make sure the vehicle battery is in a good state of charge. A defective or poorly charged battery will cause the various components of the ignition system to read incorrectly when they are being tested. Second, make sure all wiring connections are clean and tight, not only at the battery, but also at the distributor cap, ignition coil, and at the electronic control module.

Since the only change between electronic and conventional ignition systems is in the distributor component area, it is imperative to check the secondary ignition circuit first. If the secondary circuit checks out properly, then the engine condition is probably not the fault of the ignition system. To check the secondary ignition system, perform a simple spark test. Remove one of the plug wires and insert some sort of extension in the plug socket. An old spark plug with the ground electrode removed makes a good extension. Using insulated pliers, hold the wire and extension about ¼ in. away from the block and crank the engine. If a normal spark occurs, then the problem is most likely *not* in the ignition system. Check for fuel system problems, or fouled spark plugs.

If, however, there is no spark or a weak spark, then further ignition system testing will have to be done. Troubleshooting techniques fall into two categories, depending on the nature of the problem. The categories are (1) Engine cranks, but won't start or (2) Engine runs, but runs rough or cuts out.

Engine Fails to Start

If the engine won't start, perform a spark test as described earlier. If no spark occurs, check for the presence of normal battery voltage at the battery (BAT) terminal in the distributor cap. The ignition switch must be in the "on" position for this test. Either a voltmeter or a test light may be used for this test. Connect the test light wire to ground and the probe end to the BAT terminal at the distributor. If the light comes on, you have voltage to the distrib-utor. If the light fails to come on, this indicates an open circuit in the ignition primary wiring leading to the distributor. In this case, you will have to check wiring continuity back to the ignition switch using a test light. If there is battery voltage at the BAT terminal, but no spark at the plugs, then the problem lies within the distributor assembly. Go on to the distributor components test section.

Engine Runs, but Runs Rough or Cuts Out

Make sure the plug wires are in good shape first. There should be no obvious cracks or breaks. You can check the plug wires with an ohmmeter, but *do not* pierce the wires with a probe. Check the chart for the correct plug wire resistance.

If the plug wires are OK, remove the cap assembly, and check for moisture, cracks, chips, or carbon tracks, or any other high voltage leaks or failures. Replace the cap if you find any defects. Make sure the timer wheel rotates when the engine is cranked. If everything is all right so far go on to the distributor components test section.

HEI Plug Wire Resistance Chart

Wire Length	Minimum	Maximum
0–15 inches	3000 ohms	10,000 ohms
15–25 inches	4000 ohms	15,000 ohms
25–35 inches	6000 ohms	20,000 ohms
Over 35 inches	6000 ohms	25,000 ohms

Distributor Components Testing

If the trouble has been narrowed down to the units within the distributor, the following tests can help pinpoint the defective component. An ohmmeter with both high and low ranges should be used. These tests are made with the cap assembly removed and the battery wire disconnected.

1. Connect an ohmmeter between the TACH and BAT terminals in the distributor cap. The primary coil resistance should be less than one ohm (zero or nearly zero).

2. To check the coil secondary resistance, connect an ohmmeter between the rotor button and the BAT terminal. Then connect the ohmmeter between the ground terminal and the rotor button. The resistance in both cases should be between 6,000 and 30,000 ohms.

3. Replace the coil *only* if the readings in step one and two are infinite.

NOTE: *These resistance checks will not disclose shorted coil windings. This condition can be detected only with scope analysis or a suitably designed coil tester. If these instruments are unavailable, replace the coil with a known good coil as a final coil test.*

4. To test the pick-up coil, first disconnect the white and green module leads. Set the ohmmeter on the high scale and connect it between a ground and either the white or green lead. Any resistance measurement *less* than infinity requires replacement of the pickup coil.

5. Pick-up coil continuity is tested by connecting the ohmmeter (on low range) between the white and green leads. Normal resistance is between 500 and 1500 ohms. Move the vacuum advance arm while performing this test. This will detect any break in coil continuity. Such a condition can cause intermittent misfiring. Replace the pick-up coil if the reading is outside the specific limits.

6. If no defects have been found at this time, and you still have a problem, then the module will have to be checked. If you do not have access to a module tester, the only possible alternative is a substitution test. If the module fails the substitution test, replace it.

COMPONENT REPLACEMENT ON 4–2000, 6–2800 ENGINES

Integral Ignition Coil

1. Disconnect the feed and module wire terminal connectors from the distributor cap.

2. Remove the ignition set retainer.

3. Remove the 4 coil cover-to-distributor cap screws and coil cover.

4. Remove the 4 coil-to-distributor cap screws.

5. Using a blunt drift, press the coil wire spade terminals up out of the distributor cap.

6. Lift the coil up out of the distributor cap.

7. Remove and clean the coil spring, rubber seal washer and coil cavity of the distributor cap.

8. Coat the rubber seal with a dielectric lubricant furnished in the replacement ignition coil package.

9. Reverse the above procedures to install.

Distributor Cap

1. Remove the feed and module wire terminal connectors from the distributor cap.

2. Remove the retainer and spark plug wires from the cap.

3. Depress and release the 4 distributor cap-to-housing retainers and lift off the cap assembly.

4. Remove the 4 coil cover screws and cover.

5. Using a finger or a blunt drift, push the spade terminals up out of the distributor cap.

6. Remove all 4 coil screws and lift the coil,

coil spring and rubber seal washer out of the cap coil cavity.

7. Using a new distributor cap, reverse the above procedures to assemble, being sure to clean and lubricate the rubber seal washer with dielectric lubricant.

Rotor

1. Disconnect the feed and module wire connectors from the distributor.

2. Depress and release the 4 distributor cap to housing retainers and lift off the cap assembly.

3. Remove the two rotor attaching screws and rotor.

4. Reverse the above procedure to install.

Vacuum Advance

1. Remove the distributor cap and rotor as previously described.

2. Disconnect the vacuum hose from the vacuum advance unit.

3. Remove the two vacuum advance retraining screws, pull the advance unit outward, rotate and disengage the operating rod from its tang.

4. Reverse the above procedure to install.

Module

1. Remove the distributor cap and rotor as previously described.

2. Disconnect the harness connector and pick-up coil spade connectors from the module. Be careful not to damage the wires when removing the connector.

3. Remove the two screws and module from the distributor housing.

4. Coat the bottom of the new module with dielectric lubricant supplied with the new module. Reverse the above procedure to install.

NOTE: *The dielectric silicone grease helps dissipate heat when the module is operating.*

COMPONENT REPLACEMENT ON 4–1950 ENGINE

Distributor Disassembly and Assembly

1. Remove the cap.

2. Remove the rotor. Remove the gasket.

3. Remove the static shield.

4. Unbolt and remove the vacuum advance unit.

5. Disconnect the wiring harness.

6. Remove the reluctor assembly from the shaft by carefully prying with two screwdrivers.

7. Unbolt and remove the breaker plate.

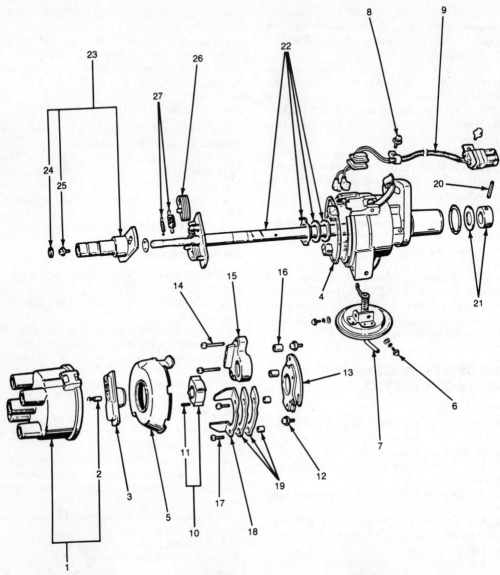

1. Cap assembly	10. Pole piece	19. Magnet set
2. Carbon point	11. Roll pin	20. Roll pin
3. Rotor head	12. Screw	21. Collar
4. Packing	13. Breaker plate assembly	22. Shaft assembly
5. Cover	14. Screw	23. Rotor shaft assembly
6. Screw	15. P/U coil module assembly	24. Packing
7. Vacuum control assembly	16. Spacer	25. Screw
8. Screw	17. Screw	26. Governor weight
9. Harness assembly	18. Stator	27. Governor spring

HEI distributor components, 4-1950

8. Remove the module from the breaker plate.

9. Installation is the reverse of removal.

Reluctor Air Gap

Use a non-magnetic feeler gauge such as brass or plastic for this procedure.

Place a feeler gauge between the pole piece and the stator. Measure the air gap. Gap should be .012–.022 in. To adjust the air gap, loosen the screws and move the pole piece. When the gap is correct, tighten the screws. Recheck the air gap after tightening.

Ignition Timing

Timing should be checked at each tune-up. It isn't likely to change much with HEI. The tim-

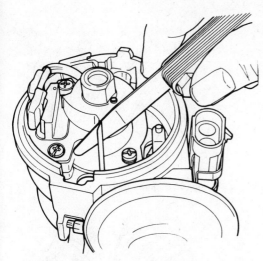

Checking the air gap on the 4-1950 distributor

ing marks consist of a notch on the rim of the crankshaft pulley or vibration damper and a graduated scale attached to the engine front (timing) cover. A stroboscopic flash (dynamic) timing light must be used, as a static light is too inaccurate for emission controlled engines.

There are three basic types of timing light available. The first is a simple neon bulb with two wire connections. One wire connects to the spark plug terminal and the other plugs into the end of the spark plug wire for the No. 1 cylinder, thus connecting the light in series with the spark plug. This type of light is pretty dim and must be held very closely to the timing marks to be seen. Sometimes a dark corner has to be sought out to see the flash at all. This type of light is very inexpensive. The second type operates from the vehicle battery—two alligator clips connect to the battery terminals, while an adapter enables a third clip to be connected to the No. 1 spark plug and wire. This type is a bit more expensive, but it provides a nice bright flash that you can see even in bright sunlight. It is the type most often seen in professional shops. The third type replaces the battery power source with 110 volt current.

Some timing lights have other features built into them, such as dwell meters or tachometers. These are convenient, in that they reduce the tangle of wires under the hood when you're working, but may duplicate the functions of tools you already have. One worthwhile feature, which is becoming more of a necessity with higher voltage ignition systems, is an inductive pickup. The inductive pickup clamps around the No. 1 spark plug wire, sensing the surges of high voltage electricity as they are sent to the plug. The advantage is that no mechanical connection is inserted between the wire and the plug, which eliminates false signals to the timing light. A timing light with an inductive pickup should be used on HEI systems.

To check and adjust the timing:

1. Warm up the engine to normal operating temperature. Stop the engine and connect the timing light to the No. 1 (left front on V6 front on 4 cylinder) wire. You can also use the No. 6 wire, if it is more convenient. Numbering is illustrated in Chapter 3. Under no circumstances should the spark plug wire be pierced to hook up a timing light. Clean off the timing marks and mark the pulley or damper notch and timing scale with white chalk. The timing notch on the pulley or damper can be elusive. The best way to get it to an accessible position for marking is to "bump" the engine around using either the ignition key or a remote starter.

2. Disconnect and plug the vacuum line at the distributor. This is done to prevent any distributor vacuum advance. A short screw, pencil, or a golf tee can be used to plug the line.

3. Start the engine and adjust the idle speed to that specified in the "Tune-Up Specifications" chart. With automatic transmission, set the specified idle speed in Park. It will be too high, since it is normally (in most cases) adjusted in Drive. However, it is safer to adjust the timing in Park and to reset the idle speed after all timing work is done. Some trucks require that the timing be set with the transmission in Neutral. Refer to the "Tune-up Specifications" chart or the underhood sticker for details. You can disconnect the idle solenoid, if any, to get the speed down. Otherwise, adjust the idle speed crew. This is done to prevent any centrifugal (mechanical) advance. All tachometer connections are to the TACH terminal. Some tachometers must connect to the TACH terminal and to the positive battery terminal. Some tachometers won't work with HEI.

CAUTION: *Never ground the HEI TACH terminal; serious system damage will result.*

4. Aim the timing light at the pointer marks. Be careful not to touch the fan, because it may appear to be standing still. Keep the timing light wires clear of the fan, belts, and pulleys. If the pulley or damper notch isn't aligned with the proper timing mark (see the "Tune-Up Specifications" chart), the timing will have to be adjusted.

NOTE: *TDC or Top Dead Center corresponds to 0 degrees. B, or BTDC, or Before Top Dead Center may be shown as BEFORE. A, or ATDC, or After Top Dead Center may be shown as AFTER.*

5. Loosen the distributor base clamp locknut. You can buy a special wrench which makes this task a lot easier on V6s. Turn the distribu-

tor slowly to adjust the timing, holding it by the body and not the cap. Turn the distributor in the direction of rotor rotation (found in the "Firing Order" illustration) to retard, and against the direction of rotation to advance.

6. Tighten the locknut. Check the timing again, in case the distributor moved slightly as you tightened it.

7. Replace the distributor vacuum line. Correct the idle speed.

8. Stop the engine and disconnect the timing light.

Diesel Injection Timing

NOTE: *This procedure requires the use of a dial indicator and adapter. DO NOT attempt any injection timing adjustments without this tool.*

1. Check that notched line on the injection pump flange is in alignment with notched line on the injection pump front bracket.

2. Bring the piston in No. 1 cylinder to top dead center on compression stroke by turning the crankshaft as necessary.

3. With the timing pulley housing cover removed, check that timing belt is properly tensioned and that timing marks are aligned.

4. Disconnect the injection pipe from the injection pump and remove the distributor head screw, then install static timing gauge. Set the lift approximately 1 mm (0.04 in.) from the plunger.

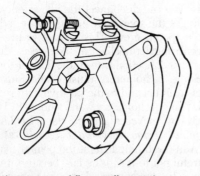

Injection pump and flange alignment

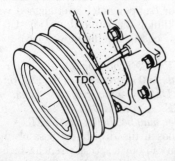

No. 1 piston at TDC

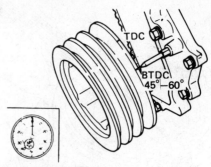

No. 1 piston 45–60 degrees BTDC

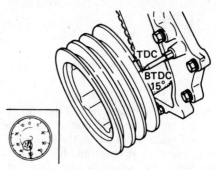

No. 1 piston 15 degrees BTDC

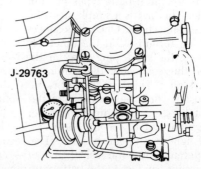

Static timing gauge installed

5. Use a wrench to hold the delivery holder when loosening the sleeve nuts on the injection pump side.

6. Bring the piston in No. 1 cylinder to a point 45–60 degrees before top dead center by turning the crankshaft, then calibrate the dial indicator to zero.

7. Turn the crankshaft pulley slightly in both directions and check that gauge indication is stable.

8. Turn the crankshaft in normal direction of rotation, and take the reading of the dial indicator when the timing mark (15 degrees) on the crankshaft pulley is in alignment with the pointer. Reading should be 0.020 in.

9. If the reading of dial indicator deviates from the specified range, hold crankshaft in position 15 degrees before top dead center and loosen two nuts on injection pump flange.

10. Move the injection pump to a point where dial indicator gives reading of 0.020 in., then tighten pump flange nuts.

Valve Lash

Valve adjustment determines how far the valves enter the cylinder and how long they stay open and closed.

NOTE: *While all valve adjustments must be made as accurately as possible, it is better to have the valve adjustment slightly loose than slightly tight, as a burned valve may result from overly tight adjustments.*

ADJUSTMENT

1950cc and 2238cc Diesel

NOTE: *The valves are adjusted with the engine cold.*

1. Make sure that the cylinder head and camshaft retaining bolts are tightened to the proper torque.

2. Remove the camshaft carrier side cover.

3. Turn the crankshaft with a wrench on the front pulley attaching bolt or by bumping the engine with the starter or remote starter button until the No. 1 piston is at TDC of the compression stroke. You can tell when the piston is coming up on the compression stroke by removing the spark plug and placing your thumb over the hole and you will feel air being forced out of the spark plug hole past your thumb. Stop turning the crankshaft when the TDC timing mark on the crankshaft pulley is directly aligned with the timing mark pointer.

4. With the No. 1 piston at TDC of the compression stroke, check the clearance between the rocker arm and the camshaft with the proper thickness feeler gauge on Nos. 1 and 2 intake valves and Nos. 1 and 3 exhaust valves.

5. Adjust the clearance by loosening the locknut with an open-end wrench, turning the adjuster screw with a phillips head screwdriver and retightening the locknut. The proper thickness feeler gauge should pass between the camshaft and the rocker with a slight drag when the clearance is correct.

6. Turn the crankshaft one full turn to position the No. 4 piston at TDC of its compression stroke. Adjust the remaining valves: No. 2 and 4 exhaust and Nos. 3 and 4 intake in the same manner as outlined in step 5.

7. Install the camshaft carrier sidecover.

Idle Speed and Mixture Adjustment

1950cc ENGINE

In order to adjust the idle mixture you must first remove the plug that covers the mixture screw.

1. To remove the plug, first remove the carburetor and turn it upside down.

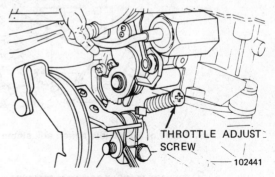

THROTTLE ADJUST SCREW

102441

4-1950 idle adjustment

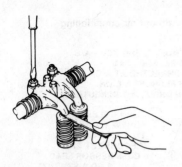

Valve clearance adjustment

Number of Cylinders	1		2		3		4	
Valve Arrangement	Exh.	In.	In.	Exh.	Exh.	In.	In.	Exh.
When piston in No. 1 cylinder is held at T.D.C.	0	0	0			0		
When piston in No. 4 cylinder is held at T.D.C.				0		0	0	0

Valve adjusting sequence

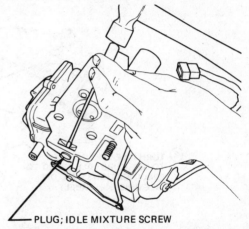

PLUG; IDLE MIXTURE SCREW

Removing the mixture screw plug on the 4-1950

2. Remove the plug carefully with a hammer and screwdriver, (see illustration).

3. Reinstall the carburetor and adjust as necessary.

4. Turn the mixture screw all the way in, and then back it out 2 turns (Federal) and 1 turn (California).

5. Readjust the idle if necessary.

2000cc, 2800cc ENGINES

1. See the underhood sticker for those procedures necessary prior to setting the idle speed.

2. With the truck prepared, turn the idle speed screw to adjust the speed to specifications.

3. On trucks with air conditioning, disconnect the air conditioning compressor lead wire. Turn the air conditioning on and place the transmission in drive (AT) or neutral (MT). Make sure that the handbrake is fully set. Open the throttle slightly to extend the solenoid plunger. Turn the solenoid screw to establish the specified rpm. Reconnect the compressor lead wire.

DIESEL ENGINE

Slow Idle Speed Adjustment

1. Set parking brake and block drive wheels.
2. Place transmission in neutral.
3. Start and warm up the engine. Engine coolant temperature above 80°C (176°F).
4. Connect a diesel tachometer according to the manufacturer's instructions.

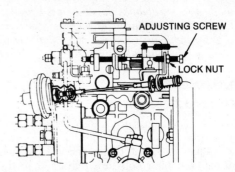

Diesel idle speed adjustment points

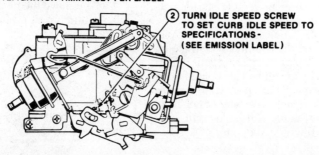

4-2000 or 6-2800 idle speed adjustment on trucks without air conditioning

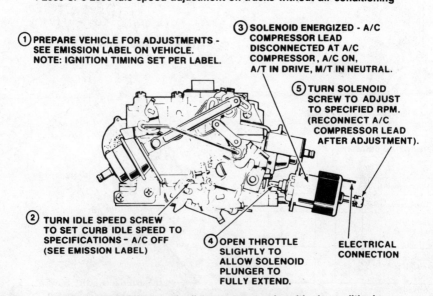

4-2000 or 6-2800 idle speed adjustment on trucks with air conditioning

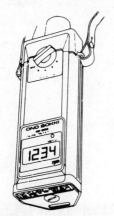

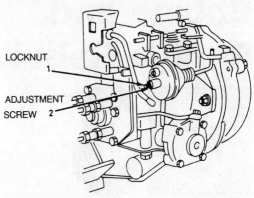

Diesel engine fast idle speed adjustments—1984 and later

Diesel tachometer

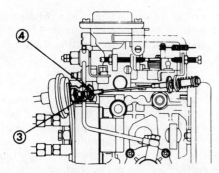

Diesel fast idle adjustment—1982–83 models

5. If the idle speed deviates from the specified range of 700–800 rpm, loosen the idle speed adjusting screw lock nut.

6. Turn the adjusting screw in or out until the idle speed is in the correct range. After tightening the lock nut, lock it in place.

Fast Idle Speed Adjustment

1. Start and warm up the engine. Engine coolant temperature above 80°C (176°F).

2. Connect a diesel tachometer according to the manufacturers instructions.

3. Disconnect the hoses from the vacuum switch valve, then connect a pipe (4 mm dia.) in position between the hoses.

4. Loosen adjust nut and adjust engine idle speed by moving the nut. Fast idle should be 900–950 rpm.

5. Tighten the lock nut.

6. Remove engine tachometer.

Engine and Engine Rebuilding

3

ENGINE ELECTRICAL

Distributor

REMOVAL

1950cc ENGINE

1. Disconnect the negative battery cable, then remove the high-tension wires from the distributor cap terminal towers, after tagging each one for reassembly.

2. Remove the primary lead from the coil terminal (small wire).

3. Disconnect the vacuum line.

4. Unlatch the two distributor cap retaining clips and remove the distributor cap.

5. Note the position of the rotor in relation to the base. Scribe a mark on the base of the distributor and on the engine block to facilitate reinstallation. Align the marks with the direction the metal tip of the rotor is pointing.

6. Remove the bolt and bracket which holds the distributor to the engine.

7. Lift the distributor assembly from the engine. Do not crank the engine with the distributor removed.

8. Insert the distributor shaft and assembly into the engine. Line up the mark on the distributor and the one on the engine with the metal tip of the rotor. Make sure that the vacuum advance diaphragm is pointed in the same direction as it was pointed originally. This will be done automatically if the marks on the engine and the distributor are lined up with the rotor.

9. Install the distributor hold-down bolt and clamp. Leave the screw loose enough so that you can move the distributor with heavy hand pressure.

10. Connect the primary wire to the coil. Install the distributor cap on the distributor housing. Secure the distributor cap with the spring clips.

11. Install the spark plug wires. Make sure that the wires are pressed all the way into the top of the distributor cap and firmly onto the spark plug.

12. Check and adjust the timing if necessary.

NOTE: *If the crankshaft has been turned or the engine disturbed in any manner (i.e., disassembled and rebuilt) while the distributor was removed, or if the marks were not drawn, it will be necessary to initially time the engine. Follow the procedure given below.*

1. It is necessary to place the No. 1 cylinder in the firing position to correctly install the distributor. To locate this position, the ignition timing marks on the crankshaft front pulley are used.

2. Remove the No. 1 cylinder spark plug. Turn the crankshaft until the piston in the No. 1 cylinder is moving up on the compression stroke. This can be determined by placing your thumb over the spark plug hole and feeling the air being forced out of the cylinder. Stop turning the crankshaft when the timing marks that are used to time the engine are aligned.

3. Oil the distributor housing lightly where the distributor bears on the cylinder block.

4. Install the distributor so that the rotor, which is mounted on the shaft, points toward the No. 1 spark plug terminal tower position when the cap is installed. Of course you won't be able to see the direction in which the rotor is pointing if the cap is on the distributor, and make a mark on the side of the distributor housing just below the No. 1 spark plug terminal. Make sure that the rotor points toward that mark when you install the distributor.

5. When the distributor shaft has reached the bottom of the hole, move the rotor back and forth slightly until the driving lug on the end of the shaft enters the slots cut in the end

of the oil pump shaft and the distributor assembly slides down into place.

6. When the distributor is correctly installed, line up the marks that you made before the distributor was removed from the engine.

7. Install the distributor hold-down bolt and bracket.

8. Install the spark plug into the No. 1 spark plug hole and continue from step 3 of the distributor installation procedure.

2000cc Engine

1. Disconnect the negative battery cable.

2. Tag and disconnect all wires leading from the distributor cap.

3. Remove the air cleaner housing as previously detailed.

4. Remove the distributor cap.

5. Disconnect the AIR pipe-to-exhaust manifold hose at the air management valve.

6. Unscrew the rear engine lift bracket bolt and nut lift it off the stud and then position the entire assembly out of the way to facilitate better access to the distributor.

7. Mark the position of the distributor, relative to the engine block and then scribe a mark on the distributor body indicating the initial position of the rotor.

8. Remove the hold-down nut and clamp from the base of the distributor. Remove the distributor from the engine. The drive gear on the distributor shaft is helical and the shaft will rotate slightly as the distributor is removed. Note and mark the position of the rotor at this second position. *Do not crank the engine while the distributor is removed.*

9. To install the distributor, rotate the shaft until the rotor aligns with the second mark you made (when the shaft stopped moving). Lubricate the drive gear with clean engine oil and install the distributor into the engine. As the distributor is installed, the rotor should move to the first mark that you made. This will ensure proper timing. If the marks do not align properly, remove the distributor and try again.

10. Install the clamp and hold-down nut.

NOTE: *You may wish to use a magnet attached to an extension bar to position the clamp on the stud.*

11. Installation of the remaining components is in the reverse order of removal. Check the ignition timing.

2800cc Engine

1. Disconnect the negative battery cable and wiring harness connectors at the side of the distributor cap.

2. Disconnect the vacuum advance line, if equipped.

3. Scribe a mark on the engine in line with the rotor and then mark the distributor body so all marks align with the rotor.

4. Remove the distributor hold-down clamp and nut.

5. Lift the distributor from the engine. Do not rotate or crank the engine with the distributor removed.

CAUTION: *Do not clamp the distributor body tightly in a steel-jawed vise during service procedures. Excessive pressure can crack or distort the distributor body.*

To install the distributor with the engine undisturbed:

6. Reinsert the distributor into its opening, aligning the previously-made marks on the housing and the engine block.

7. The rotor may have to be turned either way a slight amount to align the rotor-to-housing marks.

8. Install the retaining clamp and bolt. Install the distributor cap, primary wire, and the vacuum hose.

9. Start the engine and check the ignition timing.

To install the distributor with the engine disturbed:

10. Turn the engine so the No. 1 piston is at the top of its compression stroke. This may be determined by covering the No. 1 spark plug hole with your thumb and slowly turning the engine over. When the timing mark on the crankshaft pulley aligns with the 0 on the timing scale and your thumb is pushed out by compression, No. 1 piston is at top-dead-center (TDC).

11. Install the distributor to the engine block so that the vacuum advance unit points in the correct direction.

12. Turn the rotor so that it will point to the No. 1 terminal in the cap.

13. Install the distributor into the engine block. It may be necessary to turn the rotor a little in either direction in order to engage the gears.

14. Tap the starter a few times to ensure that the oil pump shaft is mated to the distributor shaft.

15. Bring the engine to No. 1 TDC again and check to see that the rotor is indeed pointing toward the No. 1 terminal of the cap.

16. After correct positioning is assured, turn the distributor housing so that all scribed marks made earlier align. Tighten the retaining clamp.

17. Install the cap and primary wire. Check the ignition timing. Install the vacuum hose.

NOTE: *On engines with electronic spark timing, make sure the timing marks agree with the specifications on the underhood emission control sticker.*

ALTERNATOR PRECAUTIONS

To prevent damage to the on-board computer, alternator and regulator, the following precautionary measures must be taken when working with the electrical system.

• Never reverse battery connections. Always check the battery polarity visually. This is to be done before any connections are made to be sure that all of the connections correspond to the battery ground polarity.

• Booster batteries for starting must be connected properly. Make sure that the positive cable of the booster battery is connected to the positive terminal of the battery that is getting the boost. This applies to both negative and ground cables.

• Make sure the ignition switch is OFF when connecting or disconnecting any electrical component, especially on trucks equipped with an on-board computer control system.

• Disconnect the battery cables before using a fast charger; the charger has a tendency to force current through the diodes in the opposite direction for which they were designed. This burns out the diodes.

• Never use a fast charger as a booster for starting the vehicle.

• Never disconnect the voltage regulator while the engine is running.

• Do not ground the alternator output terminal.

• Do not operate the alternator on an open circuit with the field energized.

• Do not attempt to polarize an alternator.

REMOVAL AND INSTALLATION

1. Disconnect the negative battery cable.
2. Remove the air pump, if necessary, to gain access to the alternator. Remove the drive belt.
3. Disconnect the alternator circuit at the connector and disconnect the cable from the "A" terminal.
4. Remove the mounting bolts on the lower part of the alternator and the fan belt adjusting bolt and remove the alternator.
5. Install the alternator in the reverse order of removal and tighten the fan belt and air pump belt tension.

Starter

REMOVAL AND INSTALLATION

All Engines

1. Disconnect the battery cables.
2. Disconnect and tag all wires at the starter.
3. Raise and support the vehicle on jackstands.

4. Remove any braces, shields or skid plates that are in the way.
5. Unbolt and remove the starter. Be careful; it's heavy.
6. Installation is the reverse of removal.

STARTER DRIVE REPLACEMENT

1. Remove the drive housing by removing the through bolts.
2. Remove the thrust collar from the end of the retaining shaft.
3. Using a ½ in. pipe or another suitable tool, drive the retainer toward the armature end of the snap-ring.
4. Remove the snap-ring from the groove in the shaft using pliers. If the snap-ring is badly distorted, it will have to be replaced.
5. Slide the drive mechanism off the armature shaft.

To assemble the starter drive, use the following procedure.

1. Slide the drive assembly onto the armature shaft after it has been lubricated with a silicone lubricant.
2. The retainer is positioned on the shaft, with the cupped surface facing away from the pinion.
3. Place the snap-ring on the end of the shaft and slide it into its groove.
4. Place the thrust collar on the shaft with its shoulder next to the snap-ring.
5. Using two pliers, one on either side, force the snap-ring into the retainer.
6. Lubricate the drive housing bushing and slide the armature shaft into the starter housing.
7. Assemble the commutator end of the starter after lubricating the bushing and placing the leather brake washer in position.

SOLENOID REPLACEMENT

1 Remove the screw and washer from the motor connector strap terminal.
2. Remove the two solenoid retaining screws.
3. Twist the solenoid housing clockwise to remove the flange key from the keyway in the housing. Then remove the housing.
4. To re-install the unit, place the return spring on the plunger and place the solenoid body on the drive housing. Turn counterclockwise to engage the flange key. Place the two retaining screws in position and install the screw and washer which secures the strap terminal. Install the unit on the starter.

ENGINE MECHANICAL

NOTE: *The following procedures require the use of an engine hoist with sufficient capacity to safely lift and support 500–1000 lbs.*

Engine Removal and Installation

Gasoline Engine

1. Raise the hood and disconnect the battery cables.
2. Remove the skid plate and drain both the cooling system and the oil pan.
3. Remove the air cleaner assembly and vacuum hoses. Mark the vacuum hoses for reinstallation.
4. Disconnect all hoses, tubing and electrical leads from the engine and mark them for reinstallation.
5. Remove the radiator and fan blade assembly.
6. Disconnect the exhaust pipe from the exhaust manifold.
7. Raise the vehicle and, if equipped with a manual transmission, remove the clutch return spring and cable.
8. Remove the starter motor.
9. Remove the flywheel cover pan.
10. Remove the bell housing bolts and support the transmission with a suitable jack.
11. Attach the engine hoist securely. Lift the engine slightly and remove the engine mount nuts.
12. Make certain that all lines, hoses, wires and cables have been disconnected from the engine and the frame.
13. Remove the engine from the vehicle with the front of the engine raised slightly.
14. Installation is the reverse of removal.

Diesel Engine

2-WHEEL DRIVE

1. Raise engine hood.
2. Disconnect the battery ground cable.
3. Remove the hood.
4. Remove the battery assembly.
5. Remove under cover and drain the cooling system by opening the drain plugs on the radiator and on the cylinder block.
6. Remove the air cleaaner assembly as follows:
   a. Remove the intake silencer.
   b. Remove the bolts fixing the air cleaner and loosen the clamp bolt.
   c. Lift the air cleaner slightly and disconnect the breather hose, then remove the air cleaner assembly.
7. Disconnect the upper water hose at the engine side.
8. Loosen the compressor drive belts by moving the power steering oil pump or idler (if so equipped).
9. Remove the cooling fan and fan shroud.
10. Disconnect the lower water hose at the engine side.
11. Remove the radiator grille.
12. Remove the radiator attaching bolts and remove the radiator.
13. Disconnect the accelerator control cable from the injection pump side.
14. Disconnect the air conditioner compressor control cable (if so equipped).
15. Disconnect the fuel hoses from the injection pump.
NOTE: *See the Fuel Section for precautions and service procedures on the diesel engine injection pump and lines.*
16. Disconnect the battery cable from the cylinder body.
17. Disconnect the transmission wiring.
18. Disconnect the vacuum hose from the fast idle actuator.
19. Disconnect the connector at fuel cut solenoid.
20. Disconnect the A/C compressor wiring.
21. Disconnect the heater hoses extending from the heater unit from the dash panel side.
22. Disconnect the hose for master-vac from the vacuum pump.
23. Disconnect vacuum hose from the vacuum pump.
24. Disconnect the generator wiring at the connector.
25. Disconnect the exhaust pipe from the exhaust manifold at the flange.
26. Remove the exhaust pipe mounting brake from the engine back plate.
27. Disconnect the starter motor wiring.
28. Disconnect the battery cable from starter motor.
29. Slide the gearshift lever boot upwards on the lever. Remove 2 gearshift lever attaching bolts and remove lever.
30. Place a pan under transmission to receive oil, disconnect speedometer cable at the transmission then disconnect the ground cable.
31. Disconnect the driveshaft at differential side.
32. Remove the driveshaft.
33. Remove return spring from clutch fork.
34. Disconnect clutch cable from hooked portion of clutch fork and pull it out forward through stiffener bracket.
35. Remove two bracket to transmission rear mount bolts and nuts.
36. Raise engine and transmission as required and remove (4) crossmember to frame bracket bolts.
37. Remove the rear mounting nuts from the transmission rear extension.
38. Disconnect electrical connectors at CRS switch and back-up lamp switch.
39. Remove the engine mounting bolt and nuts. Check that the engine is slightly lifted before removing the engine mounting bolt and nuts.

40. Engine removal,

a. Check to make certain all the parts have been removed or disconnected from the engine that are fastened to the frame side.

b. Remove the engine toward front of the vehicle by maneuvering the hoist, so that front part of the engine is lifted slightly.

4-WHEEL DRIVE MODELS

1. Raise engine hood.
2. Disconnect the battery ground cable.
3. Remove the engine hood.
4. Remove the battery assembly.
5. Remove under cover and drain the cooling system by opening the drain plugs on the radiator and on the cylinder block.
6. Remove the air cleaner as follows:

a. Remove the intake silencer.

b. Remove the bolts fixing the air cleaner and loosen the clamp bolt.

c. Lift the air cleaner slightly and disconnect the breather hose, then remove the air cleaner assembly.

7. Disconnect the upper water hose at the engine side.
8. Loosen the compressor drive belts by moving the power steering oil pump or idler (if so equipped).
9. Remove the cooling fan and fan shroud.
10. Disconnect the lower water hose at the engine side.
11. Remove the radiator grille.
12. Remove the radiator attaching bolts and remove the radiator.
13. Disconnect the accelerator control cable from the injection pump side.
14. Disconnect the air conditioner compressor control cable (if so equipped).
15. Disconnect the fuel hoses from the injection pump.
16. Disconnect the battery cable from the cylinder body.
17. Disconnect the transmission wiring.
18. Disconnect the vacuum hose from the fast idle actuator.
19. Disconnect the connector at fuel cut solenoid.
20. Disconnect the A/C compressor wiring.
21. Disconnect the heater hoses extending from the heater unit from the dash panel side.
22. Disconnect the hose for master-vac from the vacuum pump.
23. Disconnect the vacuum hose from the vacuum pump.
24. Disconnect the generator wiring at the connector.
25. Disconnect the exhaust pipe from the exhaust manifold at the flange.
26. Remove the exhaust pipe mounting brake from the engine back plate.

27. Disconnect the starter motor wiring.
28. Disconnect the battery cable from starter motor.
29. Slide the transmission and transfer gearshift lever boot upwards on each lever, remove gearshift lever attaching bolts.
30. Remove return spring from transfer gear shift lever then remove levers.
31. Remove the transmission.
32. Remove the engine mounting bolts and nuts. Check that the engine is slightly lifted before removing the engine mounting bolts and nuts.
33. Engine removal:

a. Check to make certain all the parts have been removed or disconnected from the engine that are fastened to the frame side.

b. Remove the engine toward front of the vehicle by maneuvering the hoist, so that front part of the engine is lifted slightly.

Rocker Arms and Push Rods
REMOVAL AND INSTALLATION
1950cc Engine

1. Remove the camshaft carrier as outlined under Cylinder Head Removal.
2. Remove the rocker spring from the pivot and lift the rocker from the cylinder head. Be careful not to lose the rocker guide resting on the top of each of the valves.
3. Install in the reverse order of removal.

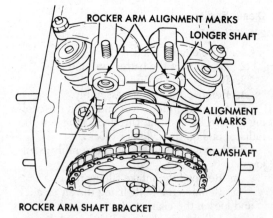

ROCKER ARM ALIGNMENT MARKS
LONGER SHAFT
ALIGNMENT MARKS
CAMSHAFT
ROCKER ARM SHAFT BRACKET
103000

4-1950 rocker arm shaft installation

2238cc Diesel Engine

1. Remove the rocker cover.
2. Remove the 8 bolts fixing the rocker arm brackets in sequence commencing with the outer ones.
3. Remove the rocker arm, bracket and shaft assembly.

General Engine Specifications

Engine Displacement cc (cu. in)	Fuel System	Horsepower @ rpm SAE Net	Net Torque ft. lb. @ rpm	Bore and Stroke (in.)	Compression Ratio	Oil Pressure @ 1400 rpm psi
1950 (118.9)	2-bbl	84 @ 4600	101 @ 3000	3.43 x 3.23	8.4:1	57
2000 (121)	2-bbl	83 @ 4600	108 @ 2400	3.50 x 3.15	9.3:1	45
2238 (136.6)	Diesel	58 @ 4300	93 @ 2200	3.46 x 3.62	21.0:1	55
2800 (173)	2-bbl	110 @ 4800	148 @ 2000	3.50 x 2.99	8.5:1	45

Crankshaft and Connecting Rod Specifications
(All measurements in inches)

Engine Displacement cc (cu. in)	Crankshaft					Connecting Rod	
	Main Bearing Journal Dia.	Main Bearing Oil Clearance	Crankshaft End-play	Thrust on No.	Journal Dia.	Oil Clearance	Side Clearance
1950 (118.9)	2.2050	0.0008–0.0025	0.0117 max.	3	1.9290	0.0007–0.0030	0.0137 max.
2000 (121)	①	②	0.0020–0.0071	3	1.9990	0.0010–0.0031	0.0039–0.0240
2238 (136.6)	2.3590	0.0011–0.0033	0.0018	3	2.0837	0.0016–0.0047	0.0024
2800 (173)	2.4940	0.0017–0.0030	0.0020–0.0067	3	1.9980	0.0014–0.0032	0.0063–0.0173

① Nos. 1, 2, 3, 4: 2.4940–2.4950   No. 5: 2.4930–2.4950
② Nos. 1, 2, 3, 4: 0.0006–0.0019   No. 5: 0.0014–0.0027

Piston and Ring Specifications

Engine Displacement cc (cu. in.)	Piston to Bore Clearance	Ring Side Clearance			Ring End Gap		
		Top Compression	Middle Compression	Oil Control	Top Compression	Middle Compression	Oil Control
1950 (118.9)	.0018–.0026	.0059 max.	.0059 max.	.0059 max.	.012–.020	.008–.016	.008–.035
2000 (121)	.0008–.0018	.0012–.0027	.0012–.0038	.0078 max.	.010–.020	.010–.020	.020–.055
2238 (136.6)	.0062–.0070	.0018–.0028	.0012–.0021	.0008–.0021	.008–.016	.008–.016	.008–.016
2800 (173)	.0017–.0027	.0012–.0028	.0016–.0037	.0078 max.	.010–.020	.010–.020	.020–.055

Valve Specifications

Engine Displacement cc (cu. in)	Seat Angle (deg)	Face Angle (deg)	Spring Test Pressure (lbs. @ in.)		Stem-to-Guide Clearance (in.)		Stem Diameter (in.)	
			Outer	Inner	Intake	Exhaust	Intake	Exhaust
1950 (118.9)	45	45	35 @ 1.614	20 @ 1.516	.0009–.0022	.0015–.0031	.3102 min.	.3091 min.
2000 (121)	46	45	182 @ 1.330	—	.0011–.0026	.0014–.0031	.3410–.3416	.3410–.3416
2238 (136.6)	45	45	145 @ 1.535	44 @ 1.457	.0015–.0027	.0025–.0037	.3150	.3150
2800 (173)	46	45	195 @ 1.180	—	.0010–.0027	.0010–.0027	.3410–.3416	.3410–.3416

Camshaft Specifications

| Engine | Journal Diameter | | | | Bearing Clearance | Lobe Lift | | Camshaft End Play |
	1	2	3	4		Intake	Exhaust	
4-1950	1.3365	1.3365	1.3365	1.3365	.0016–.0035	NA	NA	.0020–.0059
4-2000	1.8687	1.8687	1.8687	1.8687	.0010–.0040	.262	.262	NA
4-2238	1.8898	1.8898	1.8898	1.8898	.0020–.0047	NA	NA	.0032–.0079
6-2800	1.8687	1.8687	1.8687	1.8687	.0010–.0040	.231	.231	NA

NA: Information not available

Torque Specifications
(All readings in ft. lbs. unless noted)

| Engine Displacement cc (cu. in.) | Cylinder Head Bolts | Rod Bearing Bolts | Main Bearing Bolts | Crankshaft Pulley Bolts | Flywheel to Crankshaft Bolts | Manifolds | |
						Intake	Exhaust
1950 (118.9)	72	43	75	87	76	17	16
2000 (121)	70	37	70	75	50	23	25
2238 (136.6)	60	65	116–130	125–150	70	15	15
2800 (173)	70	37	70	75	50	23	25

4. To install, follow the removal procedure in reverse order.

5. Tighten the bracket fixing bolts evenly in sequence commencing with the inner ones to 15 ft. lbs.

2000cc Engine

1. Remove the air cleaner. Remove the cylinder head cover.

2. Remove the rocker arm nut and ball. Lift the rocker arm off the stud. *Always keep the rocker arm assemblies together and install them on the same stud.* Remove the push rods.

To install:

3. Coat the bearing surfaces of the rocker arms and the rocker arm balls with "Molykote" or its equivalent.

NOTE: *At time of installation, flanges must be free of oil. A bead of sealant must be applied to flanges and sealant must be wet to touch when bolts are torqued.*

4. Install the push rods making sure that they seat properly in the lifter.

5. Install the rocker arms, balls and nuts. Tighten the rocker arm nuts until all lash is eliminated.

6. Adjust the valves when the lifter is on the base circle of a camshaft lobe:

a. Crank the engine until the mark on the crankshaft pulley lines up with the '0' mark on the timing tab. Make sure that the engine is in the No. 1 firing position. Place your fingers on the No. 1 rocker arms as the mark on the crank pulley comes near the '0' mark. If the valves are not moving, the engine is in the No. 1 firing position. If the valves move,

the engine is in the No. 4 firing position; rotate the engine one complete revolution and it will be in the No. 1 position.

b. When the engine is in the No. 1 firing position, adjust the following valves:
- Exhaust—1,3
- Intake—1,2

c. Back the adjusting nut out until lash can be felt at the push rod, then turn the nut until all lash is removed (this can be determined by rotating the push rod while turning the adjusting nut). When all lash has been removed, turn the nut in 1½ additional turns, this will center the lifter plunger.

d. Crank the engine one complete revolution until the timing tab and the '0' mark are again in alignment. Now the engine is in the No. 4 firing position. Adjust the following valves:
- Exhaust—2,4
- Intake—3,4

7. Installation of the remaining components is in the reverse order of removal.

2800cc Engine

NOTE: *Some engines are assembled using RTV (Room Temperature Vulcanizing silicone sealant in place of rocker arm cover gasket. If the engine was assembled using RTV, never use a gasket when reasembling. Conversely, if the engine was assembled using a rocker arm cover gasket, never replace it with RTV.*

When using RTV an ⅛ inch bead is sufficient. Always run the bead on the inside of the bolt holes.

Rocker arms are removed by removing the adjusting nut. Be sure to adjust valve lash after replacing rocker arms.

NOTE: *When replacing an exhaust rocker, move an old intake rocker arm to the exhaust rocker arm stud and install the new rocker arm on the intake stud.*

Cylinder heads use threaded rocker arm studs. If the threads in the head are damaged or stripped, the head can be retapped and a helical type insert installed.

NOTE: *If engine is equipped with the A.I.R. exhaust emission control system, the interfering components of the system must be removed. Disconnect the lines at the air injection nozzles in the exhaust manifolds.*

Intake Manifold

REMOVAL AND INSTALLATION

1950cc Engine

1. Disconnect the battery ground cable and remove the air cleaner assembly.

2. Remove the EGR pipe clamp bolt at the rear of the cylinder head.

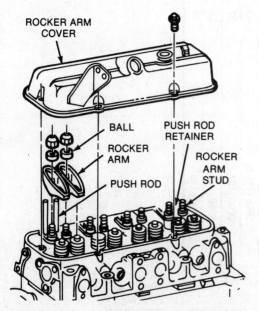

ROCKER ARM COVER

BALL

ROCKER ARM

PUSH ROD

PUSH ROD RETAINER

ROCKER ARM STUD

4-2000 rocker arm removal and installation

3. Raise the vehicle and remove the EGR pipe from the intake and exhaust manifolds.

4. Remove the EGR valve and bracket assembly from the intake manifold.

5. Lower the vehicle and drain the cooling system.

6. Remove the upper coolant hoses from the manifold.

7. Disconnect the accelerator linkage, vacuum lines, electrical wiring and fuel line from the intake manifold.

8. Remove the retaining nuts and remove the manifold from the cylinder head.

9. Remove the lower heater hose while holding the manifold away from the engine. Remove the manifold from the vehicle.

10. Installation is the reverse of removal.

2238 cc Diesel Engine

1. Raise engine hood.

2. Remove the bolts fixing the air cleaner and loosen the clamp bolt.

3. Lift the air cleaner slightly and disconnect the breather hose, then remove the air cleaner assembly.

4. Remove the 2 bolts and 4 nuts fixing the intake manifold.

5. Remove the intake manifold.

6. Installation is the reverse of removal. Torque the bolts to 15 ft. lbs., starting from the center and working outward.

2000cc Engine

1. Disconnect the negative battery cable.

2. Remove the air cleaner. Drain the cooling system.

3. Tag and disconnect all necessary vacuum lines and wires. Remove the idler pulley.

4. Remove the A.I.R. drive belt. If equipped with power steering, remove the drive belt and then remove the pump with the lines attached. Position the pump out of the way.

5. Remove the A.I.R. bracket-to-intake manifold bolt. Remove the air pump pulley.

6. If equipped with power steering, remove the A.I.R. thru-bolt and then the power steering adjusting bracket.

7. Loosen the lower bolt on the air pump mounting bracket so that the bracket will rotate.

8. Disconnect the fuel line at the carburetor. Disconnect the carburetor linkage and then remove the carburetor.

9. Lift off the Early Fuel Evaporation (EFE) heater grid.

10. Remove the distributor.

11. Remove the mounting bolts and nuts and remove the intake manifold. Make sure to disconnect the heater hose and condenser from the bottom of the intake manifold before you lift it all the way out.

12. Using a new gasket, replace the manifold, tightening the nuts and bolts to specification.

13. Installation of the remaining components is in the reverse order of removal. Adjust all necessary drive belts and check the ignition timing.

2800cc Engine

1. Remove the rocker covers.

2. Drain the cooling system.

3. If equipped, remove the AIR pump and bracket.

4. Remove the distributor cap. Mark the position of the ignition rotor in relation to the distributor body, and remove the distributor. Do not crank the engine with the distributor removed.

5. Remove the heater and radiator hoses from the intake manifold.

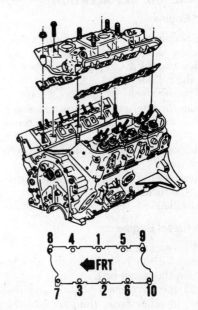

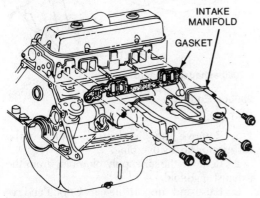

4-2000 intake manifold

3-2800 intake manifold showing torque sequence

6. Remove the power brake vacuum hose.

7. Disconnect and label the vacuum hoses. Remove the EFE pipe from the rear of the manifold.

8. Remove the carburetor linkage. Disconnect and plug the fuel line.

9. Remove the manifold retaining bolts and nuts.

10. Remove the intake manifold. Remove and discard the gaskets, and scrape off the old silicone seal from the front and rear ridges.

To install:

1. The gaskets are marked for right and left side installation; do not interchange them. Clean the sealing surface of the engine block, and apply a 3/16 in. bead of silicone sealer to each ridge.

2. Install the new gaskets onto the heads. The gaskets will have to be cut slightly to fit past the center pushrods. Do not cut any more material than necessary. Hold the gaskets in place by extending the ridge bead of sealer 1/4 in. onto the gasket ends.

3. Install the intake manifold. The area between the ridges and the manifold should be completely sealed.

4. Install the retaining bolts and nuts, and tighten in sequence to 23 ft. lbs. Do not overtighten; the manifold is made from aluminum, and can be warped or cracked with excessive force.

5. The rest of installation is the reverse of removal. Adjust the ignition timing after installation, and check the coolant level after the engine has warmed up.

Exhaust Manifold

REMOVAL AND INSTALLATION

1950cc Engine

1. Disconnect the battery ground cable and remove the air cleaner assembly.

2. Remove the EGR pipe clamp bolt at the rear of the cylinder head.

3. Raise the vehicle and remove the EGR pipe from the intake and exhaust manifolds.

4. Separate the exhaust pipe from the manifold.

5. Remove the manifold shield and remove the heat stove.

6. Remove the manifold retaining nuts and remove the manifold from the engine.

7. Installation is the reverse of removal.

2238cc Diesel Engine

1. Raise engine hood.

2. Remove the bolts fixing the air cleaner and loosen the clamp bolt.

3. Lift the air cleaner slightly and disconnect the breather hose, then remove the air cleaner assembly.

4. Disconnect the exhaust pipe from the exhaust manifold at the flange.

5. Remove the 3 nuts fixing the exhaust manifold, then remove the engine hanger and exhaust manifold.

6. Installation is the reverse of removal. Torque the bolts to 15 ft. lbs.

2000cc Engine

1. Disconnect the negative battery cable.

2. Remove the air cleaner. Remove the exhaust manifold shield. Raise and support the front of the vehicle.

3. Disconnect the exhaust pipe at the manifold and then lower the vehicle.

4. Disconnect the air management-to-check valve hose and remove the bracket. Disconnect the oxygen sensor lead wire.

5. Remove the alternator belt. Remove the alternator adjusting bolts, loosen the pivot bolt and pivot the alternator upward.

6. Remove the alternator brace and the A.I.R. pipes bracket bolt.

7. Unscrew the mounting bolts and remove the exhaust manifold. The manifold should be removed with the A.I.R. plumbing as an assembly. If the manifold is to be replaced, transfer the plumbing to the new one.

8. Clean the mating surfaces on the manifold and the head, position the manifold and tighten the bolts to the proper specifications.

9. Installation of the remaining components is in the reverse order of removal.

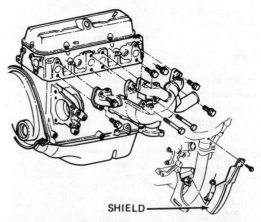

SHIELD

4-2000 exhaust manifold

2800cc Engine

LEFT SIDE

1. Remove the air cleaner. Remove the carburetor heat stove pipe.

2. Remove the air supply plumbing from the exhaust manifold.

3. Raise and support the car. Unbolt and remove the exhaust pipe at the manifold.

ENGINE OVERHAUL

Most engine overhaul procedures are fairly standard. In addition to specific parts replacement procedures and complete specifications for your individual engine, this chapter also is a guide to accepted rebuilding procedures. Examples of standard rebuilding practice are shown and should be used along with specific details concerning your particular engine.

Competent and accurate machine shop services will ensure maximum performance, reliability and engine life. Procedures marked with the symbol shown above should be performed by a competent machine shop, and are provided so that you will be familiar with the procedures necessary to a successful overhaul.

In most instances it is more profitable for the do-it-yourself mechanic to remove, clean and inspect the component, buy the necessary parts and deliver these to a shop for actual machine work.

On the other hand, much of the rebuilding work (crankshaft, block, bearings, pistons, rods, and other components) is well within the scope of the do-it-yourself mechanic.

Tools

The tools required for an engine overhaul or parts replacement will depend on the depth of your involvement. With a few exceptions, they will be the tools found in a mechanic's tool kit (see Chapter 1). More indepth work will require any or all of the following:
• a dial indicator (reading in thousandths) mounted on a universal base
• micrometers and telescope gauges
• jaw and screw-type pullers
• scraper
• valve spring compressor
• ring groove cleaner
• piston ring expander and compressor
• ridge reamer
• cylinder hone or glaze breaker

• Plastigage®
• engine stand

Use of most of these tools is illustrated in this chapter. Many can be rented for a one-time use from a local parts jobber or tool supply house specializing in automotive work.

Occasionally, the use of special tools is called for. See the information on Special Tools and the Safety Notice in the front of this book before substituting another tool.

Inspection Techniques

Procedures and specifications are given in this chapter for inspecting, cleaning and assessing the wear limits of most major components. Other procedures such as Magnaflux and Zyglo can be used to locate material flaws and stress cracks. Magnaflux is a magnetic process applicable only to ferrous materials. The Zyglo process coats the material with a flourescent dye penetrant and can be used on any material. Check for suspected surface cracks can be more readily made using spot check dye. The dye is sprayed onto the suspected area, wiped off and the area sprayed with a developer. Cracks will show up brightly.

Overhaul Tips

Aluminum has become extremely popular for use in engines, due to its low weight. Observe the following precautions when handling aluminum parts:
• Never hot tank aluminum parts (the caustic hot-tank solution will eat the aluminum)
• Remove all aluminum parts (identification tag, etc.) from engine parts prior to hot-tanking.
• Always coat threads lightly with engine oil or anti-seize compounds before installation, to prevent seizure.
• Never over-torque bolts or spark plugs, especially in aluminum threads.

Stripped threads in any component can be repaired using any of several commercial repair kits (Heli-Coil, Microdot, Keenserts, etc.)

When assembling the engine, any parts that will be in frictional contact must be pre-lubed to provide lubrication at initial start-up. Any product specifically formulated for this purpose can be used, but engine oil is not recommended as a pre-lube.

When semi-permanent (locked, but removable) installation of bolts or nuts is desired, threads should be cleaned and coated with Loctite® or other similar, commercial non-hardening sealant.

Repairing Damaged Threads

Several methods of repairing damaged threads are available. Heli-Coil® (shown here), Keenserts® and Microdot® are among the most widely used. All involve basically the same principle—drilling out stripped threads, tapping the hole and installing a prewound insert—making welding, plugging and oversize fasteners unnecessary.

Two types of thread repair inserts are usually supplied—a standard type for most Inch Coarse, Inch Fine, Metric Coarse and Metric Fine thread sizes and a spark plug type to fit most spark plug port sizes. Consult the individual manufacturer's catalog to determine exact applications. Typical thread repair kits will contain a selection of prewound threaded inserts, a tap (corresponding to the outside diameter threads of the insert) and an installation tool. Spark plug inserts usually differ because they require a tap equipped with pilot threads and a combined reamer/tap section. Most manufacturers also supply blister-packed thread repair inserts separately in addition to a master kit containing a variety of taps and inserts plus installation tools.

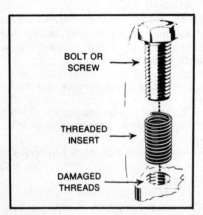

Damaged bolt holes can be repaired with thread repair inserts

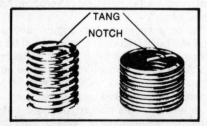

Standard thread repair insert (left) and spark plug thread insert (right)

Before effecting a repair to a threaded hole, remove any snapped, broken or damaged bolts or studs. Penetrating oil can be used to free frozen threads; the offending item can be removed with locking pliers or with a screw or stud extractor. After the hole is clear, the thread can be repaired, as follows:

Drill out the damaged threads with specified drill. Drill completely through the hole or to the bottom of a blind hole

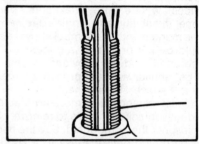

With the tap supplied, tap the hole to receive the thread insert. Keep the tap well oiled and back it out frequently to avoid clogging the threads

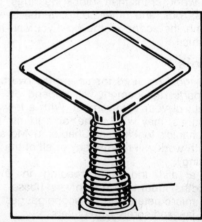

Screw the threaded insert onto the installation tool until the tang engages the slot. Screw the insert into the tapped hole until it is ¼–½ turn below the top surface. After installation break off the tang with a hammer and punch

Standard Torque Specifications and Fastener Markings

In the absence of specific torques, the following chart can be used as a guide to the maximum safe torque of a particular size/grade of fastener.
- There is no torque difference for fine or coarse threads.
- Torque values are based on clean, dry threads. Reduce the value by 10% if threads are oiled prior to assembly.
- The torque required for aluminum components or fasteners is considerably less.

U.S. Bolts

SAE Grade Number	1 or 2			5			6 or 7		
Number of lines always 2 less than the grade number.									
	Maximum Torque			Maximum Torque			Maximum Torque		
Bolt Size (Inches)—(Thread)	Ft./Lbs.	Kgm	Nm	Ft./Lbs.	Kgm	Nm	Ft./Lbs.	Kgm	Nm
¼—20	5	0.7	6.8	8	1.1	10.8	10	1.4	13.5
—28	6	0.8	8.1	10	1.4	13.6			
⁵⁄₁₆—18	11	1.5	14.9	17	2.3	23.0	19	2.6	25.8
—24	13	1.8	17.6	19	2.6	25.7			
⅜—16	18	2.5	24.4	31	4.3	42.0	34	4.7	46.0
—24	20	2.75	27.1	35	4.8	47.5			
⁷⁄₁₆—14	28	3.8	37.0	49	6.8	66.4	55	7.6	74.5
—20	30	4.2	40.7	55	7.6	74.5			
½—13	39	5.4	52.8	75	10.4	101.7	85	11.75	115.2
—20	41	5.7	55.6	85	11.7	115.2			
⁹⁄₁₆—12	51	7.0	69.2	110	15.2	149.1	120	16.6	162.7
—18	55	7.6	74.5	120	16.6	162.7			
⅝—11	83	11.5	112.5	150	20.7	203.3	167	23.0	226.5
—18	95	13.1	128.8	170	23.5	230.5			
¾—10	105	14.5	142.3	270	37.3	366.0	280	38.7	379.6
—16	115	15.9	155.9	295	40.8	400.0			
⅞—9	160	22.1	216.9	395	54.6	535.5	440	60.9	596.5
—14	175	24.2	237.2	435	60.1	589.7			
1—8	236	32.5	318.6	590	81.6	799.9	660	91.3	894.8
—14	250	34.6	338.9	660	91.3	849.8			

Metric Bolts

Relative Strength Marking	4.6, 4.8			8.8		
Bolt Markings						
	Maximum Torque			Maximum Torque		
Bolt Size Thread Size x Pitch (mm)	Ft./Lbs.	Kgm	Nm	Ft./Lbs.	Kgm	Nm
6 x 1.0	2–3	.2–.4	3–4	3–6	.4–.8	5–8
8 x 1.25	6–8	.8–1	8–12	9–14	1.2–1.9	13–19
10 x 1.25	12–17	1.5–2.3	16–23	20–29	2.7–4.0	27–39
12 x 1.25	21–32	2.9–4.4	29–43	35–53	4.8–7.3	47–72
14 x 1.5	35–52	4.8–7.1	48–70	57–85	7.8–11.7	77–110
16 x 1.5	51–77	7.0–10.6	67–100	90–120	12.4–16.5	130–160
18 x 1.5	74–110	10.2–15.1	100–150	130–170	17.9–23.4	180–230
20 x 1.5	110–140	15.1–19.3	150–190	190–240	26.2–46.9	160–320
22 x 1.5	150–190	22.0–26.2	200–260	250–320	34.5–44.1	340–430
24 x 1.5	190–240	26.2–46.9	260–320	310–410	42.7–56.5	420–550

CHECKING ENGINE COMPRESSION

A noticeable lack of engine power, excessive oil consumption and/or poor fuel mileage measured over an extended period are all indicators of internal engine wear. Worn piston rings, scored or worn cylinder bores, blown head gaskets, sticking or burnt valves and worn valve seats are all possible culprits here. A check of each cylinder's compression will help you locate the problems.

As mentioned in the "Tools and Equipment" section of Chapter 1, a screw-in type compression gauge is more accurate than the type you simply hold against the spark plug hole, although it takes slightly longer to use. It's worth it to obtain a more accurate reading. Follow the procedures below for gasoline and diesel-engined cars.

Gasoline Engines

1. Warm up the engine to normal operating temperature.
2. Remove all spark plugs.

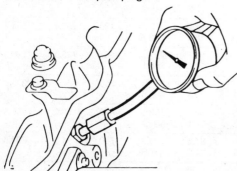

The screw-in type compression gauge is more accurate

3. Disconnect the high-tension lead from the ignition coil.
4. On carbureted cars, fully open the throttle either by operating the carburetor throttle linkage by hand or by having an assistant "floor" the accelerator pedal. On fuel-injected cars, disconnect the cold start valve and all injector connections.
5. Screw the compression gauge into the No. 1 spark plug hole until the fitting is snug.
   NOTE: *Be careful not to crossthread the plug hole. On aluminum cylinder heads use extra care, as the threads in these heads are easily ruined.*
6. Ask an assistant to depress the accelerator pedal fully on both carbureted and fuel-injected cars. Then, while you read the compression gauge, ask the assistant to crank the engine two or three times in short bursts using the ignition switch.

7. Read the compression gauge at the end of each series of cranks, and record the highest of these readings. Repeat this procedure for each of the engine's cylinders. Compare the highest reading of each cylinder to the compression pressure specifications in the "Tune-Up Specifications" chart in Chapter 2. The specs in this chart are maximum values.

A cylinder's compression pressure is usually acceptable if it is not less than 80% of maximum. The difference between each cylinder should be no more than 12–14 pounds.

8. If a cylinder is unusually low, pour a tablespoon of clean engine oil into the cylinder through the spark plug hole and repeat the compression test. If the compression comes up after adding the oil, it appears that that cylinder's piston rings or bore are damaged or worn. If the pressure remains low, the valves may not be seating properly (a valve job is needed), or the head gasket may be blown near that cylinder. If compression in any two adjacent cylinders is low, and if the addition of oil doesn't help the compression, there is leakage past the head gasket. Oil and coolant water in the combustion chamber can result from this problem. There may be evidence of water droplets on the engine dipstick when a head gasket has blown.

Diesel Engines

Checking cylinder compression on diesel engines is basically the same procedure as on gasoline engines except for the following:

1. A special compression gauge adaptor suitable for diesel engines (because these engines have much greater compression pressures) must be used.
2. Remove the injector tubes and remove the injectors from each cylinder.
   NOTE: *Don't forget to remove the washer underneath each injector; otherwise, it may get lost when the engine is cranked.*

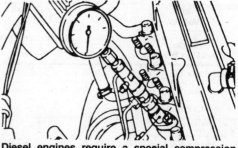

Diesel engines require a special compression gauge adaptor

3. When fitting the compression gauge adaptor to the cylinder head, make sure the bleeder of the gauge (if equipped) is closed.
4. When reinstalling the injector assemblies, install new washers underneath each injector.

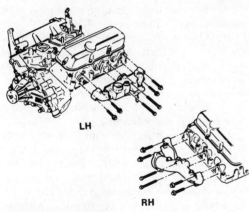

6-2800 exhaust manifold

4. Unbolt and remove the manifold.

To install:

1. Clean the mating surfaces of the cylinder head and manifold. Install the manifold onto the head, and install the retaining bolts finger tight.

2. Tighten the manifold bolts in a circular pattern, working from the center to the ends, to 25 ft. lbs. in two stages.

3. Connect the exhaust pipe to the manifold.

4. The remainder of installation is the reverse of removal.

RIGHT SIDE

1. Raise and support the car.

2. Tighten the exhaust pipe-to-manifold flange bolts until they break off. Remove the pipe from the manifold. Later models are equipped with flange bolts.

3. Lower the car. Remove the spark plug wires from the plugs. Number them first if they are not already labeled.

4. Remove the air supply pipes from the manifold. Remove the PULSAIR bracket bolt from the rocker cover, on models so equipped, then remove the pipe assembly.

5. Remove the manifold retaining bolts and remove the manifold.

To install:

1. Clean the mating surfaces of the cylinder head and manifold. Position the manifold against the head and install the retaining bolts finger tight.

2. Tighten the bolts in a circular pattern, working from the center to the ends, to 25 ft. lbs. in two stages.

3. Install the air supply system.

4. Install the spark plug wires.

5. Raise and support the car. Connect the exhaust pipe to the manifold and install new flange bolts.

Cylinder Head

REMOVAL AND INSTALLATION

1950cc Engine

1. Remove cam cover.

2. Remove EGR pipe clamp bolt at rear of cylinder head.

3. Raise vehicle on hoist.

4. Disconnect exhaust pipe at exhaust manifold.

5. Lower vehicle on hoist.

6. Drain cooling system.

7. Disconnect heater hoses at intake manifold and at front of cylinder head.

8. Remove A/C and/or P/S compressor or pump and lay them aside.

9. Disconnect accelerator linkage at carburetor, fuel line at carburetor, all necessary electrical connections, spark plug wires and necessary vacuum lines.

10. Rotate camshaft until #4 cylinder is in firing position. Remove distributor cap and mark rotor to housing relationship. Remove the distributor.

11. Remove the fuel pump.

12. Lock the shoe on automatic adjuster in fully retracted position by depressing the adjuster lock lever with a screwdriver or equivalent in direction as indicated in the drawing.

13. Remove timing sprocket to camshaft bolt and remove the sprocket and the fuel pump drive cam from the camshaft. Keep the sprocket on the chain damper and tensioner—do not remove the sprocket from the chain.

14. Disconnect AIR hose and check valve at air manifold.

15. Remove cylinder head to timing cover bolts.

16. Remove cylinder head bolts using Extension Bar Wrench J-24239-01, remove bolts in progressional sequence, beginning with the outer bolts.

17. With the aid of an assistant, remove cylinder head, intake and exhaust manifold as an assembly.

18. Clean all gasket material from cylinder head and block surfaces.

NOTE: *The gasket surfaces on both the head and block must be clean of any foreign matter and free of picks or heavy scratches. Cyl-*

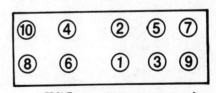

4-1950 head bolt torque sequence

inder bolt threads in the block and threads on the bolts must be cleaned (dirt will affect bolt torque).

19. Place new gasket over dowel pins with "TOP" side of gasket up.

20. Reverse removal Steps 1–17.

Tighten cylinder head bolts a little at a time in the sequence shown, torque to 60 lb. ft. and then retighten to specified torque of 72 ft. lb.

2000cc Engine

NOTE: *The engine should be "overnight" cold before removing the cylinder head.*

1. Disconnect the negative battery cable.

2. Drain the cooling system into a clean container; the coolant can be reused if it is still good.

3. Remove the air cleaner. Raise and support the front of the vehicle.

4. Remove the exhaust shield. Disconnect the exhaust pipe.

5. Remove the heater hose from the intake manifold and then lower the car.

6. Unscrew the mounting bolts and remove the engine lift bracket (includes air management).

7. Remove the distributor. Disconnect the vacuum manifold at the alternator bracket.

8. Tag and disconnect the remaining vacuum lines at the intake manifold and thermostat.

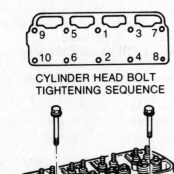

CYLINDER HEAD BOLT
TIGHTENING SEQUENCE

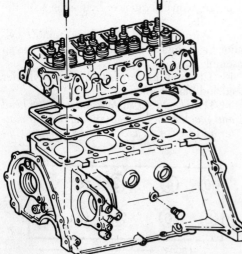

4-2000 head bolt torque sequence

9. Remove the air management pipe at the exhaust check valve.

10. Disconnect the accelerator linkage at the carburetor and then remove the linkage bracket.

11. Tag and disconnect all necessary wires. Remove the upper radiator hose at the thermostat.

12. Remove the bolt attaching the dipstick tube and hot water bracket.

13. Remove the idler pulley. Remove the A.I.R. and power steering pump drive belts.

14. Remove the A.I.R. bracket-to-intake manifold bolt. If equipped with power steering, remove the air pump pulley, The A.I.R. thru-bolt and the power steering adjusting bracket.

15. Loosen the A.I.R. mounting bracket lower bolt so that the bracket will rotate.

16. Disconnect and plug the fuel line at the carburetor.

17. Remove the alternator. Remove the alternator brace from the head and then remove the upper mounting bracket.

18. Remove the cylinder head cover. Remove the rocker arms and push rods.

19. Remove the cylinder head bolts in the order given in the illustration. Remove the cylinder head with the carburetor, intake and exhaust manifolds still attached. To install, the gasket surfaces on both the head and the block must be clean of any foreign matter and free of any nicks or heavy scratches. Cylinder bolt threads in the block and the bolt must be clean.

20. Place a new cylinder head gasket in position over the dowel pins on the block. Carefully guide the cylinder head into position.

21. Coat the cylinder bolts with sealing compound and install them finger tight.

22. Using a torque wrench, gradually tighten the bolts in the sequence shown in the illustration to the proper specifications.

23. Installation of the remaining components is in the reverse order of removal.

2238cc Diesel Engine

NOTE: *The injection timing must be reset after this procedure. See the Fuel Section for details and special tools required*

1. Follow the intake and exhaust manifold removal steps.

2. Remove the intake and exhaust manifold gasket.

3. Drain the cooling system by opening the drain plugs on the radiator and on the cylinder block.

4. Disconnect the upper water hose at the engine side.

5. Remove the cooling fan and fan shroud.

6. Remove the sleeve nuts and disconnect the injection pipes.

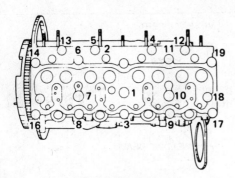

4-2238 diesel head bolt torque sequence

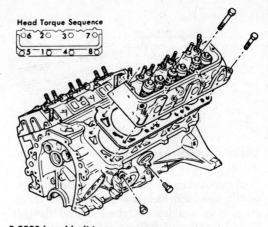

6-2800 head bolt torque sequence

7. Remove the nozzle holder fixing nuts and remove the nozzle holder assembly.

8. Follow the rocker arm, bracket and shaft assembly removal steps.

9. Remove the pushrods.

10. Remove the joint bolt and disconnect the leak-off pipe.

11. Remove the 19 bolts fixing the cylinder head, then remove the cylinder head and gasket.

12. Install the cylinder head gasket with the TOP mark side up on the cylinder body by aligning the holes with the dowels.

13. Install the cylinder head.

14. Install the pushrod in position on the cylinder head.

15. Install the rocker arm assembly on the cylinder head. Tighten the bracket fixing bolts evenly in sequence commencing with the inner ones.

16. Follow the intake and exhaust manifold installation steps.

17. Install the cooling fan and fan shroud.

18. Connect the upper water hose to engine side.

19. Fill the engine cooling system.

2800cc Engine

LEFT SIDE

1. Raise and support the truck.

2. Drain the coolant from the block and lower the car.

3. Remove the intake manifold.

4. Remove the crossover.

5. Remove the alternator and AIR pump brackets.

6. Remove the dipstick tube.

7. Loosen the rocker arm bolts and remove the pushrods. Keep the pushrods in the same order as removed.

8. Remove the cylinder head bolts in stages and in the reverse order of the tightening sequence.

9. Remove the cylinder head. Do not pry on the head to loosen it.

10. Installation is the reverse of removal.

The words "This side Up" on the new cylinder head gasket should face upward. Coat the cylinder head bolts with sealer and torque to specifications in the sequence shown. Make sure the pushrods seat in the lifter seats and adjust the valves.

RIGHT SIDE

1. Raise the car and drain the coolant from the block.

2. Disconnect the exhaust pipe and lower the car.

3. If equipped, remove the cruise control servo bracket.

4. Remove the air management valve and hose.

5. Remove the intake manifold.

6. Remove the exhaust crossover.

7. Loosen the rocker arm nuts and remove the pushrods. Keep the pushrods in the order in which they were removed.

8. Remove the cylinder head bolts in stages and in the reverse order of the tightening sequence.

9. Remove the cylinder head, do not pry on the cylinder head to loosen it.

10. Installation is the reverse of removal. The words "This Side Up" on the new cylinder head gasket should face upwards. Coat the cylinder head bolts with sealer and tighten them to specifications in the sequence shown. Make sure the lower ends of the pushrods seat in the lifter seats and adjust the valves.

INSPECTION

1. Remove all traces of carbon from the head, using a decarbon-type wire brush mounted in an electric drill.

2. If the engine has high mileage, it's a good idea to send the head out to a qualified machine shop to be cleaned and leak-tested.

3. Lay a straight-edge across the cylinder

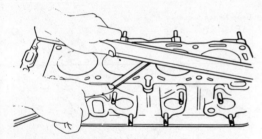

Checking cylinder head distortion

head face and check between the straight-edge and the head with feeler gauges. Make the check at six points at least. Cylinder head flatness should be within .0078 in. If the gap is between .0078 and .0157 in. the head flatness may be corrected by resurfacing at a machine shop. If the gap exceeds .0157 in., the head must be replaced.

4. Check the valve seats as outlined later.
5. Check the valve guides as outlined later.

Valves

REMOVAL AND INSTALLATION

All Engines

1. Remove the cylinder head.
2. Using a valve spring compressor, available at most auto parts stores, compress the valve spring and remove the valve keys and retaining ring.
3. Release the compressor and remove the spring and valve stem seal. Keep the valves in order for installation.
4. Installation is the reverse of removal. Use new seals.

NOTE: *Keep all parts in order so that they may be assembled in their original locations.*

INSPECTION

Check the valve face for cracks, chips or excessive pitting, scoring or wear. Check the stem for wear. Reface the valve if a refacer is available. If not, take the valves to a competent machine shop. Remember to number the valves for reference. It's best to clean the valves before taking them for refacing. Remove all carbon with a drill-mounted brush.

Valve Seats

REMOVAL AND INSTALLATION

1950cc and 2238cc Engines

NOTE: *Special tools are required for this procedure.*
1. Weld pieces of welding rod to several points around the seat.
2. Allow the head to cool for about 5 min-

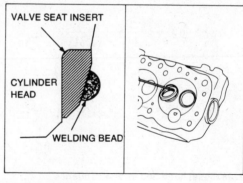

Valve seat removal

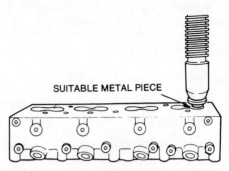

Valve seat installation using a bench press

utes and pull the seats with a slide hammer attached to the welding rods.
3. Clean the valve seat recess carefully.
4. Place the new valve seat in dry ice while heating the recess in the head with steam. Take about five minutes for this procedure. Perform the heating and cooling simultaneously.
5. Using protective gloves, insert the seat in the recess. The seat depth below combustion chamber face should be .0031–.0047 in.
6. Cut the valve seat to the angle shown in the valve specifications chart. Valve seat contact width should be .0472–.0630 in.
7. Polish the seat with lapping compound and suction type lapper.
8. Smear the seat and the face of a correctly ground and cleaned valve with a dye such as Prussian blue. Insert the valve and let it contact the seat. Turn the valve against the seat several times, remove the valve and check that the dye shows an even contact.

2000cc and 2800cc Engines

These engines do not have replaceable seats. The seats should be cut and cleaned only. See the valve specifications chart for proper seat angle. Cut the seats, polish them with lapping compound and a suction type lapper. Coat the seat with a dye such as Prussian blue and insert a clean and properly ground valve. Turn the valve against the seat several times and remove the valve. Check that there is a uniform coating of dye on the valve face.

Valve Guides

REMOVAL AND INSTALLATION

1950cc and 2238cc Engines

NOTE: *Special tools will be needed for this procedure.*

1. Insert a guide remover such as tool J-26512, into the guide from the combustion chamber side. Drive the guide upward and out. Remove the lower valve spring seat.

2. Apply clean engine oil to the outside of the new guide and position it on the head top side. Tool J-26512 is also an installer. Drive the guide in until it bottoms.

NOTE: *If the guides are replaced, the valves should be replaced also.*

3. The guide should protrude 12mm (.4724 in.) above the head surface. Grind the end of the guide to achieve this height. Make certain that the guide has bottomed before grinding.

2000cc and 2800cc Engines

These guides are not replaceable. The guides should be reamed to accommodate valves with

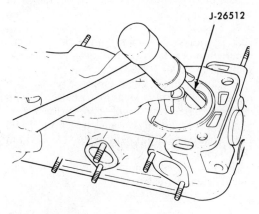

Valve guide removal

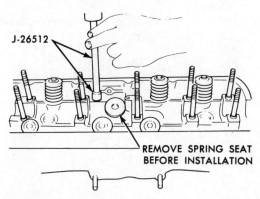

Valve guide installation

oversized stems. Oversized stems are available in .089, .394 and .775mm.

Timing Gear (Front) Cover

REMOVAL AND INSTALLATION

1950cc Engine

1. Remove cylinder head as outlined previously.

2. Remove oil pan as outlined previously.

3. Remove oil pickup tube from oil pump.

4. Remove harmonic balancer as outlined previously.

5. Remove AIR pump drive belt.

6. Air Conditioned Vehicles—Remove compressor and lay it to one side. Remove compressor mounting brackets. If equipped with power steering, remove pump and bracket and lay aside.

CAUTION: *Do not remove any refrigerant lines from the A/C compressor.*

7. Remove distributor cap and then remove distributor.

8. Remove front cover attaching bolts and remove front cover.

9. Remove and discard front cover to block gasket.

10. Install new gasket onto cylinder block.

11. Align the oil pump drive gear punch mark with the oil filter side of cover; then align the center of dowel pin with alignment mark on oil pump case.

12. Rotate crankcase until No. 1 and No. 4 cylinders are at top dead center.

13. Install the front cover by engaging the pinion gear with the oil pump drive gear on the crankshaft.

14. Check that the punch mark on the oil pump drive gear is turned to the rear side as viewed through clearance between front cover and cylinder block.

15. Check that the slit at the end of oil pump shaft is parallel with front face of cylinder block and that it is offset forward.

16. With all parts correctly installed, install and tighten front cover bolts.

17. Reverse Steps 1–7 of Removal procedure.

18. Check engine timing.

19. Check for leaks.

Diesel Engine

1. Remove the radiator.

2. Remove the compressor drive belt by moving the powersteering oil pump or idler (if so equipped).

3. Loosen the generator adjust plate bolt and fixing bolt, then remove the fan belt.

4. Remove the 4 bolts fixing the crankshaft pulley and remove the crankshaft pulley.

5. Remove the bolts fixing the timing pulley housing covers, then remove the covers.

6. Installation is the reverse of removal.

2800cc Engine

CAUTION: *The engines use a harmonic balancer. Breakage may occur if the balancer is hammered back onto the crankshaft. A press or special installation tool is necessary.*

1. Remove the water pump.

2. Remove the compressor without disconnecting any A/C lines and lay it aside.

3. Remove harmonic balancer, using a puller. Note: *The outer ring (weight) of the harmonic balancer is bonded to the hub with rubber. The balancer must be removed with a puller which acts on the inner hub only. Pulling on the outer portion of the balancer will break the rubber bond or destroy the tuning of the torsional damper.*

4. Disconnect the lower radiator hose and heater hose.

5. Remove timing gear cover attaching screws, and cover and gasket.

6. Clean all the gasket mounting surfaces on the front cover and block. Apply a continuous ³⁄₃₂ in. bead of sealer (1052357 or equivalent) to front cover sealing surface and around coolant passage ports and central bolt holes.

7. Apply a bead of silicone sealer to the oil pan-to-cylinder block joint.

8. Install a centering tool jn the crankcase snout hole in the front cover and install the cover.

9. Install the front cover bolts finger tight, remove the centering tool and tighten the cover bolts. Install the harmonic balancer, pulley, water pump, belts, radiator, and all other parts.

2000cc Engine

NOTE: *The following procedure requires the use of a special tool.*

1. Remove the engine drive belts.

2. Although not absolutely necessary, removal of the right front inner fender splash shield will facilitate access to the front cover.

3. Unscrew the center bolt from the crankshaft pulley and slide the pulley and hub from the crankshaft.

4. Remove the alternator lower bracket.

5. Remove the oil pan-to-front cover bolts.

6. Remove the front cover-to-block bolts and then remove the front cover. If the front cover is difficult to remove, use a plastic mallet.

7. The surfaces of the block and front cover must be clean and free of oil. Apply a ⅛ in. bead of RTV sealant to the cover. The sealant must be wet to the touch when the bolts are torqued down.

NOTE: *When applying RTV sealant to the front cover, be sure to keep it out of the bolt holes.*

8. Position the front cover on the block using a centering tool (J-23042) and tighten the screws.

9. Installation of the remaining components is in the reverse order of removal. The oil seal can be replaced with the cover either on or off the engine. If the cover is on the engine, remove the crankshaft pulley and hub first. Pry out the seal using a large screwdriver, being careful not to distort the seal mating surface. Install the new seal so that the open side or helical side is towards the engine. Press it into place with a seal driver made for the purpose. Install the hub if removed.

Timing Chains, Sprockets, and Tensioners

REMOVAL AND INSTALLATION

1950cc Engine

1. Remove front cover assembly as outlined previously.

2. Lock the shoe on automatic adjuster in fully retracted position by depressing the adjuster lock lever in direction as shown.

3. Remove timing chain from crankshaft sprocket.

4. Check timing sprockets for wear or damage. If crankshaft sprocket must be replaced, remove sprocket and pinion gear from crankshaft using Puller J-25031.

5. Check timing chain for wear or damage; replace as necessary. Measure distance (L) with chain stretched with a pull of approximately 98 N (22 lbs.). Standard (L) value is 381mm (15.00 in.); replace chain if (L) is greater than 385mm (15.16 in.).

6. Remove attaching bolt and remove automatic chain adjuster.

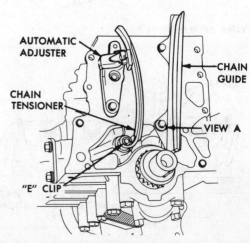

4-1950 timing chain guide and tensioner

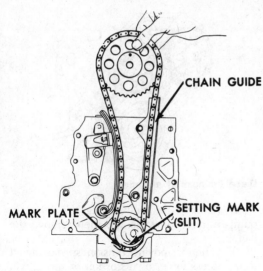

CHAIN GUIDE

MARK PLATE   SETTING MARK (SLIT)

4-1950 timing chain alignment

7. Check that the shoe becomes locked when shoe is pushed in with the lock lever released.

8. Check that lock is released when the shoe is pushed in. The adjuster assembly must be replaced if rack teeth are found to be worn excessively.

9. Remove "E" clip and remove chain tensioner. Check tensioner for wear or damage; replace as necessary.

10. Inspect tensioner pin for wear or damage. If replacement is necessary, remove pin from cylinder block using locking pliers. Lubricate NEW pin tensioner with clean engine oil. Start new pin in block, place tensioner over appropriate pin. Place "E" clip on pin and then tap pin into block, using a hammer, until clip just clears tensioner. Check tensioner and adjuster for freedom of rotation on pins.

11. Inspect guide for wear or damage and plugged lower oil jet. If replacement or cleaning is necessary, remove guide bolts, guide and oil jet. Install new guide and upper attaching bolt. Install lower oil jet and bolt so that oil port is pointed toward crankshaft as shown.

12. Install timing sprocket and pinion gear (groove side toward front cover). Align key grooves with key on crankshaft, then drive into position using Installing Tool J-26587.

13. Turn crankshaft so that key is turned toward cylinder head side (No. 1 and No. 4 pistons at top dead center).

14. Install the timing chain by aligning mark plate on chain with mark on crankshaft timing sprocket. The side of the chain with the mark plate is on the front side and the side of chain with the most links between mark plates is on the chain guide side. Keep the timing chain engaged with the camshaft timing sprocket un-

til the camshaft timing sprocket is installed on camshaft.

15. Install the camshaft timing sprocket so that marked side of sprocket faces forward and so that the triangular mark aligns with the chain mark plate.

16. Install the automatic chain adjuster.

17. Release lock by depressing the shoe on adjuster by hand, and check to make certain the chain is properly tensioned when lock is released.

18. Install front cover assembly as outlined previously.

2800cc Engine

To replace the chain, remove the crankcase front cover. This will allow access to the timing chain. Crank the engine until the marks punched on both sprockets are closest to one another and in line between the shaft centers. Take out the three bolts that hold the camshaft sprocket to the camshaft. This sprocket is a light press fit on the camshaft and will come off readily. It is located by a dowel. The chain comes off with the camshaft sprocket. A gear puller will be required to remove the camshaft sprocket.

Without disturbing the position of the engine, mount the new crank sprocket on the shaft, then mount the chain over the camshaft sprocket. Arrange the camshaft sprocket in such a way that the timing marks will line up between the shaft centers and the camshaft locating dowel will enter the dowel hole in the cam sprocket.

Place the cam sprocket, with its chain mounted over it, in position on the front of the camshaft and pull up with the three bolts that hold it to the camshaft.

After the sprockets are in place, turn the en-

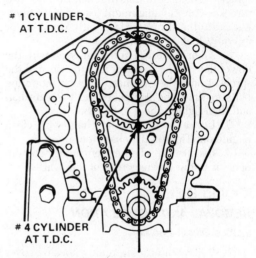

1 CYLINDER AT T.D.C.

4 CYLINDER AT T.D.C.

6-2800 timing chain alignment

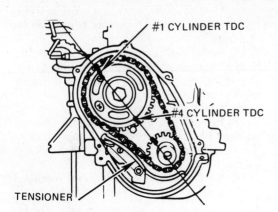

4-2000 timing chain alignment

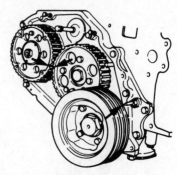

Diesel timing mark alignment

gine two full revolutions to make certain that the timing marks are in correct alignment between the shaft centers.

2000cc Engine

1. Remove the front cover as previously detailed.

2. Place the No. 1 piston at TDC of the compression stroke so that the marks on the camshaft and crankshaft sprockets are in alignment (see illustration).

3. Loosen the timing chain tensioner nut as far as possible without actually removing it.

4. Remove the camshaft sprocket bolts and remove the sprocket and chain together. If the sprocket does not slide from the camshaft easily, a light blow with a soft mallet at the lower edge of the sprocket will dislodge it.

5. Use a gear puller (J-2288-8-20) and remove the crankshaft sprocket.

6. Press the crankshaft sprocket back onto the crankshaft.

7. Install the timing chain over the camshaft sprocket and then around the crankshaft sprocket. Make sure that the marks on the two sprockets are in alignment (see illustration). Lubricate the thrust surface with Molykote or its equivalent.

8. Align the dowel in the camshaft with the dowel hole in the sprocket and then install the sprocket onto the camshaft. Use the mounting bolts to draw the sprocket onto the camshaft and then tighten them to 27–33 ft. lbs.

9. Lubricate the timing chain with clean engine oil. Tighten the chain tensioner.

10. Installation of the remaining components is in the reverse order of removal.

Timing Belt

REMOVAL AND INSTALLATION

2238cc Diesel Engine

1. Follow the timing pulley housing cover removal steps.

2. Remove the bolts fixing the injection pump timing pulley flange, then remove the flange.

3. When removing tension spring, avoid using excess force, or distortion of spring will result.

4. Remove the fixing nut of the tension pulley, then remove the tension pulley and tension center.

5. Remove the timing belt. Avoid twisting or kinking the belt and keep it free from water, oil, dust and other foreign matter.

NOTE: *No attempt should be made to readjust belt tension. If the belt has been loosened through service of the timing system, it should be replaced with a new one.*

6. Check that the setting marks on the crank pulley, injection pump timing pulley, and camshaft timing pulley are in alignment, then install the timing belt in sequence of crankshaft timing pulley, camshaft timing pulley, and injection pump timing pulley.

7. Make an adjustment, so that slackness

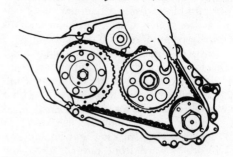

Installing the diesel timing belt

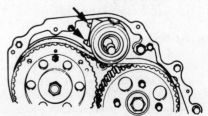

Tension pulley making proper contact with the two pins on the housing

Torquing the tension pulley

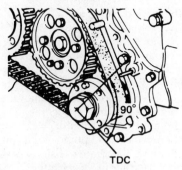

Bringing #1 cylinder to TDC

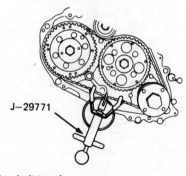

Checking belt tension

of the belt is taken up by the tension pulley. When installing the belt, care should be taken so as not to damage the belt.

8. Install the tension center and tension pulley, making certain the end of the tension center is in proper contact with two pins on the timing pulley housing.

9. Hand-tighten the nut, so that tension pulley can slide freely.

10. Install the tension spring correctly and semitighten the tension pulley fixing nut.

11. Turn the crankshaft 2 turns in normal direction of rotation to permit seating of the belt. Further rotate the crankshaft 90 degrees beyond top dead center to settle the injection pump. Never attempt to turn the crankshaft in reverse direction.

NOTE: *If the engine is turned past the tim-*

ing marks, keep rotating the engine in the normal direction of rotation until the marks align properly.

12. Loosen the tension pulley fixing nut completely, allowing the pulley to take up looseness of the belt. Then, tighten the nut to 78–95 ft. lbs.

13. Install the flange on the injection pump pulley. The hole in the outer circumference of the flange should be aligned with the timing mark "△" on the injection pump pulley.

14. Turn the crankshaft 2 turns in normal direction of rotation to bring the piston in no. 1 cylinder to top dead center on compression stroke and check that the mark "△" on the timing pulley is in alignment with the hole in the flange.

15. The belt tension should be checked at a point between the injection pump pulley and crankshaft pulley using tool J-29771, to 33–55 lbs. as read on the scale.

16. Adjust valve clearances.

17. Install remaining parts in the reverse order of removal.

18. Check the injection timing.

Camshaft

REMOVAL AND INSTALLATION

1950 cc Engine

1. Remove cam cover as outlined previously.

2. Rotate camshaft until No. 4 cylinder is in firing position. Remove distributor cap and mark rotor to housing position. Remove distributor.

3. Remove the fuel pump.

4. Lock the shoe on automatic adjuster in fully retracted position by depressing the adjuster lock lever with a screwdriver or equivalent in direction as indicated. After locking the automatic adjuster, check that the chain is in free state.

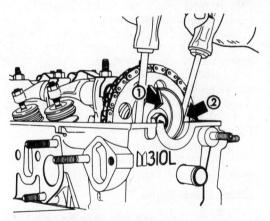

Depressing the adjusting lock lever

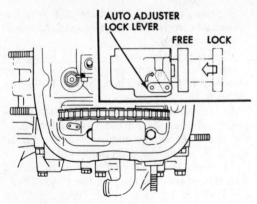

Locking the timing chain adapter

5. Remove the timing sprocket to camshaft bolt and remove the sprocket and fuel pump drive cam from the camshaft. Keep the timing sprocket on the chain damper and tensioner without removing the chain from the sprocket.

6. Remove rocker arm, shaft and bracket assembly as outlined previously.

7. Remove the camshaft assembly.

8. Apply a generous amount of clean engine oil to the camshaft and journals of cylinder head.

9. Install the camshaft assembly.

10. Install the rocker arm, shaft and bracket assembly as outlined previously.

11. Check that the mark on the No. 1 rocker arm shaft bracket is in alignment with the mark on the camshaft and that the crankshaft pulley groove is aligned with the TDC mark ("O" mark) on the front cover.

12. Assemble the timing sprocket to the camshaft by aligning it with the pin on the camshaft; use care not to remove the chain from the sprocket.

13. Install the fuel pump drive cam and install the sprocket retaining bolt and washer. Remove the half-moon seal in front end of head; then install torque wrench and torque bolt to 60 ft. lb. replace half-moon seal in cylinder head.

14. Install the distributor.

15. Release lock by depressing the shoe on adjuster with a screwdriver or equivalent, check timing chain for proper tension.

16. Check valve timing, rotor and mark on distributor housing should be in alignment when No. 4 piston is in firing position. Timing mark on crank pulley should align with TDC mark ("O" mark) on front cover.

17. Reinstall distributor cap.

18. Reinstall cam cover as outlined previously.

2238cc Diesel Engine

1. Remove the camshaft carrier as outlined under the "Cylinder Head Removal and Installation" procedure.

2. Remove the two bolts retaining the thrust plate in position on the front of the camshaft carrier.

3. Remove the thrust plate and carefully slide the camshaft out through the front of the carrier.

4. Install the camshaft in the carrier in the reverse order of removal, coating it liberally with engine oil before sliding it into position. Exercise care not to damage the camshaft bearing journals during the installation.

2000 cc Engine

1. Remove the engine.

2. Remove the intake manifold.

3. Remove the cylinder head cover, pivot the rocker arms to the sides, and remove the pushrods, keeping them in order. Remove the valve lifters, keeping them in order. There are special tools which make lifter removal easier.

4. Remove the front cover.

5. Remove the distributor.

6. Remove the fuel pump and its pushrod.

7. Remove the timing chain and sprocket as described earlier in this chapter.

8. Carefully pull the camshaft from the block, being sure that the camshaft lobes do not contact the bearings.

9. To install, lubricate the camshaft journals with clean engine oil. Lubricate the lobes with Molykote or the equivalent. Install the camshaft into the engine, being extremely careful not to contact the bearings with the cam lobes.

10. Install the timing chain and sprocket. Install the fuel pump and pushrod. Install the timing cover. Install the distributor.

11. Install the valve lifters. If a new camshaft has been installed, new lifters should be used to ensure durability of the cam lobe.

12. Install the pushrods and rocker arms and the intake manifold. Adjust the valve lash after installing the engine. Install the cylinder head cover.

2800cc Engines

Follow the 2800cc engine removal procedure then remove the camshaft as follows:

1. Remove the intake manifold, valve lifters and timing chain cover as described in this section. If the car is equipped with air conditioning, unbolt the condenser and move it aside *without disconnecting any lines.*

2. Remove fuel pump and pump pushrod.

3. Remove camshaft sprocket bolts, sprocket and timing chain. A light blow to the lower edge of a tight sprocket should free it (use a plastic mallet).

4. Install two bolts in cam bolt holes and pull cam from block with a suitable slide hammer tool.

5. To install, reverse removal procedure after aligning the sprocket timing marks.

Pistons and Connecting Rods

1950cc and 2238cc ENGINES

Removal

1. Remove the cylinder head.
2. Remove the oil pan.
3. Remove any carbon buildup from the cylinder wall at the top end of the piston travel with a ridge reamer tool.
4. Position the piston to be removed at the bottom of its stroke so that the connecting rod bearing cap can be reached easily from under the engine.
5. Unscrew the connecting rod bearing cap and remove the cap and lower half of the bearing.
6. Push the piston and connecting rod up and out of the cylinder block with a length of wood. Use care not to scratch the cylinder wall with the connecting rod or the wooden tool.

Inspection

Check the pistons for scuffs, cracking or wear. Replace the pistons with new ones if found to be defective.

Measure clearance between pistons and cylinder wall as follows:

1. With an outside micrometer, measure the diameter of the piston at a point 40mm (1.575 in.) below the piston head grading position) in direction at a right angle to the piston pin.
2. With a cylinder bore indicator, measure the cylinder bore diameter at the lower section where the amount of wear is smallest. Compare the value obtained with the cylinder bore diameter to determine the clearance. If the amount of clearance deviates from the 0.045–

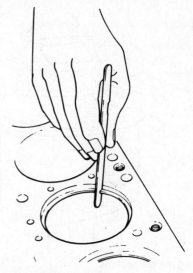

Measuring piston ring gap

0065mm (0.0018–0.0026 in.), replace the pistons with new ones.

NOTE: *The following measurement may be used only for reference purpose as it does not give an exact value.*

3. Hold a feeler gage against the cylinder wall and insert the piston into the cylinder bore, so that larger diameter side of the piston is turned to the feeler gauge.
4. Check the effort required to pull out the feeler gauge using a pull scale. Thickness of the feeler gauge corresponds directly with the clearance being measured when reading of the pull scale is within 1.1–2.2 lbs.

Piston pin clearance is normal when the piston pin is snugly fitted into the piston and piston turns smoothly. Replace the piston pin and piston if a considerable amount of play exists between the parts.

NOTE: *The piston rings should be replaced with new ones whenever the engine is overhauled or if found to be worn or damaged.*

5. Insert the piston rings into the cylinder

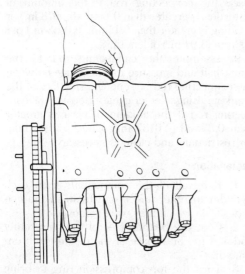

Piston removal

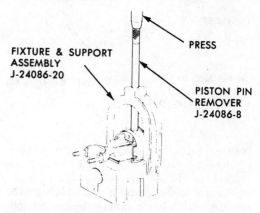

FIXTURE & SUPPORT ASSEMBLY J-24086-20

PRESS

PISTON PIN REMOVER J-24086-8

Removing piston pin

Removing the piston rings

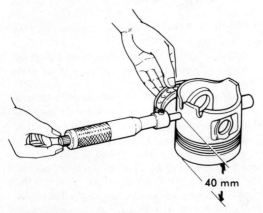

40 mm

Measuring the piston diameter

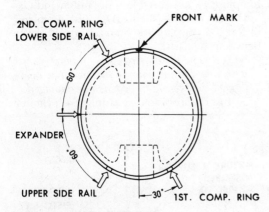

4-1950 piston ring positioning

2ND. COMP. RING
LOWER SIDE RAIL

FRONT MARK

60°

EXPANDER

60°

UPPER SIDE RAIL

30°   1ST. COMP. RING

bore and push them down to the skirt (portion where bore diameters is smallest) using the piston head. This will position piston rings at a right angle to the cylinder wall. Measure the ring gap with a feeler gauge. Replace the pis-

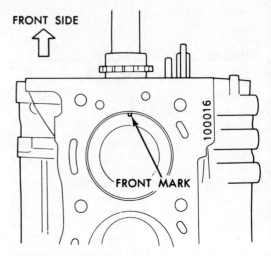

FRONT SIDE

100016

FRONT MARK

Piston correctly installed

ton rings with new ones if the measured value is beyond the limit shown in the chart.

6. With a feeler gauge, measure the clearance between the piston ring and ring grooves in the piston at several points around the circumference of the piston. Replace the piston rings together with the piston if the measured value is greater than 0.15mm (0.0059 in.) or if abnormal contact is noticeable on the upper or lower face of the piston rings.

7. Measure the tension of the piston rings using a piston ring tester. Replace the piston rings with new ones if tension is less than 3.1 lbs. on compression rings or 6.2 lbs. on oil control ring with expander.

8. If distortion of connecting rod is suspicious, remove piston from the connecting rod and check for parallelism. Check the connecting rods for distortion and bending by installing on a connecting rod aligner. Correct or replace the connecting rod if the amount of distortion is greater than 0.2mm (0.0078 in.) or bending is greater than 0.15mm (0.0058 in.) per 100mm (3.94 in.) of length.

9. Assemble the connecting rod to the crankshaft and measure the clearance between the connecting rod big-end and side face of the crankpin using a feeler gauge. Replace the connecting rod if the amount of wear is greater than 0.35mm (0.0137 in.). Check oil jet hole for restrictions and clean as necessary.

Installation

1. Keep all of the components from each cylinder together and install them in the cylinder from which they were removed.

2. Coat the bearing face of the connecting rod and the outer face of the pistons with engine oil.

3. Turn the top compression ring to bring

its gap to the side of the piston marked "Front." Set the remaining rings to that their gaps are positioned 120° apart around the piston.

4. Turn the crankcase until the rod journal of the particular cylinder you are working on is brought to the TDC position.

5. With the piston and rings clamped in a ring compressor, the notched mark on the head of the piston toward the front of the engine, and the marked side of the connecting rod toward the jackshaft, push the piston and connecting rod assembly into the cylinder bore until the big bearing end of the connecting rod contacts and is seated on the rod journal of the crankshaft. Use care not to scratch the cylinder wall with the connecting rod.

6. Push down farther on the piston and turn the crankshaft while the connecting rod rides around on the crankshaft rod journal. Turn the crankshaft until the crankshaft rod journal is at BDC (bottom dead center).

7. Align the mark on the connecting rod bearing cap with that on the connecting rod and tighten the bearing cap bolts to the specified torque.

8. Install all of the piston/connecting rod assemblies in the manner outlined above and assemble the oil pan and cylinder head to the engine in the reverse order of removal.

2000CC ENGINE

Removal

1. Remove the cylinder head.

2. Examine the cylinder bores above the ring travel. If bores are worn so that a shoulder or ridge exists at the top of the cylinder, remove the ridges with a ridge reamer to avoid damaging rings or cracking ring lands in pistons during removal.

3. Use a silver pencil or quick drying paint to mark the cylinder number on all pistons, connecting rods and caps.

4. Remove rod bearing cap and bearing.

5. Install guide hose over threads of rod bolts. This is to prevent damage to bearing journal and rod bolt threads.

6. Remove rod and piston assembly through the top of the cylinder bore.

Disassembly

Remove compression rings and oil ring. Install piston and connecting rod assembly on fixture and support J-24086-20 and place in an arbor press. Press pin out of connecting rod.

Inspection

1. Inspect cylinder walls for scoring, roughness, or ridges which indicate excessive wear. Check cylinder bores for taper and out-of-round with an accurate cylinder gauge at top, middle and bottom of bore, both parallel and at right angles to the cylinder bores at any point may be measured with an inside micrometer or setting the cylinder gauge dial at "O" and measuring across the gauge contact points with outside micrometer while the gage is at same "O" setting.

2. If a cylinder bore is moderately rough or slightly scored but is not out-of-round or tapered, it is usually possible to remedy the situation by honing the bore to fit a standard service piston since standard service pistons are high limit production pistons. If cylinder bore is very rough or deeply scored, however, it may be necessary to rebore the cylinder to fit an oversize piston in order to insure satisfactory results.

3. If cylinder bore is tapered 0.1mm (.003 in.) or more or is out-of-round 0.1mm (.003 in.) or more, it is advisable to rebore for the smallest possible oversize piston and rings. Below these limits, the cylinder bore can be trued up with honing.

4. Clean carbon from piston surfaces and under side of piston heads. Clean carbon from ring grooves with suitable tool and remove any gum or varnish from piston skirts with suitable solvent.

5. Carefully examine pistons for rough or scored surfaces; cracks in skirt of head; cracked or broken ring lands, chipped or uneven wearing pistons would cause rings to seat improperly or have excessive clearance in ring grooves. Damaged or faulty pistons should be replaced. The pistons are cam ground, which means that the diameter at a right angle to the wrist pin is greater than the diameter parallel to the wrist pin. When a piston is checked for size, it must be done at points 90° to the piston pin. The piston should be checked (for fitting purposes) on a plane equal to the piston pin centerline.

6. Inspect surfaces of wrist pins and check for wear by measuring worn or unworn surfaces with micrometers. Occasionally pins will be found tight due too gum or varnish deposits. This may be corrected by removing the deposit with a suitable solvent. if piston bosses are worn out-of-round or oversize, the piston and pin assembly must be replaced. Oversize pins are not practical due to the pin being a press fit in the connecting rod. Piston pins must fit the piston with an easy finger push at 70°F (21°C) (.0065–.0091 mm clearance).

7. Examine all piston rings for scores, chips, or cracks. Check compression rings for tension compression rings by placing rings in bore at bottom of ring travel. Measure gap with feeler gauge. Gap should be between 0.25mm–0.50mm (.009–.019 in.).

If gaps are over .50mm (.019 in.), it indicates the rings have worn considerably and should be replaced. Bore wear should be checked before rings are replaced, .125mm (.004 in.) bore wear will result in .380mm (.014 in.) increase in ring gap.

Assembly

There is a hole and notch cast in the top of all pistons to facilitate proper installation. The piston assemblies should always be installed with the hole toward the front of the engine.

1. Lubricate piston pin holes in the piston and connecting rod lightly with engine oil.
2. Position connecting rod in its respective piston. Hold in place with piston pin guide and piston pin. Place assembly on fixture and support assembly J-24086-20.
3. Press the piston pin into the piston and connecting rod.

NOTE: *After installer hub bottoms on support assembly, do not exceed 5000 psi pressure, as this could cause structural damage to the tool.*

4. Remove piston and connecting rod, assembly from tool and check piston pin for freedom of movement on piston.

Installation

Cylinder bores must be clean before piston installation. This may be accomplished with a hot water and detergent wash or with a light honing as necessary. After cleaning, the bores should be swabbed several times with light engine oil and a clean dry cloth.

1. Lubricate connecting rod bearings and install in rods and rod caps.
2. Lightly coat pistons, rings and cylinder walls light engine oil.
3. With bearing caps removed, install guide hose over connecting rod bolts. These guide hoses protect the crankpin journal from damage during installation of connecting rod and piston assembly.
4. Make sure the ring gaps are positioned as shown.
5. Install each connecting rod and piston assembly in its respective bore. Install with connecting rod bearing tang slots on side opposite camshaft. Use Tool J-8037 or J-8910 to compress the rings. Guide the connecting rod into place on the crankshaft journal.

NOTE: *Use a hammer handle and light blows to install the piston into the bore. Hold the ring compressor firmly against the cylinder block until all piston rings have entered the cylinder bore.*

6. *Install the bearing caps and torque nuts to specifications. If bearing replacement is required refer to "Connecting Rod Bearings."*

Be sure to install new pistons in the same cylinders for which they were fitted, and used pistons in the same cylinder from which they were removed.

ENGINE LEFT   ENGINE FRONT   ENGINE RIGHT

"A" OIL RING SPACER GAP
(Tang in Hole or Slot within Arc)

"B" OIL RING RAIL GAPS

"C" 2ND COMPRESSION RING GAP

"D" TOP COMPRESSION RING GAP

4-2000 piston ring positioning

2800cc ENGINE

Removal

1. Remove cylinder heads.
2. Examine the cylinder bores above the ring travel. If bores are worn so that a shoulder or ridge exists at the top of the cylinder, remove the ridges with a ridge reamer to avoid damaging rings or cracking ring lands in pistons during removal.
3. Use a silver pencil or quick drying paint to mark the cylinder number on all pistons, connecting rods and caps. Starting at the front end of the crankcase the cylinders in the right bank are numbered 1-3-5 and those in the left bank are numbered 2-4-6.
4. Remove rod bearing cap and bearing.
5. Install guide hose over threads of rod bolts. This is to prevent damage to bearing journal and rod bolt threads.
6. Remove rod and piston assembly through the top of the cylinder bore.

Disassembly

1. Remove compression rings and oil ring.
2. Install piston and connecting rod assembly on fixture and support J-24086-20 and place in an arbor press. Press pin out of connecting rod.

Inspection

1. Inspect cylinder walls for scoring, roughness, or ridges which indicate excessive wear. Check cylinder bores for taper and out-of-round with an accurate cylinder gauge at top, middle and bottom of bore. Both parallel and right angles to the cylinder bores at any point may be measured with an inside micrometer while the gauge is at same "O" setting.

2. If a cylinder bore is moderately rough or slightly scored but is not out-of-round or tapered, it is usually possible to remedy the situation by honing the bore to fit a standard service piston since standard service pistons are high limit production pistons. If cylinder bore is very rough or deeply scored, however, it may be necessary to rebore the cylinder to fit an oversize piston in order to insure satisfactory results.

3. If cylinder bore is tapered 0.1mm or more or is out-of-round 0.1mm or more, it is advisable to rebore for the smallest possible oversize piston and rings. Below these limits, the cylinder bore can be trued up with honing.

4. Clean carbon from piston surfaces and under side of piston heads. Clean carbon from ring grooves with suitable tool and remove any gum or varnish from piston skirts with suitable solvent.

5. Carefully examine pistons for rough or scored surfaces; cracks in skirt or head; cracked or broken ring lands; chipped or uneven wearing pistons would cause rings to seat improperly or have excessive clearance in ring grooves. Damaged or faulty pistons should be replaced. The pistons are cam ground, which means that the diameter at a right angle to the wrist pin is greater than the diameter parallel to the wrist pin. When a piston is checked for size, it must be done at points 90° to the piston pin. The piston should be checked (for fitting purposes) in a plane through the piston pin centerline.

6. Inspect surfaces of wrist pins and check for wear by measuring worn or unworn surfaces with micrometers. Occasionally pins will be found tight due to gum or varnish deposits. This may be corrected by removing the deposit with a suitable solvent. If piston bosses are worn out-of-round or oversize, the piston and pin assembly must be replaced. Oversize pins are not practical due to the pin being a press fit in the connecting rod. Piston pins must fit the piston with an easy finger push at 70°F (21°C) with .0065–.0091mm clearance.

7. Examine all piston rings for scores, chips or cracks. Check compression rings for tension by comparing with new rings. Check gap of compression rings by placing rings in bore at bottom of ring travel. Measure gap with feeler gauge. Gap should be between 0.25mm and 0.50mm. If gaps are excessive (over 0.50mm) it indicates the rings have worn considerably and should be replaced. Bore wear should be checked before rings are replaced .125mm bore wear will result in .39mm increase in ring gap.

Assembly

There is machined hole or a cast notch in the top of all pistons to facilitate proper installation. The piston assemblies should always be installed with the hole toward the front of the engine.

1. Lubricate piston pin holes in piston and connecting rod light with engine oil.
2. Position connecting rod in its respective piston. Hold in place with piston pin guide and piston pin. Place assembly on fixture and support assembly J-24086-20.
3. Press the piston pin into the piston and connecting rod.

NOTE: *After installer hub bottoms on support assembly, do not exceed 5000 psi pressure, as this could cause structural damage to the tool.*

4. Remove piston and connecting rod assembly from tool and check piston pin for freedom of movement on piston.

Installation

Cylinder bores must be clean before piston installation. This may be accomplished with a hot water and detergent wash or with a light honing as necessary. After cleaning, the bores should be swabbed several times with light engine oil and a clean dry cloth.

1. Lubricate connecting rod bearings and install in rods and rod caps.
2. Lightly coat pistons, rings and cylinder walls with light engine oil.
3. With bearing caps removed, install guide hose over connecting rod bolts. These guide hoses protect the crankpin journal from damage during installation of connecting rod and piston assembly.
4. Make sure the gap in the oil ring rails in "up" position toward center of engine and the gaps of the compression rings are positioned as shown.
5. Install each connecting rod and piston assembly in its respective bore. Install with connecting rod bearing tang slots on side opposite camshaft. Use Tool J-8037 or J-8910 to com-

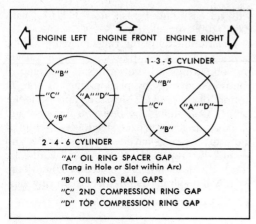

ENGINE LEFT   ENGINE FRONT   ENGINE RIGHT

1 - 3 - 5 CYLINDER

"B"
"C" "A" "D"
"B"

"B"
"C" "A" "D"
"B"

2 - 4 - 6 CYLINDER

"A" OIL RING SPACER GAP
(Tang in Hole or Slot within Arc)
"B" OIL RING RAIL GAPS
"C" 2ND COMPRESSION RING GAP
"D" TOP COMPRESSION RING GAP

6-2800 piston ring positioning

HONED SURFACE

1. Cross Hatch Angle 22°-32°
2. Uniformly Cut in Both Directions
3. Clean Cut Not Sharp Free of Torn and Folded Metal
4. Micro Ave. 20-30 Range 15-35
5. Cross Hatch Ave. .0004"-.0006" Wide Range .0002"-.0009"
6. Cross Hatch Ave. .00015"-.00025" Deep Range .0001"-.0003"
7. Plateau to be ½ to ⅔ of Surface
8. Free of Burnish or Glaze
9. Free of Imbedded Particles

Cylinder honing specification

press the rings. Guide the connecting rod into place on the crankshaft journal.

Use a hammer handle and light blows to install the piston into the bore. Hold the ring compressor firmly against the cylinder block until all piston rings have entered the cylinder bore.

6. Install the bearing caps and torque nuts to specifications. If bearing replacement is required refer to "Connecting Rod Bearings."

Be sure to install new pistons in the same cylinders for which they were fitted, and used pistons in the same cylinder from which they were removed. Each connecting rod and bearing cap should be marked, beginning at the front of the engine. On V-6 engines, 1, 3 and 5 are in the right bank and 2, 4 and 6 are in the left bank. The numbers on the connecting rod and bearing cap must be on the same side when installed in the cylinder bore. If a connecting rod is ever transposed from one block or cylinder to another, new bearings should be fitted and the connecting rod should be numbered to correspond with the new cylinder number.

HONING OR REBORING CYLINDERS

If one or more cylinder bores are rough, scored or worn beyond limits, it will be necessary to smooth or true up such bores to fit new pistons.

If relatively few bores require correction, it will not be necessary to rebore all cylinders to the same oversize in order to maintain engine balance. All oversize service pistons are held to the same weights as standard size pistons.

No attempt should be made to cut down oversize pistons to fit cylinder bores as this will destroy the surface treatment and affect the weight. The smallest possible oversize service pistons should be used and the cylinder bores

should be honed to size for proper clearances.

Before the honing or reboring operation is started, measure all new pistons with micrometer contacting at points exactly 90 degrees from piston pin centerline; then select the smallest piston for the first fitting. The slight variation usually found between pistons in a set may provide for correction in case the first piston is fitted too free.

If wear at top of cylinder does not exceed 0.10 mm on the diameter or exceed 0.10mm out-of-round, honing is recommended for truing the bore. If wear or out-of-round exceeds these limits, the bore should be trued up with a boring bar of the fly cutter type, then finish honed.

When reboring cylinders, all crankshaft bearing caps must be in place and tightened to proper torque to avoid distortion of bores in final assembly. Always be sure the crankshaft is out of the way of the boring cutter when boring each cylinder. When taking the final cut with boring bar, leave .025mm on the diameter for finish honing to give the required clearance specified.

When honing cylinders, use clean sharp stones of proper grade for the amount of metal to be removed, in accordance with instructions of the hone manufacturer. Dull or dirty stones cut unevenly and generate excessive heat. When using coarse or medium grade stones use care to leave sufficient metal so that all stone marks may be removed with the fine stones used for finishing to provide proper clearance.

It is of the greatest importance that refinished cylinder bores are trued up to have not over .02mm out-of-round or taper. Each bore must be final honed to remove all stone or cutter marks and provide a smooth surface. During final honing, each piston must be fitted individually to the bore in which it will be installed and should be marked to insure correct installation.

After final honing and before the piston is checked for fit, each cylinder bore must be thoroughly washed to remove all traces of abrasive and then dried thoroughly. The dry bore should then be brushed clean with a power-driven fibre brush. If all traces of abrasive are not removed, rapid water of new pistons and rings will result.

FITTING PISTONS

1. Remove all rings from pistons which will be fitted. It is not necessary to separate rods from pistons. If an excess amount of varnish or carbon appears as a ridge at the top of the cylinder, remove by scraping or sanding.

2. Wipe bores and pistons clean, removing oil or other foreign material. Select a piston-rod assembly for the bore to be fitted (or piston and pin if a new piston is being fitted) and position down into the bore with the top of piston down. The piston should fall free by its own weight through the bore when the bottom of the piston skirt is 12 to 25mm (½ to 1 in.) from top of block.

CAUTION: *Make sure piston is not damaged when it "falls" through the cylinder. If it doesn't, the piston fit is too tight and another piston should be selected until the piston will slide freely through the bore without any force being applied. Mark piston and bore for proper assembly.*

3. After a piston has been selected, which will slide freely through a bore, it must be determined if piston fit will be too loose. This is done by placing a .060mm (.025 in.) feeler gauge for used pistons and at least 150mm (6 in.) long and not over 12mm (½ in.) wide, down into the same bore with selected piston while holding feeler to top of the bore.

Position selected piston and feeler down into the bore until the bottom of the skirt is again 12 to 25mm (½ to 1 in.) from top of block, being sure that the feeler gauge is 90 degrees from the pin. If the piston hangs on the feeler gauge and does not fall free, it indicates that the piston is correctly fitted to that respective bore. Mark both piston and bore before going to the next bore. If the piston fell free during this check with the .060mm (.0025 in.) feeler gauge (.050mm (.002 in.) feeler gauge for new pistons) then that particular piston is too small for the bore and a larger diameter piston will be required.

When checking more than one bore, it is very possible that what may be a piston too small for one will be a correct fit in another.

PISTON RINGS

When new piston rings are installed without reboring cylinders, the glazed cylinder walls should be slightly dulled, but without increasing the bore diameter, by means of the finest grade of stones in a cylinder hone.

New piston rings must be checked for clearance in piston grooves and for gap in cylinder bores. The cylinder bores and piston grooves must be clean, dry and free of carbon and burrs.

NOTE: *With rings installed, check clearance in grooves by inserting feeler gauges between each ring and its lower land. Any wear that occurs forms a step at inner portion of the lower land.*

If the piston grooves have worn to the extent that relatively high steps exist on the lower lands, the piston should be replaced because the steps will interfere with the operation of new rings and the ring clearances will be excessive. Piston rings are not furnished in oversize widths to compensate for ring groove wear.

All compression rings are marked on the upper side of the ring. When installing compression rings, make sure the marked side is toward the top of the piston. The top ring is treated with molybdenum for maximum life. The oil control rings are of three pieces type, consisting of two segments (rails) and a spacer.

Fitting Rings to Piston

1. Select rings comparable in size to the piston being used.

2. Slip the compression ring in the cylinder bore: then press the ring down into the cylinder bore about 6mm (.24 in.) (above ring travel). Be sure ring is square with cylinder wall.

3. Measure the space or gap between the end of the ring with a feeler gauge.

4. If the gap between the ends of the ring is below specifications, remove the ring and try another fit.

5. Fit each compression ring to the cylinder in which it is going to be used.

6. If the pistons have not been cleaned and inspected as previously outlined, do so.

7. Slip the outer surface of the top and second compression ring into the respective piston ring groove and roll the ring entirely around the groove. If binding occurs at any point, the cause should be determined. If there's a ring groove, remove by dressing with a fine cut file. If the binding is caused by a distorted ring, check a new ring.

Installation

1. Install oil ring spacer in groove being sure ends are butted and not overlapped.

2. Hold spacer ends butted and install lower steel oil ring rail.

3. Install upper steel oil ring rail with gap staggered.

4. Flex the oil ring assembly to make sure ring is free. If binding occurs, the cause should be determined. If caused by ring groove, remove by dressing groove with a fine cut file. If binding is caused by a distorted ring, check a new ring.

5. Install second compression ring. Stagger gap from other rings.

6. Install top compression ring with gap properly located.

Crankshaft and Main Bearings

NOTE: *Special tools are required for this procedure.*

REMOVAL
All Engines

1. Remove the engine from the truck.
2. Remove the spark plugs.
3. Remove the front cover.
4. Remove the crankshaft pulley and sprocket.
5. Remove the oil pan and pump.
6. Remove the Flywheel.
7. Mark and remove the connecting rod bearing caps. Push the pistons to the tops of the bores.
8. Mark the main bearing caps. Remove the caps, beginning at the ends and working towards the middle.
9. Remove the crankshaft.
10. If they're being replaced, remove the upper and lower bearing halves.

INSPECTION

1. Wash the crankshaft in a safe solvent. Check the shaft for any signs of damage, wear, pitting, scuffing or cracks.
2. Measure the main bearing journals and crankpins with a micrometer for out-of-round, taper or undersize.
3. If the journals are found to have some surface damage, they can be reground at some well-equipped machine shops.
4. Replace or recondition the crankshaft as necessary.

INSTALLATION

1. Replace the rear main seal.
2. Install the upper main bearing halves in the block and lubricate them thoroughly with clean engine oil. Install the lower bearing halves in the caps.
3. Position the crankshaft on the upper bearing halves.

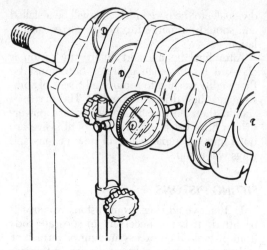
Checking crankshaft journal runout

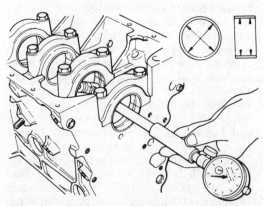
Checking main bearing journal diameter

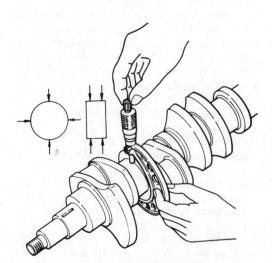
Measuring main bearing diameter

4. Lay a piece of Plastigage across the lower bearing halves. Install the bearing caps and torque them to specification. Remove the caps and check the width of the Plastigage. The measured width should correspond to the

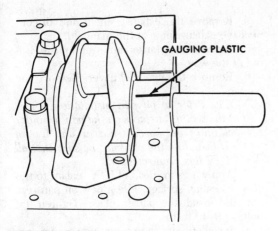

Using Pastigage

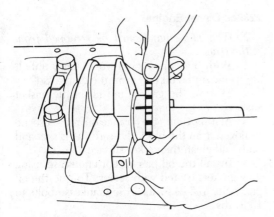

Measuring plastigage after bearing cap removal

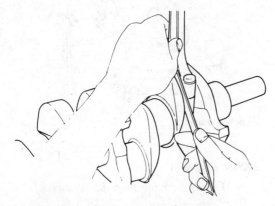

Measuring connecting rod side clearance

bearing clearance given in the Crankshaft Specifications chart. If not, oversized bearings may be needed.

5. Perform the same clearance test with the connecting rod bearings.

6. On the 2000cc or 2800cc engine, apply a thin coat of RTV sealant to the block mating surface of the rear main cap. Do not allow any sealer to get into the crankcase.

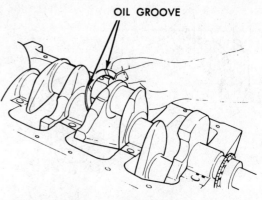

4-1950, 2238 thrust bearing location

7. On the 1950cc, or 2238cc diesel, make sure that the thrust bearing is installed with the oil groove turned outward. Make sure that all other bearings are properly seated. Bearings are installed with the corresponding tongues in grooves. Caps are installed with the stamped arrow facing front and the numbers aligned. Coat all parts with clean engine oil or engine oil supplement. Torque the bearing caps to 50 ft. lb. as follows: 3, 4, 2, 5, 1. Turn the crankshaft one full revolution, then torque the caps to 75 ft. lb. in the same sequence. Make sure that the crankshaft turns smoothly. Install all other parts in reverse of removal.

8. On the 2000cc engine, install all bearing caps with the arrows facing forward. Torque all main caps, except No. 4, to specification. Torque number 4 to 10–12 ft. lb., then tap the end of the crankshaft, first rearward, then forward, with a lead or wood hammer. This will line up the rear main bearing and crankshaft thrust surfaces. Torque all main caps to the specification shown in the Torque Specifications chart. Install all other parts in reverse of removal.

9. On the 2800cc engine, follow the procedure for the 2000cc engine in step 8. Instead of bearing number 4, the bearing on the V6 is No. 3. Install all other parts in reverse of removal.

Oil Pan
REMOVAL AND INSTALLATION
1950cc Engine

NOTE: *On 4-wheel drive the engine must be removed before removing the oil pan.*

1. Disconnect the negative battery terminal.
2. Jack up your vehicle and support it with jack stands.
3. Drain the oil.
4. Remove the front splash shield.
5. Remove the front crossmember, if necessary.

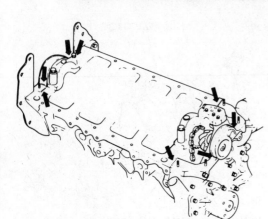

4-1950 oil pan sealer location

6. Disconnect the relay rod at the idler arm and lower the relay rod.

7. Remove the left side bellhousing bracket.

8. Remove the vacuum line at the oil pan.

9. Remove the oil pan bolts and the pan.

NOTE: *It may be necessary to remove the motor mounts and jack up the engine in order to remove the oil pan.*

10. Installation is the reverse of removal. Tighten the retaining bolts to 43 in. lbs.

2000cc Engine

1. Disconnect the negative battery cable.

2. Drain the crankcase. Raise and support the front of the vehicle with jack stands.

3. Remove the A/C brace if so equipped.

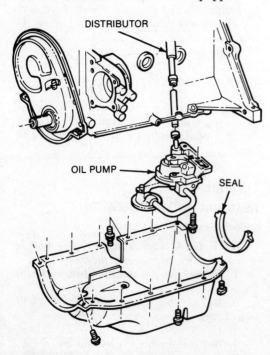

4-2000 oil pan

4. Remove the exhaust shield and disconnect the exhaust pipe at the manifold.

5. Remove the starter motor and position it out of the way.

6. Remove the flywheel cover. Remove the oil pan.

NOTE: *Prior to oil pan installation, check that the sealing surfaces on the pan, cylinder block and front cover are clean and free of oil. If installing the old pan, be sure that all old RTV has been removed.*

7. Apply a ⅛ in. bead of RTV sealant to the oil pan sealing surface. Use a new oil pan rear seal and install the pan in place. Tighten the bolts to 9–13 ft. lbs.

8. Installation of the remaining components is in the reverse order of removal.

2238cc Diesel Engine

NOTE: *The engine must be removed from the truck.*

1. With the engine on a work stand, unbolt and remove the oil pan from the crankcase.

2. Discard the gasket and clean the gasket surfaces.

3. At this time, the crankcase may also be removed from the block. Discard the gasket and seals and clean the gasket surfaces.

4. Install the oil pan and/or crankcase using new gaskets coated with sealer. Torque the oil pan bolts to 5–9 ft. lbs.; the crankcase bolts to 15 ft. lbs.

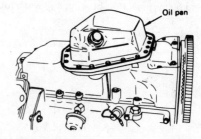

Diesel oil pan

2800cc Engine

NOTE: *The engine must be removed from the truck.*

1. With the engine on a work stand, unbolt and remove the pan.

2. Discard the gasket and clean the gasket surfaces.

3. The oil pan does not use a preformed gasket. Rather it is sealed with RTV gasket material. Make sure that the sealing surfaces are free of oil and old RTV material.

4. Run a ⅛ in. bead of sealer along the entire sealing surface of the pan.

5. Place the pan on the engine and finger

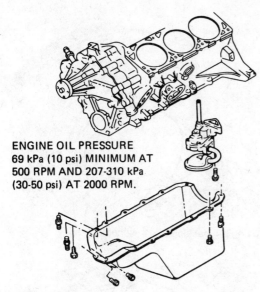

ENGINE OIL PRESSURE
69 kPa (10 psi) MINIMUM AT
500 RPM AND 207-310 kPa
(30-50 psi) AT 2000 RPM.

6-2800 oil pan

tighten the bolts. Torque the smaller bolts to 6–9 ft. lbs.; the larger bolts to 15–22 ft. lbs.

Oil Pump

REMOVAL AND INSTALLATION

1950cc Engine

1. Drain and remove the oil pan.
2. Disconnect the oil feed pipe.
3. Remove the two bolts securing the oil pump to the cylinder block and remove the oil pump.
4. Install in the reverse order of removal.

2238cc Diesel Engine

1. Follow the engine assembly removal steps.
2. Remove the 20 bolts fixing the crankcase and remove the crankcase together with the oil pan.

NOTE: *Pry off the crankcase by fitting a screwdriver into the slots in the crankcase.*

3. Remove the oil pipe sleeve nut.
4. Remove the 2 bolts fixing the oil pump and remove the oil pump with oil pipe.
5. Install the oil pipe and leave the joints semi-tight.
6. Fully tighten the oil pump fixing screws, then tighten the oil pipe joints.
7. Reverse the removal procedure for the remaining parts.

2000cc Engine

1. Remove the engine oil pan.
2. Remove the pump attaching bolts and carefully lower the pump.
3. Install in reverse order. To ensure immediate oil pressure on start-up, the oil pump

gear cavity should be packed with petroleum jelly. Installation torque is 26–35 ft. lbs.

2800cc Engine

1. Remove the oil pan as described earlier.
2. Unbolt and remove the oil pump and pickup.
3. Installation is the reverse of removal. Torque the pump bolts to 26–35 ft. lbs.

Oil Cooler

REMOVAL AND INSTALLATION

2238cc Diesel Engine

1. Place a suitable size tray under the oil filter to receive oil and water flowing out from the filter.
2. Drain the cooling system by opening the drain plugs on the radiator and on the cylinder block.
3. Remove the oil cooler water drain plug and drain the water.
4. Disconnect the oil cooler hoses at the cooler side.
5. Remove the oil filter cartridge using filter wrench.
6. Remove the nut fixing the oil cooler, then remove the oil cooler assembly.
7. Install the cooler using a new O-ring. Torque to 55–60 ft. lbs.

Rear Main Oil Seal

REPLACEMENT

1950cc Engine

1. Disconnect the negative battery terminal.
2. Remove the oil pan as previously described.
3. Remove the transmission.

NOTE: *On manual transmissions, remove the clutch assembly.*

4. Unbolt the starter and tie it out of the way.
5. Remove the flywheel.

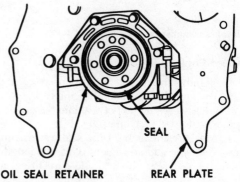

SEAL

OIL SEAL RETAINER   REAR PLATE

4-1950 rear main seal

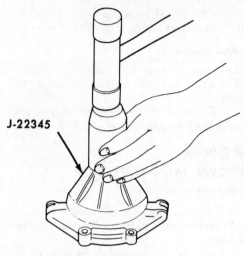

J-22345

4-1950 rear main seal installation

6. Remove the rear main seal retainer.
7. Remove the oil seal and discard it.
8. Install the new oil seal.
9. Installation is the reverse of removal. Fill the space between the seal lips with grease and lubricate the seal lips with engine oil.

2238cc Diesel Engine

1. Follow the engine removal steps.
2. Remove the 6 bolts mounting the flywheel and remove the flywheel assembly.

When loosening the flywheel bolts, hold the crankshaft front bolt with a wrench to prevent turning of the crankshaft.

3. Remove the crankshaft rear seal.
4. Install the new seal with seal installer J-22928 or equivalent. Reverse removal procedures for all other parts.

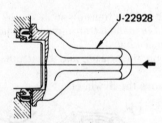

J-22928

Diesel rear main seal installation

2000cc Engine

1. Remove the oil pan and pump.
2. Remove the rear main bearing cap.
3. Gently pack the upper seal into the groove approximately ¼ inch on each side.
4. Measure the amount the seal was driven in on one side and add ¹⁄₁₆ in. Cut this length from the old lower cap seal. Be sure to get a sharp cut. Repeat for the other side.
5. Place the piece of cut seal into the groove

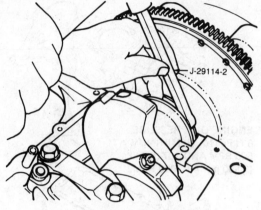

J-29114-2

Using the packing tool—4-2000, 6-2800

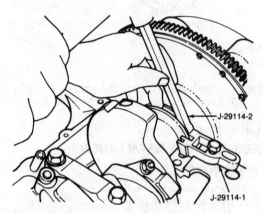

J-29114-2

J-29114-1

Using the guide tool—4-2000, 6-2800

and pack the seal into the block. Do this for each side.

6. Install a piece of Plastigage or the equivalent on the bearing journal. Install the rear cap and tighten to 75 ft. lbs. Remove the cap and check the gauge for bearing clearance. If out of specification, the ends of the seal may be frayed or not flush, preventing the cap from proper seating. Correct as required.

7. Clean the journal, and apply a thin film of sealer to the mating surfaces of the cap and tighten to 70 ft. lbs. Install the pan and pump.

2800cc Engine

1. Remove the oil pan and pump.
2. Remove the rear main bearing cap.
3. Gently pack the upper seal into the groove approximately ¼ inch on each side.
4. Measure the amount the seal was driven in one one side and add ¹⁄₁₆ in. Cut this length from the old lower cap seal. Be sure to get a sharp cut. Repeat for the other side.
5. Place the piece of cut seal into the groove and pack the seal into the block. Do this for each side.

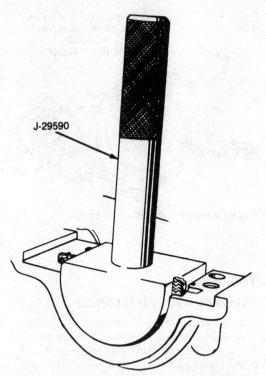

J-29590

After positioning the seal on the 4-2000 or 6-2800, cut the ends flush

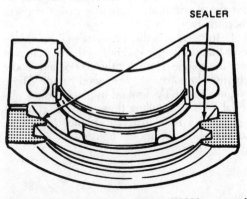

SEALER

Applying sealer to the 4-2000 or 6-2800 rear main cap

NOTE: *GM makes a guide tool (J-29114-1) which bolts to the block via an oil pan bolt hole, and a packing tool (J-29114-2) which are machined to provide a built-in stop for the installation of the short cut pieces. Using the packing tool, work the short pieces of seal onto the guide tool, then pack them into the block with the packing tool.*

6. Install a new lower seal in the rear main cap.

7. Install a piece of Plastigage or the equivalent on the bearing journal. Install the rear cap and tighten to 70 ft. lbs. Remove the cap and check the gauge for bearing clearance. If

out of specification, the ends of the seal may be frayed or not flush, preventing the cap from proper sealing. Correct as required.

8. Clean the journal, and apply a thin film of sealer to the mating surfaces of the cap and block. Do not allow any sealer to get onto the journal or bearing. Install the bearing cap and tighten to 70 ft. lbs. Install the pan and pump.

Flywheel
REMOVAL AND INSTALLATION
All Engines

1. Remove the transmission and clutch, or torque converter.
2. Unbolt and remove the flywheel.
3. If the ring gear is to be replaced, split it with a cold chisel or electric drill and remove it. Wear eye protection.
4. Heat the new ring gear in an oven at about 450°F for 20 minutes. Using protective gloves, hammer the hot ring gear into position and allow it to cool.
5. Installation is the reverse of removal.
NOTE: *Using a torch to heat the ring gear can weaken the metal.*

Water Pump
REMOVAL AND INSTALLATION
1950cc and 2238cc Engines

1. Disconnect the battery ground. Drain the cooling system.
2. Remove the front cover. Disconnect the hoses at the pump.
3. On models without air conditioning, remove the fan.
4. On models with air conditioning, remove the fan belt, fan pulley, fan, air pump pulley and fan set plate.
5. Unbolt and remove the pump.
6. Clean the gasket surfaces thoroughly.
7. Installation is the reverse of removal. Always use a new gasket.

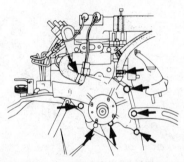

4-1950 water pump mounting bolts—diesel engine similar

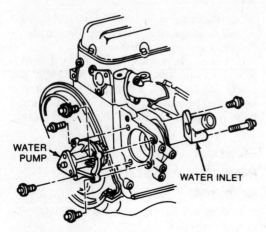

WATER
PUMP

WATER INLET

4-2000 water pump

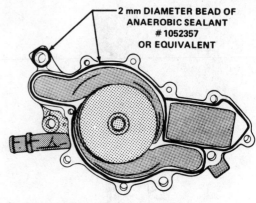

2 mm DIAMETER BEAD OF
ANAEROBIC SEALANT
1052357
OR EQUIVALENT

Applying sealer to the V6 water pump

2000cc Engine

1. Disconnect the battery ground.
2. Drain the cooling system.
3. Remove all drive belts. Disconnect the hoses at the pump.
4. Remove the alternator.
5. Unbolt and remove the pump.
6. Thoroughly clean the gasket surfaces. Discard the old gasket.
7. Using a new gasket, install the pump and assemble all other components in reverse order of removal.

2800cc Engine

1. Disconnect the battery ground.
2. Drain the cooling system.
3. Disconnect the hoses at the pump.
4. Unbolt and remove the pump.
5. Thoroughly clean the sealing surfaces of old gasket material. This engine uses RTV sealant in place of a gasket.
6. Place a $3/32$ in. bead of sealer on the water pump mating surface. Coat the bolt threads with pipe compound and mount the pump on the engine.
7. Assemble all other components in reverse order of removal.

Thermostat
REMOVAL AND INSTALLATION

1. Drain the cooling system.
2. Disconnect any wires or hoses in the way of thermostat removal. The thermostat is located under the engine water outlet housing. This housing is the point at which the upper radiator hose connects to the engine.
3. Remove the thermostat housing and lift out the thermostat. Clean the gasket surfaces thoroughly.
4. Installation is the reverse of removal. Make sure that the larger end of the thermostat goes into the engine. Note that the 2000cc and 2800cc engines do not use a preformed gasket. These engines use RTV formed-in-place gasket material. When installing these gaskets, run a $1/8$ in. bead of RTV material around the sealing surface of the thermostat housing.

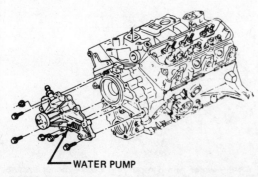

WATER PUMP

6-2800 water pump

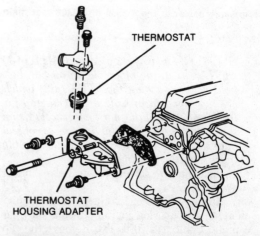

THERMOSTAT

THERMOSTAT
HOUSING ADAPTER

4-2000 thermostat

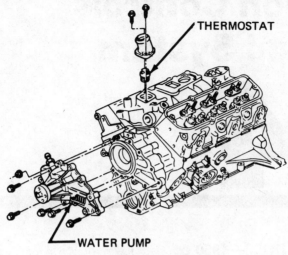

6-2800 thermostat

Radiator

REMOVAL AND INSTALLATION

1. Disconnect the battery ground.
2. Drain the cooling system.
3. Disconnect the hoses from the radiator.
4. On models with automatic transmission, disconnect the cooler lines.
5. Remove the fan shroud.
6. Unbolt and remove the radiator.
7. Installation is the reverse of removal.

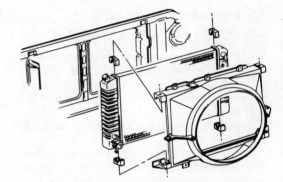

Typical radiator and shroud installation

Emission Controls and Fuel System

4

EMISSION CONTROLS—1950 cc ENGINE

Air Injection Pump (AIR)
INSPECTION AND REPLACEMENT

Check the air pump for any abnormal noise or seizing and replace if found to be defective.

NOTE: *The air pump is non-serviceable, it must be replaced as an assembly if found defective.*

1. Remove air pump drive belt from air pump pulley.
2. Disconnect hoses from air switching valve.
3. Remove attaching bolts from engine mount and jack up mount.
4. Remove air pump mounting bolts and remove air pump and air switching valve.
5. Remove air switching valve from air pump.
6. Reverse procedure to install.

Air Switching Valve (ASV)
INSPECTION AND REPLACEMENT

If air switching valve is normal, the secondary air continues to blow out from the valve for a

CHECK VALVE — AIR CLEANER

◄ FRT

AIR MANIFOLD

AIR PUMP

AIR SWITCHING VALVE

HOSE (CALIF)

HOSE (FED)

Air Injection Reactor (AIR) on the 4-1950

few seconds when the accelerator pedal is depressed all the way to floor and released quickly. If the secondary air continues to blow out for more than 5 seconds, replace the air switching valve.

1. Remove the hoses from the air switching valve.
2. Remove mounting hardware and remove the valve.
3. Reverse the procedure to install.

Check Valve

Remove the check valve from the air manifold. Test it for leakage by blowing air into the valve from the air pump side and from the air manifold side. If check valve is normal, air passes only from the air pump side. If air passes from the air manifold side, it indicates the need for replacing check valve. A small amount of air leakage may be overlooked. To remove the valve, release clamp and disconnect the air hose from the check valve. Unscrew the check valve from the air injection pipe. Reverse the procedure to install the check valve.

Mixture Control (Anti-Backfire) Valve
INSPECTION AND REPLACEMENT

Disconnect rubber hose connecting mixture control valve with intake manifold, and plug intake manifold side. If mixture control valve is normal, the secondary air continues to blow out from the mixture control valve for a few seconds when the accelerator pedal is depressed all the way to floor and released quickly. If the secondary air continues to blow out for more than 5 seconds, replace mixture control valve.

For replacement, remove valve from clamp bracket and remove hose.

Air Hoses and Injector Pipes

INSPECTION AND REPLACEMENT

Check around air manifold for air leakage with engine running at 2000 rpm. If air is leaking from the nozzle sleeve nuts, retighten them.

Check and replace hoses if found to be fatigued or cracked. Also check hose joints and clips. Be sure that hoses are not in contact with adjacent parts.

Vacuum Switching Valve (VSV)

REPLACEMENT

1. Disconnect electrical connector.
2. Remove hoses from valve.
3. Remove vacuum switching valve.
4. Reverse procedure to install valve.

Exhaust Gas Recirculation (EGR)

INSPECTION

Check vacuum diaphragm function by applying an outside vacuum source to the vacuum supply tube at the top of vacuum diaphragm. The diaphragm should not "leak down" and should move to the fully up position at about 13 kPa (3.9 in. Hg.).

EGR VALVE REPLACEMENT

1. Disconnect EGR pipe from adaptor.
2. Disconnect EGR valve vacuum hose at valve.
3. Remove bolts holding EGR valve on manifold adaptor and remove valve.

4. Clean EGR mounting surface.
5. Install replacement EGR valve using new gasket.
6. Connect vacuum hose.
7. Connect EGR pipe.

BACK PRESSURE TRANSDUCER REPLACEMENT

1. Remove back pressure transducer from clamp bracket.
2. Remove hoses from transducer.
3. Reverse procedure to install transducer.

THERMAL VACUUM VALVE TESTING

Put the thermo sensing portion into hot water, 46° to 54°C (115° to 129°F) for M/T or 45° to 55°C (113° to 131°F) for A/T and check the valve opening by blowing air. If air does not pass, replace the thermal vacuum valve.

Early Fuel Evaporation (EFE)

EFE HEATER REPLACEMENT

1. Remove air cleaner.
2. Disconnect all electrical, vacuum, and fuel connections from carburetor.
3. Disconnect EFE Heater electrical connector.
4. Remove carburetor.
5. Replace EFE heater insulator assembly.
6. Reinstall carburetor.
7. Reconnect EFE Heater electrical connection.

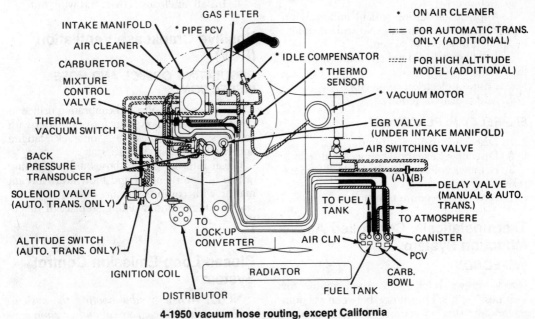

4-1950 vacuum hose routing, except California

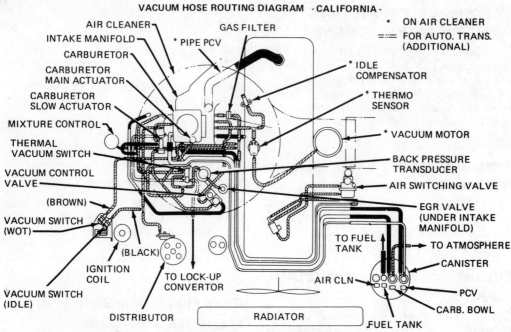

VACUUM HOSE ROUTING DIAGRAM · CALIFORNIA ·

* ON AIR CLEANER
=== FOR AUTO. TRANS. (ADDITIONAL)

4-1950 California vacuum hose routing

8. Reconnect electrical, vacuum and fuel connections to carburetor.

9. Replace air cleaner.

10. Start engine and check for vacuum leaks.

EFE Temperature Switch

REPLACEMENT

1. Drain coolant below level of engine coolant outlet housing.

2. Disconnect electrical connector.

3. Remove switch.

4. Apply a soft setting sealant uniformly on replacement switch threads. No sealant should be applied to sensor of switch.

5. Install switch and tighten to 14 Nm (10 ft. lbs.)

6. Connect electrical connector.

7. Add coolant as required.

EFE RELAY REPLACEMENT

1. Disconnect battery ground.

2. Disconnect electrical connector at relay.

3. Remove bolts holding relay and remove relay.

4. Reverse procedure to install.

Thermostatically Controlled Air Induction System

INSPECTION

Check screws retaining vacuum motor for looseness, and rubber hoses between vacuum motor and thermo sensor for loose connec-

tions. Check idle compensator and thermo sensor fasteners for looseness. Check rubber hose between thermo sensor and intake manifold for loose connections. Check other hoses for loose connections.

AIR CLEANER ELEMENT REPLACEMENT

1. Remove wing nut and air cleaner cover.

2. Remove element.

3. Install new element in air cleaner with either end up.

4. Install air cleaner cover and wing nut.

Positive Crankcase Ventilation (PCV)

REGULATING ORIFICE AND HOSE INSPECTION

Clean hoses internally and calibrating orifice in detergent oil and blow away foreign matter with compressed air. Check hoses for cracks, fatigue and swelling, replace if necessary.

Clean internal part of hoses and regulating orifice in detergent oil and blow away foreign matter with compressed air. Check hoses for cracks, fatigue and swelling; replace if defective.

Closed Loop Emission Control System

NOTE: *When troubleshooting the system, always check the electrical and vacuum con-*

nectors which may be the source of a problem before testing or replacing a component.

TEMPERATURE SWITCH REPLACEMENT

1. Disconnect electrical connection at temperature switch.
2. Remove temperature switch.

3. Install switch and tighten to 72 in. lbs.
4. Connect electrical connector.

VACUUM CONTROLLER REPLACEMENT

1. Disconnect electrical connector.
2. Disconnect vacuum hoses from vacuum regulator and solenoid.

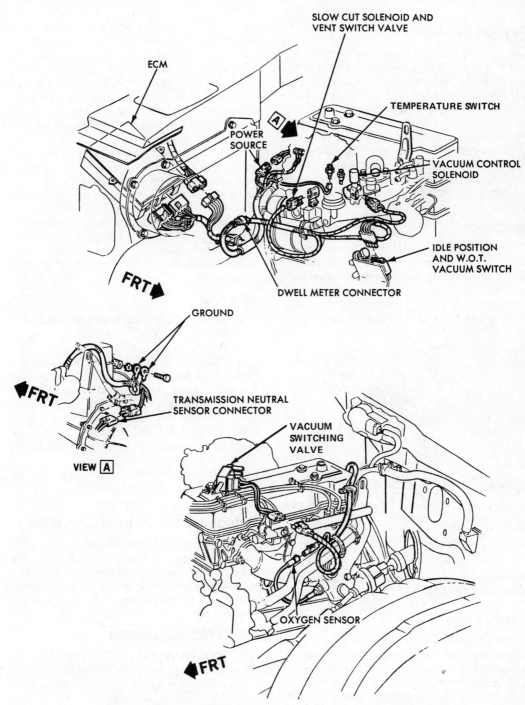

4-1950 closed loop emission system engine compartment components

3. Remove vacuum controller.

4. Reverse procedure for installation.

IDLE AND WOT VACUUM SWITCH REPLACEMENT

1. Disconnect electrical connector.
2. Disconnect vacuum hoses from sensors.
3. Remove idle and WOT vacuum switch.
4. Reverse procedure for installation.

Oxygen Sensor

The oxygen sensor uses a permanently attached pig-tail and connector. This pig-tail should not be removed from the oxygen sensor. Damage or removal of pig-tail or connector could affect proper operation of the oxygen sensor.

Care must be taken when handling an oxygen sensor in order to preserve the efficiency. The in-line electrical connector and louvered end must be kept free of grease or other contaminants. Do not use cleaning solvents of any type.

REMOVAL

The oxygen sensor may be difficult to remove when engine temperature is below 48°C (120°F). Excessive force may damage threads in exhaust manifold or exhaust pipe. Disconnect electrical connector and any attaching hardware. Remove oxygen sensor with a suitable tool.

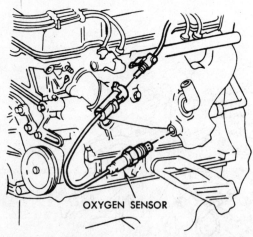

OXYGEN SENSOR

4-1950 oxygen sensor location in exhaust manifold—others similar

INSTALLATION

A new oxygen sensor is pre-coated with anti-seize compound, but if same oxygen sensor is being installed, coat threads of oxygen sensor with anti-seize compound P/N 5613695 (or equivalent). Install sensor and torque to 30 ft.

lbs. Connect electrical connector and attaching hardware if used.

EMISSION CONTROLS—2000cc ENGINE

Positive Crankcase Ventilation (PCV)

An engine which is operated without any crankcase ventilation can be damaged seriously. Therefore, it is important to replace the PCV valve at recommended intervals.

NOTE: *If an engine is idling rough, this may be caused by a clogged ventilator valve or plugged hose; therefore, never adjust the carburetor idle without first checking the PCV valve and hose.*

With this system, any blow-by in excess of the system capacity (from a badly-worn engine, sustained heavy load, etc.) is exhausted into the air cleaner and is drawn into the engine. Proper operation of the PCV System is dependent upon a sealed engine. If oil sludging or dilution is noted, and the PCV System is functioning properly, check engine for possible cause and correct to insure that the system will function as intended.

REMOVAL

1. Remove PCV valve from intake manifold or rocker arm cover.
2. Run the engine at idle.
3. Place your thumb over the end of the valve to check for vacuum. If there is no vacuum at the valve, check for plugged hoses or valve. Replace plugged or deteriorated hoses.
4. Shut off the engine and remove PCV valve. Shake valve and listen for the rattle of check needle inside the valve. If valve does not rattle, replace it.
5. After installing a new PCV valve, readjust base engine idle if necessary.

Exhaust Gas Recirculation (EGR)

This vehicle uses a negative back pressure EGR valve. The valve opening is determined by the amount of vacuum received from a ported source on the carburetor and the amount of backpressure in the exhaust system. The EGR System requires the use of unleaded fuel.

CHECKING EGR SYSTEM

1. Place finger under EGR valve and push on diaphragm plate. Diaphragm should move freely from open to closed position. If it does not more freely, replace valve.

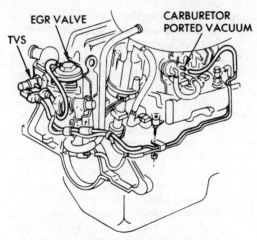

4-2000 EGR system

CAUTION: *If valve is hot, it may be necessary to wear gloves to avoid burning fingers.*

2. Hook up vacuum gauge between EGR signal tube and vacuum hose.

3. With vehicle in PARK or NEUTRAL and engine running, open throttle to obtain at least 17 kPa Hg. (5 in. of vacuum) at EGR. Engine must be at coolant operating temperature (approx. 195°F or 90°C).

4. Remove vacuum hose from EGR signal tube and check for diaphragm plate to move downward (valve closed). This should be accompanied by an increase in engine speed.

5. Replace vacuum hose and check for diaphragm plate to move upward (valve open). Engine speed should decrease.

NOTE: *A vibration of the diaphragm plate may be noticed on back pressure EGR valves. This does not indicate a bad valve or require correction.*

Diaphragm Doesn't Move:

1. Check engine vacuum, it should be at least 17 kPa (5 in. Hg.) at EGR valve with engine running and throttle open.

2. Make sure engine is at operating temperature.

3. Check for vacuum at EGR hose. If no vacuum is present, find the cause (hose routing not correct, plugged or leaking hose or carburetor port).

4. Check transducer control valve operation (See Checking EGR Valve).

Diaphragm Moves with No Change in Engine Speed:

Check EGR manifold passages for blockage (clean if blocked). If cause is not found, check EGR valve.

CHECKING EGR VALVE

1. Check hose routing (Refer to Vehicle Emission Control Information Label).

2. Check EGR valve signal tube orifice for obstructions.

3. Hook up vacuum gage between EGR valve and carburetor and check vacuum (engine must be at operating temperature approx. 195°F or 90°C.) With engine running at approximately 3000 RPM there should be at least 17 kPa Hg. (5 in. of vacuum).

4. Check EGR solenoid for correct operation.

5. Valve check (valve can be left on or removed from engine).

   a. Depress the valve diaphragm.

   b. With diaphragm still depressed hold a finger over source tube and release diaphragm.

   c. Check diaphragm and seat for movement. Valve is good if it takes over 20 seconds for the diaphragm to move to the seated position (valve closed).

   d. Replace EGR valve if it takes less than 20 seconds to move to the seated position.

EGR VALVE REPLACEMENT

1. Disconnect EGR valve vacuum hose at valve.

2. Remove bolts or nuts holding EGR valve on manifold.

3. Remove EGR valve from manifold.

4. Clean EGR mounting surfaces.

5. Reassemble replacement EGR valve on intake manifold using new gasket(s). Install spacer (if used). Torque attachments to correct torque.

6. Install bolts and tighten to 25 ft. lbs.

7. Connect vacuum hose to valve.

EGR MANIFOLD PASSAGE

If inspection of EGR passages in the inlet manifold indicates excessive build-up of deposits, the passages should be cleaned. Care should be taken to ensure that all loose particles are completely removed to prevent them from clogging the EGR valve or from being ingested into the engine.

EGR VALVE CLEANING

NOTE: *Do not wash valve assembly in solvents or degreaser—permanent damage to valve diaphragm may result. Also, sand blasting of the valve is recommended since this can affect the operation of the valve.*

1. Remove EGR valve and 2 attaching bolts, discarding the gasket.

2. With a wire wheel, buff the exhaust de-

posits from the mounting surface and around the valve.

3. Depress the valve diaphragm and look at the valve seating area through the valve outlet for cleanliness. If valve and/or seat are not completely clean, repeat Step 2.

4. Look for exhaust deposits in the valve outlet. Remove deposit build-up with a screwdriver.

5. Clean mounting surfaces of intake manifold and valve assembly, then using a new gasket install the valve assembly to the intake manifold. Torque the bolts to 25 ft. lbs.

6. Connect vacuum hoses.

Thermostatic Air Cleaner (Thermac)

CHECKING THERMAC AIR CLEANER

1. Inspect system to be sure all hoses and ducts are connected. Check for kinked, plugged or deteriorated hoses.

2. If engine is warm above 27°C (80°F), remove air cleaner. Allow it to cool to room temperature, below 27°C (80°F). Placing a cool, wet rag on the temperature sensor will aid in cooling.

3. Install cooled air cleaner with cold air intake disconnected from snorkel.

4. Start engine. Watch damper door in air cleaner snorkel. When engine is first started, damper door should be closed. As air cleaner warms up, damper door should open slowly.

Some air cleaner temperature sensors contain a check valve that delays the opening of the damper door. Length of delay depends on temperature, varying from several minutes at −18°C (0°F) to a few seconds at 21°C (70°F).

5. Apply at least 23 kPa (7 in. Hg.) of vacuum to the vacuum diaphragm motor through hose disconnected at the temperature sensor. Damper door should completely block off snorkel passage when vacuum is applied. If not, check to see if linkage is hooked up correctly.

6. With vacuum still applied, trap vacuum in vacuum diaphragm motor by bending hose. Damper door should remain closed. If not, replace vacuum diaphragm motor assembly. (Failure of the vacuum diaphragm motor assembly is more likely to be caused from binding linkage or a corroded snorkel than from a failed diaphragm. This should be checked first, before replacing the diaphragm.)

7. Reinstall air cleaner. As the engine warms up, the damper door should start to allow outside air and heated air to enter the carburetor.

8. If the air cleaner fails to operate as described above, or if correct operation of the air cleaner is still in doubt, perform thermometer check of sensor.

THERMOMETER CHECK OF SENSOR

1. Start test with air cleaner temperature below 38°C (100°F). If engine has been run recently, remove air cleaner cover and place Thermometer as close as possible to the sensor. Let air cleaner cool until thermometer reads below 35°C (95°F) about 5 to 10 minutes. Reinstall air cleaner on engine and continue to Step 2 below.

2. Start and idle engine. Damper door should move to close the snorkel passage immediately

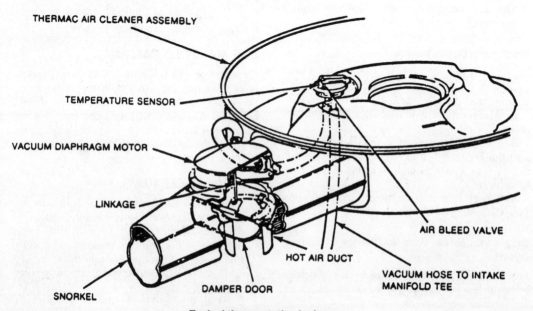

Typical thermostatic air cleaner

if engine is cool enough. When damper door starts to open the snorkel passage (in a few minutes), remove air cleaner cover and read. It must read 7–38°C (20–100°F) thermometer.

3. If the damper door does not start to open up the snorkel passage at temperature indicated, temperature sensor is malfunctioning and must be replaced.

AIR CLEANER ELEMENT REPLACEMENT

1. Remove air cleaner cover.
2. Remove element.
3. Install new element in air cleaner with either end up.
4. Install air cleaner cover. Do not overtorque nut.

Vacuum Diaphragm Motor

REMOVAL

1. Remove air cleaner.
2. Disconnect vacuum hose from motor.
3. Drill out the two spot welds initially with a 1.6mm (1/16 in.) hole, then enlarge as required to remove the retaining strap. Do not damage the snorkel tube.
4. Remove motor retaining strap.
5. Lift up motor, cocking it to one side to unhook the motor linkage at the control damper assembly.

INSTALLATION

1. Drill a 2.8 mm (7/64 in.) hole in snorkel tube at center of vacuum motor retaining strap.
2. Insert vacuum motor linkage into control damper assembly.
3. Use the motor retaining strap and sheet metal screw provided in the motor service package to secure the retaining strap and motor to the snorkel tube.
4. Make sure the screw does not interfere with the operation of the damper assembly. Shorten screw if required.
5. Connect vacuum hose to motor and install air cleaner.

Sensor

REMOVAL

1. Remove air cleaner.
2. Detach hoses at sensor.
3. Pry up tabs on sensor retaining clip; remove clip and sensor from air cleaner. Note position of sensor for installation.

INSTALLATION

1. Install sensor and gasket assembly in original position.

2. Press retainer clip on hose connectors.
3. Connect vacuum hoses and install air cleaner on engine.

Thermal Vacuum Switch (TVS)

The TVS is located on the engine coolant outlet housing.

REPLACEMENT

1. Drain coolant below level of engine coolant outlet housing.
2. Disconnect hoses at TVS ports.
3. Remove TVS.
4. Apply a soft setting sealant uniformly on replacement TVS male threads. No sealant should be applied to sensor end of TVS.
5. Install TVS, tighten to 120 inch lbs. as required to align TVS to accommodate hoses.
6. Connect hoses to TVS ports.
7. Add coolant as required.

Early Fuel Evaporation System (EFE)

EFE HEATER REPLACEMENT

1. Remove air cleaner.
2. Disconnect all electrical, vacuum, and fuel connections from carburetor.
3. Disconnect EFE Heater electrical connector.
4. Remove carburetor.
5. Remove and replace EFE heater isolator assembly.

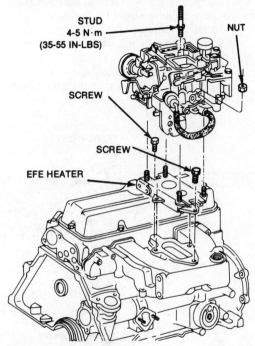

4-2000 EFE heater grid

6. Reinstall carburetor.
7. Reconnect EFE Heater electrical connection.
8. Reconnect electrical, vacuum and fuel connections to carburetor.
9. Replace air cleaner.
10. Start engine and check for leaks.

EFE HEATER RELAY REPLACEMENT

1. Disconnect battery ground.
2. Remove bracket at fender skirt.
3. Remove relay electrical connections.
4. Remove bolts holding relay and remove relay.
5. Reverse procedure to install.

Air Management System

AIR PUMP REMOVAL

1. Disconnect battery cable.
2. Mark front of pump pulley so it can be installed in the same direction.
3. Remove air pump pulley as outlined under air pump pulley replacement.
4. Disconnect hoses, vacuum and electrical connections from air management valve.
5. Remove air pump mounting bolts and remove pump assembly.
6. If pump is being replaced, transfer air management valve to new pump.

INSTALLATION

1. Install air pump assembly and tighten mounting bolts.
2. Reconnect hoses, vacuum and electrical connections to air management valve.
3. Install air pump pulley.
4. Install pump belt and adjust to correct tension.
5. Reconnect battery cable.
6. Check air management system for proper operation.

AIR PUMP DRIVE BELT ADJUSTMENT AND REPLACEMENT

1. Inspect drive belt for wear, cracks or deterioration.
2. Loosen pump adjustment and pivot bolts.
3. Replace belt if required.
4. Move air pump until drive belt is at proper tension, then retighten bolts.
5. Check belt tension using a belt tension gage.

AIR PUMP PULLEY REPLACEMENT

1. Hold pump pulley from turning by compressing drive belt, then loosen pump pulley bolts.
2. Loosen pump through bolt and adjusting bolt.
3. Remove drive belt, pump pulley and pulley spacer.
4. Install pump pulley and spacer with retaining bolts hand tight.
5. Install drive belt and adjust to proper tension.
6. Hold pump pulley from turning by compressing drive belt, then torque pump pulley bolts to 24 ft. lbs.
7. Recheck belt tension and adjust if required.

AIR PUMP FILTER FAN REPLACEMENT

Before starting this operation note the following:
* Do not allow any filter fragments to enter the air pump intake hole.
* Do not remove filter fan by inserting a screwdriver between pump and filter fan. Air damage to sealing lip pump will result.
* Do not remove metal drive hub from filter fan.
* It is seldom possible to remove the filter fan without destroying it.

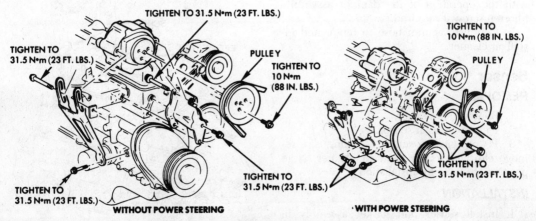

TIGHTEN TO 31.5 N•m (23 FT. LBS.)

TIGHTEN TO 31.5 N•m (23 FT. LBS.)

PULLEY
TIGHTEN TO 10 N•m (88 IN. LBS.)

TIGHTEN TO 31.5 N•m (23 FT. LBS.)

WITHOUT POWER STEERING

TIGHTEN TO 10 N•m (88 IN. LBS.)

PULLEY

TIGHTEN TO 31.5 N•m (23 FT. LBS.)

TIGHTEN TO 31.5 N•m (23 FT. LBS.)

WITH POWER STEERING

4-2000 air pump

1. Remove drive belt, pump pully and spacer.

2. Insert needle nose pliers and pull filter fan from hub.

3. Position new filter fan on pump hub.

4. Position spacer and pump pulley against centrifugal filter fan.

5. Install pump pulley bolts and tighten equally to 80 inch lbs. This will compress the centrifugal filter fan into the pump hole. Do not drive filter fan on with a hammer.

A slight amount of interference with the housing bore is normal. After a new filter fan has been installed, it may squeal upon initial operation or until O.D. sealing lip has worn in. This may require a short period of pump operation at various engine speeds.

6. Install pump drive belt and adjust.

AIR HOSES AND INJECTION PIPES INSPECTION AND REPLACEMENT

1. Inspect all hoses for deterioration or holes.

2. Inspect all air injection pipes for cracks or holes.

3. Check all hose and pipe connections.

4. Check pipe and hose routing. Interference may cause wear.

5. If a leak is suspected on the pressure side of the system or any hose has been disconnected on the pressure side, the connection should be checked for leaks with a soapy water solution.

6. If hose and/or manifold and pipe assembly replacement is required, note routing, then remove hose and/or those as required.

7. Install new hose and/or manifold and pipe assembly, routing them as when removed.

8. Tighten hose and pipe connections.

CHECK VALVE INSPECTION

1. The check valve should be inspected whenever the hose is disconnected from the

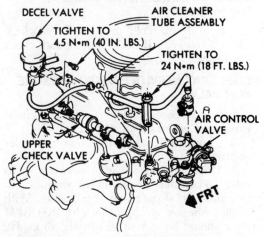

4-2000 upper check valve and hoses

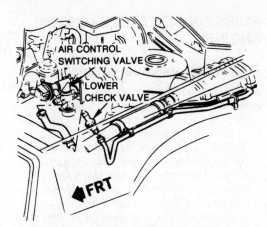

4-2000 lower check valve and hoses

check valve or whenever check valve failure is suspected (A pump that had become inoperative and had shown indications of having exhaust gases in the pump would indicate check valve failure).

2. Blow through the check valve (toward the cylinder head) then attempt to suck back through check valve. Flow should only be in one direction (toward the exhaust manifold). Replace valve which does not function this way.

REPLACEMENT

1. Release clamp and disconnect air hoses from check valve.

2. Unscrew check valve from air injection pipe.

3. Screw check valve onto air injection pipe.

4. Position air hose on check valve and secure with clamp.

DECELERATION VALVE REMOVAL

1. Remove vacuum and air hoses from valve.

2. Remove deceleration valve from bracket.

3. Reverse procedure for installation.

AIR MANAGEMENT VALVE REMOVAL

1. Disconnect battery ground cable.

2. Disconnect vacuum hoses at valve.

3. Disconnect air outlet hoses from valve.

4. Disconnect electrical connections from valve.

5. Remove bolts holding control valve to bracket.

6. Remove control valve bracket.

INSTALLATION

1. Install control valve to bracket.

2. Connect electrical connectors to valve.

3. Install bolts and locks to elbow.

4. Tighten bolts to elbow and control valve.

5. Connect vacuum and air outlet hoses to valve.

6. Reconnect battery ground cable.

EMISSION CONTROLS—2800cc ENGINE

Positive Crankcase Ventilation

An engine which is operated without any crankcase ventilation can be damaged seriously. Therefore, it is important to replace the PCV valve at recommended intervals.

NOTE: *If an engine is idling too slow or rough, this may be caused by a clogged ventilator valve or plugged hose; therefore, never adjust the carburetor idle without first checking the PCV valve and hose.*

With this system, any blow-by in excess of the system capacity (from a badly-worn engine, sustained heavy load, etc.) is exhausted into the air cleaner and is drawn into the engine. Proper operation of the PCV System is dependent upon a sealed engine. If oil sludging or dilution is noted, and the PCV System is functioning properly, check engine for possible cause and correct to insure that system will function as intended.

REPLACEMENT

1. Remove PCV valve from rocker arm cover.
2. Run the engine at idle.
3. Place your thumb over end of valve to check for vacuum. If there is no vacuum at valve, check for plugged hoses or valve. Replace plugged or deteriorated hoses.
4. Shut off the engine and remove PCV valve. Shake valve and listen for the rattle of check needle inside the valve. If valve does not rattle, replace it.
5. After installing a new PCV valve, readjust engine idle if necessary.

6-2800 PCV system

Exhaust Gas Recirculation (EGR)

Backpressure EGR valves are used on all engines. The valve opening is determined by the amount of vacuum received from a ported source on the carburetor and the amount of backpres-

sure in the exhaust system. The EGR System requires the use of unleaded fuel.

CHECKING EGR SYSTEM

CAUTION: *If valve is hot, it may be necessary to wear gloves to avoid burning fingers.*

1. Place finger under EGR valve and push on diaphragm plate. Diaphragm should move freely from open to closed position. If it does not move freely, replace valve.
2. Hook up vacuum gage between EGR signal tube and vacuum hose.
3. With vehicle in PARK or NEUTRAL and engine running, open throttle to obtain at least 17 kPa Hg. (5 in. Hg. of vacuum) at EGR. Engine must be fully warmed up.
4. Remove vacuum hose from EGR signal tube and check for diaphragm plate to move downward (valve closed). This should be accompanied by an increase in engine speed.
5. Replace vacuum hose and check for diaphragm plate to move upward (valve open). Engine speed should decrease.

NOTE: *A vibration of the diaphragm plate may be noticed on back pressure EGR valves. This does not indicate a bad valve or require correction.*

Diaphragm Doesn't Move:

1. Check engine vacuum, it should be at least 17 kPa (5 in. Hg.) at EGR valve with engine running and throttle open.
2. Make sure engine is at operating temperature.
3. Check for vacuum at EGR hose. If no vacuum is present, find the cause (hose routing not correct, plugged or leaking hose or carburetor port.)
4. Check transducer control valve operation (See Checking Negative Backpressure EGR Valve.)

Diaphragm Moves With No Change in Engine Speed:

Check EGR manifold passages for blockage (clean if blocked). If cause is not found, check EGR valve.

CHECKING NEGATIVE BACKPRESSURE EGR VALVE

1. Check hose routing (Refer to Vehicle Emission Control Information Label).
2. Check EGR valve signal tube orifice for obstructions.
3. Hook up vacuum gage between EGR valve and carburetor and check vacuum (engine must be at operating temperature. With engine running at approximately 3000 RPM there should be at least 17 kPa Hg. (5 in. Hg of vacuum).

4. Check EGR bleed solenoid for correct operation.

5. Valve check (valve can be left on or removed from engine).

　a. Depress the valve diaphragm.

　b. With diaphragm still depressed hold a finger over source tube and release diaphragm.

　c. Check diaphragm and seat for movement. Valve is good if it takes over 20 seconds for the diaphragm to move to the seated position (valve closed).

　d. Replace EGR valve if it takes less than 20 seconds to move to the seated position.

EGR VALVE REPLACEMENT

1. Disconnect EGR valve vacuum hose at valve.

2. Remove bolts or nuts holding EGR valve on manifold.

3. Remove EGR valve from manifold.

4. Clean EGR mounting surfaces.

5. Reassemble replacement EGR valve on intake manifold using new gasket(s). Install spacer (if used). Torque attachments to correct torque.

6. Connect vacuum hose to valve.

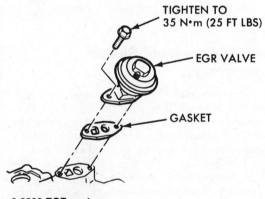

TIGHTEN TO
35 N•m (25 FT LBS)

EGR VALVE

GASKET

6-2800 EGR system

EGR MANIFOLD PASSAGE

If inspection of EGR passages in the inlet manifold indicates excessive build-up of deposits, the passages should be cleaned. Care should be taken to ensure that all loose particles are completely removed to prevent them from clogging the EGR valve or from being ingested into the engine.

EGR VALVE CLEANING

NOTE: *Do not wash valve assembly in solvents or degreaser—permanent damage to valve diaphragm may result. Also, sand blasting of the valve is recommended since this can affect the operation of the valve.*

1. Remove EGR valve and 2 attaching bolts, discarding the gasket.

2. With a wire wheel, buff the exhaust deposits from the mounting surface and around the valve.

3. Depress the valve diaphragm and look at the valve seating area through the valve outlet for cleanliness. If valve and/or seat are not completely clean, repeat Step 2.

4. Look for exhaust deposits in the valve outlet. Remove deposit build-up with a screwdriver.

5. Clean mounting surfaces of intake manifold and valve assembly, then using a new gasket install the valve assembly to the intake manifold. Torque the bolts to 25 ft. lbs.

6. Connect vacuum hoses.

Early Fuel Evapoartion (EFE) System

CHECKING EFE

Federal

1. Disconnect electrical connector from EFE heater switch.

2. Connect a 12 volt test lamp across the connector terminals.

3. If lamp glows when ignition switch is on and engine off, EFE heater is good.

4. If lamp does not glow, reconnect heater switch connector. With engine temperature below 60°C (140°F), measure voltage across the EFE heater by inserting test probes in rear of connector body (black wire is Negative). The voltage should be approximately 11 to 13 volts.

5. If voltage is not 11 to 13 volts across the heater terminals, check black wire voltage to ground. If voltage is not zero, the black (ground) wire is an open circuit. Repair the open circuit.

6. If voltage is zero, check voltages to vehicle ground from each heater switch terminal—voltage should be 11 to 13 volts at each switch terminal.

7. If 11 to 13 volts is measured at one switch terminal but low or zero at the other, inspect the connector for deformed terminals and repair as required.

8. If connector is making proper contact, replace heater switch.

9. If voltage is not 11 to 13 volts at both switch terminals, inspect wiring circuit between heater switch and ignition switch and repair as required.

10. Start engine and allow it to warm up to above 76.7°C (170°F). Check voltage across the EFE heater terminals. The voltage should be zero. If voltage is not zero, replace the temperature switch.

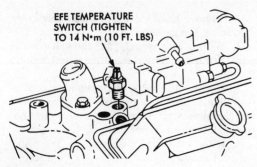

6-2800 EFE temperature switch

EFE Switch Replacement

1. Drain coolant below level of engine coolant outlet housing.
2. Disconnect electrical connector.
3. Remove temperature switch.
4. Apply a soft setting sealant uniformly on replacement TVS threads. No sealant should be applied to sensor and temperature switch.
5. Install a switch, tighten to 120 inch lbs. and then hand torque clockwise as required to align electrical connector.
6. Connect electrical connector.
7. Add coolant as required.

CHECKING EFE

California Models

EFE HEATER RELAY REPLACEMENT

1. Disconnect battery ground.
2. Remove relay electrical connections.
3. Remove bolts holding relay and remove relay.
4. Reverse procedure for installation.

EFE HEATER REPLACEMENT

1. Remove air cleaner.
2. Disconnect all electrical, vacuum, and fuel connections from carburetor.

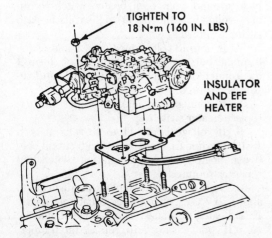

6-2800 EFE heater

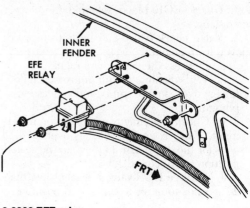

6-2800 EFE relay

3. Disconnect EFE Heater electrical connector.
4. Remove carburetor.
5. Replace EFE heater insulator assembly.
6. Reinstall carburetor.
7. Reconnect EFE Heater electrical connection.
8. Reconnect electrical, vacuum and fuel connections to carburetor.
9. Replace air cleaner.
10. Start engine and check for leaks.

Air Management System
INSPECTION

Accelerate engine to approximately 1500 rpm and observe air flow from hoses(s). If air flow increases as engine is accelerated, pump is operating satisfactorily. If air flow does not increase or is not present, proceed as follows:

1. Check for proper drive belt tension. The Air Management System is not completely noiseless. Under normal conditions, noise rises in pitch as engine speed increases. To determine if excessive noise is the fault of the air injection reactor system, operate the engine with the pump drive belt removed. If excessive noise does not exist with the belt removed, proceed as follows:
2. Check for a seized Air Injection Pump. Do not oil air pump.
3. Check hoses, pipes and all connections for leaks and proper routing.
4. Check air control valve.
5. Check air injection pump for proper mounting and bolt torque.
6. Repair irregularities in these components as necessary.
7. If no irregularities exist and the air injection pump noise is still excessive, remove and replace pump.

AIR INJECTION PUMP REMOVAL

1. Mark front of pump pulley so it can be installed in the same direction.
2. Remove air pump pulley as outlined under air pump pulley replacement.
3. Disconnect hose from rear of air pump.
4. Remove air pump mounting bolts and remove pump assembly.

INSTALLATION

1. Install air pump assembly and tighten mounting bolts.
2. Reconnect hose at rear of air pump.
3. Install air pump pulley.
4. Install pump belt and adjust to correct tension.
5. Check air management system for proper operation.

AIR PUMP DRIVE BELT ADJUSTMENT AND REPLACEMENT

1. Inspect drive belt for wear, cracks or deterioration.
2. Loosen pump adjustment and pivot bolts.
3. Replace belt if required.
4. Move air pump until drive belt is at proper tension.
5. Check belt tension using a belt tension gage.

AIR PUMP PULLEY REPLACEMENT

1. Hold pump pulley from turning by compressing drive belt, then loosen pump pulley bolts.
2. Loosen pump through bolt and adjusting bolt.
3. Remove drive belt and pump pulley.
4. Install pump pulley with retaining bolts hand tight.
5. Install drive belt and adjust to proper tension.
6. Hold pump pulley from turning by compressing drive belt, then torque pump pulley bolts to 90 inch lbs.
7. Recheck belt tension and adjust if required.

AIR PUMP FILTER FAN REPLACEMENT

Before starting this operation note the following

• Do not allow any filter fragments to enter the air pump intake hole.
• Do not remove filter fan by inserting a screwdriver between pump and filter fan. Air damage to sealing lip pump will result.
• Do not remove metal drive hub from filter fan.
• It is seldom possible to remove the filter fan without destroying it.

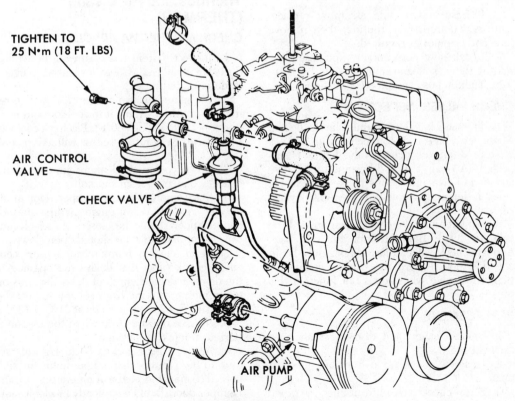

TIGHTEN TO 25 N•m (18 FT. LBS)

AIR CONTROL VALVE

CHECK VALVE

AIR PUMP

6-2800 AIR system

1. Remove drive belt and pump pulley.

2. Insert needle nose pliers and pull filter fan from hub.

3. Position new filter fan on pump hub.

4. Position pump pulley against centrifugal filter fan.

5. Install pump pulley bolts and tighten equally to 90 inch lbs. This will compress the centrifugal filter fan onto the pump hole. Do not drive filter fan on with a hammer. A slight amount of interference with the housing bore is normal. After a new filter fan has been installed, it may squeal upon initial operation or until O.D. sealing lip has worn in. This may require a short period of pump operation at various engine speeds.

6. Install pump drive belt and adjust.

AIR HOSES AND INJECTION PIPES INSPECTION AND REPLACEMENT

1. Inspect all hoses for deterioration or holes.

2. Inspect all air injection pipes for cracks or holes.

3. Check all hose and pipe connections.

4. Check pipe and hose routing. Interference may cause wear.

5. If a leak is suspected on the pressure side of the system or any hose has been disconnected on the pressure side, the connection should be checked for leaks with a soapy water solution.

6. If hose and/or pipe assembly replacement is required, note routing, then remove hose and/or pipes as required.

7. Install new hose and/or pipe assembly, routing them as when removed.

8. Tighten hose and pipe connections.

CHECK VALVES INSPECTION

1. The check valves should be inspected whenever a hose is disconnected from a check valve or whenever a check valve failure is suspected. (A pump that had become inoperative and had shown indications of having exhaust gases in the pump would indicate a check valve failure.)

2. Blow through the check valve (toward the cylinder head) then attempt to suck back through check valve. Flow should only be in one direction (toward the exhaust manifold). Replace a valve which does not function this way.

REPLACEMENT

1. Release clamp and disconnect air hose from check valve.

2. Unscrew check valve from air injection pipe.

3. Screw check valve onto air injection pipe.

4. Position air hose on check valve and secure with clamp.

AIR CONTROL VALVE REMOVAL

1. Disconnect battery ground cable (California).

2. Remove carburetor air cleaner.

3. Disconnect vacuum hose or hoses at valve.

4. Disconnect air inlet and outlet hoses from valve.

5. Disconnect electrical connections from valve (California).

6. Remove bolts holding air control valve and remove valve.

INSTALLATION

1. Install control valve.

2. Connect electrical connector to valve (California).

3. Connect vacuum and air inlet and outlet hoses to valve.

4. Reconnect battery ground cable (California).

5. Check system operation.

DECELERATION VALVE

1. Remove vacuum and air hose from valve.

2. Remove deceleration valve from bracket.

3. Reverse procedure for installation.

Thermostatic Air Cleaner (THERMAC)

CHECKING THERMA AIR CLEANER

1. Inspect system to be sure all hoses and ducts are connected. Check for kinked, plugged or deteriorated hoses.

2. If engine is warm above 27°C (80°F), remove air cleaner. Allow it to cool to room temperature, below 27°C (80°F). Placing a cool wet rag on the temperature sensor will aid in cooling.

3. Install cooled air cleaner with cold air intake disconnected from snorkel.

4. Start engine. Watch damper door in air cleaner snorkel. When engine is first started, damper door should be closed. As air cleaner warms up, damper door should open slowly.

Some air cleaner temperature sensors contain a check valve that delays the opening of the damper door. Length of delay depends on temperature, varying from several minutes at −18°C (0°F) to a few seconds at 21°C (70°F).

5. If valve doesn't close when the engine is started, remove air cleaner.

6. Apply at least 23 kPa (7 in. Hg.) of vacuum to the vacuum diaphragm motor through hose disconnected at the temperature sensor. Damper door should completely block off snor-

kel passage when vacuum is applied. If not, check to see if linkage is hooked up correctly.

7. With vacuum still applied, trap vacuum in vacuum diaphragm motor by bending hose. Damper door should remain closed. If not, replace vacuum diaphragm motor assembly. (Failure of the vacuum diaphragm motor assembly is more likely to be caused from binding linkage or a corroded snorkel than from a failed diaphragm. This should be checked first, before replacing the diaphragm.)

8. Reinstall air cleaner. As the engine warms up, the damper door should start to allow outside air and heated air to enter the carburetor.

9. If the air cleaner fails to operate as described above, or if correct operation of the air cleaner is still in doubt, perform thermometer check of sensor.

THERMOMETER CHECK OF SENSOR

1. Start test with air cleaner temperature below 80°F (27°C). If engine has been run recently, remove air cleaner cover and place thermometer as close as possible to the sensor. Let air cleaner cool until thermometer reads below 79°F (26°C) about 5 to 10 minutes. Reinstall air cleaner on engine and continue to Step 2 below.

2. Start and idle engine. Damper door should move to close the snorkel passage immediately if engine is cool enough. When damper door starts to open the snorkel passage (in a few minutes), remove air cleaner cover and read. It must read 100°F ± 20°F (38°C ± 7°C) thermometer.

3. If the damper door does not start to open up the snorkel passage at temperature indicated, temperature sensor is malfunctioning and must be replaced.

AIR CLEANER ELEMENT REPLACEMENT

1. Remove air cleaner cover.
2. Remove element.
3. Install new element in air cleaner with either end up.
4. Install air cleaner cover. Do not overtorque nut.

VACUUM DIAPHRAGM MOTOR REMOVAL

1. Remove air cleaner.
2. Disconnect vacuum hose from motor.
3. Drill out the two spot welds initially with a 1.6mm (1/16 in.) hole, then enlarge as required to remove the retaining strap. Do not damage the snorkel tube.
4. Remove motor retaining strap.
5. Lift up motor, cocking it to one side to

unhook the motor linkage at the control damper assembly.

Oxygen Sensor

The oxygen sensor uses a permanently attached pig-tail and connector. This pig-tail should not be removed from the oxygen sensor. Damage or removal of pig-tail or connector could affect proper operation of the oxygen sensor.

Care must be taken when handling an oxygen sensor in order to preserve the efficiency. The in-line electrical connector and louvered end must be kept free of grease or other contaminants. Do not use cleaning solvents of any type.

REMOVAL

The oxygen sensor may be difficult to remove when engine temperature is below 48°C (120°F). Excessive force may damage threads in exhaust manifold or exhaust pipe. Disconnect electrical connector and any attaching hardware. Remove oxygen sensor using a suitable tool.

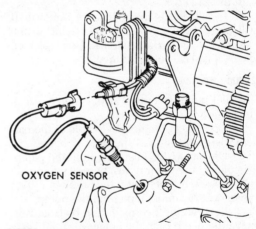

OXYGEN SENSOR

6-2800 oxygen sensor

INSTALLATION

A new oxygen sensor is pre-coated with anti-seize compound, but if same oxygen sensor is being installed, coat threads of oxygen sensor with anti-seize compound. Install sensor and torque to 30 ft. lbs. Connect electrical connector and attaching hardware if used.

GASOLINE ENGINE FUEL SYSTEM

Fuel Pump

All engines use a mechanical fuel pump, driven off the camshaft and located on the engine block.

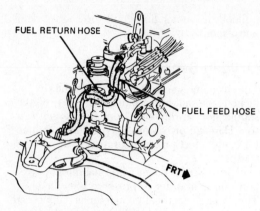

FUEL RETURN HOSE

FUEL FEED HOSE

FRT

4-1950 fuel pump and hoses

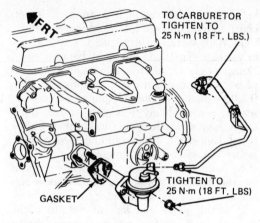

FRT

TO CARBURETOR
TIGHTEN TO
25 N·m (18 FT. LBS.)

TIGHTEN TO
25 N·m (18 FT. LBS)

GASKET

4-2000 fuel pump

REMOVAL AND INSTALLATION

1950cc Engine

1. Disconnect the battery ground.
2. Remove the distributor.
3. Disconnect the fuel hoses at the pump.
4. Remove the engine lifting hook.
5. Unbolt and remove the fuel pump. Discard the gasket.
6. Installation is the reverse of removal. It will be easier if you rotate the engine so the cam lobe is on a down stroke. Use sealer on the new gasket. Set the timing.

2000cc Engine

The fuel pump is located at the center rear of the engine.

1. Disconnect the negative cable at the battery. Raise and support the car.
2. Disconnect the inlet hose from the pump. Disconnect the vapor return hose, if equipped.
3. Loosen the fuel line at the carburetor, then disconnect the outlet pipe from the pump.
4. Remove the two mounting bolts and remove the pump from the engine.
5. To install, place a new gasket on the pump and install the pump on the engine. Tighten the two mounting bolts alternately and evenly.
6. Install the pump outlet pipe. This is easier if the pipe is disconnected from the carburetor. Tighten the fitting while backing up the pump nut with another wrench. Install the pipe at the carburetor.
7. Install the inlet and vapor hoses. Lower the car, connect the negative battery cable, start the engine, and check for leaks.

2800cc Engine

1. Disconnect the battery ground.
2. Disconnect the fuel hoses at the pump.
3. Unbolt and remove the pump. Discard the gasket.
4. Installation is the reverse of removal. Use

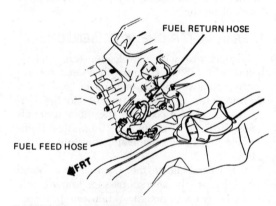

FUEL RETURN HOSE

FUEL FEED HOSE

FRT

6-2800 fuel pump and hoses

sealer on the new gasket. It will be easier if you rotate the engine so that the cam lobe is on a down stroke.

TESTING THE MECHANICAL FUEL PUMP

To determine if the pump is in good condition, tests for both volume and pressure should be performed. The tests are made with the pump installed, and the engine at normal operating temperature and idle speed. Never replace a fuel pump without first performing these simple tests.

Be sure that the fuel filter has been changed at the specified interval. If in doubt, install a new filter first.

Pressure Test

1. Disconnect the fuel line at the carburetor and connect a fuel pump pressure gauge.
2. Start the engine and check the pressure with the engine at idle. If the pump has a vapor return hose, squeeze it off so that an accurate reading can be obtained. Pressure should not be below 4.5 psi.
3. If the pressure is incorrect, replace the pump. If it is ok, go on to the volume test.

Volume Test

4. Disconnect the pressure gauge. Run the fuel line into a graduated container.

5. Run the engine at idle until one pint of gasoline has been pumped. One pint should be delivered in 30 seconds or less. There is normally enough fuel in the carburetor float bowl to perform this test, but refill it if necessary.

6. If the delivery rate is below the minimum, check the lines for restrictions or leaks, then replace the pump.

Fuel Tank

REMOVAL AND INSTALLATION

1. Drain the tank.
2. Raise and support the truck on jackstands.
3. Disconnect the wiring and ground strap at the tank.
4. Disconnect the filler neck hose and vent hose at the tank.
5. Disconnect the fuel feed line and vapor line at the tank.
6. Place a floor jack under the tank to take up its weight.
7. Remove the fuel tank support bolts and lower the tank.
8. Installation is the reverse of removal.

Fuel Filter

REMOVAL AND INSTALLATION

All models use a paper filter behind the inlet nut in the carburetor. Using two wrenches, disconnect the fuel line, unscrew the nut and replace the filter. Do not overtighten the inlet nut. It is easily stripped.

Carburetor

REMOVAL AND INSTALLATION

1950cc Engine

1. Remove the PCV valve from the rocker arm cover.
2. Disconnect the ECS hose from the air cleaner.
3. Disconnect the AIR hose from the pump.
4. On California models, disconnect the air hose from the slow carburetor.
5. Unbolt the air cleaner, lift it slightly, disconnect the hoses and remove the unit.
6. Disconnect the rubber piping from the TVS switch.
7. Disconnect the vacuum advance hose at the distributor.
8. On models with automatic transmission, disconnect the vacuum hose from the converter housing.

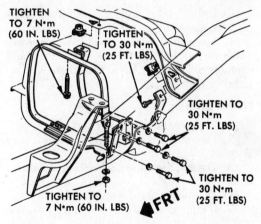

Fuel tank

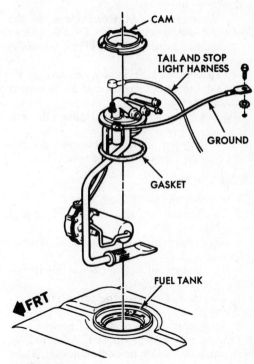

Fuel meter

9. On California models, disconnect the vacuum hoses from the slow and main actuator.
10. Disconnect the carburetor solenoid lead wire.
11. Disconnect the accelerator control cable.
12. Disconnect the cruise control cable.
13. On automatic transmission models, disconnect the detent control cable.
14. Disconnect the fuel line at the carburetor.
15. Disconnect the ECS hose at the carburetor.

16. Unbolt and remove the carburetor. Discard the mounting gasket.

17. Installation is the reverse of removal. Make sure all linkage is properly adjusted and operates smoothly. Check that there are no leaks.

2000cc Engine

1. Remove the air cleaner and gasket.
2. Disconnect the fuel pipe and all vacuum lines.
3. Tag and disconnect all electrical connections.
4. Disconnect the downshift cable.
5. If equipped with cruise control, disconnect the linkage.
6. Unscrew the carburetor mounting bolts and remove the carburetor.
7. Before installing the carburetor, fill the float bowl with gasoline to reduce the battery strain and the possibility of backfiring when the engine is started again.
8. Inspect the EFE heater for damage. Be sure that the throttle body and EFE mating surfaces are clean.
9. Install the carburetor and tighten the nuts alternately.
10. Installation of the remaining components is in the reverse order of removal.

2800cc Engine

1. Remove the air cleaner.
2. Disconnect the fuel and vacuum lines at the carburetor.
3. Disconnect all wiring from the carburetor.
4. Disconnect all linkage from the carburetor.
5. Unbolt and remove the carburetor. Discard the gasket.
6. Installation is the reverse of removal. Always use a new gasket. Check that the linkage works smoothly and is properly adjusted. Make sure there are no leaks.

ADJUSTMENTS
1950cc Engine
FLOAT LEVEL

The fuel level is normal if it is seen to be within the mark on the float bowl window. If not, remove the top of the carburetor and bend the float seat to regulate the level.

PRIMARY THROTTLE VALVE

When the choke plate is completely closed, the primary throttle valve should be opened by the fast idle screw to an angle of 16° (MT), or 18° (AT). To check this adjustment:

1. Close the choke plate completely and

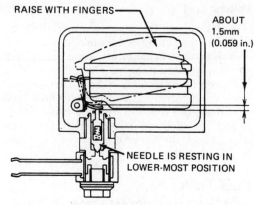

RAISE WITH FINGERS
ABOUT 1.5mm (0.059 in.)
NEEDLE IS RESTING IN LOWER-MOST POSITION

4-1950 float level adjustment

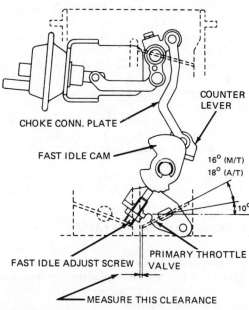

COUNTER LEVER
CHOKE CONN. PLATE
FAST IDLE CAM
16° (M/T)
18° (A/T)
10°
FAST IDLE ADJUST SCREW
PRIMARY THROTTLE VALVE
MEASURE THIS CLEARANCE

4-1950 primary throttle valve adjustment

measure between Throttle plate and the air horn wall. Clearance should be .050–.059 in. for MT or .059–.069 in. for AT. Measurement should be made at the center point of the choke plate.

2. If necessary, adjust the opening by turning the fast idle screw.

THROTTLE LINKAGE

1. Turn the primary throttle valve plate until the adjustment plate is in contact with the kickdown lever. This is a primary throttle plate opening of about 47°.

2. Measure the clearance between the center point of the primary throttle plate and the air horn wall. Clearance should be .24–.30 in. If not, bend the kickdown lever tab until it is.

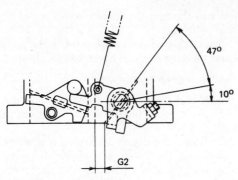

4-1950 linkage adjustment

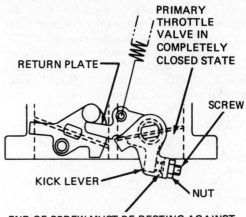

END OF SCREW MUST BE RESTING AGAINST
RETURN PLATE

4-1950 kick lever adjustment

KICKDOWN LEVER ADJUSTMENT

1. Turn the primary throttle lever until plate is completely closed. Back off the throttle adjustment screw if necessary.

2. Loosen the locknut on the kickdown lever screw and turn the screw until it just contacts the return plate. Tighten the locknut.

2000cc and 2800cc Engines

FLOAT LEVEL

1. With the engine cold, remove the top of the carburetor.

2. While holding a finger lightly, but firmly, on the float retainer, press down lightly on the float tab to seat the needle valve.

3. Measure the distance between the float bowl gasket surface and the point on the float farthest from the needle valve.

4. If the measurement is not correct, remove the float and bend the tab until it is.

PUMP

1. With the throttle closed and the fast idle screw off the steps of the fast idle cam, measure the distance from the air horn casting to the top of the pump stem.

2. To adjust, remove the retaining screw and

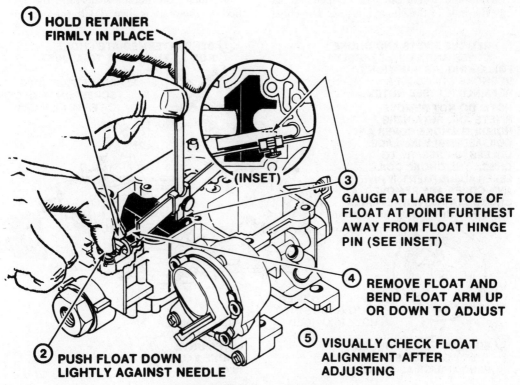

① **HOLD RETAINER FIRMLY IN PLACE**

(INSET)

③ **GAUGE AT LARGE TOE OF FLOAT AT POINT FURTHEST AWAY FROM FLOAT HINGE PIN (SEE INSET)**

④ **REMOVE FLOAT AND BEND FLOAT ARM UP OR DOWN TO ADJUST**

② **PUSH FLOAT DOWN LIGHTLY AGAINST NEEDLE**

⑤ **VISUALLY CHECK FLOAT ALIGNMENT AFTER ADJUSTING**

4-2000, 6-2800 float adjustment

washer and remove the pump lever. Bend the end of the lever to correct the stem height. Do not twist the lever or bend it sideways.

3. Install the lever, washer and screw and check the adjustment. When correct, open and close the throttle a few times to check the linkage movement and alignment.

FAST IDLE

1. Set the ignition timing and curb idle speed, and disconnect and plug hoses as directed on the emission control decal.

2. Place the fast idle screw on the highest step of the cam.

3. Start the engine and adjust the engine speed to specification with the fast idle screw.

CHOKE COIL LEVER

1. Remove the three retaining screws and remove the choke cover and coil. On models with a riveted choke cover, drill out the three rivets and remove the cover and choke coil.

NOTE: *A choke stat cover retainer kit is required for reassembly.*

2. Place the fast idle screw on the high step of the cam.

3. Close the choke by pushing in on the intermediate choke lever. On front wheel drive models, the intermediate choke lever is behind the choke vacuum diaphragm.

4. Insert a drill or gauge of the specified size into the hole in the choke housing. The choke

lever in the housing should be up against the side of the gauge.

5. If the lever does not just touch the gauge, bend the intermediate choke rod to adjust.

FAST IDLE CAM (CHOKE ROD)

NOTE: *A special angle gauge should be used.*

1. Adjust the choke coil lever and fast idle first.

2. Rotate the degree scale until it is zeroed.

3. Close the choke and install the degree scale onto the choke plate. Center the leveling bubble.

4. Rotate the scale so that the specified degree is opposite the scale pointer.

5. Place the fast idle screw on the second step of the cam (against the high step). Close the choke by pushing in the intermediate lever.

6. Push on the vacuum break lever in the direction of opening choke until the lever is against the rear tang on the choke lever.

7. Bend the fast idle cam rod at the U to adjust angle to specifications.

AIR VALVE ROD

1. Align the zero degree mark with the pointer on an angle gauge.

2. Close the air valve and place a magnet on top of it.

3. Rotate the bubble until it is centered.

4. Rotate the degree scale until the specified degree mark is aligned with the pointer.

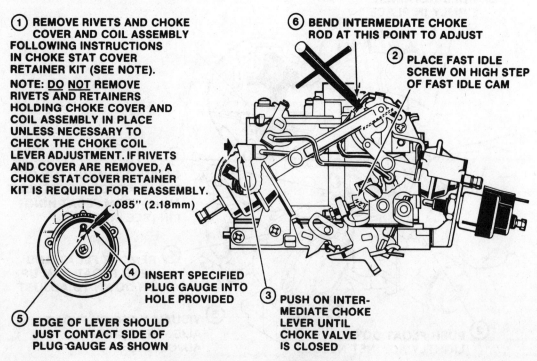

① REMOVE RIVETS AND CHOKE COVER AND COIL ASSEMBLY FOLLOWING INSTRUCTIONS IN CHOKE STAT COVER RETAINER KIT (SEE NOTE).

NOTE: DO NOT REMOVE RIVETS AND RETAINERS HOLDING CHOKE COVER AND COIL ASSEMBLY IN PLACE UNLESS NECESSARY TO CHECK THE CHOKE COIL LEVER ADJUSTMENT. IF RIVETS AND COVER ARE REMOVED, A CHOKE STAT COVER RETAINER KIT IS REQUIRED FOR REASSEMBLY.

.085" (2.18mm)

④ INSERT SPECIFIED PLUG GAUGE INTO HOLE PROVIDED

⑤ EDGE OF LEVER SHOULD JUST CONTACT SIDE OF PLUG GAUGE AS SHOWN

⑥ BEND INTERMEDIATE CHOKE ROD AT THIS POINT TO ADJUST

② PLACE FAST IDLE SCREW ON HIGH STEP OF FAST IDLE CAM

③ PUSH ON INTERMEDIATE CHOKE LEVER UNTIL CHOKE VALVE IS CLOSED

4-2000, 6-2800 choke coil lever adjustment

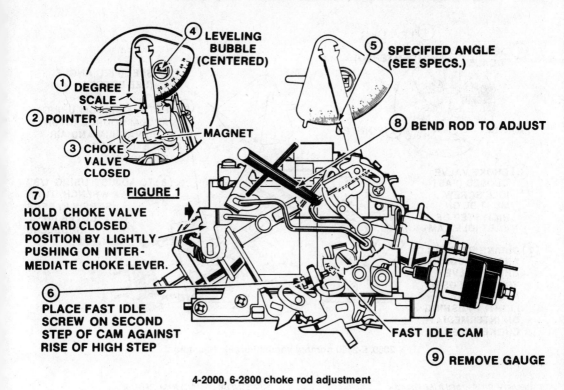

① **DEGREE SCALE**

② **POINTER**

③ **CHOKE VALVE CLOSED**

④ **LEVELING BUBBLE (CENTERED)**

⑤ **SPECIFIED ANGLE (SEE SPECS.)**

⑧ **BEND ROD TO ADJUST**

MAGNET

FIGURE 1

⑦ **HOLD CHOKE VALVE TOWARD CLOSED POSITION BY LIGHTLY PUSHING ON INTER-MEDIATE CHOKE LEVER.**

⑥ **PLACE FAST IDLE SCREW ON SECOND STEP OF CAM AGAINST RISE OF HIGH STEP**

FAST IDLE CAM

⑨ **REMOVE GAUGE**

4-2000, 6-2800 choke rod adjustment

5. Seat the vacuum diaphragm using an external vacuum source.

6. On four cylinder models plug the end cover. Unplug after adjustment.

7. Apply light pressure to the air valve shaft in the direction to open the air valve until all the slack is removed between the air link and plunger slot.

8. Bend the air valve link until the bubble is centered.

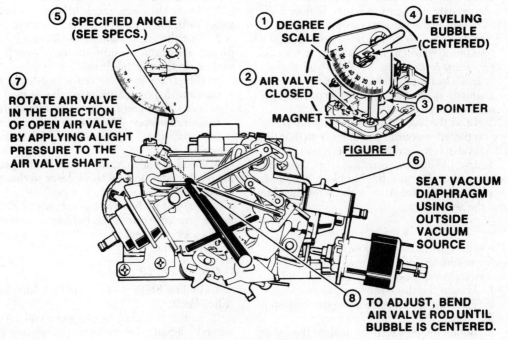

⑤ **SPECIFIED ANGLE (SEE SPECS.)**

⑦ **ROTATE AIR VALVE IN THE DIRECTION OF OPEN AIR VALVE BY APPLYING A LIGHT PRESSURE TO THE AIR VALVE SHAFT.**

① **DEGREE SCALE**

② **AIR VALVE CLOSED**

MAGNET

④ **LEVELING BUBBLE (CENTERED)**

③ **POINTER**

FIGURE 1

⑥ **SEAT VACUUM DIAPHRAGM USING OUTSIDE VACUUM SOURCE**

⑧ **TO ADJUST, BEND AIR VALVE ROD UNTIL BUBBLE IS CENTERED.**

4-2000, 6-2800 air valve rod adjustment

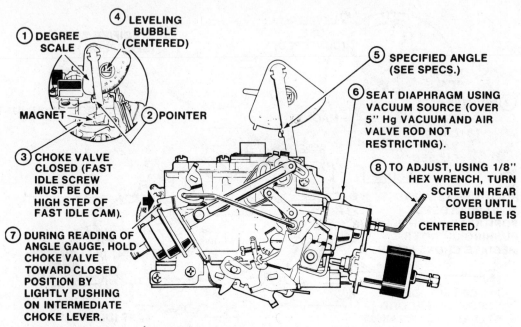

① **DEGREE SCALE**

④ **LEVELING BUBBLE (CENTERED)**

MAGNET

② **POINTER**

③ **CHOKE VALVE CLOSED (FAST IDLE SCREW MUST BE ON HIGH STEP OF FAST IDLE CAM).**

⑤ **SPECIFIED ANGLE (SEE SPECS.)**

⑥ **SEAT DIAPHRAGM USING VACUUM SOURCE (OVER 5" Hg VACUUM AND AIR VALVE ROD NOT RESTRICTING).**

⑧ **TO ADJUST, USING 1/8" HEX WRENCH, TURN SCREW IN REAR COVER UNTIL BUBBLE IS CENTERED.**

⑦ **DURING READING OF ANGLE GAUGE, HOLD CHOKE VALVE TOWARD CLOSED POSITION BY LIGHTLY PUSHING ON INTERMEDIATE CHOKE LEVER.**

4-2000, 6-2800 primary vacuum break adjustment

PRIMARY SIDE VACUUM BREAK

NOTE: *Prior to adjustment, remove the vacuum break from the carburetor. Place the bracket in a vise and using the proper safety precautions, grind off the adjustment screw cap then reinstall the vacuum break.*

1. Rotate the degree scale on the measuring gauge until the zero is opposite the pointer.

2. Seat the choke vacuum diaphragm by applying an external vacuum source of over 5 in. Hg vacuum to the vacuum break.

NOTE: *If the air valve rod is restricting the vacuum diaphragm from seating it may be necessary to bend the air valve rod slightly to gain clearance. Make an air valve rod adjustment after the vacuum break adjustment.*

3. Read the angle gauge while lightly pushing on the intermediate choke lever so that the choke valve is toward the close position.

4. Use a ⅛ in. hex wrench and turn the screw in the rear cover until the bubble is centered. Apply a silicone sealant over the screw head to seal the setting.

ELECTRIC CHOKE

This procedure is only for those carburetors with choke covers retained by screws. Riveted choke covers are preset and nonadjustable.

1. Loosen the three retaining screws.

2. Place the fast idle screw on the high step of the cam.

3. Rotate the choke cover to align the cover mark with the specified housing mark.

SECONDARY VACUUM BREAK

NOTE: *Prior to adjustment, remove the vacuum break from the carburetor. Place the bracket in the vise and using the proper safety precautions, grind off the adjustment screw cap then reinstall the vacuum break.*

NOTE: *Plug the end cover using an accelerator pump plunger cup or equivalent. Remove the cup after the adjustment.*

1. Rotate the degree scale on the measuring gauge until the zero is opposite the pointer.

2. Seat the choke vacuum diaphragm by applying an external vacuum source of over 5 in. vacuum to the vacuum break.

NOTE: *If the air valve rod is restricting the vacuum diaphragm from seating it may be necessary to bend the air valve rod slightly to gain clearance. Make an air valve rod adjustment after the vacuum break adjustment.*

3. Read the angle gauge while lightly pushing on the intermediate choke lever so that the choke valve is toward the close position.

4. Use a ⅛ in. hex wrench and turn the screw in the rear cover until the bubble is centered. Apply a silicone sealant over the screw head to seal the setting.

CHOKE UNLOADER

1. Follow Steps 1–4 of the Fast Idle Cam Adjustment.

2. Install the choke cover and coil, if removed, aligning the marks on the housing and cover as specified.

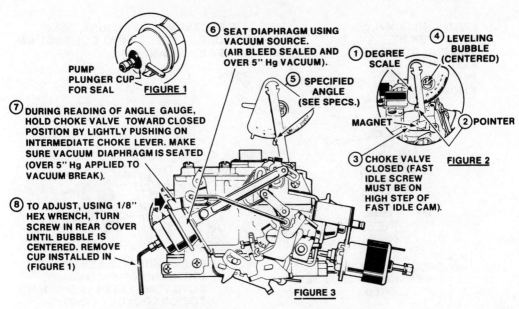

PUMP PLUNGER CUP FOR SEAL   FIGURE 1

⑥ SEAT DIAPHRAGM USING VACUUM SOURCE. (AIR BLEED SEALED AND OVER 5" Hg VACUUM).

⑤ SPECIFIED ANGLE (SEE SPECS.)

④ LEVELING BUBBLE (CENTERED)

① DEGREE SCALE

MAGNET   ② POINTER

③ CHOKE VALVE CLOSED (FAST IDLE SCREW MUST BE ON HIGH STEP OF FAST IDLE CAM).   FIGURE 2

⑦ DURING READING OF ANGLE GAUGE, HOLD CHOKE VALVE TOWARD CLOSED POSITION BY LIGHTLY PUSHING ON INTERMEDIATE CHOKE LEVER. MAKE SURE VACUUM DIAPHRAGM IS SEATED (OVER 5" Hg APPLIED TO VACUUM BREAK).

⑧ TO ADJUST, USING 1/8" HEX WRENCH, TURN SCREW IN REAR COVER UNTIL BUBBLE IS CENTERED. REMOVE CUP INSTALLED IN (FIGURE 1)

FIGURE 3

4-2000, 6-2800 secondary vacuum break adjustment

3. Hold the primary throttle wide open.

4. If the engine is warm, close the choke valve by pushing in on the intermediate choke lever.

5. Bend the unloader tang until the bubble is centered.

SECONDARY LOCKOUT

1. Pull the choke wide open by pushing out on the intermediate choke lever.

2. Open the throttle until the end of the secondary actuating lever is opposite the toe of the lockout lever.

3. Gauge clearance between the lockout lever and secondary lever should be as specified.

4. To adjust, bend the lockout lever where it contacts the fast idle cam.

OVERHAUL—4-1950CC ENGINE
Disassembly

1. Remove main and assist return spring.
2. Disconnect accelerating pump lever.

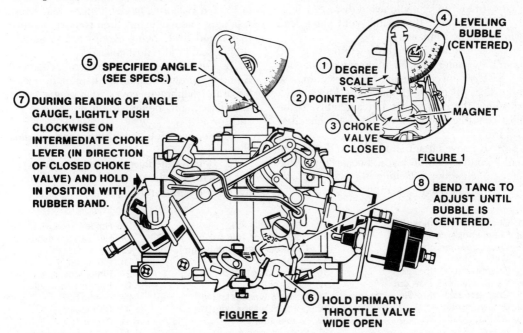

⑤ SPECIFIED ANGLE (SEE SPECS.)

⑦ DURING READING OF ANGLE GAUGE, LIGHTLY PUSH CLOCKWISE ON INTERMEDIATE CHOKE LEVER (IN DIRECTION OF CLOSED CHOKE VALVE) AND HOLD IN POSITION WITH RUBBER BAND.

④ LEVELING BUBBLE (CENTERED)

① DEGREE SCALE

② POINTER

③ CHOKE VALVE CLOSED

MAGNET

FIGURE 1

⑧ BEND TANG TO ADJUST UNTIL BUBBLE IS CENTERED.

⑥ HOLD PRIMARY THROTTLE VALVE WIDE OPEN

FIGURE 2

4-2000, 6-2800 choke unloader adjustment

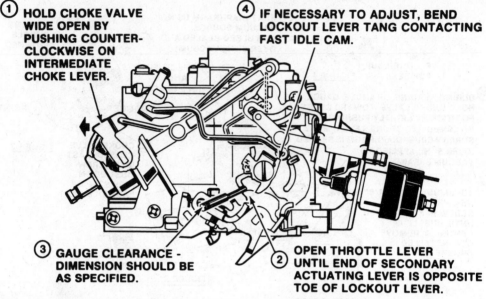

① HOLD CHOKE VALVE WIDE OPEN BY PUSHING COUNTER-CLOCKWISE ON INTERMEDIATE CHOKE LEVER.

④ IF NECESSARY TO ADJUST, BEND LOCKOUT LEVER TANG CONTACTING FAST IDLE CAM.

③ GAUGE CLEARANCE - DIMENSION SHOULD BE AS SPECIFIED.

② OPEN THROTTLE LEVER UNTIL END OF SECONDARY ACTUATING LEVER IS OPPOSITE TOE OF LOCKOUT LEVER.

4-2000, 6-2800 secondary lockout adjustment

3. On California model, disconnect rubber pipe from the slow-actuator.

4. Remove throttle return spring(s). Flatten the harness clips under the choke housing and at the choke chamber and then remove lead wire from clips.

5. Remove the connector (Federal model 3P, California model 1P) from the connector hanger and disconnect the automatic choke lead wire from the connector.

Remove the fuel nipple and strainer; remove strainer carefully to avoid distorting it.

6. Disconnect the switch vent valve lead wire from the connector.

7. Disconnect the choke connecting rod from the counter lever by removing circuit clip.

8. Disconnect automatic choke vacuum hose from float chamber. Remove the four screws attaching the choke chamber assembly to the float chamber and remove the choke chamber assembly.

9. Remove circuit clip between diaphragm and secondary trottle lever. Loosen three diaphragm chamber attaching screws, then remove the diaphragm assembly.

10. Separate float chamber assembly from the throttle chamber assembly.

11. Remove slow-actuator.

12. Remove accelerating pump plunger assembly.

13. Remove the float needle valve assembly.

14. On Federal model, remove three screws retaining level gage cover, then remove level gage, and float, being careful not to damage rubber seal or lose float collar.

15. On California model, remove four screws retaining main-actuator, then remove main-actuator and float, being careful not to damage rubber seal or lose float collar.

16. Disassembly of diaphragm chamber. Remove screws retaining diaphragm cover. Separate diaphragm cover, diaphragm spring and diaphragm, being careful not to lose ball and spring.

17. Remove jets on upper part of float chamber.

18. Remove the injector weight plug and take out injector weight and check ball. On California model, also remove spring.

1. Chamber asm., choke	12. Washer, idle adj.	23. Holder, lead wire
2. Plate, choke, connecting	13. Seal, rubber, idle adj.	24. Hanger, connector
3. Lever, counter, choke	14. Chamber asm., diaphragm	25. Lever, fast idj.
4. Valve, solenoid, sw. vent.	15. Diaphragm	26. Float, fuel
5. Chamger asm., float	16. Spring, diaphragm	27. Plate, lock, drain plug
6. Valve, solenoid, slow cut	17. Gasket kit	28. Hanger, connector
7. Chamber asm., throttle	18. Screw & washer kit (A)	29. Connector
8. Screw, throttle adj.	19. Screw & washer kit (B)	30. Connector
9. Spring, throttle adj.	20. Nipple, fuel	31. Connector
10. Screw, idle adj.	21. Plate, stopping	32. Rubber, mounting
11. Spring, idle adj.	22. Cam, fast idle	33. Plate, mt. rubber

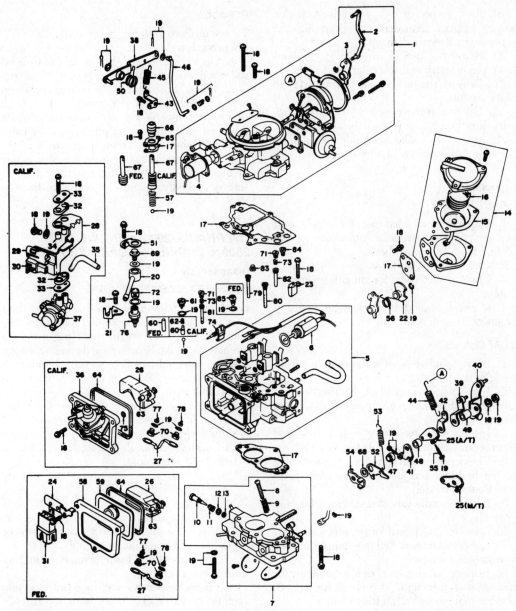

34. Collar, mt. rubber	52. Plate, return	69. Screw, nipple set
35. Hose, rubber	53. Spring, throttle, "S"	70. Plug, drain fuel
36. Actuator, main	54. Lever, adj.	71. Plug, taper
37. Actuator, slow	55. Screw, fast idle	72. Filter
38. Lever, pump	56. Spring, cam	73. Spring, slow jet
39. Lever, accele	57. Spring, piston return	74. Connector, lead wire
40. Lever, cruise	58. Cover, level gauge	75. O-ring
41. Lever, kick	59. Gauge, level	76. Valve, needle
42. Hanger, spring "A"	60. Weight, injector	77. Jet, main, "P"
43. Hanger, spring "B"	61. Screw, pump set	78. Jet, main, "S"
44. Spring, main	62. Spring, injector	79. Bleed, air main. "P"
45. Spring, assist	63. Collar, "C"	80. Bleed, air main, "S"
46. Rod, pump	64. Seal, rubber	81. Jet, slow, "P"
47. Sleeve	65. Plate, cyl.	82. Jet, slow, "S"
48. Collar, shaft "A"	66. Cover, dust	83. Bleed, air, slow, "P"
49. Collar, shaft "B"	67. Piston	84. Bleed, air, slow, "S"
50. Spring, pump lever	68. Washer, throttle shaft	85. Valve, power
51. Lever, lock		

4-1950 carburetor, exploded view

19. Remove power jet. On Federal model, be sure to place screwdriver properly into slot to prevent valve rod damage.

20. Removing two main jet plugs and remove the primary and secondary main jets.

21. Remove the primary slow air bleed from choke chamber.

22. Do not remove screws retaining primary throttle valve, secondary throttle valve and choke valve. On California model, do not remove slow and main actuators.

Inspection

CHOKE CHAMBER

1. Inspect choke chamber for cracks and damage, paying particular attention to the jointing face of the chamber.

2. Check shaft holes for wear.

3. Check choke valve for smoothness of operation.

4. On Federa model, check vacuum piston for smoothness of operation.

FLOAT CHAMBER

1. Inspect and remove carbon deposit from inside of the body.

2. Inspect body for cracks, jointing face for damage, and thread portions for damage and corrosion.

3. Inspect jets mounting holes, threaded portions and screwdriver slots for damage.

4. Check power valve for leaks, power valve rod for bending and for smoothness of operation (Federal model).

5. Inspect needle valve for sticking, dirt, and corrosion.

6. Carefully check float for pin hole and wear.

7. Inspect strainer in fuel pipe nipple for dirt, corrosion and damage.

8. Inspect accelerating pump plunger for damage and distortion. Also check for smooth plunger movement within the cylinder.

9. Check rubber boot of accelerating pump for damage.

THROTTLE CHAMBER

1. Check slow port, idle port and others for clogging.

2. Check primary and secondary throttle valve for presence of carbon deposit and wear.

3. Check throttle valve shaft holes for wear.

4. Check mixture adjusting screw seating face for step wear and threaded portion for damage.

5. Check diaphragm for deterioration and damage.

SOLENOID

Inspect for looseness of attaching parts and damage of wire harness connection.

Assembly

To assemble carburetor, reverse the disassembly procedures.

1. On Federal model, be careful not to bend valve rod when installing the power jet valve.

2. When reassembly of the accelerator pump is completed, fill cylinder with fuel and check to be sure fuel is injected smoothly. When reassembling accelerating pump parts be careful not to bend piston connecting rod.

3. When reassembling main actuator, apply grease to O–ring, then tighten the attaching screws carefully to prevent cracks of the O–ring.

OVERHAUL—2000cc ENGINE AND 2800cc ENGINE 2SE CARBURETOR

Disassembly

IDLE SPEED SOLENOID REMOVAL

Bend back retaining tabs on lockwasher; then remove large solenoid retaining nut using suitable wrench. Use care in removing nut with wrench to avoid bending or damaging choke linkage, solenoid bracket, vacuum break unit or throttle lever. Remove lockwasher and solenoid unit from bracket.

NOTE: *The solenoid should not be immersed in any type of carburetor cleaner and should always be removed before complete carburetor overhaul. Immersion in cleaner will damage solenoid.*

AIR HORN

1. Remove clip from hole in pump lever. Do not remove pump lever retaining screw or pump lever from air horn assembly.

2. Remove hose from primary side vacuum break assembly.

3. Remove screws securing primary side vacuum break bracket to air horn and throttle body, then, rotate vacuum break and bracket assembly to disengage vacuum break link from slot in vacuum break and choke lever and air valve rod from slot in air valve lever.

NOTE: *Do not place vacuum break assembly in carburetor cleaner. Immersion in cleaner will damage vacuum break diaphragm.*

4. If necessary to remove air valve rod from vacuum break, remove and discard retaining clips from end of air valve rod. New retaining clip is required for reassembly. Remove plastic bushing used on rods and retain for later reuse.

5. Remove secondary side idle speed solenoid-vacuum break bracket attaching screws from throttle body. Then, rotate bracket to re-

move secondary side vacuum break link from slot in break and choke lever.

NOTE: *Do not place vacuum break assembly and solenoid in carburetor cleaner. Immersion in cleaner will damage vacuum break diaphragm.*

6. Remove and discard retaining clip from intermediate choke rod at choke lever. A new retaining clip is required for reassembly. Remove choke rod and plastic bushing from choke lever, and save the bushing for later re-use.

7. Remove small screws that retain the hot idle compensator valve (if used). Remove valve and seal from air horn. Discard seal. Hot idle compensator valve must be removed to gain access to short air horn to bowl attaching screw.

8. Remove the air horn to bowl attaching screws and lockwashers. Remove vent and screen assembly.

9. Rotate fast idle cam to the full UP position and remove air horn assembly by tilting to disengage fast idle cam and pump rod from hole in pump lever. If pump plunger remains with air horn, remove. The air horn gasket should remain on the float bowl for removal later.

Do not remove fast idle cam screw and cam from float bowl. These parts are not serviced separately and are to remain permanently in place. The new service replacement float bowl will include the secondary lockout lever, fast idle cam and screw installed as required.

10. Remove fast idle cam rod from choke lever by rotating rod to align squirt on rod with small slot in lever.

AIR HORN DISASSEMBLY

1. Remove pump plunger stem seal by inverting air horn and use a small screwdriver to remove staking holding the seal retainer in place. Remove and discard retainer and seal.

NOTE: *Use care in removing the pump plunger stem seal retainer to prevent damage to air horn casting. A new seal and retainer are required at time of reassembly.*

2. Further disassembly of the air horn is not required for cleaning purposes or air horn replacement. The new service air horn assembly includes the secondary metering rod-air valve assembly and is pre-set at the factory. No attempt should be made to change this adjustment in the field. The air valve and choke valve screws are staked in place and should not be removed.

FLOAT BOWL DISASSEMBLY

1. Remove air horn gasket. Gasket is pre-cut for easy removal around metering rod and hanger assembly.

2. Remove pump plunger from pump well (if not removed with air horn).

3. Remove pump return spring from pump well.

4. Remove plastic filler block over float valve.

5. Remove float assembly and float valve by pulling up on retaining pin.

6. Remove float valve seat and gasket using a wide-blade screwdriver.

7. Remove power piston and metering rod assembly by depressing piston stem and allowing it to snap free. The power piston can be easily removed by pressing the piston down and releasing it with a snap. This will cause the power piston spring to snap the piston up against the plastic retainer. This procedure may have to be repeated several times. Do not remove power piston by using pliers on metering rod holder.

8. Remove the power piston spring from the piston bore. If necessary, metering rod may be removed from power piston hanger by compressing spring on top of metering rod and aligning groove on rod with slot in holder. Use extreme care in handling the metering rod to prevent damage to metering rod tip.

9. Remove the main metering jet using a wide blade screwdriver.

10. Using a small slide hammer or equivalent, remove plastic retainer holding pump discharge spring and check ball in place. Discard plastic retainer (a new retainer is required for reassembly). Turn bowl upside down catching spring and check ball in palm of hand.

NOTICE: *Do not attempt to remove plastic retainer by prying out with a tool such as a punch or screwdriver—this will damage the sealing beads on the bowl casting surface requiring complete float bowl replacement.*

CHOKE COVER REMOVAL

NOTE: *The tamper resistant choke cover design is used to discourage readjustment of choke thermostatic cover and coil assembly in the field. However, it is necessary to remove the cover and coil assembly during normal carburetor disassembly for cleaning and overhaul using the procedure that follows.*

1. Support float bowl and throttle body as an assembly on a suitable holding fixture such as Tool J-9789-118. Carefully align a No. 21 drill (.159 in.) on rivet head and drill only enough to remove rivet head. After removing rivet heads and retainers, use a drift and small hammer to drive the remainder of the rivets out of the choke housing. Use care in drilling to prevent damage to choke cover or housing.

2. Remove the choke cover assembly from choke housing.

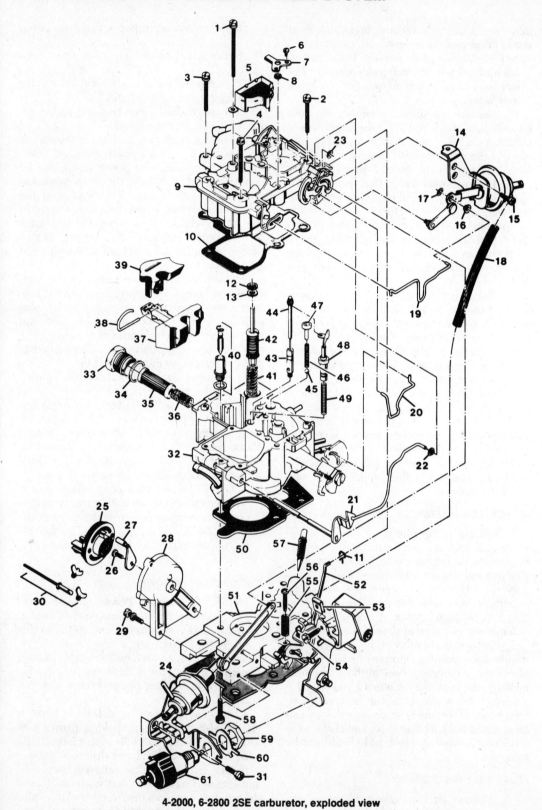

4-2000, 6-2800 2SE carburetor, exploded view

3. Remove screw from end of intermediate choke shaft inside choke housing.

4. Remove choke coil lever from shaft.

5. Remove intermediate choke shaft and lever assembly from float bowl by sliding rearward out throttle lever side.

6. Remove choke housing by removing two attaching screws in throttle body.

DISASSEMBLY OF REMAINING FLOAT BOWL PARTS

Remove fuel inlet nut, gasket, check valve/filter assembly, and spring. Discard gasket and filter.

THROTTLE BODY DISASSEMBLY

1. Remove throttle body to bowl attaching screws and lockwashers and remove throttle body assembly.

2. Remove throttle body to bowl insulator gasket.

3. Place throttle body assembly on carburetor holding fixture to avoid damaging throttle valves.

4. Hold primary throttle lever wide-open and disengage pump rod from throttle lever by rotating rod until squirt on rod aligns with slot in lever.

5. Further disassembly of the throttle body is not required for cleaning purposes.

The primary and secondary throttle valve screws are permanently staked in place and should not be removed. The throttle body is serviced as a complete assembly.

Do not remove plugs covering idle mixture needle unless it is necessary to replace the mixture needle or normal soaking and air pressure fails to clean the idle mixture passages.

Idle mixture should be adjusted only if required at time of major carburetor overhaul, throttle body replacement, or high emissions as determined by official inspections.

If necessary, remove idle mixture needle and plug as follows:

a. Invert throttle body and place on carburetor holding fixture-manifold side up.

b. Make two parallel cuts in throttle body on either side of the locator points beneath the idle mixture needle plug (manifold side) with a hack saw. The cuts should reach down to the steel plug but should not extend more than $1/8''$ beyond the locator points. The distance between the saw marks depends on the size of the punch to be used.

c. Place a flat punch at a point near the ends of the saw marks in the throttle body.

AIR HORN PARTS

1. Screw—air horn (long) (2)
2. Screw—air horn (large)
3. Screw—air horn (short) (3)
4. Screw—air horn (medium)
5. Vent stack assembly
6. Screw—hot idle compensator (2)
7. Hot idle compensator
8. Gasket—hot idle compensator
9. Air horn assembly
10. Gasket—air horn
11. Retainer—pump link
12. Seal—pump stem
13. Retainer—stem seal

CHOKE PARTS

14. Vacuum break and bracket assembly—primary
15. Screw—vacuum break attaching
16. Bushing—air valve—link
17. Retainer—air valve link
18. Hose—vacuum break—primary
19. Link—air valve
20. Link—fast idle cam
21. Intermediate choke shaft/lever/link assembly
22. Bushing—intermediate choke shaft link
23. Retainer—intermediate choke shaft link
24. Vacuum break and bracket assembly—secondary
25. Choke cover and coil assembly
26. Screw—choke lever
27. Choke lever and contact assembly
28. Choke housing
29. Screw—choke housing (2)
30. Stat cover retainer kit
31. Screw—vacuum break attaching (2)

FLOAT BOWL PARTS

32. Float bowl assembly
33. Nut—fuel inlet
34. Gasket—fuel inlet nut
35. Filter—fuel inlet
36. Spring—fuel filter
37. Float assembly
38. Hinge pin—float
39. Insert—float bowl
40. Needle and seat assembly
41. Spring—pump return
42. Pump—assembly
43. Jet—main metering
44. Rod—main metering assembly
45. Ball—pump discharge
46. Spring—pump discharge
47. Retainer—pump discharge spring
48. Power piston assembly
49. Spring—power piston

THROTTLE BODY PARTS

50. Gasket—throttle body
51. Throttle body assembly
52. Pump rod
53. Clip—cam screw
54. Screw—cam
55. Spring—throttle stop screw
56. Screw—throttle stop
57. Idle needle and spring
58. Screw—throttle body attaching (4)
59. Nut—idle solenoid
60. Retainer—idle solenoid
61. Idle solenoid

4-2000, 6-2800 2SE carburetor, exploded view

Holding the punch at a 45 degree angle, drive it into the throttle body until the casting breaks away, exposing the steel plug.

d. Holding a center punch vertical, drive it into the steel plug. Then, holding the punch at a 45 degree angle, drive the plug out of the casting.

Hardened plug will shatter rather than remaining intact. It is not necessary to remove the plug completely; remove loose pieces.

e. Using Tool J-29030, remove idle mixture needle and spring from throttle body.

f. Using Tool J-29030-B, remove idle mixture needle, and spring from throttle body.

Cleaning and Inspection

The carburetor parts should be cleaned in a cold immersion-type cleaner such as Carbon X (X-55) or its equivalent.

NOTE: *The solenoid, electric choke, rubber parts, plastic parts, diaphragms, pump plunger, plastic filler block should NOT be immersed in carburetor cleaner as they will swell, harden or distort.*

1. Thoroughly clean all metal parts and blow dry with compressed air. Make sure all fuel passages and metering parts are free of burrs and dirt. Do not pass drills or wires through jets and passages.

2. Inspect upper and lower surface of carburetor castings for damage.

3. Inspect holes in levers for excessive wear or out of round conditions. If worn, levers should be replaced. Inspect plastic bushings for damage and excessive wear. Replace as required.

4. Check, repair, or replace parts if the following problems are encountered:

A. Flooding

1. Inspect float valve and seat for dirt, deep wear grooves, scores, and proper seating.

2. Inspect float valve pull clip for proper installation. Be careful not to bend pull clip.

3. Inspect float, float arms and hinge pin for distortion, binds, and burrs. Check density of material in the float; if heavier than normal, replace float.

4. Replace fuel inlet filter and check valve assembly.

B. Hesitation

1. Inspect pump plunger and cup for cracks, scores, or cup excessive wear. A used pump cup will shrink when dry. If dried out, soak in fuel for 8 hours before testing.

2. Inspect pump duration and return springs for being weak or distorted.

3. Check all pump passages and jet for dirt, improper seating of discharge check ball and scores in pump well. Check condition of pump discharge check ball spring.

4. Check pump linkage for excessive wear; repair or replace as necessary.

C. Hard Starting—Poor Cold Operation

1. Check choke valve and linkage for excessive wear, binds or distortion.

2. Inspect choke vacuum diaphragms for leaks.

3. Replace carburetor fuel filter.

4. Inspect float valve for sticking, dirt, etc.

5. Also check items under "Flooding."

D. Poor Performance—Poor Gas Mileage

1. Clean all fuel and vacuum passages in castings.

2. Check choke valve for freedom of movement.

3. Check power piston, metering rod, and jet for dirt, sticking, binding, damaged parts or excessive wear.

4. Check air valve and secondary metering rod for binding conditions.

If air valve or metering rod is damaged, the air horn assembly must be replaced. Also, check air valve spring for proper installation (tension against air valve lever).

E. Rough Idle

1. Inspect gasket and gasket mating surfaces on castings for damage to sealing beads, nicks, burrs and other damage.

2. Clean all idle fuel passages.

3. If removed, inspect idle mixture needle for ridges, burrs, or being bent.

4. Check throttle lever and valves for bind, nicks and other damage.

5. Check all diaphragms for possible ruptures or leaks.

6. Clean plastic parts only in low volatile cleaning solvent—never in gasoline.

Assembly

THROTTLE BODY

1. Holding primary throttle lever wide open, install lower end of pump rod in throttle lever by aligning squirt on rod with slot in lever. End of rod should point outward toward throttle lever.

2. If removed, install idle mixture needle and spring using tool J-29030-B; lightly seat needle and then back out 3 turns as a preliminary idle mixture adjustment. Final idle mixture adjustment must be made on-vehicle using the procedure described under Idle Mixture Adjustment.

FLOAT BOWL ASSEMBLY

If a new float bowl assembly is used, stamp or engrave the model number on the new float bowl.

1. Install new throttle body to bowl insulator gasket over two locating dowels on bowl.

2. Holding fast idle cam so that cam steps

face fast idle screw on throttle lever when properly installed, install throttle body making certain throttle body is properly located over dowels on float bowl; then install throttle body to bowl screws and lockwashers and tighten evenly and securely.

Inspect linkage to insure lockout tang is located properly to engage slot in secondary lockout lever and that linkage moves freely and does not bind.

3. Place carburetor on proper holding fixture such as J-9789-118 or equivalent.

4. Install fuel inlet filter spring, new filter assembly, new gasket and inlet nut and tighten nut to 18 ft. lbs.

When installing a service replacement filter, make sure the filter is the type that includes the check valve to meet U.S. Motor Vehicle Safety Standards (M.V.S.S.). When properly installed, hole in filter faces toward inlet nut. Ribs on closed end of filter element prevent filter from being installed incorrectly unless forced. Tightening beyond specified torque can damage nylon gasket and cause fuel leak.

5. Install choke housing on throttle body, making sure raised boss and locating lug on rear of housing fit into recesses in float bowl casting. Install choke housing attaching screws and lockwashers in throttle body and tighten screws evenly and securely.

6. Install intermediate choke shaft and lever assembly in float bowl by pushing through from throttle lever side.

7. With intermediate choke lever in the UP (12 o'clock) position, install thermostatic coil lever inside choke housing onto flats on intermediate choke shaft. Coil is properly aligned when the coil pick-up tang is at the top (12 o'clock) position. Install retaining screw into end of intermediate choke shaft and tighten securely.

8. Install pump discharge steel check ball and spring in passage next to float chamber. Insert end of new plastic retainer into end of spring and install retainer in float bowl, tapping lightly in place until top of retainer is flush with bowl casting surface.

9. Using a wide-blade screwdriver, install main metering jet and the float valve seat (with gasket) into bottom of float bowl. Tighten jet and seat securely.

10. To make adjustment easier, carefully bend float arm upward at notch in arm before assembly.

11. Install float valve onto float arm by sliding float lever under pull clip. Correct installation of the pull clip is to hook the clip over the edge of the float on the float arm.

12. Install float retaining pin into float arm with end of loop of pin facing pump well. Then,

install float assembly by aligning valve in the seat and float retaining pin into locating channels in float bowl.

13. Float Level Adjustment:

a. Hold float retaining pin firmly in place and push down lightly on float arm at outer end against top of float valve.

b. Using adjustable "T" scale, measure from top of float bowl casting surface (air horn gasket removed) to top of float at toe.

c. Bend float arm as necessary for proper adjustment by pushing on pontoon (see adjustment chart for specifications).

d. Visually check float alignment after adjustment.

14. Install power piston spring into piston bore.

15. If removed, assemble metering rod to holder on power piston. Spring must be on top of arm when assembled correctly.

16. Install power piston and metering rod assembly into the float bowl and main metering jet. Use care installing the metering rod into the jet to prevent damaging the metering rod tip. Press down firmly on plastic power piston retainer to make sure the retainer is seated in recess in bowl and the top is flush with the top of the bowl casting. If necessary, tap retainer lightly in place using a drift and small hammer.

17. Install plastic filler block over float valve, pressing downward until properly seated (flush with bowl casting surface).

18. Install air horn gasket on float bowl by carefully sliding slit portion of gasket over power piston, locating gasket over two dowel locating pins on bowl.

19. Install pump return spring in pump well.

20. Install pump plunger assembly in pump well.

AIR HORN ASSEMBLY

1. Install new pump plunger stem seal and retainer in air horn casting. Lightly stake seal retainer in three places, choosing locations different from the original stakings.

2. Install fast idle cam rod in lower hole of vacuum break and choke lever, aligning squirt on rod with small slot in lever (squirt end of rod points inward toward air horn).

AIR HORN TO BOWL INSTALLATION

1. Rotate fast idle cam to the full UP position and tilt the air horn assembly to engage lower end of fast idle cam rod in slot in fast idle cam and install pump rod end into hole in pump lever. Then, holding down on the pump plunger assembly, carefully lower air horn assembly onto float bowl, guiding pump plunger stem through hole in air horn casting. Do not force air horn

assembly onto bowl, but rather lightly lower in place.

2. Install vent and screen assembly over vent stack in air horn. Then, install air horn to bowl attaching screws and lockwashers—tighten evenly and securely.

3. Install new retainer clip through hole in end of pump rod.

4. Install new seal in recess of air horn, then install hot idle compensator valve and retain with small attaching screws. Tighten screws securely.

5. Install plastic bushing in upper hole in vacuum break and choke lever, making sure small end of bushing faces retaining clip when installed. With inner coil lever and intermediate choke lever at the 12 o'clock position, install intermediate choke rod in bushing. Retain rod with new clip, pressing clip securely in place with needlenose pliers. Make sure clip has full contact on rod but is not seated tightly against bushing. Rod to bushing clearance should be .8mm (.030 in.).

6. Install idle speed solenoid, lockwasher and retaining nut on secondary side vacuum break. Tighten nut securely. Then, bend back two (2) retaining tabs on lockwasher to fit slots in bracket.

7. Rotate secondary side vacuum break and bracket assembly and insert end ("T" pin) of vacuum break link into upper slot of vacuum break and choke lever. Install bracket on throttle body and install countersunk screws. Tighten screws securely.

8. If air valve rod has been removed from primary side vacuum break plunger, install plastic bushings in hole in primary side vacuum break plunger, making sure small end of bushing faces retaining clip when installed. Then, insert end of air valve rod through bushing. Retain with new clip, pressing clip in place using needlenose pliers. Make sure clip has full contact on rod but is not sealed tightly against the bushing. Rod to bushing clearance should be .8mm (.030 in.).

9. Rotate primary side vacuum break assembly and bracket and insert end of air valve rod into slot of air valve lever and end of "T" pin of vacuum break link into lower slot of vacuum break and choke lever. Position bracket over locating lug on air horn and install (2) countersunk screws and tighten securely.

10. Reinstall hose to primary side vacuum break assembly and throttle body tube.

11. Perform choke coil lever adjustment procedure as specified in carburetor adjustment section.

12. Install the choke cover and coil assembly in the choke housing, aligning notch in cover with raised casting projection on housing cover

flange. Make sure choke coil lever is located inside the "trapped stat" coil tang when installing the choke cover and coil assembly.

Ground contact for the electric choke is provided by a metal plate located at the rear of the choke cover assembly. Do not install a choke cover gasket between the electric choke assembly and the choke housing.

A choke cover retainer kit is required to attach choke cover to choke housing. Install proper retainers and rivets contained in kit, using a suitable blind rivet installing tool.

OVERHAUL—2000cc ENGINE AND 2800cc ENGINE E2SE CARBURETOR

Disassembly

SECONDARY VACUUM BREAK REMOVAL

1. Remove secondary vacuum break and bracket assembly attaching screws from throttle body. Then, rotate assembly to disengage vacuum break link ("T Pin") from choke lever slot.

NOTE: *Do not immerse the idle speed solenoid or vacuum break units in any type of carburetor cleaner. These items must always be removed before complete cleaning or damage to components will result.*

AIR HORN REMOVAL

1. Remove clip from hole in pump rod.

NOTE: *Do not remove pump lever retaining screw or pump lever from air horn assembly.*

2. Remove and discard retaining clip from intermediate choke link at choke lever. A new retaining clip is required for reassembly. Remove choke link and plastic bushing from choke lever and save the bushing for later reuse.

3. Remove three mixture control solenoid screws in air horn; then, using a slight twisting motion, carefully lift solenoid out of air horn. Remove and discard solenoid gasket.

4. Remove seal retainer and rubber seal from end of solenoid stem, being careful not to damage or nick end of solenoid stem. Discard seal and retainer. Retain spacer for use at time of reassembly.

5. Remove the seven air horns to bowl attaching screws and lockwashers.

6. Rotate fast idle cam to the full UP position and remove air horn assembly by tilting to disengage fast idle cam rod from slot in fast idle cam and pump rod from hole in pump lever. If pump plunger comes out of float bowl with air horn removal, remove pump plunger from air horn. The air horn gasket should remain on the float bowl for removal later. Do not remove fast idle cam screw and cam from float bowl. These parts are not serviced separately and are to re-

main permanently in place as installed by the factory. The new service replacement float bowl will include the secondary lockout lever, fast idle cam and screw installed as required.

7. Remove fast idle cam link from choke lever by rotating rod to align upset on link with small slot in lever.

AIR HORN DISASSEMBLY

1. Remove Throttle Position Sensor (T.P.S.) plunger by pushing it downward through seal in air horn.

NOTE: *Use fingers only to remove plunger*

to prevent damage to sealing surface of plunger.

2. Remove T.P.S. seal by inverting air horn and use a small screwdriver to remove staking holding seal retainer in place. Remove and discard retainer and seal.

3. Remove pump plunger stem seal by inverting air horn and use a small screwdriver to remove staking holding the seal retainer in place. remove and discard retainer and seal.

NOTE: *Use care in removing the T.P.S. plunger seal retainer and pump plunger stem seal retainer to prevent damage to air horn*

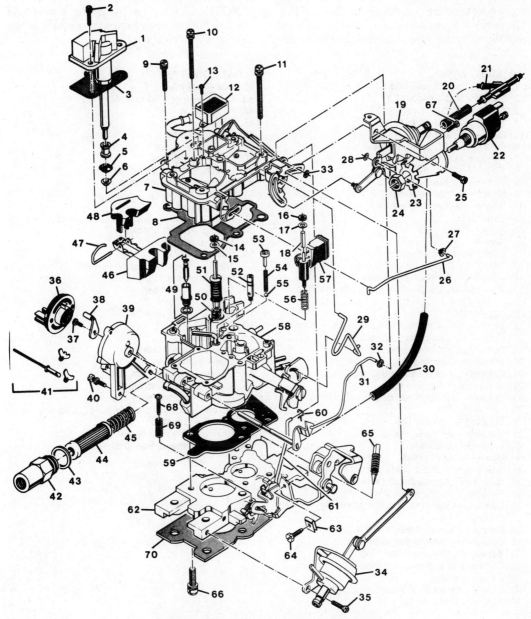

4-2000, 6-2800 E2SE carburetor, exploded view

casting. New seals and retainers are required for reassembly.

4. Remove the vent/screen assembly by removing the two small attaching screws.

5. Further disassembly of the air horn is not required for cleaning purposes or air horn replacement. A new service air horn assembly includes the secondary metering rod-air valve assembly with adjustments pre-set to factory specifications. No attempt should be made to change air valve settings. The air valve and choke valve attaching screws are staked in place and are not removable. A new service air horn assembly will also include a T.P.S. adjustment screw (refer to "on Vehicle Service," section or proper adjustment procedure for the T.P.S.). The new service air horn assembly will also have the thermostatic pump bypass assembly in-

stalled, this temperature sensitive device is pressed permanently in place and is not serviceable separately.

FLOAT BOWL DISASSEMBLY

1. Remove air horn gasket.

2. Remove pump plunger from pump well (if not removed with air horn).

3. Remove pump return spring from pump well.

4. Push up from bottom on electrical connector and remove Throttle Position Sensor (T.P.S.) and Connector Assembly from float bowl. Remove spring from bottom of T.P.S. well in bowl.

NOTE: *Use care in removing sensor and connector assembly to prevent damage to this critical electrical part.*

AIR HORN PARTS
 1. Mixture control solenoid
 2. Screw—M/C solenoid (3)
 3. Gasket—M/C solenoid
 4. Spacer—M/C solenoid
 5. Seal—M/C solenoid
 6. Retainer—M/C solenoid seal
 7. Air horn assembly
 8. Gasket—air horn
 9. Screw—air horn—short (2)
10. Screw—air horn—long (3)
11. Screw—air horn—large
12. Vent stack
13. Screw—vent stack (2)
14. Seal—pump plunger
15. Retainer—pump plunger seal
16. Seal—T.P.S. plunger
17. Retainer—T.P.S. plunger seal
18. Plunger—T.P.S. (throttle position sensor)

CHOKE PARTS
19. Vacuum break and bracket assembly—primary
20. Hose—vacuum break connection
21. Tee—vacuum break connecting
22. Solenoid—idle speed
23. Retainer—idle speed solenoid
24. Nut—idle speed solenoid
25. Screw—vacuum break bracket attaching
26. Link—air valve
27. Bushing—air valve link
28. Retainer—air valve link
29. Link—fast idle cam
30. Hose—vacuum break
31. Intermediate choke shaft/lever/link assembly
32. Bushing—intermediate choke link
33. Retainer—intermediate choke link
34. Vacuum break and bracket assembly—secondary
35. Screw—vacuum break attaching (2)
36. Choke—cover and coil assembly
37. Screw—choke lever attaching
38. Choke lever and contract assembly
39. Choke housing
40. Screw—choke housing attaching (2)
41. Stat cover retainer kit

FLOAT BOWL PARTS
42. Nut—fuel inlet
43. Gasket—fuel inlet nut
44. Filter—fule inlet
45. Spring—fuel filter
46. Float assembly
47. Hinge pin—float
48. Insert—float bowl
49. Needle and seat assembly
50. Spring—pump return
51. Pump—assembly
52. Metering jet
53. Retainer—pump spring and check ball
54. Spring—pump check ball
55. Ball—pump check
56. Spring—T.P.S.
57. T.P.S.—(throttle position sensor)
58. Float bowl assembly
59. Gasket—float bowl

THROTTLE BODY PARTS
60. Clip—pump rod
61. Pump rod
62. Throttle body assembly
63. Clip—cam screw
64. Screw—fast idle cam
65. Idle needle and spring
66. Screw—throttle body attaching
67. Screw—vacuum break bracket attaching (new)
68. Screw—idle stop
69. Spring—idle stop screw
70. Gasket—intake manifold

4-2000, 6-2800 E2SE carburetor, exploded view

5. Remove plastic filler block over float valve.

6. Remove float assembly and float valve by pulling up hinge pin (hold float valve clip in place with a finger while tilting float to clear bowl vapor purge tube).

7. Using a removal tool or a wide-blade screwdriver remove the float valve seat (with gasket) and the extended metering jet from the float bowl.

NOTE: *Do not remove or change adjustment of the small calibration screw located deep inside the metering jet during routine servicing. The adjustment screw is pre-set at the factory and no attempt should be made to change this adjustment in the field except as the result of a Computer Command Control system performance check.*

8. Using small slidehammer or equivalent, remove plastic retainer holding pump discharge spring and check ball in place. Discard plastic retainer (a new retainer is required for reassembly).

NOTE: *Do not attempt to remove plastic retainer by prying out with a tool such as a punch or screwdriver as this will damage the sealing beads on the bowl casting surface and require complete float bowl replacement.*

Turn bowl upside down catching pump discharge spring and check ball in palm of hand. Return bowl to upright position.

9. Remove fuel inlet nut, gasket, check valve filter assembly, and spring.

CHOKE DISASSEMBLY

A tamper resistant choke cover design is used to discourage readjustment of the choke thermostatic coil assembly in the field. However, it is necessary to remove the cover and coil assembly during normal carburetor disassembly for cleaning and overhaul using procedures as follows:

1. Support float bowl and throttle body as an assembly on a suitable holding fixture.

2. Carefully align a No. 21 drill (.159 in.) on rivet head and drill only enough to remove rivet head. After removing rivet heads and retainers, use a drift and a small hammer to drive the remainder of the rivets out of the choke housing.

NOTE: *Use care in drilling to prevent damage to choke cover or housing.*

3. Remove screw from end of intermediate choke shaft inside choke housing.

4. Remove choke coil lever from end of shaft.

5. Remove intermediate choke shaft assembly from float bowl by sliding shaft rearward and out throttle lever side.

6. Remove choke housing by removing two attaching screws.

THROTTLE BODY REMOVAL

1. Remove four throttle body to bowl attaching screws and remove throttle body assembly from float bowl.

2. Remove throttle body gasket.

THROTTLE BODY DISASSEMBLY

1. Place throttle body assembly on carburetor holding fixture to avoid damaging throttle valves.

2. Hold primary throttle lever wide-open and disengage pump rod from throttle lever by rotating rod until upset on rod aligns with slot in lever.

Further disassembly of the throttle body is not required for cleaning purposes.

NOTE: *The primary and secondary throttle valve screws are permanently staked in place and should not be removed. The throttle body is serviced as a complete assembly.*

3. DO NOT remove plugs covering idle mixture needle unless it is necessary to replace the mixture needle or normal soakings and air pressure fails to clean the idle mixture passages. If necessary, remove idle mixture plug and needle as follows:

a. Invert throttle body and place on suitable holding fixture—manifold side up.

b. Make two parallel cuts in throttle body on either side of the locator point beneath the idle mixture needle plug (manifold side) with a hacksaw. The cuts should reach down to the steel plug, but should not extend more than $\frac{1}{8}$ in. beyond the locator point. The distance between the saw marks depends on the size of the punch to be used.

c. Place a flat punch at a point near the ends of the saw marks in the throttle body. Holding the punch at a 45 degree angle, drive it into the throttle body until the casting breaks away, exposing the steel plug.

d. Holding a center punch vertical, drive it into the steel plug. Then holding the punch at a 45 degree angle, drive the plug out of the casting.

NOTE: *Hardened plug will break rather than remaining intact. It is not necessary to remove the plug whole: instead, remove loose pieces to allow use of idle mixture adjusting Tool J-29030 or BT-7610B.*

4. Using Tool J29030 or BT-7610B, remove idle mixture needle and spring from throttle body.

Cleaning and Inspection

The carburetor parts should be cleaned in a cold immersion-type cleaner such as Carbon X (X-55) or its equivalent.

NOTE: *The idle speed solenoid, mixture*

control solenoid, throttle position sensor, electric choke, rubber parts, plastic parts, diaphragms, pump plunger, plastic filler block, should NOT be immersed in carburetor cleaner as they will harden, swell, or distort.

The plastic bushing in the throttle lever will withstand normal cleaning in carburetor cleaner.

1. Thoroughly clean all metal parts and blow dry with shop air. Make sure all fuel passages and metering parts are free of burrs and dirt. Do not pass drills or wires through jets and passages.

2. Inspect upper and lower surface of carburetor castings for damage.

3. Inspect holes in levers for excessive wear or out of round conditions. If worn, levers should be replaced. Inspect plastic bushings in levers for damage and excessive wear. Replace as required.

4. Check, repair, or replace parts if the following problems are encountered:

A. FLOODING

1. Inspect float valve and seat for dirt, deep wear grooves, scores and improper sealing.

2. Inspect float valve pull clip for proper installation. Be careful not to bend pull clip.

3. Inspect float, float arms and hinge pin for distortion, binds, and burrs. Check density of material in the float; if heavier than normal, replace float.

4. Clean or replace fuel inlet filter and check valve assembly.

B. HESITATION

1. Inspect pump plunger for cracks, scores, or cup excessive wear. A used pump cup will shrink when dry. If dried out, soak in fuel for 8 hours before testing.

2. Inspect pump duration and return springs for weakness or distortion.

3. Check pump passages and jet(s) for dirt, improper seating of discharge checkball, or temperature bypass disc and scores in pump well. Check condition of pump discharge check ball spring. replace as necessary.

4. Check pump linkage for excessive wear; repair or replace as necessary.

C. HARD STARTING—POOR COLD OPERATION

1. Check choke valve and linkage for excessive wear, binds or distortion.

2. Test vacuum break diaphragm(s) for leaks.

3. Clean or replace fuel filter.

4. Inspect float valve for sticking, dirt, etc.

5. Also check items under "Flooding."

D. POOR PERFORMANCE—POOR GAS MILEAGE

1. Clean all fuel and vacuum passages in castings.

2. Check choke valve for freedom of movement.

3. Check Mixture Control Solenoid for sticking, binding, or leaking as follows:

   a. Connect one end of a jumper wire to either terminal of the solenoid connector and the other end to the positive (+) terminal of a 12-volt battery source.

   b. Connect a jumper wire to the other terminal of the solenoid connector and the other end to a known good ground.

   c. With rubber seal, retainer and spacer removed from the end of the solenoid stem, attach a hose from a hand vacuum pump.

   d. With the solenoid fully energized (lean position), apply 25 in. Hg of vacuum and time the leak-down rate from 20 in. Hg to 15 in. Hg. Leak-down rate should not exceed 5 in. Hg in 5 seconds. If leakage exceeds that amount, replace solenoid.

   e. To check solenoid for sticking in the down position. remove jumper lead to 12-volt source and observe hand vacuum pump reading. Reading should go to zero in less than one second.

4. Inspect metering jet for dirt, loose parts, or damage.

NOTE: *DO NOT attempt to readjust the mixture screw located inside the metering jet. The screw is factory adjusted and a change can upset fuel system calibration. NO ATTEMPT should be made to change this adjustment in the field except as the result of a Computer Command Control system performance check.*

5. Check air valve and secondary metering rod for binding conditions. If air valve or metering rod is damaged or metering rod adjustment is changed from the factory setting, the air horn assembly must be replaced. Also check air valve lever spring for proper installation (tension against air valve shaft pin).

E. ROUGH IDLE

1. Inspect gasket and gasket mating surfaces on castings for nicks, burrs or damage to sealing beads.

2. Check operation and sealing of mixture control solenoid.

3. Clean all idle fuel passages.

4. If removed, inspect idle mixture needle for ridges, burrs, or being bent.

5. Check throttle lever and valves for binds, nicks or other damage.

6. Check all diaphragms for possible ruptures or leaks.

Assembly

THROTTLE BODY ASSEMBLY

1. Holding primary throttle lever wide open, install lower end of pump rod in throttle lever

by aligning squirt on rod with slot in lever. End of rod should point outward toward throttle lever.

2. If removed, install idle mixture needle and spring using Tool J-29030 or equivalent. Lightly seat needle and then back out three turns as a preliminary idle mixture adjustment. Final idle mixture adjustment must be made on-car. Refer to "On-Vehicle Service" section for idle mixture adjustment procedures.

FLOAT BOWL ASSEMBLY

NOTE: *If a new float bowl assembly is used, stamp or engrave the model number on the new float bowl.*

1. Install new throttle to bowl gasket over two locating dowels on bowl.

2. Rotate fast idle cam so that steps face fast idle screw on throttle lever when properly installed, install throttle body making certain throttle body is properly located over dowels on float bowl; then install four throttle body to bowl screws and lockwashers and tighten evenly and securely.

Inspect linkage to insure lockout tang is located properly to engage slot in secondary lockout lever and that linkage moves freely and does not bind.

3. Place carburetor on suitable holding fixture.

4. Install fuel inlet filter spring, filter assembly, new gasket and inlet nut and tighten nut to 18 ft. lbs.

When installing a service replacement filter, make sure the filter is the type that includes the check valve to meet U.S. Motor Vehicle Safety Standards (M.V.S.S.).

When properly installed, hole (check valve end) in filter faces toward inlet nut.

NOTE: *Tightening beyond specified torque can damage nylon gasket to cause fuel leak.*

5. Install choke housing on throttle body, making sure raised boss and locating lug on rear of housing fit into recesses in float bowl casting. Install choke housing attaching screws and lockwashers and tighten screws evenly and securely.

6. Install intermediate choke shaft assembly in float bowl by pushing shaft through from throttle lever side.

7. With intermediate choke lever in the UP (12 o'clock) position, install choke coil lever inside choke housing onto flats on intermediate choke shaft. Choke coil lever is properly aligned when the coil pick-up tang is in the UP position. Install choke coil lever retaining screw into end of intermediate choke shaft and tighten securely.

8. Install pump discharge check ball, spring and new plastic retainer in float bowl. Tap lightly

in place until top of retainer is flush with bowl casting surface.

9. Using a wide-blade screwdriver install the float valve seat (with gasket) and the metering jet. Tighten securely.

10. To make adjustment easier, carefully bend float arm upward at notch in arm before assembly.

11. Install float valve onto float arm by sliding float lever under pull clip. Correct installation of the pull clip is to hook the clip over the edge of the float on the float arm facing the float pontoon.

12. Install float hinge pin into float arm with end of loop of pin facing pump well. Then, install float assembly by aligning valve in the seat and float hinge pin into locating channels in float bowl.

13. Float Level Adjustment.

   a. Hold float hinge pin firmly in place and push down lightly on arm at outer end against top of float valve.

   b. Using adjustment "T" scale, measure from top of float bowl casting surface (air horn gasket removed) to top of float at toe.

   c. Bend float arm as necessary for proper adjustment by pushing on pontoon (see Adjustment Chart for specifications).

   d. Visually check float alignment after adjustment.

14. Install plastic filler block over float valve pressing downward until properly seated (flush with bowl casting surface).

15. Install Throttle Position Sensor return spring in bottom of well in float bowl.

16. Install throttle position sensor (T.P.S.) and connector assembly in float bowl by aligning groove in electrical connector with "V" in float bowl casting, push down on connector and sensor assembly so that connector wires and sensor are located below the bowl casting surface.

NOTE: *Care must be taken when installing throttle position sensor to assure that electrical integrity is maintained. Make sure that the wires between connector and sensor assembly are not pinched or insulation broken upon final assembly. Accidental electrical grounding of the T.P.S. must be avoided.*

17. Install air horn gasket on float bowl, locating gasket over two dowel locating pins on bowl.

18. Install pump return spring in pump well.

19. Install pump plunger assembly in pump well.

AIR HORN ASSEMBLY

1. Install new pump plunger stem seal and retainer in air horn casting. Lightly stake seal retainer in three places, choosing locations different from the original stakings.

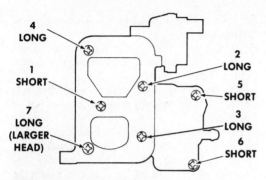

2SE or E2SE air horn tightening sequence

2. Install new Throttle Position Sensor actuator plunger seal and retainer in air horn casting. Lightly stake seal retainer in three places, choosing locations different from the original stakings.

3. Install vent/screen assembly by installing the two small attaching screws. Tighten securely.

4. Inspect the air valve shaft pin for lubrication, apply a liberal quantity of lithium base grease to the air valve shaft pin. Make sure to lubricate pin surface contacted by windup spring.

5. Install fast idle cam rod in lower hole of choke lever, aligning squirt on rod with small slot in lever.

6. Install T.P.S. plunger through seal in air horn until about one half of the plunger extends above the surface of the air horn casting. Seal pressure should hold plunger in place during air horn installation on float bowl.

AIR HORN TO BOWL INSTALLATION

1. Rotate fast idle cam to the full up position and tilt the air horn assembly to engage lower end of fast idle cam rod in slot in fast idle cam and install pump rod end into hole in pump lever; check intermediate choke rod for position then, holding down on the pump plunger assembly, carefully lower air horn assembly onto float bowl, guiding pump plunger stem through seal in air horn casting.

Do not force air horn assembly onto bowl, but rather lightly lower in place. Make sure T.P.S. actuator plunger engages sensor plunger in bowl by checking plunger movement.

2. Install air horn to bowl attaching screws and lockwashers, tighten evenly and securely.

3. Install new retainer clip through hole in end of pump rod extending through pump lever, making sure clip is securely locked in place.

4. If not tested previously, test mixture control solenoid for sticking, binding, or leaking following steps noted in cleaning and inspection procedure. Then, install spacer and new rubber seal on mixture control solenoid

stem making sure seal is up against the spacer. Then using a 3/16 in. socket and light hammer, carefully drive a new retainer on stem. Drive retainer on stem only far enough to retain rubber seal on stem leaving a slight clearance between the retainer and seal to allow for seal expansion.

5. Prior to installing the mixture control solenoid, lightly coat the rubber seal on the end of the solenoid stem with a silicone grease or light engine oil. Using a new mounting gasket, install mixture control solenoid on air horn, carefully aligning soleniod stem with recess in bottom of bowl. Use a slight twisting motion of the solenoid during installation to ensure rubber seal on stem is guided into recess in the bottom of the bowl to prevent distortion or damage to the rubber seal. Install solenoid attaching screws and tighten securely.

6. Install plastic bushing in hole in choke lever, making sure small end of bushing faces retaining clip when installed.

With inner coil lever and intermediate choke lever at the 12 o'clock position, install intermediate choke rod in bushing. Retain rod with new clip, pressing clip securely in place with needlenose pliers. Make sure clip has full contact on rod, but is not seated tightly against bushing. Rod to bushing clearance should be .88mm (.030 in.).

7. Install secondary vacuum break assembly. Rotate assembly and insert end ("T" Pin) of vacuum break link into upper slot of choke lever. Attach bracket to throttle body with countersunk screws. Tighten screws securely.

8. If air valve rod has been removed from primary side vacuum break plunger, install plastic bushing in hole in primary side vacuum break plunger, making sure small end of bushing faces retaining clip when installed. Then insert end of air valve rod through bushing. Retain with new clip, pressing clip in place using needlenose pliers. Make sure clip has full contact on rod, but is not seated tightly against the bushing. Rod to bushing clearance should be 8mm (.030 in.).

9. Rotate primary side vacuum break assembly (with idle speed solenoid and bracket), insert end of air valve rod into slot of air valve lever and end ("T" Pin) of vacuum break link into lower slot of choke lever. Connect primary vacuum break hose to tube on throttle body and tube on vacuum break unit. Position bracket over locating lug on air horn and install two countersunk screws in air horn and screw with lockwasher in throttle body. Tighten screws securely.

10. Carry out choke coil lever adjustment procedure as specified in carburetor adjustment section.

11. Install the choke cover and coil assembly in the choke housing, aligning notch in cover with raised casting projection on housing cover flange. Make sure coil pick-up tang engages the inside choke coil lever.

The tang on the thermostatic coil is the "trapped stat" design. This means that the coil tang is formed so that it will completely encircle the coil pick-up lever. Make sure the coil pick-up lever is located inside the coil tang when installing the choke cover and coil assembly.

NOTE: *Ground contact for the electric choke is provided by a metal plate located at the rear of the choke cover assembly. Do not install a choke cover gasket between the electric choke assembly and the choke housing. A choke cover retainer kit is required to attach choke cover to choke housing. Install proper retainers and rivets contained in kit, using suitable blind rivet installing tool.*

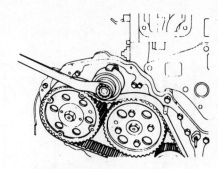

Loosening tension pulley

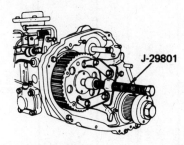

J-29801

Removing timing pulley

DIESEL ENGINE FUEL SYSTEM

CAUTION: *The following procedure should not be attempted unless all tools necessary to adjust the injection pump timing are available.*

Injection Pump

REMOVAL

1. Raise engine hood.
2. Disconnect the battery ground cable.
3. Remove the battery.
4. Remove the under cover.
5. Drain the cooling system by opening the drain plugs on the radiator and on the cylinder block.
6. Disconnect the upper water hose at the engine side.
7. Loosen the compressor drive belt by moving the power steering oil pump or idler. (If so equipped.)
8. Remove the cooling fan and fan shroud.
9. Disconnect the lower water hose at the engine side.
10. Remove the air conditioner compressor. (If so equipped.)
11. Remove the fan belt.
12. Remove the crankshaft pulley.
13. Remove the timing pulley housing covers.
14. Remove the tension spring and fixing bolt, then remove the tension center and pulley.
15. Remove the timing belt.
16. Remove the engine control cable and wiring harness of the fuel cut solenoid.
17. Remove the fuel hoses and injection

pipes. Use a wrench to hold the delivery holder when loosening the sleeve nuts on the injection pump side.

18. Install a 6 mm bolt (with pitch of 1.25) into threaded hole in the timing pulley housing through the hole in pulley to prevent turning of the pulley.

Remove the bolts fixing the injection pump timing pulley, then remove the pulley using pulley puller.

19. Remove injection pump flange fixing nuts and rear bracket bolts, then remove the injection pump.

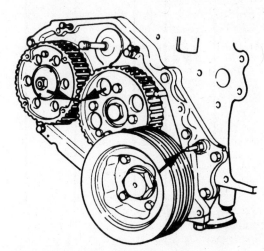

Correct timing mark alignment at TDC

Carburetor Specifications

Type DCH340 4-1950cc Engine

Primary Throttle Plate Gap (in.)	Primary Main Jet Number	Secondary Main Jet Number	Primary Slow Jet Number	Secondary Slow Jet Number	Power Jet Number	Primary Main Air Bleed Number	Secondary Main Air Bleed Number	Slow Air Bleed Number
.050–.059 (MT) .059–.069 (AT)	114 Fed. 85 Cal.	170	50 Fed. 54 Cal.	100	50	120 Fed. 110 Cal.	70 Fed. 90 Cal.	150 Fed. 130 Cal.

Type 2SE 4-2000 6-2800 exc. Cal.

Carb. Number	Float Level (in.)	Fast Idle Cam (deg.)	Primary Vacuum Break (deg.)	Air Valve Rod (deg.)	Secondary Vacuum Break (deg.)	Choke Unloader (deg.)
17082348	$7/16$	22	26	1	32	40
17082349	$7/16$	22	28	1	32	40
17082350	$7/16$	22	26	1	32	40
17082351	$7/16$	22	28	1	32	40
17082353	$7/16$	22	28	1	35	30
17082355	$7/16$	22	28	1	35	30
17083348	$7/16$	22	30	1	32	40
17083349	$7/16$	22	30	1	32	40
17083350	$7/16$	22	30	1	32	40
17083351	$7/16$	22	30	1	32	40
17083352	$7/16$	22	30	1	35	40
17083353	$7/16$	22	30	1	35	40
17083354	$7/16$	22	30	1	35	40
17083355	$7/16$	22	30	1	35	40
17083360	$7/16$	22	30	1	32	40

17083361	7/16	22	28	1	32	40
17083362	7/16	22	30	1	32	40
17083363	7/16	22	28	1	32	40
17083364	7/16	22	30	1	35	40
17083365	7/16	22	30	1	35	40
17083366	7/16	22	30	1	35	40
17083367	7/16	22	30	1	35	40
17083390	13/32	28	30	1	35	38
17083391	13/32	28	30	1	35	38
17083392	13/32	28	30	1	35	38
17083393	13/32	28	30	1	35	38
17083394	13/32	28	30	1	35	38
17083395	13/32	28	30	1	35	38
17083396	13/32	28	30	1	35	38
17083397	13/32	28	30	1	35	38
17084410	11/32	15	23	1	38	42
17084412	11/32	15	23	1	38	42
17084425	11/32	15	26	1	36	40
17084427	11/32	15	26	1	36	40
17084560	11/32	15	24	1	34	38
17084562	11/32	15	24	1	34	38
17084569	11/32	15	24	1	34	38

Type E2SE 6-2800 Cal.

Carb. Number	Float Level (in.)	Fast Idle Cam (deg.)	Primary Vacuum Break (deg.)	Air Valve Rod (deg.)	Secondary Vacuum Break (deg.)	Choke Unloader (deg.)
17082356	13/32	22	25	1	30	30
17082357	13/32	22	25	1	32	30
17082358	13/32	22	25	1	30	30
17082359	13/32	22	25	1	32	30
17072683	9/32	28	25	1	35	45
17074812	9/32	28	25	1	35	45
17084356	9/32	22	25	1	30	30
17084357	9/32	22	25	1	30	30
17084358	9/32	22	25	1	30	30
17084359	9/32	22	25	1	30	30
17084368	1/8	22	25	1	30	30
17084370	1/8	22	25	1	30	30
17084430	11/32	15	26	1	38	42
17084431	11/32	15	26	1	38	42

CHILTON'S
FUEL ECONOMY
& TUNE-UP TIPS

Tune-up • Spark Plug Diagnosis • Emission Controls

Fuel System • Cooling System • Tires and Wheels

General Maintenance

CHILTON'S FUEL ECONOMY & TUNE-UP TIPS

Fuel economy is important to everyone, no matter what kind of vehicle you drive. The maintenance-minded motorist can save both money and fuel using these tips and the periodic maintenance and tune-up procedures in this Repair and Tune-Up Guide.

There are more than 130,000,000 cars and trucks registered for private use in the United States. Each travels an average of 10-12,000 miles per year, and, and in total they consume close to 70 billion gallons of fuel each year. This represents nearly ⅔ of the oil imported by the United States each year. The Federal government's goal is to reduce consumption 10% by 1985. A variety of methods are either already in use or under serious consideration, and they all affect you driving and the cars you will drive. In addition to "down-sizing", the auto industry is using or investigating the use of electronic fuel delivery, electronic engine controls and alternative engines for use in smaller and lighter vehicles, among other alternatives to meet the federally mandated Corporate Average Fuel Economy (CAFE) of 27.5 mpg by 1985. The government, for its part, is considering rationing, mandatory driving curtailments and tax increases on motor vehicle fuel in an effort to reduce consumption. The government's goal of a 10% reduction could be realized — and further government regulation avoided — if every private vehicle could use just 1 less gallon of fuel per week.

How Much Can You Save?

Tests have proven that almost anyone can make at least a 10% reduction in fuel consumption through regular maintenance and tune-ups. When a major manufacturer of spark plugs sur-

TUNE-UP

1. Check the cylinder compression to be sure the engine will really benefit from a tune-up and that it is capable of producing good fuel economy. A tune-up will be wasted on an engine in poor mechanical condition.

2. Replace spark plugs regularly. New spark plugs alone can increase fuel economy 3%.

3. Be sure the spark plugs are the correct type (heat range) for your vehicle. See the Tune-Up Specifications.

Heat range refers to the spark plug's ability to conduct heat away from the firing end. It must conduct the heat away in an even pattern to avoid becoming a source of pre-ignition, yet it must also operate hot enough to burn off conductive deposits that could cause misfiring.

The heat range is usually indicated by a number on the spark plug, part of the manufacturer's designation for each individual spark plug. The numbers in bold-face indicate the heat range in each manufacturer's identification system.

Manufacturer	Typical Designation
AC	R **45** TS
Bosch (old)	WA **145** T30
Bosch (new)	HR **8** Y
Champion	RBL **15** Y
Fram/Autolite	**415**
Mopar	P-**62** PR
Motorcraft	BRF-**42**
NGK	BP **5** ES-15
Nippondenso	W **16** EP
Prestolite	14GR **5** 2A

Periodically, check the spark plugs to be sure they are firing efficiently. They are excellent indicators of the internal condition of your engine.

On AC, Bosch (new), Champion, Fram/Autolite, Mopar, Motorcraft and Prestolite, a higher number indicates a hotter plug. On Bosch (old), NGK and Nippondenso, a higher number indicates a colder plug.

4. Make sure the spark plugs are properly gapped. See the Tune-Up Specifications in this book.

5. Be sure the spark plugs are firing efficiently. The illustrations on the next 2 pages show you how to "read" the firing end of the spark plug.

6. Check the ignition timing and set it to specifications. Tests show that almost all cars have incorrect ignition timing by more than 2°.

veyed over 6,000 cars nationwide, they found that a tune-up, on cars that needed one, increased fuel economy over 11%. Replacing worn plugs alone, accounted for a 3% increase. The same test also revealed that 8 out of every 10 vehicles will have some maintenance deficiency that will directly affect fuel economy, emissions or performance. Most of this mileage-robbing neglect could be prevented with regular maintenance.

Modern engines require that all of the functioning systems operate properly for maximum efficiency. A malfunction anywhere wastes fuel. You can keep your vehicle running as efficiently and economically as possible, by being aware of your vehicle's operating and performance characteristics. If your vehicle suddenly develops performance or fuel economy problems it could be due to one or more of the following:

PROBLEM	POSSIBLE CAUSE
Engine Idles Rough	Ignition timing, idle mixture, vacuum leak or something amiss in the emission control system.
Hesitates on Acceleration	Dirty carburetor or fuel filter, improper accelerator pump setting, ignition timing or fouled spark plugs.
Starts Hard or Fails to Start	Worn spark plugs, improperly set automatic choke, ice (or water) in fuel system.
Stalls Frequently	Automatic choke improperly adjusted and possible dirty air filter or fuel filter.
Performs Sluggishly	Worn spark plugs, dirty fuel or air filter, ignition timing or automatic choke out of adjustment.

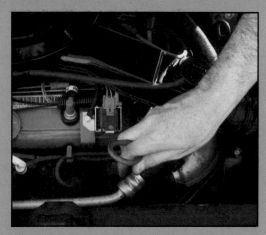

Check spark plug wires on conventional point type ignition for cracks by bending them in a loop around your finger.

Be sure that spark plug wires leading to adjacent cylinders do not run too close together. (Photo courtesy Champion Spark Plug Co.)

7. If your vehicle does not have electronic ignition, check the points, rotor and cap as specified.

8. Check the spark plug wires (used with conventional point-type ignitions) for cracks and burned or broken insulation by bending them in a loop around your finger. Cracked wires decrease fuel efficiency by failing to deliver full voltage to the spark plugs. One misfiring spark plug can cost you as much as 2 mpg.

9. Check the routing of the plug wires. Misfiring can be the result of spark plug leads to adjacent cylinders running parallel to each other and too close together. One wire tends to

pick up voltage from the other causing it to fire "out of time".

10. Check all electrical and ignition circuits for voltage drop and resistance.

11. Check the distributor mechanical and/or vacuum advance mechanisms for proper functioning. The vacuum advance can be checked by twisting the distributor plate in the opposite direction of rotation. It should spring back when released.

12. Check and adjust the valve clearance on engines with mechanical lifters. The clearance should be slightly loose rather than too tight.

SPARK PLUG DIAGNOSIS

Normal

APPEARANCE: This plug is typical of one operating normally. The insulator nose varies from a light tan to grayish color with slight electrode wear. The presence of slight deposits is normal on used plugs and will have no adverse effect on engine performance. The spark plug heat range is correct for the engine and the engine is running normally.

CAUSE: Properly running engine.

RECOMMENDATION: Before reinstalling this plug, the electrodes should be cleaned and filed square. Set the gap to specifications. If the plug has been in service for more than 10-12,000 miles, the entire set should probably be replaced with a fresh set of the same heat range.

Oil Deposits

APPEARANCE: The firing end of the plug is covered with a wet, oily coating.

CAUSE: The problem is poor oil control. On high mileage engines, oil is leaking past the rings or valve guides into the combustion chamber. A common cause is also a plugged PCV valve, and a ruptured fuel pump diaphragm can also cause this condition. Oil fouled plugs such as these are often found in new or recently overhauled engines, before normal oil control is achieved, and can be cleaned and reinstalled.

RECOMMENDATION: A hotter spark plug may temporarily relieve the problem, but the engine is probably in need of work.

Incorrect Heat Range

APPEARANCE: The effects of high temperature on a spark plug are indicated by clean white, often blistered insulator. This can also be accompanied by excessive wear of the electrode, and the absence of deposits.

CAUSE: Check for the correct spark plug heat range. A plug which is too hot for the engine can result in overheating. A car operated mostly at high speeds can require a colder plug. Also check ignition timing, cooling system level, fuel mixture and leaking intake manifold.

RECOMMENDATION: If all ignition and engine adjustments are known to be correct, and no other malfunction exists, install spark plugs one heat range colder.

Photos Courtesy Fram Corporation

Carbon Deposits

APPEARANCE: Carbon fouling is easily identified by the presence of dry, soft, black, sooty deposits.

CAUSE: Changing the heat range can often lead to carbon fouling, as can prolonged slow, stop-and-start driving. If the heat range is correct, carbon fouling can be attributed to a rich fuel mixture, sticking choke, clogged air cleaner, worn breaker points, retarded timing or low compression. If only one or two plugs are carbon fouled, check for corroded or cracked wires on the affected plugs. Also look for cracks in the distributor cap between the towers of affected cylinders.

RECOMMENDATION: After the problem is corrected, these plugs can be cleaned and reinstalled if not worn severely.

MMT Fouled

APPEARANCE: Spark plugs fouled by MMT (Methycyclopentadienyl Maganese Tricarbonyl) have reddish, rusty appearance on the insulator and side electrode.

CAUSE: MMT is an anti-knock additive in gasoline used to replace lead. During the combustion process, the MMT leaves a reddish deposit on the insulator and side electrode.

RECOMMENDATION: No engine malfunction is indicated and the deposits will not affect plug performance any more than lead deposits (see Ash Deposits). MMT fouled plugs can be cleaned, regapped and reinstalled.

High Speed Glazing

APPEARANCE: Glazing appears as shiny coating on the plug, either yellow or tan in color.

CAUSE: During hard, fast acceleration, plug temperatures rise suddenly. Deposits from normal combustion have no chance to fluff-off; instead, they melt on the insulator forming an electrically conductive coating which causes misfiring.

RECOMMENDATION: Glazed plugs are not easily cleaned. They should be replaced with a fresh set of plugs of the correct heat range. If the condition recurs, using plugs with a heat range one step colder may cure the problem.

Ash (Lead) Deposits

APPEARANCE: Ash deposits are characterized by light brown or white colored deposits crusted on the side or center electrodes. In some cases it may give the plug a rusty appearance.

CAUSE: Ash deposits are normally derived from oil or fuel additives burned during normal combustion. Normally they are harmless, though excessive amounts can cause misfiring. If deposits are excessive in short mileage, the valve guides may be worn.

RECOMMENDATION: Ash-fouled plugs can be cleaned, gapped and reinstalled.

Detonation

APPEARANCE: Detonation is usually characterized by a broken plug insulator.

CAUSE: A portion of the fuel charge will begin to burn spontaneously, from the increased heat following ignition. The explosion that results applies extreme pressure to engine components, frequently damaging spark plugs and pistons.

Detonation can result by over-advanced ignition timing, inferior gasoline (low octane) lean air/fuel mixture, poor carburetion, engine lugging or an increase in compression ratio due to combustion chamber deposits or engine modification.

RECOMMENDATION: Replace the plugs after correcting the problem.

Photos Courtesy Champion Spark Plug Co.

EMISSION CONTROLS

13. Be aware of the general condition of the emission control system. It contributes to reduced pollution and should be serviced regularly to maintain efficient engine operation.

14. Check all vacuum lines for dried, cracked or brittle conditions. Something as simple as a leaking vacuum hose can cause poor performance and loss of economy.

15. Avoid tampering with the emission control system. Attempting to improve fuel econ-

FUEL SYSTEM

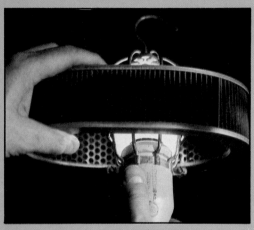

Check the air filter with a light behind it. If you can see light through the filter it can be reused.

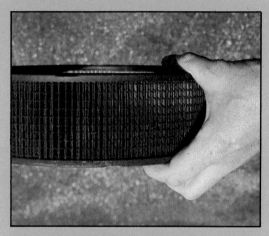

Extremely clogged filters should be discarded and replaced with a new one.

18. Replace the air filter regularly. A dirty air filter richens the air/fuel mixture and can increase fuel consumption as much as 10%. Tests show that ⅓ of all vehicles have air filters in need of replacement.

19. Replace the fuel filter at least as often as recommended.

20. Set the idle speed and carburetor mixture to specifications.

21. Check the automatic choke. A sticking or malfunctioning choke wastes gas.

22. During the summer months, adjust the automatic choke for a leaner mixture which will produce faster engine warm-ups.

COOLING SYSTEM

29. Be sure all accessory drive belts are in good condition. Check for cracks or wear.

30. Adjust all accessory drive belts to proper tension.

31. Check all hoses for swollen areas, worn spots, or loose clamps.

32. Check coolant level in the radiator or expansion tank.

33. Be sure the thermostat is operating properly. A stuck thermostat delays engine warm-up and a cold engine uses nearly twice as much fuel as a warm engine.

34. Drain and replace the engine coolant at least as often as recommended. Rust and scale

TIRES & WHEELS

38. Check the tire pressure often with a pencil type gauge. Tests by a major tire manufacturer show that 90% of all vehicles have at least 1 tire improperly inflated. Better mileage can be achieved by over-inflating tires, but never exceed the maximum inflation pressure on the side of the tire.

39. If possible, install radial tires. Radial tires deliver as much as ½ mpg more than bias belted tires.

40. Avoid installing super-wide tires. They only create extra rolling resistance and decrease fuel mileage. Stick to the manufacturer's recommendations.

41. Have the wheels properly balanced.

omy by tampering with emission controls is more likely to worsen fuel economy than improve it. Emission control changes on modern engines are not readily reversible.

16. Clean (or replace) the EGR valve and lines as recommended.

17. Be sure that all vacuum lines and hoses are reconnected properly after working under the hood. An unconnected or misrouted vacuum line can wreak havoc with engine performance.

23. Check for fuel leaks at the carburetor, fuel pump, fuel lines and fuel tank. Be sure all lines and connections are tight.

24. Periodically check the tightness of the carburetor and intake manifold attaching nuts and bolts. These are a common place for vacuum leaks to occur.

25. Clean the carburetor periodically and lubricate the linkage.

26. The condition of the tailpipe can be an excellent indicator of proper engine combustion. After a long drive at highway speeds, the inside of the tailpipe should be a light grey in color. Black or soot on the insides indicates an overly rich mixture.

27. Check the fuel pump pressure. The fuel pump may be supplying more fuel than the engine needs.

28. Use the proper grade of gasoline for your engine. Don't try to compensate for knocking or "pinging" by advancing the ignition timing. This practice will only increase plug temperature and the chances of detonation or pre-ignition with relatively little performance gain.

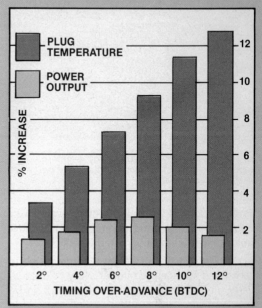

Increasing ignition timing past the specified setting results in a drastic increase in spark plug temperature with increased chance of detonation or preignition. Performance increase is considerably less. (Photo courtesy Champion Spark Plug Co.)

that form in the engine should be flushed out to allow the engine to operate at peak efficiency.

35. Clean the radiator of debris that can decrease cooling efficiency.

36. Install a flex-type or electric cooling fan, if you don't have a clutch type fan. Flex fans use curved plastic blades to push more air at low speeds when more cooling is needed; at high speeds the blades flatten out for less resistance. Electric fans only run when the engine temperature reaches a predetermined level.

37. Check the radiator cap for a worn or cracked gasket. If the cap does not seal properly, the cooling system will not function properly.

42. Be sure the front end is correctly aligned. A misaligned front end actually has wheels going in differed directions. The increased drag can reduce fuel economy by .3 mpg.

43. Correctly adjust the wheel bearings. Wheel bearings that are adjusted too tight increase rolling resistance.

Check tire pressures regularly with a reliable pocket type gauge. Be sure to check the pressure on a cold tire.

GENERAL MAINTENANCE

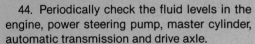

Check the fluid levels (particularly engine oil) on a regular basis. Be sure to check the oil for grit, water or other contamination.

A vacuum gauge is another excellent indicator of internal engine condition and can also be installed in the dash as a mileage indicator.

44. Periodically check the fluid levels in the engine, power steering pump, master cylinder, automatic transmission and drive axle.

45. Change the oil at the recommended interval and change the filter at every oil change. Dirty oil is thick and causes extra friction between moving parts, cutting efficiency and increasing wear. A worn engine requires more frequent tune-ups and gets progressively worse fuel economy. In general, use the lightest viscosity oil for the driving conditions you will encounter.

46. Use the recommended viscosity fluids in the transmission and axle.

47. Be sure the battery is fully charged for fast starts. A slow starting engine wastes fuel.

48. Be sure battery terminals are clean and tight.

49. Check the battery electrolyte level and add distilled water if necessary.

50. Check the exhaust system for crushed pipes, blockages and leaks.

51. Adjust the brakes. Dragging brakes or brakes that are not releasing create increased drag on the engine.

52. Install a vacuum gauge or miles-per-gallon gauge. These gauges visually indicate engine vacuum in the intake manifold. High vacuum = good mileage and low vacuum = poorer mileage. The gauge can also be an excellent indicator of internal engine conditions.

53. Be sure the clutch is properly adjusted. A slipping clutch wastes fuel.

54. Check and periodically lubricate the heat control valve in the exhaust manifold. A sticking or inoperative valve prevents engine warm-up and wastes gas.

55. Keep accurate records to check fuel economy over a period of time. A sudden drop in fuel economy may signal a need for tune-up or other maintenance.

17084434	11/32	15	26	1	38	42
17084435	11/32	15	26	1	38	42
17084452	5/32	28	25	1	35	45
17084453	5/32	28	25	1	35	45
17084455	5/32	28	25	1	35	45
17084456	5/32	28	25	1	35	45
17084458	5/32	28	25	1	35	45
17084532	5/32	28	25	1	35	45
17084534	5/32	28	25	1	35	45
17084535	5/32	28	25	1	35	45
17084537	5/32	28	25	1	35	45
17084538	5/32	28	25	1	35	45
17084540	5/32	28	25	1	35	45
17084542	1/8	28	25	1	35	45
17084632	9/32	28	25	1	35	45
17084633	9/32	28	25	1	35	45
17084635	9/32	28	25	1	35	45
17084636	9/32	28	25	1	35	45

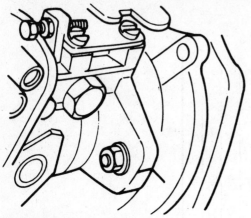

Injection pump and flange alignment

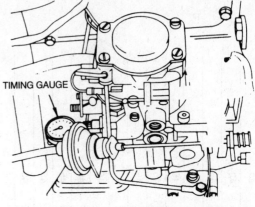

Injection timing dial gauge installed in injection pump

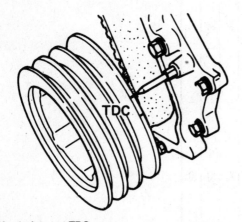

No. 1 piston at TDC

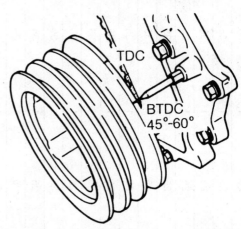

Bring the No. 1 piston to 45–60 degrees BTDC and then zero the dial gauge before adjusting the injection timing

INSTALLATION

1. Install the injection pump by aligning notched line on the flange with the line on the front bracket.

2. Install the injection pump timing pulley by aligning it with the key groove. Torque to 42–52 ft. lbs.

3. Bring the piston in No. 1 cylinder to top dead center on compression stroke and align marks on the timing pulleys.

4. Follow the timing belt installation steps.

5. Check the injection timing.

6. To install remaining parts, follow the removal steps in reverse order.

Diesel Injection Pump Timing

CHECK AND ADJUSTMENT

1. Check that notched line on the injection pump flange is in alignment with notched line on the injection pump front bracket.

2. Bring the No. 1 piston to TDC on the compression stroke by turning crankshaft as necessary.

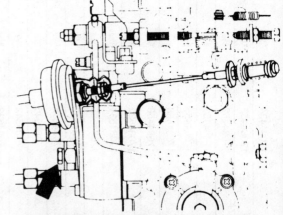

Location of distributor head screw (arrow) that must be removed to install the dial gauge

NOTE: *Make sure No. 1 cylinder is on the compression stroke; it is possible to align the timing marks incorrectly.*

3. Remove upper fan shroud, if not already done.

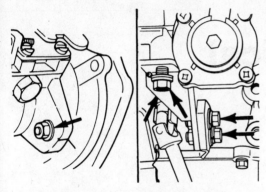

Location of injection pump flange and bracket bolts

4. With the upper cover removed, check that the timing belt is properly tensioned and that the timing marks are properly aligned. If marks are not aligned properly, timing belt will have to be removed and readjusted.

5. With the injection lines removed, remove the distributor head screw and washer from the injection pump.

6. Install the static timing gauge J-29763, or equivalent, and set lift approximately 1mm (0.04 in.) from the plunger.

7. Bring the piston, in No. 1 cylinder to a point 45–60 degrees before TDC by turning the crankshaft, then calibrate the dial indicator to zero. Turn the crankshaft pulley slightly in both directions and check that gauge indication is stable.

8. Turn the crankshaft in normal direction of rotation, and take the reading of the dial indicator when the timing mark (15 degrees) on the crankshaft pulley is in alignment with the TDC pointer. The dial indicator should read 0.5mm (0.020 in.).

9. If the reading of the dial indicator is not as described, hold the crankshaft in position 15° before TDC and loosen two nuts on the injection pump flange. Move the injection pump to a point where the dial indicator gives reading of .5mm (0.020 in.), then tighten pump flange nuts.

10. Recheck dial indicator reading and readjust the injection pump as necessary. Remove the dial indicator from the pump.

11. Install the distributor screw and washer into injection pump, then tighten.

12. Install injection lines. Do not overtighten connections.

13. Connect all the wires and hoses previously removed.

14. Install the upper dust cover.

15. If timing belt was removed, install the timing belt.

16. Install fan shroud.

17. Adjust engine idle speed and the fast idle speed as described in Chapter 2.

18. Check for leaks in the fuel system and correct as necessary.

Chassis Electrical

HEATER
Blower Motor
REMOVAL AND INSTALLATION

Without Air Conditioning

1. Disconnect the battery ground cable.
2. Disconnect all wires at the blower.
3. Remove the blower motor mounting screws and lift out the blower.
4. Installation is the reverse of removal.

With Air Conditioning

1. Disconnect the battery ground cable.
2. Remove the vacuum tank.
3. Remove the blower motor mounting screws, and lift out the blower motor.
4. Installation is the reverse of removal.

Heater Core

REMOVAL AND INSTALLATION

All Models

1. Disconnect the battery ground cable.
2. Drain the cooling system.
3. Remove the heater hoses at the core tubes on the firewall in the engine compartment.
4. Remove the core cover retaining screws.
5. Remove the retainers at each end of the core.
6. Lift out the core.
7. Installation is the reverse of removal.

NOTE: *Plug the heater core tubes to avoid spilling coolant in the passenger compartment during removal.*

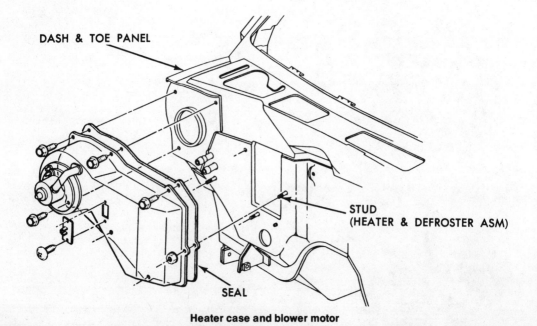

Heater case and blower motor

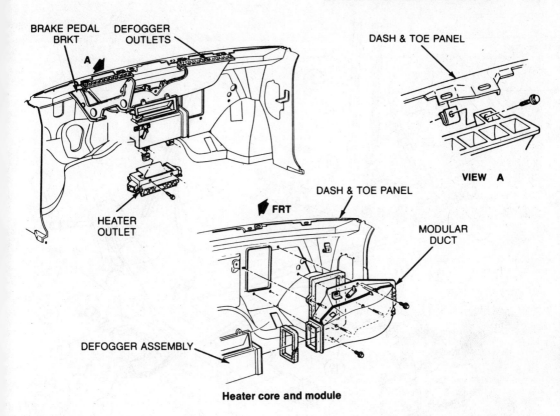

Heater core and module

RADIO

REMOVAL AND INSTALLATION

1. Disconnect the battery ground cable.
2. Remove the instrument panel center bezel.
3. Remove the four screws from the radio bracket and pull the radio forward.
4. Disconnect the antenna and electrical wires. Pull the radio out carefully.
5. Installation is the reverse of removal.
CAUTION: *It is very important when changing speakers or performing any radio work to avoid pinching the wires. A short circuit to ground from any wire will cause damage to the output circuit in the radio.*

WINDSHIELD WIPERS

Wiper Motor

REMOVAL AND INSTALLATION

1. Disconnect the battery ground cable.
2. Remove the wiper arms.
3. Remove the cowl, vent and grille.
4. Loosen, but do not remove, the nuts which hold the drive link to the motor crank arm.
5. Detach the drive link from the crank arm.

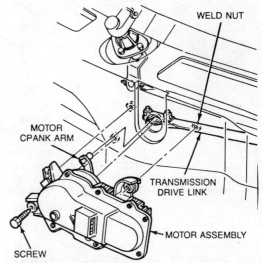

Windshield wiper motor

6. Disconnect the wiring at the motor.
7. Remove the motor mounting screws. Turn the motor upward and outward and remove it.
8. Installation is the reverse of removal. Torque the attaching screws to 50–75 inch lb.

Wiper Linkage

REMOVAL AND INSTALLATION

1. Disconnect the battery ground cable.
2. Remove the wiper arms.

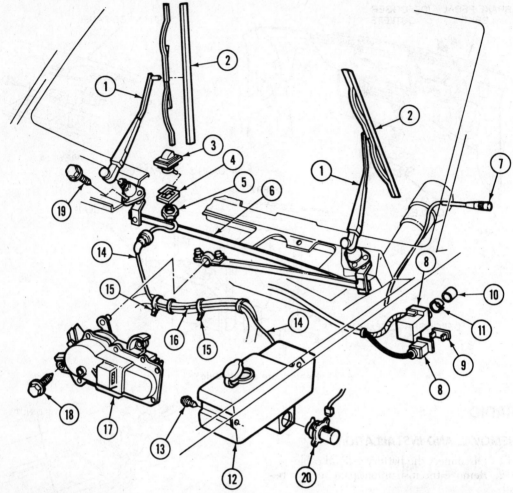

1. Arm, windshield wiper
2. Blade
   insert
3. Nozzle
4. Spacer, nozzle
5. Nut, type R stamped (M16)
6. Transmission, left hand
   transmission, right hand
7. Lever
8. Module
9. Lens, pulse switch
10. Knob, pulse switch
11. Nut, pulse module retaining
12. Reserovir
13. Bolt, (M6 × 1 × 25)
14. Hose, (5/32" ID)
15. Strap
16. Connector
17. Motor assembly
18. Bolt (M5 × .8 × 28)
19. Screw, (M6.3 × 1.69 × 20)
20. Pump

Windshield wiper system

3. Remove the cowl vent and grille.

4. Remove the nut securing the linkage to the motor.

5. Remove the screw securing the linkage to the cowl panel.

6. Installation is the reverse of removal. Torque the screws and nuts to 50–80 inch lb.

INSTRUMENT CLUSTER

REMOVAL AND INSTALLATION

1. Disconnect the battery ground cable.

2. Remove the five screws retaining the cluster trim plate and carefully lift off the plate.

3. Remove the instrument panel face plate.

4. Remove the cluster lens.

5. Disconnect the speedometer cable.

6. Disconnect the cluster electrical connector.

7. Lift out the cluster.

8. Installation is the reverse of removal.

LIGHTING

Headlight Switch

REMOVAL AND INSTALLATION

1. Disconnect the battery ground cable.

2. Pull the switch to the ON position.

3. Reach up under the instrument panel and press the switch rod retaining tab while pulling on the switch control.

4. Unscrew and remove the switch retaining plate.

5. Using a large bladed screwdriver, unscrew the switch retaining ring.

6. Disconnect the wiring from the switch.

7. Remove the switch.

8. Installation is the reverse of removal.

Brake Light Switch

REMOVAL AND INSTALLATION

1. Unplug the wiring from the switch located on the brake pedal support bracket.

2. Pull the switch from the support bracket.

3. Depress the pedal and push the new switch into the clip until the shoulder on the switch seats against the clip.

4. Let the pedal up and connect the wiring. Make sure that the switch is properly positioned and works smoothly.

FUSIBLE LINKS

Replacement

Fusible links are lengths of wire incorporated in a circuit, four gauge sizes smaller than the wire that they protect. Protection is given by the fusible link melting and separating before damage can occur to the wire or components in the circuit.

NOTE: *Replace the fusible link only after the short circuit or other problem has been corrected.*

1. Disconnect the battery ground.

2. Cut out the old fusible link.

3. Strip about ½ in. from the ends of the circuit wire.

4. Crimp the new fusible link into place and solder using resin core solder. Tape open wires thoroughly.

NOTE: *Use only resin core solder. Under no circumstances should an acid solder be used nor should link be connected in any other manner except by soldering. Use of acid core solder may result in corrosion.*

LOCATION

• At the starter BAT terminal. 14 gauge red wire.

• At the junction block in the engine compartment. 16 gauge, red link.

• In the battery feed-to-voltage regulator No. 3 terminal wire. 20 gauge red wire.

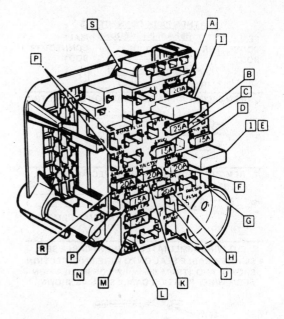

1	Circuit breaker
A	Fuse—choke
B	Fuse—heater or air condition
C	Fuse—radio
D	Fuse—stop, hazard lamps
E	Power accessory
F	Fuse—windshield wiper
G	Receptacle—power door locks
H	Fuse—horn
J	Receptacle—clock, courtesy lamp, dome lamp, I/P compt lamp & hdlp wrng buzzer
K	Fuse—tail & ctsy lamps
L	Receptacle—headlamp on warning
M	Fuse—instrument panel lamps
N	Fuse—turn & back up lamps
P	Receptacle—cruise control & auto trans
R	Fuse—ignition & gauges
S	Connector—seat belt warning buzzer & timer

Typical fuse box

FUSES AND CIRCUIT BREAKERS

These circuit protection devices are located in the fuse box, located on the firewall under the instrument panel on the driver's side. There are two circuit breakers and 10 fuses. Fuses must be replaced when tripped by a short; circuit breakers can be reset by pushing in and releasing. See the accompanying illustration for circuit breaker or fuse identification.

WIRING HARNESS SERVICE AND REPAIR

Special connectors known as Weather-Pack connectors require a special tool (J-28742) for servicing. This special tool is required to remove the pin and sleeve terminals. If removal is attempted with an ordinary pick, there is a good change that the terminal will be bent or

WEATHER PACK CONNECTORS
REPAIR PROCEDURE

FEMALE
CONNECTOR
BODY

MALE
CONNECTOR
BODY

1. OPEN SECONDARY LOCK HINGE ON CONNECTOR

2. REMOVE TERMINALS USING SPECIAL TOOL
J-28742

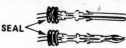

TERMINAL REMOVAL
TOOL

3. CUT WIRE IMMEDIATELY BEHIND CABLE SEAL
4. SLIP NEW CABLE SEAL ONTO WIRE (IN DIRECTION SHOWN) AND STRIP 5.00mm (.2") OF INSULATION FROM WIRE. POSITION CABLE SEAL AS SHOWN.

SEAL

Repairing Weather-Pack® terminals

deformed. Unlike standard blade-type terminals, these terminals cannot be straightened once they are bent.

Make sure that the connectors are properly seated and all of the sealing rings in place when connecting leads. The hinge-type flap provides a backup, or secondary locking feature for the terminals. They are used to improve the con-

nector reliability by retaining the terminals if the small terminal lock tangs are not positioned properly. Molded-on-connectors require complete replacement of the connection. This means splicing a new connector assembly into the harness. Environmental connections cannot be replaced with standard connections. Instructions are provided with Weather-Pack connector and terminal packages.

NOTE: *With the low current and voltage levels found in some circuits, it is important that the best possible bond at all wire splices be made by soldering the splices.*

Use care when probing the connections or replacing terminals in them, it is possible to short between opposite terminals. If this happens to the wrong terminal pair, it is possible that damage may be done to certain components. Always use jumper wires between connectors for circuit checking. Never probe through the Weather-Pack seals. When diagnosing for possible open circuits, it is often difficult to locate them by sight because oxidation or terminal misalignment are hidden by the connectors. Merely wiggling a connector on a sensor or in the wiring harness may correct the open circuit condition. This should always be considered when an open circuit is indicated while troubleshooting. Intermittent problems may also be caused by oxidized or loose connections.

When replacing wires, it is important that the correct gauge size be used. Never replace a wire with one of a smaller gauge size. Each harness and wire must be held securely in place by clips or other holding devices to prevent chafing or wearing of the insulation due to vibration.

TWISTED/SHIELDED CABLE

DRAIN WIRE

OUTER JACKET

MYLAR

1. REMOVE OUTER JACKET.
2. UNWRAP ALUMINUM/MYLAR TAPE. DO NOT REMOVE MYLAR.

3. UNTWIST CONDUCTORS. STRIP INSULATION AS NECESSARY.

DRAIN WIRE

4. SPLICE WIRES USING SPLICE CLIPS AND ROSIN CORE SOLDER. WRAP EACH SPLICE TO INSULATE.
5. WRAP WITH MYLAR AND DRAIN (UNINSULATED) WIRE.

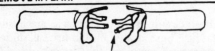

6. TAPE OVER WHOLE BUNDLE TO SECURE AS BEFORE

TWISTED LEADS

1. LOCATE DAMAGED WIRE.
2. REMOVE INSULATION AS REQUIRED.

SPLICE & SOLDER

3. SPLICE TWO WIRES TOGETHER USING SPLICE CLIPS AND ROSIN CORE SOLDER.

4. COVER SPLICE WITH TAPE TO INSULATE FROM OTHER WIRES.
5. RETWIST AS BEFORE AND TAPE WITH ELECTRICAL TAPE AND HOLD IN PLACE.

Correct method of repairing wire harness

MANUAL TRANSMISSION

Two four speed transmissions are used, as well as one five speed unit. The four speed units are identified by the distance between the mainshaft and countershaft centerlines, thus, one is called the 77mm transmission and the other, the 77.5mm transmission. The five speed is likewise identified and is called the 5-speed 77mm.

REMOVAL AND INSTALLATION

4-Speed 77.5mm

NOTE: *On 4-wheel drive models, see Transfer Case Removal and Installation.*

1. Disconnect the battery ground cable.
2. Remove the upper starter retaining nut.
3. Remove the shift lever boot attaching screws and slide the boot up the shift lever.
4. Disconnect the shift lever at the transmission.
5. Disconnect the electrical connector at the transmission.
6. Raise and support the truck on jackstands.
7. Remove the driveshaft.
8. Disconnect the exhaust pipe at the manifold.
9. Disconnect the clutch cable at the transmission.
10. Disconnect the clutch cable at the transmission.
11. Place a floor jack under the transmission to take up its weight.
12. Remove the transmission mount bolts.
13. Remove the catalytic converter hanger.
14. Remove the crossmember.
15. Remove the lower dust cover bolts.
16. Remove the lower starter bolt.
17. Unbolt the transmission from the engine and lower it on the jack.
18. Installation is the reverse of removal. Torque the transmission-to-engine bolts to 25 ft. lb. on the 4 cylinder and 55 ft. lb. on the 6 cylinder. Torque the transmission mount-to-transmission bolts to 35 ft. lb.; the crossmem-

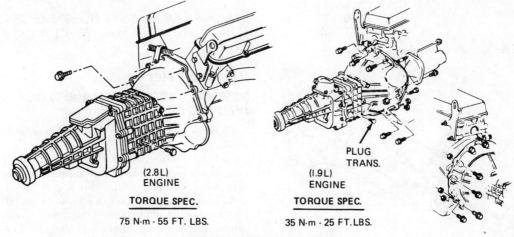

(2.8L)
ENGINE

TORQUE SPEC.

75 N·m - 55 FT. LBS.

PLUG
TRANS.

(1.9L)
ENGINE

TORQUE SPEC.

35 N·m - 25 FT.LBS.

77.5mm transmission mounting

ber-to-frame bolts to 25 ft. lb.; the dust cover bolts to 7 ft. lb.

4-Speed 77 mm and 5-Speed 77mm

NOTE: *On 4-wheel drive models, see Transfer Case Removal and Installation.*

1. Disconnect the battery ground cable.
2. Remove the shift lever boot screws and slide the boot up the lever.
3. Shift the transmission into neutral and remove the shift lever.
4. Raise and support the track on jackstands.
5. Remove the driveshaft.
6. Disconnect the speedometer cable and wiring at the transmission.
7. Disconnect the clutch cable at the transmission.
8. Place a floor jack under the transmission and take up its weight. Remove the transmission mount bolts.
9. Remove the catalytic converter hanger.
10. Remove the crossmember.
11. Remove the dust cover bolts.
12. Unbolt the transmission from the bell housing and lower the jack. It will be necessary to pull the transmission back a ways to clear the clutch. Installation is the reverse of removal. Lightly grease the input shaft splines with chassis lube. Torque the transmission mount bolts to 35 ft. lb.; the crossmember-to-

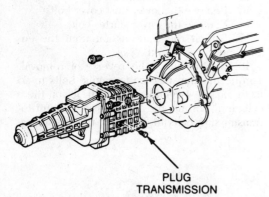

PLUG
TRANSMISSION

77mm four speed transmission mounting

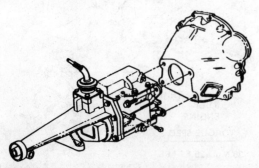

77mm five speed transmission mounting

frame bolts to 25 ft. lb.; the transmission to-bell housing bolts to 55 ft. lb.

CLUTCH

ADJUSTMENT

1. Lift up on the pedal to allow the self adjuster to adjust the cable length.
2. Depress the pedal several times to set the pawl into mesh with the detent teeth.
3. Check the linkage for lost motion caused by loose or worn swivels, mounting brackets or a damaged cable.

REMOVAL AND INSTALLATION

1. Remove the transmission.
2. Remove the flywheel housing.
3. Remove the clutch fork.
4. Insert a clutch alignment tool in the clutch hub and into the crankshaft pilot bearing.
5. Check for an X or other painted mark on the pressure plate and flywheel. If there isn't any mark, mark the assembly for installation purposes.
6. Loosen the pressure plate bolts, evenly and alternately, a little at a time until spring tension is released. Remove the pressure plate and driven plate.
7. Check the flywheel for cracks, wear, scoring or other damage. Check the pilot bearing for wear. Replace it by yanking it out with a slide hammer and driving in a new one with a wood or plastic hammer.
8. Installation is the reverse of removal. Use the alignment tool to aid installation. The raised hub of the driven plate faces the transmission. Align the mating marks and tighten the bolts evenly and alternately to 20 ft. lb.

AUTOMATIC TRANSMISSION

This truck uses the Turbo Hydra-Matic 200C or the Turbo Hydra-Matic 700-R4 transmission.

Pan and Filter

REMOVAL, INSTALLATION AND FLUID DRAINING

1. Raise and support the truck on jackstands.
2. Place a drain pan under the transmission.
3. Remove the bolts from the front and one side of the fluid pan.
4. Loosen the rear bolts a few turns and allow the pan to hang until the fluid drains. Then, remove the remaining bolts and the pan. Discard the gasket.

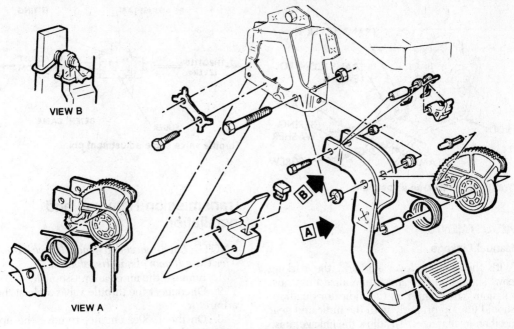

VIEW B

VIEW A

Self-adjusting clutch mechanism

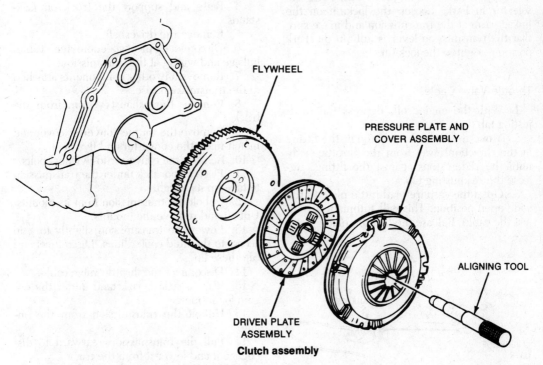

FLYWHEEL

PRESSURE PLATE AND
COVER ASSEMBLY

ALIGNING TOOL

DRIVEN PLATE
ASSEMBLY

Clutch assembly

5. Clean the pan thoroughly with a safe solvent and dry it with a lint-free rag.

6. Remove the filter-to-valve body bolts and remove the filter. Discard the gasket.

7. Installation is the reverse of removal for all parts. Always use a new gasket on the filter and pan. Torque the filter bolts to 10 ft. lb. and the pan bolts to 7ft lb. Add 7 pints of fluid.

Start the engine, run the shifter through all positions, return it to Park and check the fluid level. Add fluid, if necessary. If the converter was drained during a procedure such as transmission removal, the total fluid capacity will be 19 pints. Dispose of waste transmission fluid properly.

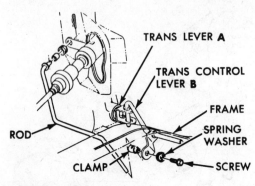

Transmission linkage adjustment

ADJUSTMENTS

Manual Linkage

With the selector lever in Park, the parking pawl should engage and immobilize the transmission. The pointer on the indicator quadrant should line up properly with the indicated gear position in all ranges. To adjust the linkage, raise and support the truck on jackstands. Place the selector in Park. Loosen the locknut on the linkage arm at the transmission and make sure that the transmission lever is fully in the Park position. Tighten the locknut.

Throttle Valve Cable

1. With the engine off, depress the readjusting tab.
2. Move the slider back through the fitting in the direction away from the throttle body until the slider stops against the fitting. Release the readjusting tab.
3. Open the carburetor throttle plate to the wide open position. This will automatically adjust the cable. Release the throttle plate.

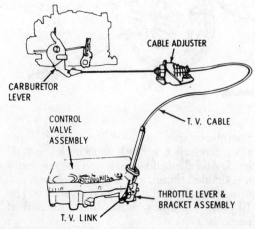

Throttle valve cable

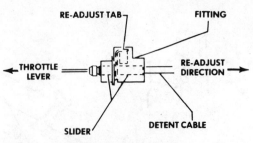

Throttle valve cable adjustment point

Transmission Removal and Installation

NOTE: *On 4-wheel drive models, see Transfer Case Removal and Installation.*

1. Remove the air cleaner assembly.
2. Disconnect the throttle valve cable at the carburetor.
3. On the 1950cc engine, remove the upper starter bolt.
4. Raise and support the truck on jackstands.
5. Remove the driveshaft.
6. Disconnect the speedometer cable, linkage and wiring at the transmission.
7. Remove any other components attached to the transmission case.
8. Remove the exhaust system from the truck.
9. Remove the torque converter cover and match-mark the converter and flywheel.
10. Remove the converter-to-flywheel bolts.
11. Place a floor jack under the transmission to take up its weight.
12. Unbolt the transmission from its mounts. Unbolt and remove the mounts.
13. Lower the transmission slightly to gain access to the fluid cooler lines. Disconnect and cap these lines.
14. Disconnect the throttle valve cable.
15. Place a jack or jackstand under the engine for support.
16. Unbolt the transmission from the engine.
17. Pull the transmission rearward to disengage it and lower it from the truck.
NOTE: *Take care to avoid dropping the converter.*
18. Installation is the reverse of removal. Match up the mating marks on the converter. Torque the transmission-to-engine bolts to 25 ft. lb. on 4-cylinder models and 55 ft. lb. on the 6-cylinder; torque the converter-to-flywheel bolts to 35 ft. lb.; torque the transmission-to-mount bolts to 35 ft. lb.; the mount-to-frame bolts to 25 ft. lb.

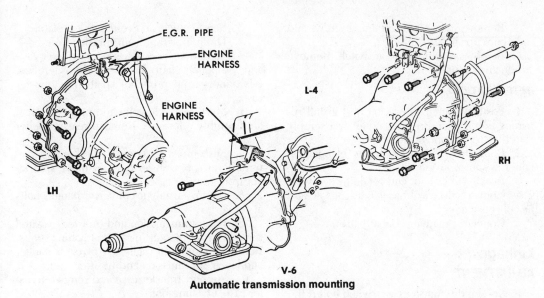

E.G.R. PIPE

ENGINE HARNESS

L-4

ENGINE HARNESS

RH

LH

V-6

Automatic transmission mounting

TRANSFER CASE

These trucks use the New Process 207. This unit is an aluminum case model with chain drive. Proper fluid for this unit is Dexron II automatic transmission fluid.

Shift Lever

REMOVAL

1. Disconnect negative cable at battery.
2. Remove console.
3. Remove shift boot.
4. Loosen jam nut at shift lever and unscrew shift lever.
5. Remove transfer case selector switch.
6. Raise vehicle.
7. Disconnect shift rod at shifter assembly.
8. Remove pivot bolt and adjusting bolt.
9. Remove shifter.

INSTALLATION

1. Position shifter and install pivot and adjusting bolt.
2. Connect shift rod.
3. Adjust shift linkage.
4. Lower vehicle.
5. Install shift lever. Screw lever down until the pawl just clears bracket. Then turndown 1½ additional turns and tighten jam nut.
6. Install selector switch.
7. Install shifter boot retaining screws and install console.
8. Connect negative cable at battery.

Selector Switch

REMOVAL

1. Disconnect negative cable at battery.
2. Remove console and disconnect electrical harness.

AUTOMATIC TRANSMISSION

ADAPTER ASM

DETENT

VIEW A

MANUAL TRANSMISSION

Transmission shifter

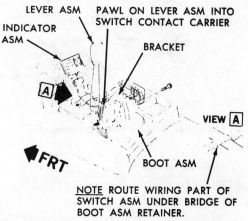

LEVER ASM   PAWL ON LEVER ASM INTO SWITCH CONTACT CARRIER

INDICATOR ASM

BRACKET

A

VIEW A

FRT

BOOT ASM

NOTE ROUTE WIRING PART OF SWITCH ASM UNDER BRIDGE OF BOOT ASM RETAINER.

Selector switch

3. Remove shifter boot retaining screws and slide boot up shifter.

4. Remove attaching bolt at switch. Remove switch and harness.

INSTALLATION

1. Position switch to bracket and install retaining bolt. Make sure pawl on lever assembly is in the switch contact carrier.

2. Route harness under bridge of boot retainer as shown in View A.

3. Install shifter boot and retaining screws.

4. Connect electrical harness at console and install console.

5. Connect negative cable at battery.

Linkage

ADJUSTMENT

1. Loosen the transfer case switch bolt d the case shift lever pivot bolt.

2. hift the transfer case to the 4H position.

3. Remove the console and slide the boot up the lever.

4. Install a ⁵⁄₁₆ in. drill bit through the shifter and into the switch bracket.

5. Install a bolt at the case lever to lock it in position.

6. Tighten the switch bracket bolt to 30 ft. lbs. and the shifter pivot bolt to 100 ft. lbs.

7. Remove the bolt you installed to lock the lever.

8. Remove the drill bit. Check the linkage action.

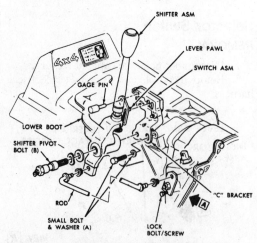

Shift lever and selector switch adjustment

Transfer Case

REMOVAL

1. Shift transfer case into 4 H.

2. Disconnect negative cable at battery.

3. Raise vehicle and remove skid plate.

4. Drain lubricant from transfer case.

5. Mark transfer case front output shaft yoke and propeller shaft for assembly reference. Disconnect front propeller shaft from transfer case.

6. Mark rear axle yoke and propeller shaft for assembly reference. Remove rear propeller shaft.

7. Disconnect speedometer cable and vacuum harness at transfer case. Remove shift lever from transfer case.

8. Remove catalytic converter hanger bolts at converter.

9. Raise transmission and transfer case and remove transmission mount attaching bolts. Remove mount and catalytic converter hanger and lower transmission and transfer case.

10. Support transfer case and remove transfer case attaching bolts.

On vehicles equipped with an automatic transmission, it will be necessary to remove the shift lever bracket mounting bolts from the transfer case adapter in order to remove the upper left transfer case attaching bolt.

11. Separate transfer case from adapter (AT) or extension housing (MT) and remove from vehicle.

INSTALLATION

1. Position new gasket on the transfer case.

2. Install transfer case, aligning splines of input shaft with transmission and slide transfer case forward until seated against transmission.

3. Install transfer case attaching bolts and torque to specification. On vehicles equipped with automatic transmission, reinstall shift lever bracket bolts.

4. Raise transmission and transfer case and install mount and hanger bracket. Install attaching bolts and torque to specification.

5. Install catalytic converter hanger bolts at converter and torque to specification.

6. Attach shift lever at transfer case. Connect speedometer cable and vacuum harness at transfer case.

7. Connect the front and install the rear propeller shaft. Be sure to align reference marks made during removal.

8. Fill transfer case with lubricant recommended in Maintenance and Lubrication.

9. Install skid plate and lower vehicle.

10. Connect negative cable at battery.

11. Road test vehicle, check to make sure vehicle shifts and operates into all ranges.

DRIVESHAFT

REMOVAL

NOTE: *Do not pound on original propeller shaft yoke ears as injection joints may fracture.*

1. Raise vehicle and support it safely. Mark relationship of shaft to pinion flange and disconnect the rear universal joint by removing retainers. If bearing cups are loose, tape together to prevent dropping and loss of bearing rollers.

2. For models with two-piece shafts remove bolts retaining center bearing support to hanger.

3. Slide propeller shaft forward disengaging trunnion from axle flange.

4. Withdraw propeller shaft slip yoke from transmission by moving shaft rearward, passing it under the axle housing. Do not allow drive shaft to drop or allow universal joints to bend to extreme angle, as this might fracture injected joint internally. Support propeller shaft during removal.

INSTALLATION

General Procedure

1. When reinstalling propeller shaft, it is necessary to place the shafts into particular positions to assure proper operation. This is called phasing.

2. The propeller shaft must be supported carefully during handling to avoid jamming or bending any of the parts.

3. Inspect outer diameter of splined yoke to ensure that it is not burred, as this will damage the transmission seal.

4. Inspect splines of slip yoke for damage or wear.

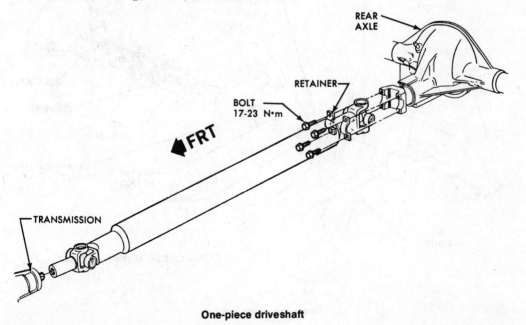

One-piece driveshaft

5. Apply engine oil to all splined propeller shaft yokes.

6. Do not drive propeller shaft in place with hammer. Check for burrs on transmission output shaft spline, twisted slip yoke splines, or possibly the wrong U-joint. Make sure the splines agree in number and fit. To prevent trunnion seal damage, do not place any tool between yoke and splines.

One Piece Propeller Shaft

1. Slide propeller shaft into transmission.

2. Position rear universal joint to rear axle pinion flange, making sure bearings are properly seated in pinion flange yoke.

When making rear shaft connection, be sure to align mark on pinion flange or end yoke with mark on drive shaft rear yoke.

3. Install rear joint fasteners and tighten evenly to torque specified.

Two Piece Propeller Shaft

1. Install front half into transmission and bolt center bearing support to crossmember.

The front propeller shaft yoke must be bottomed out in the transmission (fully forward) before installation to the support.

2. Torque center support bearing to crossmember attachment.

3. Rotate shaft so front U-joint trunnion is in correct position.

Before installing rear propeller shaft, align U-joint trunnions (a "key" in the output spline

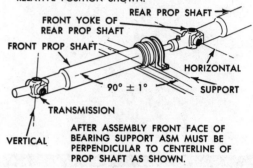

Center bearing alignment

of the front propeller shaft will align with a missing spline in the rear yoke).

4. Attach rear U-joint to axle and tighten to correct torque.

UNIVERSAL JOINTS

Nylon Injected Ring Type
DISASSEMBLY

NOTE: *Never clamp propeller shaft tubing in a vise as the tube may be dented. Always clamp on one of the yokes, and support the shaft horizontally. Avoid damaging the slip*

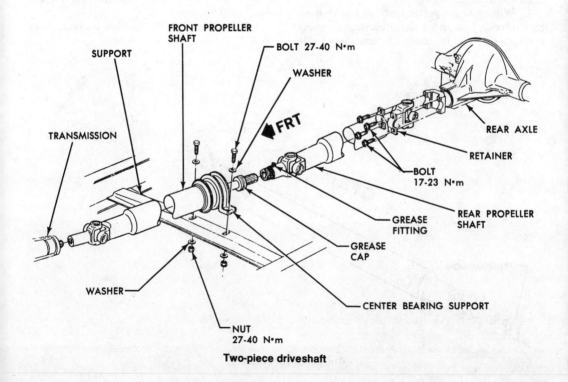

Two-piece driveshaft

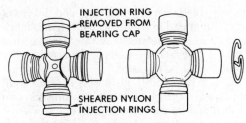

Injection ring type U-joint

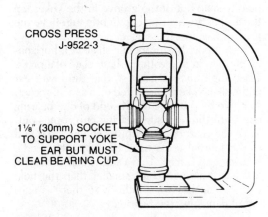

Pressing out U-joint

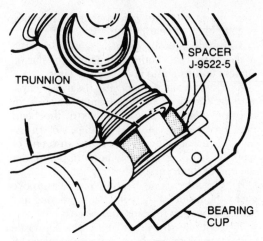

Spacer positioning

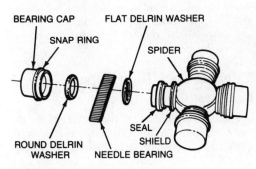

Internal snap-ring type U-joint

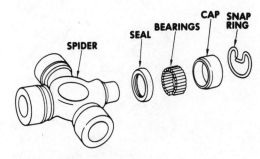

External snap-ring type U-joint

yoke sealing surface. Nicks may damage the bushing or cut the lip seal.

1. Support the propeller shaft in a horizontal position in the line with the base plate of a press. Place the universal joint so that the lower ear of the shaft yoke is supported on a 1⅛ in. socket. Place the cross press, J-9522-3, on the open horizontal bearing cups, and press the lower bearing cup out of the yoke ear. This will shear the plastic retaining ring on the lower bearing cup. If the bearing cup is not completely removed, lift the cross and insert Spacer J-9522-5 between the seal and bearing cup being removed. Complete the removal of the bearing cup by pressing it out of the yoke.

2. Rotate the propeller shaft, shear the opposite plastic retainer, and press the opposite bearing cup out of the yoke.

3. Disengage cross from yoke and remove. Production universal joints cannot be reassembled. There are no bearing retainer grooves in production bearing cups. Remove all universal joint parts.

4. If the front universal joint is being replaced, remove the pair of bearing cups from the slip yoke in the same manner.

ASSEMBLY

NOTE: *When reassembling a propeller shaft, always install a complete universal joint service kit. This kit includes one pregreased cross assembly, four service bearing cup assem-*

blies with seals, needle rollers, washers, and grease; and four bearing retainers. Make sure that the seals are in place on the service bearing cups to hold the needle rollers in place for handling.

1. Remove all of the remains of the sheared plastic bearing retainers from the grooves in the yokes. The sheared plastic may prevent the bearing cups from being pressed into place, and thus prevent the bearing retainers from being properly seated.

2. Install one bearing cup part way into one side of the yoke, and turn this yoke ear to the bottom.

3. Insert cross into yoke so that the trunnion seats freely into bearing cup.

4. Install opposite bearing cup part way. Make sure that both trunnions are started straight and true into both bearing cups.

5. Press against opposite bearing cups, working the cross all of the time to check for free movement of the trunnions of the bearings. If there seems to be a hangup, stop pressing and recheck needle rollers because one or more of them has probably been tipped under the end of the trunnion.

6. As soon as one bearing retainer groove clears the inside of the yoke, stop pressing and snap the bearing retainer into place.

7. Continue to press until the opposite bearing retainer can be snapped into place. If difficulty is encountered, strike the yoke firmly with a hammer to aid in seating bearing retainers. This springs the yoke ears slightly.

8. Assemble the other half of the universal joint in the same manner.

External Lock Ring Type
DISASSEMBLY

The universal joints are of the extended-life design and do not require periodic inspection or lubrication; however, when these joints are

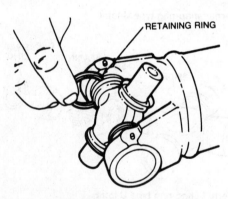

RETAINING RING

Snap-ring installation

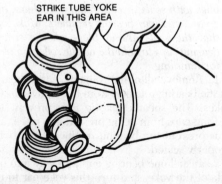

STRIKE TUBE YOKE EAR IN THIS AREA

Seating the U-joint snap-ring

disassembled, repack bearings and lubricant reservoir at end of trunnions with chassis lubricant. Use care not to loosen or damage dust seals. If dust seals are loose or damaged, entire U-joint must be replaced.

1. For reassembly purposes, indicate front of propeller shaft by marking transmission end of shaft and transmission slip yoke.

2. Remove snap ring by pinching the ends together with a pair of pliers. If ring does not readily snap out of the groove in the yoke, tap the end of the bearing cup lightly to relieve the pressure against the ring.

3. Support the propeller shaft in a horizontal position in line with the base plate of a press. Place the universal joint so that the lower ear of the shaft yoke is supported on a 1⅛ in. socket. Remove by pressing on the end of one bearing cup until the opposite bearing cup comes out. Turn the shaft over and press the exposed end of the journal cross until the opposite needle bearing cup is free. Use a soft round drift with a flat face about 1/32 in. smaller than the hole diameter in the yoke, otherwise there is danger of damaging the bearing.

ASSEMBLY

1. Clean and inspect dust seals, bearing rollers, and trunnion. Relubricate bearings.

2. In addition to packing the bearings. make sure that the lubricant reservoir at the end of each trunnion is completely filled with lubricant. In filling these reservoirs, pack lubricant into the hole so as to fill from the bottom (use of squeeze bottle is recommended). This will prevent air pockets and ensure an adequate supply of lubricant.

3. Attach transmission slip yoke on front of shaft as marked in Step 1. Failure to do so could result in driveline vibration.

4. Position trunnion into yoke. Partially install one bearing cup into yoke. Start trunnion into bearing cup. Partially install other cup. Align trunnion into cup, and press cups into yoke. Use care not to dislodge dust seal.

5. Install lock rings.

Center Support Bearing
REMOVAL AND INSTALLATION

1. Remove propeller shaft.

2. Remove strap retaining rubber cushion from bearing support.

3. Pull support bracket from rubber cushion and pull cushion from bearing.

4. Press bearing assembly from shaft.

5. Assemble bearing support as follows:

a. Install inner deflector on propeller shaft, if removed, and prick punch deflector at two opposite points to make sure it is tight on shaft.

b. Fill space between inner dust shield and bearing with lithium soap grease.

c. Start bearing and slinger assembly straight on shaft journal. Support propeller shaft and, using suitable length of pipe over splined end of shaft, press bearing and inner slinger against shoulder on shaft.

d. Install bearing retainer.

e. Install rubber cushion onto bearing.

f. Install bracket onto cushion.

g. Install retaining strap.

6. Install prop shaft.

REAR AXLE

Rear Axle Identification

The rear axle identification code and manufacturer's code must be known before attempting to adjust or repair axle shafts or rear axle case assembly. Rear axle ratio, differential type, manufacturer, and build date information is stamped on the right axle tube on the forward side. Any reports made on rear axle assemblies must include the full code letters and build date numbers.

MANUFACTURE

C - 7-1/2" (190 mm) CHEVROLET BUFFALO

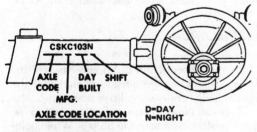

Rear axle identification

Axle Shaft

REMOVAL

1. Raise vehicle and remove wheel and brake drum.

2. Clean all dirt from area of carrier cover.

3. Drain lubricant from carrier by removing cover.

4. Remove the rear axle pinion shaft lock screw and the rear axle pinion shaft.

5. Push flanged end of axle shaft toward center of vehicle and remove "C" lock from button end of shaft.

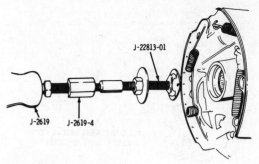

Removing axle bearing

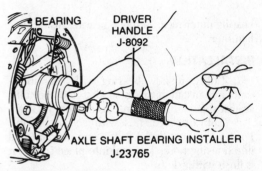

Installing axle bearing

6. Remove axle shaft from housing, being careful not to damage oil seal.

INSTALLATION

1. Slide axle shaft into place taking care that splines on end of shaft do not damage oil seal and that they engage with splines of rear axle side gear.

2. Install axle shaft "C" lock on button end of axle shaft and push shaft outward so that shaft lock seats in counterbore of rear axle side gear.

3. Position rear axle pinion shaft through case and pinions, aligning hole in shaft with lock screw hole. Install lock screw and torque to 20 ft. lbs.

4. Using a new gasket, install carrier cover and torque bolts to 20 ft. lbs.

5. Fill axle with lubricant to a level within 9.5mm (⅜ in.) of filler hole.

6. Install brake drum and wheel.

7. Lower vehicle and test operation of axle.

Oil Seal and/or Bearing Replacement (With Axle Shaft Removed)

REMOVAL

1. Remove seal from housing with a pry bar behind steel case of seal, being careful not to damage housing.

2. Insert Tool J-23689 into bore and position it behind bearing so that tangs on tool engage

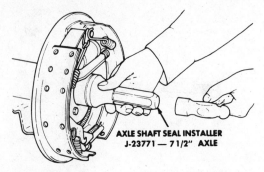

Installing axle seal

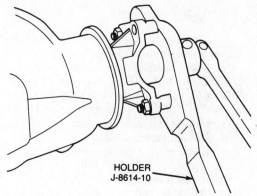

Removing pinion nut

bearing outer race. Remove bearing, using slide hammer.

INSTALLATION

1. Lubricate new bearing with gear lubricant and install bearing so that tool bottoms against shoulder in housing, using Tool J-23690.
2. Lubricate seal lips with gear lubricant. Position seal on Tool J-21128 and position seal into housing bore. Tap seal into place so that it is flush with axle tube.

Pinion Oil Seal Replacement

REMOVAL

1. Mark the drive shaft and pinion flange so they can be reassembled in the same position.
2. Disconnect drive shaft from rear axle pinion flange and support shaft up in body tunnel by wiring drive shaft to the exhaust pipe. If joint bearings are not retained by a retainer strap, use a piece of tape to hold bearings on their journals.
3. Mark the position of the pinion flange, pinion shaft and nut so the proper pinion bearing pre-load can be maintained.
4. Remove pinion flange nut and washer.
5. With suitable container in place to hold any fluid that may drain from rear axle, remove pinion flange.
6. Remove oil seal by driving it out of carrier with a blunt chisel. Do not damage carrier.

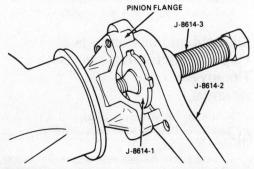

Removing pinion flange

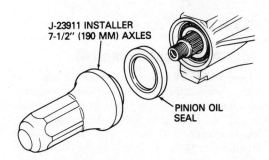

Installing pinion oil seal

7. Examine seal surface of pinion flange for tool marks, nicks, or damage, such as a groove worn by the seal. If damaged, replace flange as outlined under PINION FLANGE REPLACEMENT.
8. Examine carrier bore and remove any burrs that might cause leaks around the O.D. of the seal.

INSTALLATION

1. Install new seal.
2. Apply Special Seal Lubricant, No. 1050169 or equivalent, to the outside diameter of the pinion flange and sealing lip of new seal.
3. Install pinion flange and tighten nut to the same position as marked in Step 3. While holding pinion flange tighten nut 1.59mm (1/16 in.) beyond alignment marks.

Pinion Flange Replacement

REMOVAL

1. Raise vehicle and remove both rear wheels and drums.
2. Mark drive shaft and pinion flange, then disconnect rear joint and support drive shaft out of the way. If joint bearings are not retained by a retainer strap, use a piece of tape to hold bearings on their journals.
3. Check pre-load with an inch pound torque wrench and record. this will give combined

pinion bearing, carrier bearing, axle bearing and seal pre-load.

4. Remove pinion flange nut and washer.

5. With a suitable container in place to hold any fluid that may drain from the rear axle, remove the pinion flange.

INSTALLATION

1. Apply special seal lubricant, No. 1050169 or equivalent, to the outside diameter of the new pinion flange, then install pinion flange, washer and pinion flange nut finger tight.

2. While holding pinion flange, tighten the nut a little at a time and turn drive pinion several revolutions after each tightening to set the rollers. Check the pre-load of bearings each time with an inch pound torque wrench until pre-load is 3–5 inch pounds more than reading obtained in Step 3.

3. Connect drive shaft to rear axle pinion flange.

4. Install drums and wheels.

5. Check and add correct lubricant as necessary.

FRONT DRIVE AXLE

Tube and Shaft Assembly

REMOVAL

1. Disconnect negative battery cable.

2. Disconnect shift cable from vacuum actuator by disengaging locking spring. Then push actuator diaphragm in to release cable.

3. Unlock steering wheel at steering column so linkage is free to move.

4. Raise vehicle. If twin post hoist is used, place jack stands under frame and lower front post hoist.

5. Remove front wheels.

6. Remove engine drive belt shield.

7. Remove front axle skid plate (if equipped).

8. Place support under right hand lower control arm and disconnect right hand upper ball joint, then remove support so control arm will hang free.

9. Disconnect right hand drive axle shaft from tube assembly by removing six bolts.

Keep axle from turning by inserting a drift through opening in top of brake caliper into corresponding vane of brake rotor.

10. Disconnect four wheel drive indicator light electrical connection from switch.

11. Remove three bolts securing cable and switch housing to carrier and pull housing away to gain access to cable locking spring. Do not unscrew cable coupling nut unless cable is being replaced (Refer to Shift Cable Replacement).

12. Disconnect cable from shift fork shaft by lifting spring over slot in shift fork.

13. Remove two bolts securing tube bracket to frame.

14. Remove remaining two upper bolts securing tube assembly to carrier.

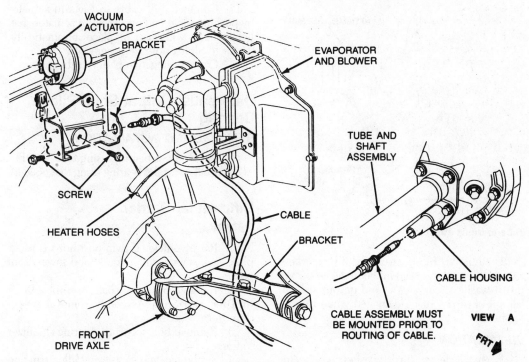

Vacuum actuator

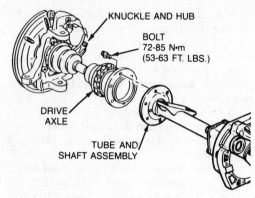

Drive axle bolts

KNUCKLE AND HUB

BOLT
72-85 N·m
(53-63 FT. LBS.)

DRIVE
AXLE

TUBE AND
SHAFT ASSEMBLY

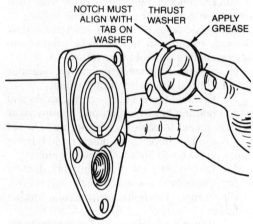

Thrust washer

NOTCH MUST
ALIGN WITH
TAB ON
WASHER

THRUST
WASHER

APPLY
GREASE

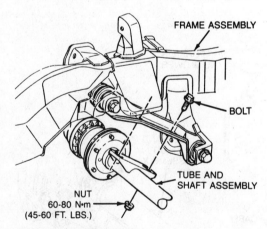

Tube-to-frame attachment

FRAME ASSEMBLY

BOLT

TUBE AND
SHAFT ASSEMBLY

NUT
60-80 N·m
(45-60 FT. LBS.)

15. Remove tube assembly by working around drive axle. Be careful not to allow sleeve, thrust washers, connector, and output shaft to fall out of carrier or be damaged when removing tube.

INSTALLATION

1. Install sleeve, thrust washers, connector and output shaft in carrier. Apply sealer No.

1052357, Locktite 514 or equivalent on tube to carrier surface. Be sure to install thrust washer. Apply grease to washer to hold it in place during assembly.

2. Install tube and shaft assembly to carrier and install bolt at one o'clock position but do not torque. Pull assembly down and install cable and switch housing, and remaining four bolts. Torque all bolts to 45–60 ft. lbs.

3. Install two bolts securing tube to frame and torque.

4. Check operation of four wheel drive mechanism using Tool J-33799. Insert tool into shift fork and check for rotation of axle shaft.

5. Remove tool and install shift cable switch housing by pushing cable through into fork shaft hole. Cable will automatically snap in place (Refer to Shift Cable Replacement).

6. Connect four wheel drive indicator light electrical connection to switch.

7. Install support under right hand lower control arm to raise arm and connect upper ball joint.

8. Install right-hand drive axle to axle tube by installing one bolt first, then, rotate axle to install remaining five bolts. Hold axle from turning by inserting a drift through opening in top of brake caliper into corresponding vane of brake rotor. Tighten bolts to 53–63 ft. lbs.

9. Install front axle skid plate, if equipped.

10. Install engine drive belt shield.

11. Install front wheels.

12. Lower vehicle.

13. Connect shift cable to vacuum actuator by pushing cable end into vacuum actuator shaft hole. Cable will snap in place automatically. (Refer to Shift Cable Replacement).

14. Connect negative battery cable.

Differential Output Shaft Pilot Bearing

REMOVAL AND INSTALLATION

1. Remove pilot bearing using tool J-34011.

2. Install new pilot bearing using tool J-33842.

Differential Carrier

REMOVAL

1. Raise vehicle. If twin post hoist is used, place jack stands under frame and lower front post.

2. Remove tube and shaft assembly. Refer to Tube and Shaft Assembly removal procedure in this section.

3. Remove bolt securing steering stabilizer to frame.

4. Scribe location of steering idler arm and then remove bolts securing arm to frame.

5. Push steering linkage towards front of vehicle.

6. Remove axle vent hose from carrier fitting.

7. Disconnect left-hand drive axle shaft from carrier by removing six bolts. Keep axle from turning by inserting a drift through opening in top of brake caliper into corresponding vane of brake rotor.

8. Disconnect front propeller shaft.

9. Remove two mounting bolts securing carrier to frame. Hold upper nut from turning by holding (through frame) with an 18mm combination wrench.

10. Remove carrier by tipping counterclockwise while lifting up to gain clearance from mounting ears.

INSTALLATION

1. Install carriers in vehicle and install two mounting bolts.

2. Install front propeller shaft.

3. Connect left-hand drive axle shaft to carrier by installing one bolt first, then, rotate axle to install remaining five bolts. Tighten bolts to 53–63 ft. lbs.

4. Connect axle vent hose to carrier.

5. Install steering idler arm in correct position marked at time of removal.

6. Install steering stabilizer to frame.

7. Install tube and shaft assembly.

8. Check axle lube, fill to level of fill plug hole.

9. Lower vehicle, test drive and recheck lubricate.

Differential Carrier Bushing
REMOVAL AND INSTALLATION

1. Remove tube and shaft assembly.

2. Remove differential carrier.

3. Remove bushing using Tool J-33791 to press bushing out of carrier ear.

4. Press new bushing into carrier using Tool J-33791. Be sure spacer, tool J-33791-3, is correctly installed between bushing and carrier ear to prevent bushing from being pressed too deep.

Shift Cable
REMOVAL AND INSTALLATION

1. Disengage shift cable from vacuum actuator by disengaging locking spring, then, push actuator diaphragm in to release cable. Squeeze the two locking fingers of the cable with pliers, then pull cable out of bracket hole.

2. Raise vehicle and remove three bolts securing cable and switch housing to carrier and pull housing away to gain access to cable locking spring. Disconnect cable from shaft fork shaft by lifting spring over slot in shift fork.

3. Unscrew cable from housing.

4. Remove cable from vehicle.

5. Install cable observing proper routing.

6. Install cable and switch housing to carrier using three attaching bolts. Torque mounting bolts to 30–40 ft. lbs.

7. Guide cable through switch housing into fork shaft hole and push cable in. Cable will automatically snap in place. Start turning coupling nut by hand, to avoid cross threading,

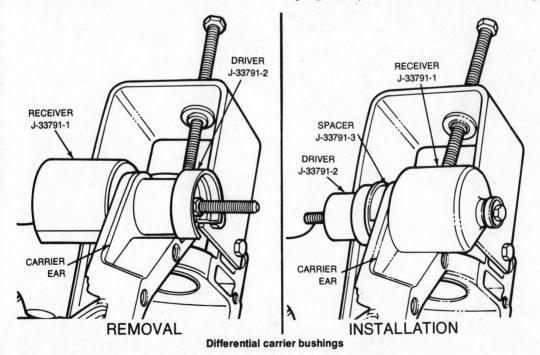

REMOVAL   INSTALLATION

Differential carrier bushings

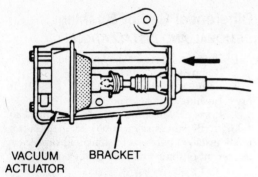

VACUUM ACTUATOR   BRACKET

Cable-to-vacuum actuator attachment

then torque nut to 71–106 inch lbs. Do not overtorque nut as this will cause thread damage to plastic housing.

8. Lower vehicle.

9. Connect shift cable to vacuum actuator by pressing cable into bracket hole. Cable and housing will snap in place automatically.

10. Check cable operation.

Differential Carrier Right Half Output Shaft and Tube
DISASSEMBLY

1. Remove right-hand output shaft from tube by striking inside of flange with a soft face hammer while holding tube.

2. Remove output shaft tube seal by prying out of tube.

3. Remove output shaft tube bearing using J-29369-2.

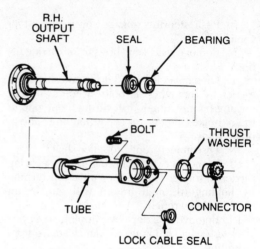

R.H. OUTPUT SHAFT   SEAL   BEARING

BOLT   THRUST WASHER

TUBE   CONNECTOR

LOCK CABLE SEAL

Right side output shaft and tube

4. Remove differential shift cable housing seal by driving out with a punch or similar tool.

ASSEMBLY

1. Install output shaft tube bearing using tool J-33844. Tool must be flush with tube when bearing is correctly installed.

2. Install output shaft tube seal using tool J-33893. Flange of seal must be flush with tube outer surface when seal is installed.

3. Install output shaft into tube and seat by striking flange with a soft face hammer.

4. Install differential shift cable housing seal using J-33799.

FRONT SUSPENSION

NOTE: *For procedures peculiar to 4-wheel drive, see Chapter 7.*

Shock Absorbers

REMOVAL

1. Raise vehicle on hoist, and with an open end wrench hold the shock absorber upper stem from turning, and then remove the upper stem retaining nut, retainer and rubber grommet.

2. Remove the two bolts retaining the lower shock absorber pivot to the lower control arm and pull the shock absorber assembly out from the bottom.

INSTALLATION

1. With the lower retainer and rubber grommet in place over the upper stem, install the shock absorber (fully extended) up through the lower control arm and spring so that the upper stem passes through the mounting hole in the upper control arm frame bracket.

2. Install the upper rubber grommet, retainer and attaching nut over the shock absorber upper stem.

3. With an open end wrench, hold the upper stem from turning and tighten the retaining nut.

4. Install the retainers attaching the shock absorber lower pivot to the lower control arm, torque and lower vehicle to floor.

Stabilizer Bar

REMOVAL AND INSTALLATION

1. Hoist vehicle.

2. Disconnect each side of stabilizer linkage by removing nut from link bolt, pull bolt from linkage and remove retainers, grommets and spacer.

3. Remove bracket to frame or body bolts

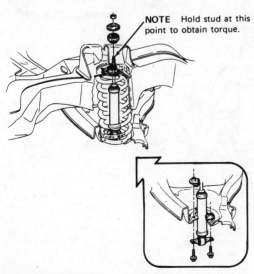

Front shock absorber attachment

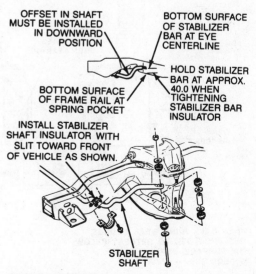

Typical stabilizer bar

and remove stabilizer shaft, rubber bushings and brackets.

4. To replace, reverse sequence of operations, being sure to install with the identification forming on the right side of the vehicle. The rubber bushings should be positioned squarely in the brackets with the slit in the bushings facing the front of car. Torque stabilizer link nut to 13 ft. lbs. and bracket bolts to 24 ft. lbs.

Ball Joints

INSPECTION

Ball joint seals should be carefully inspected for cuts or tears. Whenever cuts or tears are found, the ball joint MUST be replaced. Before checking ball joints, the wheel bearings must first be properly adjusted.

Upper Ball Joint

1. Raise the vehicle and position floor stands under the left and right lower control arm as near as possible to each lower ball joint. Vehicle must be stable and should not rock on the floor stands.

NOTE: *Upper control arm bumper must not contact frame.*

2. Position dial indicator against the wheel rim.

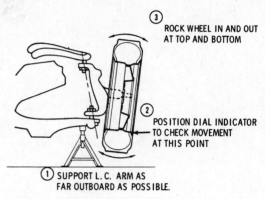

Checking upper ball joint

3. Grasp front wheel and push in on bottom of tire while pulling out at the top. Read gauge, then reverse the push-pull procedure. Horizontal deflection on dial indicator should not exceed 3.18 mm (.125 in.).

4. If dial indicator reading exceeds 3.18 mm (.125 in.) or if ball stud has been disconnected from knuckle assembly and any looseness is detected or the stud can be twisted in its socket with your fingers, replace the ball joint.

Lower Ball Joint

The lower ball joint has a visual wear indicator. Checking the condition of the ball joint is a

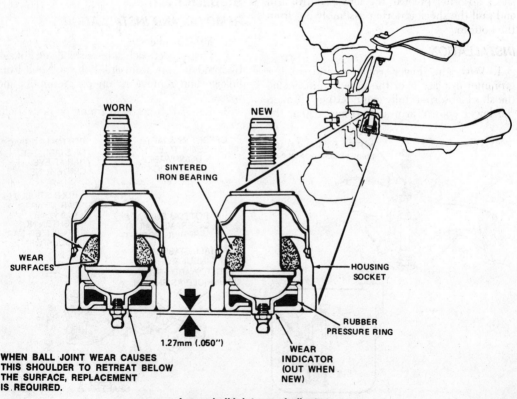

Lower ball joint wear indicator

simple procedure but must be followed accurately to prevent unnecessary ball joint replacement.

NOTE: *Vehicle must be supported by the wheels so that weight of vehicle will properly load the ball joints.*

The lower ball joint is inspected for wear by visual observation alone. Wear is indicated by the position of the 12.7mm (½ in.) diameter nipple into which the grease fitting is threaded. This round nipple projects 1.27mm (.050 in.) beyond the surface of the ball joint cover on a new, unworn joint. Normal wear will result in the surface of this nipple retreating very slowly inward.

To inspect for wear, wipe the grease fitting and nipple free of dirt and grease as for a grease job. Observe or scrape a scale, screwdriver or fingernail across the cover. If the round nipple is flush or inside the cover surface, replace the ball joint.

REMOVAL—LOWER BALL JOINT

1. Raise vehicle, support with floor stands under frame.
2. Remove tire and wheel assembly.
3. Place floor jack under control arm spring seat.

CAUTION: *Floor jack must remain under control arm spring seat during removal and installation to retain spring and control arm in position.*

4. To disconnect the lower control arm ball joint from the steering knuckle, remove the cotter pin and lower ball stud nut. Tool J-23742 can be used to break ball joint loose from knuckle.

Inspect the tapered hole in the steering

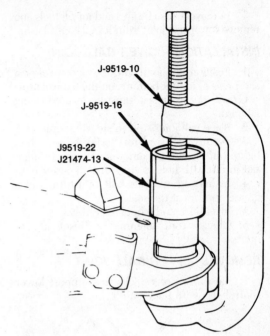

Removing lower ball joint

knuckle. Remove any dirt. If out-of-roundness, deformation or damage is noted, the knuckle MUST be replaced.

5. Guide lower control arm out of opening in splash shield with a putty knife or similar tool.

6. Block knuckle assembly out of the way by placing a wooden block between frame and upper control arm.

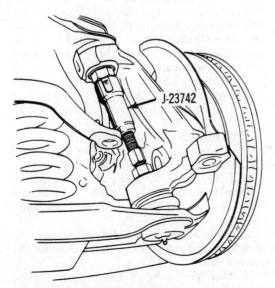

Disconnecting lower ball joint

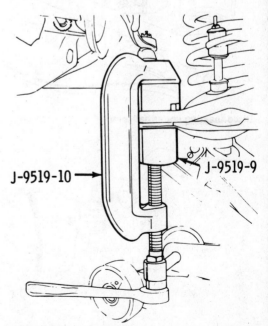

Installing lower ball joint

7. Remove grease fittings and install tools and remove lower ball joint from lower control arm.

INSTALLATION—LOWER BALL JOINT

1. Position ball joint into lower control arm and press in until it bottoms on the control arm.
Grease purge on seal must be located facing inboard.

2. Place ball joint stud in steering knuckle.

3. Torque ball stud nut to 90 ft. lbs. Then tighten an additional amount enough to align slot in nut with hole in stud. Install cotter pin.

4. Install and lubricate ball joint fitting until grease appears at the seal.

5. Install tire and wheel assembly.

6. Check front alignment. Reset as required.

REMOVAL—UPPER BALL JOINT

1. Raise front of vehicle and support lower control arm with floor stands.

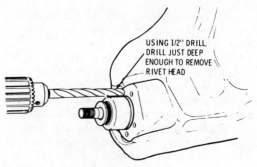

Drilling upper ball joint rivet heads

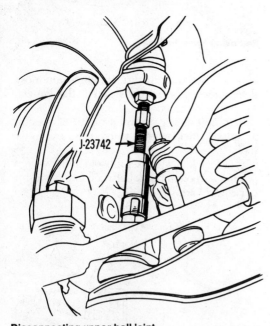

J-23742

Disconnecting upper ball joint

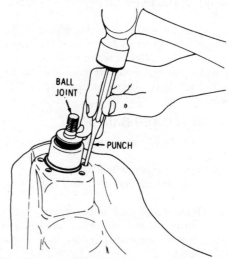

BALL JOINT

←PUNCH

Removing upper ball joint

CAUTION: *Floor jack or stand must remain under control arm spring seat during removal and installation to retain spring and control arm in position.*

Since the weight of the vehicle is used to relieve spring tension on the upper control arm, the floor stands must be positioned between the spring seats and ball joints of the lower control arms for maximum leverage.

2. Remove wheel, then loosen the upper ball joint from the steering knuckle as follows:

    a. Remove cotter pin and upper ball stud nut.

    b. Install Tool J-23742 as shown.

    c. Apply pressure on stud by expanding the tool until the stud breaks loose.

    d. Remove tool, then pull stud free from knuckle. Support the knuckle assembly to prevent weight of the assembly from damaging the brake hose.

3. With control arm in the raised position drill four rivets ¼ in. deep using an ⅛ in. diameter drill.

4. Drill off rivet heads using a ½ in. diameter drill.

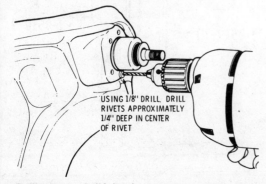

USING 1/8" DRILL, DRILL RIVETS APPROXIMATELY 1/4" DEEP IN CENTER OF RIVET

Drilling upper ball joint rivet

5. Punch out rivets using a small punch, and remove ball joint.

INSTALLATION—UPPER BALL JOINT

1. Position new ball joint in control arm and install the four attaching bolts. Torque nuts to 8 ft. lbs.

2. Remove the temporary support from knuckle assembly, then connect ball joint to steering knuckle. Torque ball stud nut to 65 ft. lbs., then tighten an additional amount to align the slot in the nut with the hole in the stud. Install cotter pin.

3. Install and lubricate ball joint fitting until grease appears at the seal.

4. Install wheel. Lower vehicle.

5. Check front alignment. Reset as required.

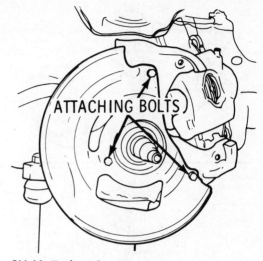

Shield attachment

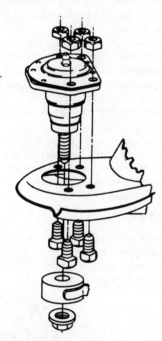

Upper ball joint attachment

Steering Knuckle

REMOVAL

1. Raise front of vehicle and support with floor stands under front lift points. Remove wheel.

NOTE: *Spring tension is needed to assist in breaking ball joint studs loose from steering knuckle. Do not place stands under lower control arm.*

2. Remove caliper.

3. Remove hub and rotor assembly.

4. Remove the three bolts attaching shield to knuckle.

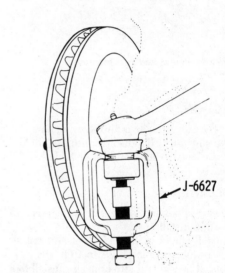

Removing tie rod end

5. Remove tie-rod end from knuckle using Tool J-6627.

6. Carefully remove knuckle seal if knuckle is to be replaced.

7. Remove ball studs from steering knuckle using tool J-23742.

CAUTION: *Floor jack must remain under control arm spring seat during removal and installation to retain spring and control arm in position.*

8. Position a floor jack under lower control arm near spring seat and raise jack until it just supports lower control arm.

9. Raise upper control arm to disengage ball joint stud from knuckle.

10. Raise knuckle from lower ball joint stud and remove knuckle.

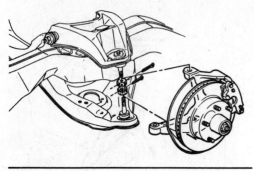

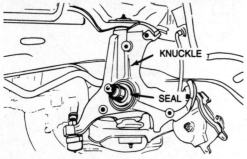

Knuckle attachment and seal location

INSPECTION

Inspect the tapered hole in the steering knuckle. Remove any dirt. If out-of-roundness, deformation, or damage is noted, the knuckle MUST be replaced.

INSTALLATION

1. Insert upper and lower ball joint studs into knuckle and install nuts.
2. Install shield to knuckle seal and splash shield. Torque attaching bolts to 10 ft. lbs.
3. Install tie rod end into knuckle. Install tool J-29193 and torque to 15 ft. lbs. Remove tool and install nut to 40 ft. lbs.
4. Replace wheel bearings. Install hub and disc assembly.
5. Adjust wheel bearings. Refer to Wheel Bearing Adjustment in Chapter 9. Install caliper.
6. Install wheel and tire assembly.
7. Remove floor stands and lower vehicle.
8. Check front alignment. Reset as required.

Coil Spring

REMOVAL

1. Raise vehicle on hoist.
2. Remove the two shock absorber screws and push shock up through control arm and into spring.
3. With the vehicle supported so that the control arms hang free, place Tool J-23028 into

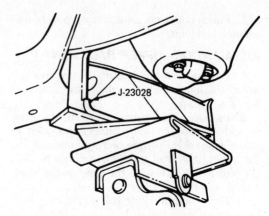

Removing spring with adapter J-23028

position cradling the inner bushings. Tool J-23028 should be secured to a suitable jack.

4. Remove stabilizer to lower control arm attachment.
5. Raise the jack to remove the tension on the lower control arm pivot bolts. Install a chain around the spring and through the control arm as a safety measure. Remove nuts and bolts— (Remove rear bolt first).
6. Lower control arm by slowly lowering jack.
7. When all compression is removed from the spring, remove safety chain and spring.

NOTE: *Do not apply force on the lower control arm and ball joint to remove spring. Proper maneuvering of the spring will allow for easy removal.*

INSTALLATION

1. Properly position spring on the control arm making sure spring insulator is in place and lift control arm with Special Tool J-23028. Take care that the spring is properly installed.

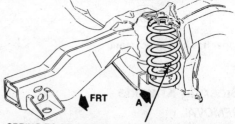

SPRING TO BE INSTALLED WITH TAPE AT LOWEST POSITION. BOTTOM OF SPRING IS COILED HELICAL, AND THE TOP IS COILED FLAT WITH A GRIPPER NOTCH NEAR END OF SPRING COIL.

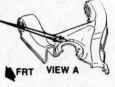

AFTER ASSEMBLY, END OF SPRING COIL MUST COVER ALL OR PART OF ONE INSPECTION DRAIN HOLE. THE OTHER HOLE MUST BE PARTLY EXPOSED OR COMPLETELY UNCOVERED. ROTATE SPRING AS NECESSARY.

Coil spring positioning

2. Position control arm into frame and install pivot bolts (front bolt first) and nuts. Torque to 85 ft. lbs. In order to maintain adequate steering linkage clearance, refer to mandatory bolt direction of installation.

3. Replace the stabilizer bar link, 13 ft. lbs. and shock absorber; top 8 ft. lbs., bottom 20 ft. lbs. Lower vehicle to floor.

Upper Control Arm

REMOVAL

1. Note the location of the shims. Alignment shims are to be installed in the same position from which they were removed. Remove nuts and shims. Raise front of vehicle and support lower control arm with floor stands.

CAUTION: *Floor jack must remain under control arm spring seat during removal and installation to retain spring and control arm in position.*

Since the weight of the vehicle is used to relieve spring tension on the upper control arm, the floor stands must be positioned between the spring seats and ball joints of the lower control arms for maximum leverage.

2. Remove wheel, then loosen the upper ball joint from the steering knuckle as previously outlined.

3. Support hub assembly to prevent weight from damaging brake hose.

4. It is necessary to remove the upper control arm attaching bolts to allow clearance to remove upper control arm assembly.

5. Remove upper control arm.

INSTALLATION

1. Position upper control arm attaching bolts loosely in the frame and install pivot shaft on the attaching bolts.

The inner pivot bolts must be installed with the bolt heads to the front (on the front bushing) and to the rear (on the rear bushing).

2. Install alignment shims in their original position between the pivot shaft and frame on their respective bolts. Torque nuts to 45 ft. lbs.

3. Remove the temporary support from the hub assembly, then connect ball joint to steering knuckle as previously outlined.

4. Install wheel, then check wheel alignment, and adjust if necessary.

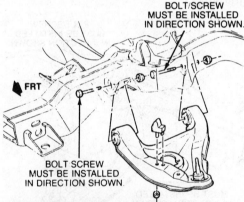

BOLT/SCREW MUST BE INSTALLED IN DIRECTION SHOWN.

FRT

BOLT SCREW MUST BE INSTALLED IN DIRECTION SHOWN.

SUGGESTED ASSEMBLY SEQUENCE
INSTALL THE FRONT LEG OF THE LOWER CONTROL ARM INTO THE CROSSMEMBER PRIOR TO INSTALLING THE REAR LEG IN THE FRAME BRACKET.

Pivot bolt installation

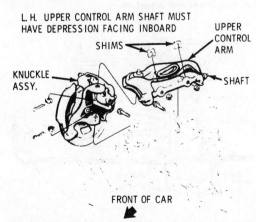

L.H. UPPER CONTROL ARM SHAFT MUST HAVE DEPRESSION FACING INBOARD

UPPER CONTROL ARM

SHIMS

KNUCKLE ASSY.

SHAFT

FRONT OF CAR

Upper control arm assembly

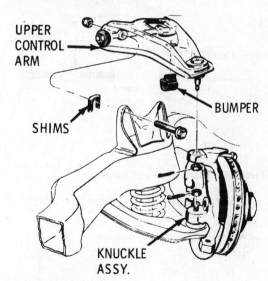

UPPER CONTROL ARM

BUMPER

SHIMS

KNUCKLE ASSY.

Upper control arm

Upper Control Arm Pivot Shaft Bushing

REMOVAL AND INSTALLATION

1. Remove upper control arm assembly from the vehicle.

2. Remove nuts from ends of pivot shaft.

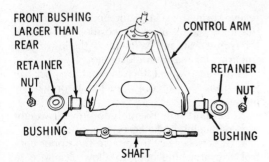

FRONT BUSHING
LARGER THAN
REAR

CONTROL ARM

RETAINER
NUT

RETAINER

NUT

BUSHING

BUSHING

SHAFT

Upper control arm components

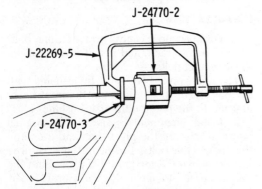

J-24770-2

J-22269-5

J-24770-3

Removing upper control arm bushings

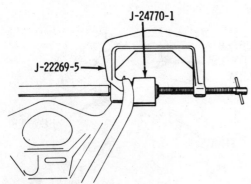

J-24770-1

J-22269-5

Installing upper control arm bushings

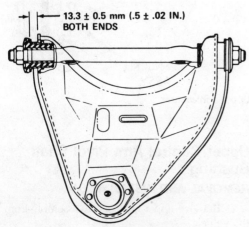

13.3 ± 0.5 mm (.5 ± .02 IN.)
BOTH ENDS

Upper control arm bushing positioning

3. Position control arm assembly and tools as shown and push bushing out of control arm.

4. Repeat Step 3 on other bushing.

5. To install bushings, place pivot shaft in control arm and push new bushing into control arm and over end of pivot shaft. Both upper control arm bushings are to be installed 13.3 ± 0.5 mm (.5 ± .02 inches) from face of the control arm to the bushing outer sleeve.

6. Repeat Step 5 on other bushing.

7. Assemble nuts to ends of pivot shaft.

8. Install the upper control arm assembly. Refer to Upper Control Arm—Installation. With weight of car on the wheels, torque pivot shaft nuts to 85 ft. lbs. Check front end alignment and adjust if necessary.

Lower Control Arm

REMOVAL

1. Remove coil spring as described earlier in this section.

2. Remove lower ball joint stud as previously outlined.

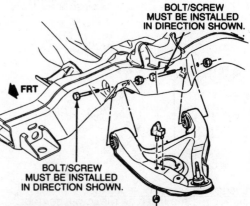

BOLT/SCREW
MUST BE INSTALLED
IN DIRECTION SHOWN.

FRT

BOLT/SCREW
MUST BE INSTALLED
IN DIRECTION SHOWN.

SUGGESTED ASSEMBLY SEQUENCE
INSTALL THE FRONT LEG OF THE LOWER CONTROL
ARM INTO THE CROSSMEMBER PRIOR TO
INSTALLING THE REAR LEG IN THE FRAME
BRACKET.

Lower control arm attachment

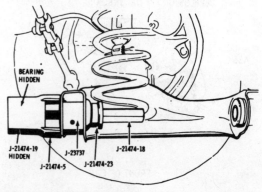

BEARING
HIDDEN

J-21474-19
HIDDEN

J-23737

J-21474-18

J-21474-5

J-21474-23

Removing front bushing

3. After stud breaks loose, hold up on lower control arm. Remove control arm.

4. Guide lower control arm out of opening in splash shield with a putty knife or similar tool.

INSTALLATION

1. Install lower ball joint stud into knuckle. Install nut as previously outlined.

2. Install spring. Refer to coil spring installation.

3. Check front alignment. Reset as required.

REAR SUSPENSION

Shock Absorbers

REMOVAL AND INSTALLATION

1. Raise vehicle on hoist, and support rear axle.

2. At the upper mounting location, disconnect shock absorber.

3. At the lower mounting location, remove nut and washer.

4. Remove shock absorbers from vehicle.

5. To install shock absorber, place into position and reattach at upper mounting location. Be sure to install parts as shown.

6. Align lower end of shock absorber with

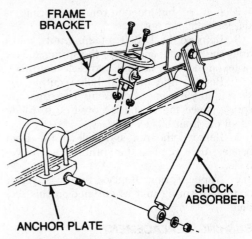

Rear shock absorber attachment

stud on anchor plate and install washer and nut, as shown.

7. Tighten fasteners to 15 ft. lbs. upper: 50 ft. lbs. lower.

8. Lower vehicle and remove from hoist.

Leaf Spring Assembly

REMOVAL

1. Raise vehicle on hoist, then support the body-chassis and axle separately, so that the load on the spring is relieved.

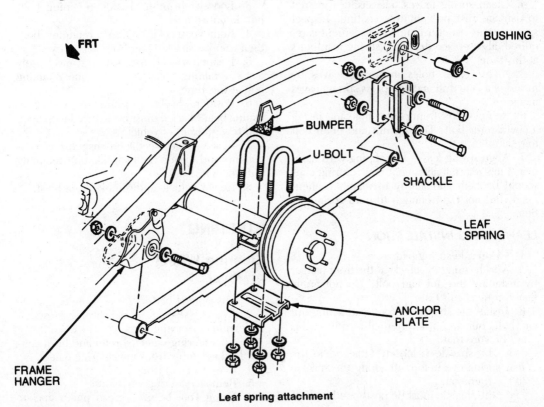

Leaf spring attachment

2. Loosen, but do not remove, spring-to-shackle retaining nut.

3. Remove the U-bolt retaining nuts, withdraw the U-bolts, and rotate the spring anchor plate, on the shock absorber, to clear the spring.

4. Remove the nut and bolt securing the shackle to the frame. Be careful to restrain the spring, since the spring is now free to rotate about the front hanger bolt.

5. Remove the nut and bolt at the front hanger, then remove the spring from the vehicle.

6. Inspect spring. Replace bushings, repair or replace spring unit as outlined in this section.

BUSHING REPLACEMENT

1. Place spring on press and press out bushing using a suitable rod, pipe or tool.

2. Press in new bushing; assure that tool presses on steel outer shell of bushing.

SPRING LEAF REPLACEMENT

1. Place spring assembly in a bench mounted vise and remove spring clip, nut, bolt and spacer.

2. Position spring in vise jaws, compressing leaves at center, adjacent to center bolt.

3. File peened end of center bolt and remove nut. Open vise slowly to allow spring assembly to expand.

4. Clean spring leaves, exercising care not to damage rust preventative coating. Inspect spring leaves to determine if replacement is required; also replace defective spring leaf liners at this time.

5. Align center holes in spring leaves by means of a long drift and compress spring leaves in a vise.

6. Remove drift from center hole and install a new center bolt. Tighten nut and peen bolt to retain nut.

7. Align spring leaves by tapping with hammer, then reinstall alignment clips. Spring clips should be bent sufficiently to maintain alignment, but not tight enough to bind spring action.

LEAF SPRING INSTALLATION

1. Clean axle spring pad.

2. Attach spring to vehicle at the front hanger by installing the nut and bolt. Do not apply final torque at this time.

3. Install the shackle-to-frame attaching nut and bolt, but do not apply final torque at this time. Be sure that:

    a. the shackle is loosely attached to the rear spring eye before attaching the shackle to the frame, and

    b. the shackle must be positioned with its open end toward the front of the vehicle, and

    c. the axle must be in position above the spring before attaching the shackle to the frame.

4. Position axle spring pad onto the spring so that the center bolt head is seated in the pilot hole of the spring pad seat.

5. Rotate the anchor plate, on shock absorber, underneath the spring assembly and install the U-bolts. Align the anchor plate, install the retaining nuts evenly (handtight), then tighten diagonally opposite nuts to 34 ft. lbs.

6. Lower the vehicle so that the weight of the vehicle is supported by the suspension components. Torque the U-bolt nuts, spring eye bolt nuts (front and rear), and shackle-to-frame bolt nuts to 85 ft. lbs.

7. Lower the vehicle and remove from the hoist.

U-BOLT AND ANCHOR PLATE INSTALLATION

A diagonal pattern is the mandatory sequence of tightening U-bolt nuts. Tighten diagonally opposite nuts to 34 ft. lbs., then tighten all nuts to 194 ft. lbs.

SHACKLE REPLACEMENT

1. Raise vehicle on hoist. Place adjustable lifting device under axle.

2. Remove load from spring by jacking frame.

3. Loosen spring-to-shackle retaining bolt, but do not remove.

4. Remove shackle-to-frame retaining bolt, then remove shackle bolt from spring eye.

5. Position shackle to spring eye and loosely install retaining bolt. Do not torque retaining bolt at this time.

6. Position shackle to frame and install retaining bolt. Shackle must be installed with open end toward front of vehicle.

7. Rest vehicle weight on suspension components and torque both shackle bolt retaining nuts to 88 ft. lbs.

8. Lower vehicle and remove from hoist.

STEERING

Steering Wheel
REMOVAL

1. Disconnect battery ground cable.

2. Remove steering wheel shroud screws on underside of steering wheel.

3. Lift steering wheel shroud and horn contact lead assembly from the steering wheel.

4. Remove snap ring.

5. Remove steering wheel nut.

6. Using Tool J-2927, thread puller anchor

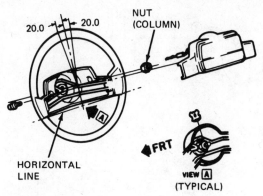

Steering wheel

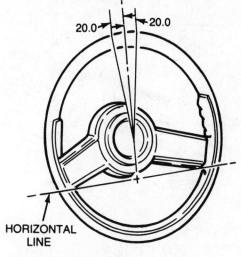

Steering wheel alignment

screws into threaded holes provided in steering wheel. Turn center bolt of tool clockwise (butting against the steering shaft) to remove steering wheel.

NOTE: *Do not hammer on puller while turning. The tool centering adapters need not be installed.*

INSTALLATION

1. With turn signal in neutral position, set wheel onto steering shaft and secure with nut. Torque to 30 ft. lbs.

NOTE: *Do not over-torque shaft nut or steering wheel rub may result.*

2. Install snap ring, making sure it is fully seated.

3. Place the steering wheel shroud onto the steering wheel while guiding the horn contact lead into the directional signal cancelling cam tower.

4. Install the shroud attaching screws on the underside of the steering wheel.

5. Connect the battery ground cable.

STEERING WHEEL ALIGNMENT AND HIGH POINT CENTERING

1. Set front wheels in straight ahead position. This can be checked by driving vehicle a short distance on a flat surface to determine steering wheel position at which vehicle follows a straight path.

2. With front wheels set straight ahead, check position of flat on wormshaft designating steering gear high point. This flat should be at the top side of the shaft at 12 o'clock position.

3. If gear has been moved off high point when setting wheels in straight ahead position, loosen adjusting sleeve clamps on both left and right hand tie rods, then turn both sleeves an equal number of turns in the same direction to bring gear back on high point.

NOTE: *Turning the sleeves an unequal number of turns or in different directions will disturb the toe-in setting of the wheels.*

4. Readjust toe-in.

5. With wheels in a straight ahead position and the steering gear on highpoint, check the steering wheel alignment. If the spokes are not within the limits specified, the wheel should be removed and centered.

Turn Signal Switch
REMOVAL AND INSTALLATION

1. Remove the steering wheel.
2. Pry out the steering shaft lock cover.
3. Remove the retaining ring and shaft lock.
4. Remove the cancelling cam and spring.
5. Remove the switch actuator arm, unscrew and remove the switch and unplug the wire connector.
6. Installation is the reverse of removal.

Ignition Lock Cylinder
REMOVAL AND INSTALLATION

1. Disconnect the battery ground.
2. Turn the lock to the RUN position.
3. Remove the turn signal switch.
4. Remove the cylinder retaining screw.
5. Pull out the cylinder.
6. Installation is the reverse of removal. Turn the cylinder to the STOP position while installing.

Wiper Switch
REMOVAL AND INSTALLATION

1. Remove the ignition switch.
2. Remove the horn contact.
3. Remove the steering shaft bearing retainer and bearing.

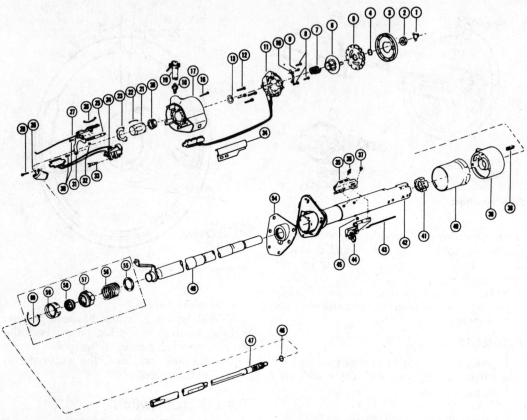

1. Retainer
2. Nut, hexagon
3. Cover, shaft lock
4. Ring, retaining
5. Lock, steering shaft
6. Cam assy, turn signal cancelling
7. Spring, upper bearing
8. Screw, binding head cross recess
9. Screw, round washer head
10. Arm assy, switch actuator
11. Switch assy, turn signal
12. Screw, hex washer head tapping
13. Washer, thrust
16. Screw, lock retaining
17. Housing, steering column
18. Sector assy, switch actuator
19. Lock cylinder set, steering column
20. Bearing assy
21. Bushing, bearing retaining
22. Contact, horn circuit
23. Retainer, upper bearing
24. Switch assy, pivot &
25. Bolt assy, spring &
26. Spring, rack preload
27. Rack assy, switch actuator rod &
28. Cover, housing
29. Screw, binding head cross recess
30. Screw, flat head cross recess
31. Gate, shift lever
32. Washer, spring thrust
33. Pin, switch actuator pivot
34. Protector, wiring
35. Switch assy, ignition
36. Stud, dimmer & ignition switch mounting
37. Screw, washer head
38. Spring, upper shift lever
39. Bowl, gearshift lever
40. Shroud, gearshift bowl
41. Bearing, bowl lower
42. Jacket assy, steering column
43. Rod, dimmer switch actuator
44. Switch assy, dimmer
45. Nut, hexagon
46. Ring, retaining
47. Shaft assy, steering
48. Tube assy, shift
54. Seal, dash
55. Washer spring thrust
56. Spring shift tube return
57. Adapter, lower bearing
58. Bearing assembly
59. Retainer bearing adapter
60. Clip, lower bearing adapter

Standard steering column components

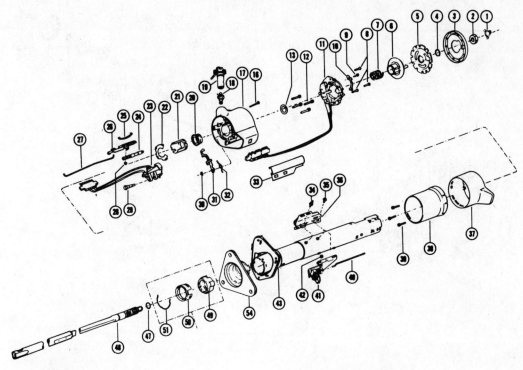

1. Retainer
2. Nut, hexagon jam
3. Cover, shaft lock
4. Ring, retaining
5. Lock, steering shaft
6. Cam assy, turn signal cancelling
7. Spring, upper bearing
8. Screw, binding head cross recess
9. Screw, round washer head
10. Arm assy, switch actuator
11. Switch assy, turn signal
12. Screw, hex washer head tapping
13. Washer, thrust
16. Screw, lock retaining
17. Housing, steering column
18. Sector assy, switch actuator
19. Lock cylinder set, steering column
20. Bearing assy
21. Bushing, bearing retaining
22. Retainer, upper bearing
23. Switch assy, pivot &
24. Bolt assy, spring &
25. Spring, rack preload
26. Rack, switch actuator

27. Rod, switch actuator
28. Washer, spring thrust
29. Pin, switch actuator pivot
30. Washer, wave
31. Lever, key release
32. Spring, key release
33. Protector, wiring
34. Stud, dimmer and ignition switch mounting
35. Screw, washer head
36. Switch assy, ignition
37. Bowl, floor shift
38. Shroud, shift bowl
39. Screw, binding head cross recess
40. Rod, dimmer switch actuator
41. Switch assy, dimmer
42. Nut, hexagon
43. Jacket assy, steering column
47. Ring, retaining
48. Shaft assy, steering
49. Bushing assy. steering shaft
50. Retainer, bearing adapter
51. Clip, lower bearing adapter
54. Bracket assy, column dash

Key release standard steering column components

4. Remove the wiper switch.
5. Installation is the reverse of removal.

Ignition Switch and Dimmer Switch

REMOVAL AND INSTALLATION

1. Remove the steering wheel, lock cylinder, turn signal switch, shift lever, shift lever bowl, shift bowl shroud and bowl lower bearing.

2. Unbolt and remove the ignition switch and dimmer switch from the column.

3. For installation, on all columns except key-release type, move the switch slider to the extreme left position, then two detents right. This is the OFF-UNLOCK position. On key-release columns, leave the slider in the extreme

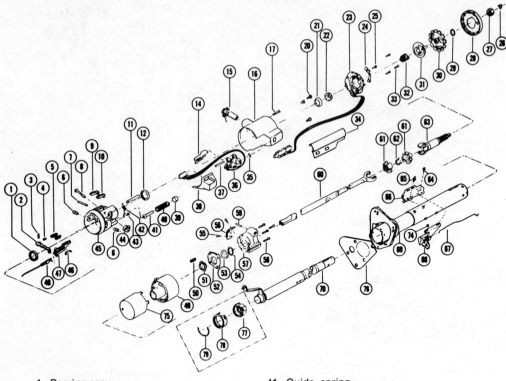

1. Bearing assy
2. Lever, shoe release
3. Pin, release lever
4. Spring, release lever
5. Spring, shoe
6. Pin, pivot
7. Pin, dowel
8. Shaft, drive
9. Shoe, steering wheel lock
10. Shoe, steering wheel lock
11. Bolt, lock
12. Bearing assy
14. Actuator, dimmer switch rod
15. Lock cylinder set, strg column
16. Cover, lock housing
17. Screw, lock retaining
20. Screw, pan head cross recess
21. Race, inner
22. Seat, upper bearing inner race
23. Switch assy, turn signal
24. Arm assy, signal switch
25. Screw, round washer head
26. Retainer
27. Nut, hex jam
28. Cover, shaft lock
29. Ring, retaining
30. Lock, shaft
31. Cam assy, turn signal cancelling
32. Spring, upper bearing
33. Screw, binding head cross recess
34. Protector, wiring
35. Spring, pin preload
36. Switch assy, pivot &
37. Pin, switch actuator pivot
38. Cap, column housing cover end
39. Retainer, spring
40. Spring, wheel tilt

41. Guide, spring
42. Spring, lock bolt
43. Screw, hex washer head
44. Sector, switch actuator
45. Housing, steering column
46. Spring, rack preload
47. Rack, switch actuator
48. Actuator assy, ignition switch
49. Bowl, gearshift lever
50. Spring, shift lever
51. Washer, wave
52. Plate, lock
53. Washer, thrust
54. Ring, shift tube retaining
55. Screw, oval head cross recess
56. Gate, shift lever
57. Support, strg column housing
58. Screw, support
59. Pin, dowel
60. Shaft assy, lower steering
61. Sphere, centering
62. Spring, joint preload
63. Shaft assy, race & upper
64. Screw, washer head
65. Stud, dimmer & ignition switch mounting
66. Switch assy, ignition
67. Rod, dimmer switch
68. Switch assy, dimmer
69. Jacket assy, steering column
70. Tube assy, shift
74. Nut, hexagon
75. Shroud, gearshift bowl
76. Seal, dash
77. Bushing assy, steering shaft
78. Retainer, bearing adapter
79. Clip, lower bearing adapter

Tilt steering column components

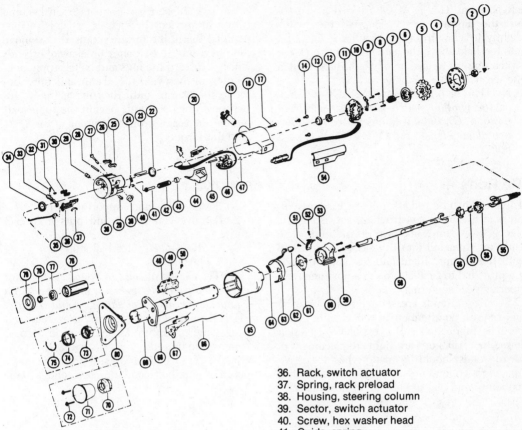

1. Retainer
2. Nut, hexagon jam
3. Cover, shaft lock
4. Ring, retaining
5. Lock, shaft
6. Cam assy, turn signal cancelling
7. Spring, upper bearing
8. Screw, binding head cross recess
9. Screw, round washer head
10. Arm assy, signal switch
11. Switch assy, turn signal
12. Seat, upper bearing inner race
13. Race, inner
14. Screw, pan head cross recess
17. Screw, lock retaining
18. Cover, lock housing
19. Lock cylinder set, steering column
20. Actuator, dimmer switch rod
22. Bearing assy
23. Bolt, lock
24. Spring, lock bolt
25. Shoe, steering wheel lock
26. Shoe, steering wheel lock
27. Shaft, drive
28. Pin, dowel
29. Pin, pivot
30. Spring, shoe
31. Spring, release lever
32. Pin, release lever
33. Lever, shoe release
34. Bearing assy
35. Actuator assy, ignition switch

36. Rack, switch actuator
37. Spring, rack preload
38. Housing, steering column
39. Sector, switch actuator
40. Screw, hex washer head
41. Guide, spring
42. Spring, wheel tilt
43. Retainer, spring
44. Cap, column housing cover end
45. Pin, switch actuator pivot
46. Switch assy, pivot &
47. Spring, pin preload
48. Switch assy, ignition
49. Stud, dimmer & ignition switch mounting
50. Screw, washer head
51. Plate, shroud retaining
52. Screw, oval head cross recess
53. Pin, dowel
54. Protector, wiring
55. Shaft assy,race & upper
56. Sphere, centering
57. Spring, joint preload
58. Shaft assy, lower steering
59. Screw, support
60. Support, steering column housing
61. Plate, lock
62. Finger pad, release lever
63. Lever, key release
64. Spring, key release
65. Shroud, steering column housing
66. Rod, dimmer switch
67. Switch assy, dimmer
68. Nut, hexagon
69. Jacket assy, steering column
73. Bushing assy, steering shaft
74. Retainer, bearing adapter
75. Clip, lower bearing adapter
80. Bracket assy, column dash

Tilt steering column with key release components

left position. This is ACCESSORIES. To adjust the dimmer switch, depress the switch slightly to allow insertion of a ³⁄₃₂ in. drill bit into the hole above the actuator rod. Force the switch upward to take up any lash, then tighten the screw.

NOTE: *On tilt columns, the ACC position on the ignition switch is the extreme right position. On these columns, move the slider two detents left to the OFF-UNLOCK position.*

Tie Rods

There are two tie rod assemblies. Each assembly is of five piece construction, consisting of a sleeve, two clamps and two tie rod ends. The ends are threaded into the sleeve and locked with the clamps. Right and left hand threads are provided to facilitate toe-in adjustment and steering gear centering.

The tie rod ends are self-adjusting for wear and require no attention in service other than periodic lubrication and occasional inspection to see that ball studs are tight. Replacement of tie rod ends should be made when excessive up and down looseness is evident or if any lost motion or end play at ball end of stud exists.

Tie rod adjuster components often become rusted in service. In such cases, it is recommended that if the torque required to remove the nut from the bolt after breakaway exceeds 7 ft. lbs. discard the nuts and bolts. Apply penetrating oil between the clamp and tube and rotate the clamps until they move freely. Install new bolts and nuts having the same part number to assure proper clamping at the specified nut torque.

REMOVAL

1. Raise vehicle and support it safely.
2. Remove cotter pins and nuts from ball studs.
3. To disconnect outer ball stud, use a tool such as J-6627.

NOTE: *Do not attempt to disengage the joint by driving a wedge between the joint and the knuckle, because seal damage could result.*

4. Disconnect inner ball stud from relay rod using same procedure as described in Step 3. Remove the tie rod.
5. To remove tie rod ends from tie rods, loosen clamp bolts and unscrew end assemblies.

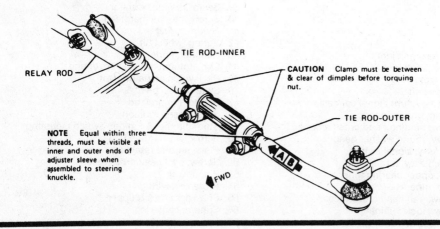

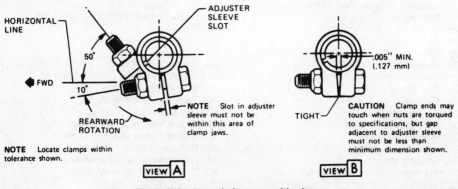

Tie rod clamp and sleeve positioning

INSTALLATION

1. If the tie rod ends were removed, lubricate the tie rod threads with EP type Chassis lube and install ends on tie rod making sure both ends are threaded an equal distance from the tie rod.

2. Make sure that the threads on the ball stud and in the ball stud nuts are clean and smooth. If threads are not clean and smooth, ball studs may turn in tie rod ends when attempting to tighten nut. In addition tapered surfaces should be clean and free from grease. Install seals on ball studs.

3. Install ball studs in steering arms and relay rod.

4. Torque nuts to 35 ft. lbs. Then tighten nuts enough to align the slot in the nut with the hole in the stud. Install cotter pins. Lubricate tie rod ends.

5. Lower vehicle to floor.

6. Adjust toe-in.

Before tightening the tie rod adjusting sleeve clamp bolts, be sure that the following conditions have been met:

    a. The sleeve clamps must be positioned between the locating dimples at either end of the sleeve.

    b. The clamps must be positioned within the angular travel indicated.

    c. The relationship of the clamp slot with the slit in the sleeve should be maintained as shown.

    d. Both inner and outer tie rod ends must rotate for their full travel. The position of each tie rod end must be maintained as the clamps are tightened to ensure free movement of each joint.

    e. All procedures for alignment, adjustment and assembly of tie rods applies to both left and right side.

Relay Rod

REMOVAL

1. Raise vehicle on hoist.

2. Disconnect inner ends of tie rods from relay rod as described under Tie Rod Removal.

3. Remove nut from relay rod ball stud attachment at pitman arm.

4. Detach relay rod from pitman arm by using tool such as J-24319-01. Shift steering linkage as required to free pitman arm from relay rod.

5. Remove nut from idler arm and remove relay rod from idler arm.

INSTALLATION

1. Install relay rod to idler arm, making certain idler stud seal is in place. Use J-29193 or

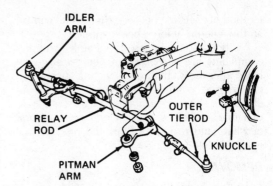

Steering linkage

J-29194 to seat the tapers. A torque of 12 ft. lbs. is required. With the tapers seated, remove the tool, then install a prevailing torque nut, and tighten to 40 ft. lbs.

2. Raise end of rod and install on pitman arm. Use J-29193 or J-29194 to seat the tapers. A torque of 20 N m is required. With the tapers seated, remove the tool, then install a prevailing torque nut, and tighten to 40 ft. lbs.

3. Install tie rod ends to relay rod as previously described under Tie Rods. Lubricate tie rod ends.

4. Lower vehicle to floor.

5. Adjust toe-in and align steering wheel as described under Steering Wheel Alignment and High Point Centering.

Idler Arm

Use of the proper diagnosis and checking procedure is essential to prevent needless replacement of good idler arms.

The proper checking procedure is as follows:

1. Raise the vehicle in such a manner as to allow the front wheels to rotate freely and the steering mechanism freedom to turn. Position the wheels in the straight ahead position.

2. Using a push pull type spring scale located as near the relay rod end of the idler arm as possible, exert a 25 lb. force upward and then downward while noticing the total distance the end of the arm moves. This distance should not exceed ⅛ inch in either direction, for total acceptable movement of ¼ inch. It is necessary to ensure that the correct load is applied to the arm since it will move more when higher loads are applied. It is also necessary that a scale or ruler be rested against the frame and used to determine the amount of movement because the actual movement can be overestimated when a scale is not used. The idler arm should always be replaced if it fails this test.

Jerking the right wheel and tire assembly back and forth, thus causing an up and down movement of the idler arm, is NOT an acceptable method of checking because there is no control on the amount of force being applied.

Caution should be used whenever shimmy complaints are suspected of being caused by loose idler arms. Before suspecting suspension or steering components, technicians should eliminate shimmy excitation factors, such as dynamic imbalance, runout or force variation of wheel and tire assemblies and road surface irregularities.

REMOVAL

1. Raise vehicle and support it safely.
2. Remove idler arm to frame nuts, washers, and bolts.
3. Remove nut from idler arm to relay rod ball stud.
4. Disconnect relay rod from idler arm by using J-24319-01 or similar puller.
5. Remove idler arm.

INSTALLATION

1. Position idler arm on frame and install mounting bolts, washers and nuts. Torque nuts to 60 ft. lbs.
2. Install relay rod to idler arm, making certain seal is on stud. Use J-29193 or J-29194 to seat the tapers. A torque of 12 ft. lbs. is required. With the tapers seated, remove the tool, then install a prevailing torque nut, and tighten to 40 ft. lbs.
3. Lower vehicle to floor.

Pitman Arm
REMOVAL

1. Raise vehicle and support it safely.
2. Remove nut from pitman arm ball stud.
3. Disconnect relay rod from pitman arm by using a tool such as J-24319-01. Pull down on relay rod to remove from stud.
4. Remove pitman arm nut from pitman shaft and mark relation of arm position to shaft.

5. Remove pitman arm with Tool J-5504 or Tool J-6632. DO NOT HAMMER ON PULLER.

INSTALLATION

1. Install pitman arm on pitman shaft, lining up the marks made upon removal.
2. Install pitman shaft nut and torque to 180 ft. lbs.
3. Position relay rod on pitman arm. Use J-29193 or J-29194 to seat the tapers. A torque of 12 ft. lbs. is required. With the tapers seated, remove the tool, then install a prevailing torque nut, and tighten to 40 ft. lbs.
4. Lower vehicle to floor.

Manual Steering Gear
ADJUSTMENT

Before any adjustments are made to the steering gear in an attempt to correct such conditions as shimmy, loose or hard steering etc., a careful check should be made of front end alignment, shock absorbers, wheel balance and tire pressure for possible cause.

Correct adjustment of the steering gear is very important. Perform adjustments following the sequence listed below.

1. Disconnect the battery ground cable.
2. Raise the vehicle.
3. Remove the pitman arm nut. Mark the relationship of the pitman arm to the pitman shaft. Remove the pitman arm with Tool J-6632 or J-5504.
4. Loosen the steering gear adjuster plug locknut and back the adjuster plug off ¼ turn.
5. Remove the horn button cap or shroud.
6. Turn the steering wheel gently in one direction until stopped by the gear; then turn back one-half turn.

NOTE: *Do not turn the steering wheel hard against the stops when the steering linkage is disconnected from the gear as damage to the ball guides could result.*

7. Measure and record "bearing drag" by

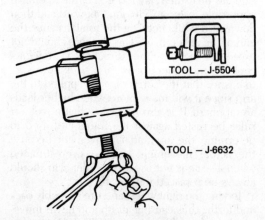

Pitman arm removal

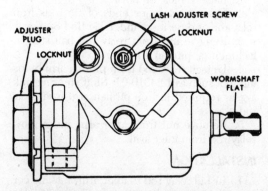

Manual steering gear adjustment points

applying a torque wrench with a ¾ inch socket on the steering wheel nut and rotating through a 90° arc. Do not use a torque wrench having a maximum torque reading of more than 50 inch lbs.

8. Adjust thrust bearing preload by tightening the adjuster plug until the proper thrust loading preload of 5–8 inch lb. is obtained. When the proper preload has been obtained, tighten the adjuster plug locknut to 85 ft. lbs. and recheck torque. If the gear feels "lumpy" after adjustment, there is probably damage in the bearings due to severe impact or improper adjustment; the gear must be disassembled for replacement of damaged parts.

9. Adjust over-center preload as follows:

a. Turn the steering wheel gently from one stop all the way to the other carefully counting the total number of turns. Turn the wheel back exactly half-way, to center position.

b. Turn the over center adjuster screw clockwise to take out all lash between the ball nut and pitman shaft sector teeth and then tighten the locknut.

c. Check the torque at the steering wheel, taking the highest reading as the wheel is turned through center position. Total over-center preload should be 16 inch lbs.

d. If necessary, loosen locknut and readjust over center adjuster screw to obtain proper torque. Tighten the locknut to 85 ft. lbs. and again check torque reading through center of travel. If maximum specification is exceeded, turn over center adjuster screw counterclockwise, then come up on adjustment by turning the adjuster lock nut in a clockwise motion.

10. Reassemble the pitman arm to the pitman shaft, lining up the marks made during disassembly. Torque the pitman shaft nut to 180 ft. lbs.

11. Install the horn button cap or shroud and

connect the battery ground cable. lower the vehicle to the floor.

REMOVAL

1. Disconnect battery ground cable and remove coupling shield if so equipped.
2. Remove retaining nuts, lock washers, and bolts at steering coupling to steering shaft flange.
3. Remove pitman arm nut and washer from pitman shaft and mark relation of arm position to shaft.
4. Remove pitman arm with Tool J-6632.
5. Remove screws securing steering gear to frame and remove gear from vehicle.

INSTALLATION

1. Place gear into position so that steering coupling mounts properly to flanged end of steering shaft. Secure gear to frame with washers and bolts. Torque all gear to frame fasteners to 65 ft. lbs.

NOTE: *Be sure coupling reinforcement is bottomed on the wormshaft so that the coupling bolt passes through the undercut on the wormshaft, or damage may occur.*

2. Secure steering coupling to flanged end of steering column with lock washers, and nuts. Torque nuts to 25 ft. lbs.
3. Install pitman arm, aligning marks made during removal, and with washer and retaining nut. Torque to 180 ft. lbs.
4. Install coupling shield and connect battery ground cable.

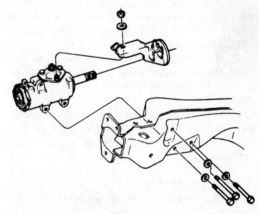

Steering gear attachment

Manual Gear Pitman Shaft Seal
REPLACEMENT

1. Rotate steering wheel from stop to stop, counting the total number of turns. Then turn back exactly halfway, placing the gear on center (the wormshaft flat should be at the 12 o'clock position).

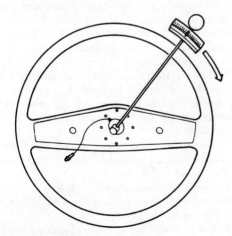

Checking wheel pull

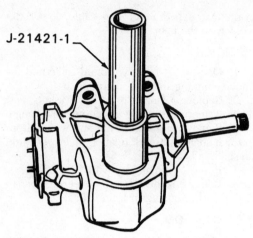

J-21421-1

Manual steering gear Pitman shaft seal replacement

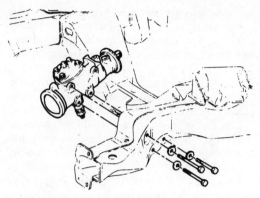

Power steering gear attachment

2. Remove the three self-locking bolts attaching side cover to the housing and lift the pitman shaft and side cover assembly from the housing.

3. Pry the pitman shaft seal from the gear housing using a screwdriver and being careful not to damage the housing bore.

NOTE: *Inspect the lubricant in the gear for contamination. If the lubricant is contaminated in any way, the gear must be removed from the vehicle and completely overhauled, or damage may occur.*

4. Coat the new pitman shaft seal with steering gear lubricant. Position the seal in the pitman shaft bore and tap into position using a suitable size socket.

5. Remove the lash adjuster lock nut. Remove the side cover from the pitman shaft assembly by turning the lash adjuster screw clockwise.

6. Place the pitman shaft in the steering gear such that the center tooth of the pitman shaft sector enters the center tooth space of the ball nut.

7. Fill the steering gear housing with steering gear lubricant.

8. Install a new side cover gasket onto the gear housing.

9. Install the side cover onto the lash adjuster screw by reaching through the threaded hole in the side cover with a small screwdriver and turning the lash adjuster screw counterclockwise until it bottoms and turn back in ¼ turn.

10. Install the side cover bolts and torque to specifications.

11. Install the lash adjuster screw locknut, perform steering gear adjustment and install the pitman arm.

Power Steering Gear
REMOVAL

Disconnect pressure and return hoses from the steering gear housing. Cap both hoses and steering gear outlets to prevent foreign material from entering the system. After service is performed and steering gear is installed, connect the pressure and return hoses to the steering gear housing. Install coupling shield. Bleed system.

1. Disconnect battery ground cable and remove coupling shield.

2. Remove retaining nuts, lock washers, and bolts at steering coupling to steering shaft flange.

3. Remove pitman arm nut and washer from pitman shaft and mark relation of arm position to shaft.

4. Remove pitman arm with Tool J-6632.

5. Remove screws securing steering gear to frame and remove gear from vehicle.

INSTALLATION

1. Place gear into position so that steering coupling mounts properly to flanged end of steering shaft. Secure gear to frame with washers and bolts. Torque all gear to frame fasteners to specifications.

NOTE: *Be sure the coupling reinforcement is bottomed on the wormshaft so that the coupling bolt passes through the undercut on the wormshaft, or damage may occur to the component.*

2. Secure steering coupling to flanged end of steering column with lock washers, and nuts. Torque nuts to 25 ft. lbs.

3. Install pitman arm, aligning marks made during removal, and with washer and retaining nut. Torque to 180 ft. lbs.

4. Install coupling shield and connect battery ground cable.

Power Steering Gear Pitman Shaft Seal

REMOVAL AND INSTALLATION

A faulty seal may be replaced without removal of steering gear from car by removing pitman arm as outlined under Maintenance and Adjustments—Steering Gear Adjustments and proceed as follows:

1. Clean end of housing to prevent contamination.

2. Remove retaining ring with snap ring pliers J-4245.

3. With rear wheels off the ground, and the engine running, turn the steering wheel all the way left. Hydraulic pressure will force the pitman shaft seal out of the housing. Catch the seal and the expelled fluid in a pan.

4. Install a new seal using J-8810 for model 605 gears, or J-6219 for model 800 gears.

5. Install seals/washers/snap rings.

6. Reinstall pitman arm as described earlier. Add fluid as required, check and bleed system until correct fluid level is obtained.

Power Steering Pump

REMOVAL

1. Disconnect hoses at pump or steering gear. When hoses are disconnected, secure ends in raised position to prevent drainage of oil. Cap or tape the ends of the hoses to prevent entrance of dirt.

2. Install two caps at hose fittings to prevent drainage of oil from pump.

3. Remove pump belt.

4. Remove pump from attaching parts and remove pump from vehicle.

INSTALLATION

1. Position pump assembly on vehicle and install attaching parts loosely.

2. Connect and tighten hose fittings.

3. Fill reservoir. Bleed pump by turning pulley backward (counter-clockwise as viewed from front) until air bubbles cease to appear.

4. Install pump belt over pulley.

5. Adjust the belt.

6. Bleed as outlined under "Bleeding Power Steering Systems."

Pump Pulley

REMOVAL

1. Install a puller on the pump. Be sure pilot bolt bottoms in the pump shaft by turning nut to the top of the pilot bolt.

2. Install puller jaws and retainer sleeve.

3. Remove pulley by holding pilot bolt and turning out counterclockwise.

INSTALLATION

1. Place pulley on end of pump shaft and install tool. Be sure pilot bolt bottoms in shaft by turning nut to the top of the pilot bolt.

2. Install pulley by holding pilot bolt and turning nut clockwise.

605

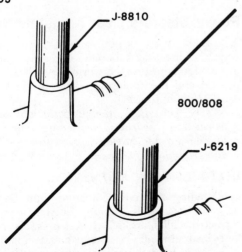

Power steering gear Pitman shaft seal replacement

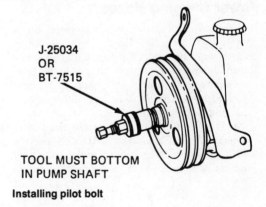

Installing pilot bolt

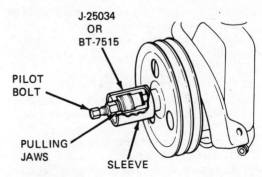

Installing puller

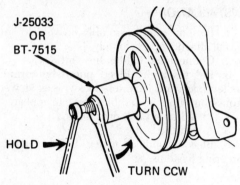

Removing power steering pump pulley

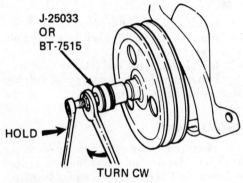

Installing power steering pump pulley

Power Steering Hoses

It is important that the power steering hoses be installed correctly. Hoses installed out of position may be subjected to chafing or other abuses during sharp turns. Always make hose installations with the front wheels in straight ahead position. Do not twist hoses unnecessarily during installation.

NOTE: *Do not start engine with any power steering hose disconnected. After connecting the power steering hoses, make sure that ample clearance has been provided between the hoses and the fan belt, sheet metal or any other components where hose rub or interference could result. If the return hose connections are removed for any reason at either connection, replace the existing crimped clamp with a worm drive clamp for proper sealing.*

Bleeding Hydraulic System

1. Fill oil reservoir to proper level and let oil remain undisturbed for at least two minutes.
2. Start engine and run momentarily.
3. Add oil if necessary.
4. Repeat above procedure until oil level remains constant after running engine.

5. Raise front end of vehicle so that wheels are off the ground.
6. Increase engine speed to approximately 1500 rpm.
7. Turn the wheels (off ground) right and left, lightly contacting the wheel stops.
8. Add oil if necessary.
9. Lower the car and turn wheels right and left on the ground.
10. Check oil level and refill as required.
11. If oil is extremely foamy, allow vehicle to stand a few minutes with engine off and repeat above procedure.
   a. Check belt tightness and check for a bent or loose pulley. (Pulley should not wobble with engine running.)
   b. Check to make sure hoses are not touching any other parts of the car, particularly sheet metal and exhaust manifold.
   c. Check oil level, filling to proper level if necessary, following operations 1 through 10. This step and step "D" are extremely important as low oil level and/or air in the oil are the most frequent causes of objectionable pump noise.
   d. Check the presence of air in the oil. If air is present, attempt to bleed system as described in operations 1 through 10. If it becomes obvious that the pump will not bleed after a few trials, proceed as outlined under Hydraulic System Checks.

Fluid Level

1. Check oil level in the reservoir by checking the dip stick when oil is at operating temperature.
2. Fill, if necessary, to proper level with power steering fluid.

Power Steering Gear Adjustments

Adjustment of the power steering gear in the vehicle is discouraged because of the difficulty involved in adjusting the worm thrust bearing preload and the confusing effects of the hydraulic fluid in the gear.

NOTE: *The effect of improperly adjusted worm thrust bearings or an improperly adjusted overcenter preload could cause a handling stability problem.*

BELT TENSION ADJUSTMENT

When adjusting a power steering pump belt, never pry against the pump reservoir or pull against the filler neck. Two systems are used for belt adjustment. On some models, the pump is loosened from the bracket and moved outward to increase the tension. On other models, a half-inch square drive hole is located in the

Wheel Alignment Specifications

Toe-In		Camber		Caster	
Range (in.)	Preferred (in.)	Range (deg)	Preferred (deg)	Range (deg)	Preferred (deg)
$\frac{1}{16}$–$\frac{3}{32}$P	$\frac{1}{16}$P	$\frac{5}{16}$–$\frac{13}{16}$P	$\frac{13}{16}$P	1½–2½P	2P

bracket, and this hole is used to rotate the pump-and-bracket assembly outward to increase belt tension.

Flex the belt at a point midway in its longest run. If the belt cannot be flexed ½ inch, but no more, proceed as follows:

1. When power steering pump is driven by a single belt:

    a. :Loosen the pump attaching bolts and adjust the belt to correct tension by moving the pump outward, away from the engine.

    b. Snug all pump mounting bolts and remove pry bar.

    c. Tighten all pump mounting bolts.

    d. Check belt tension.

2. Loosen pivot bolt and pump brace adjusting nuts.

NOTE: *Do not move pump by prying against reservoir or by pulling on filler neck, or damage may occur.*

3. Move pump, with belt in place until belt is tensioned properly.

4. Tighten pump brace adjusting nut. Then tighten pivot bolt nut.

Brakes

HYDRAULIC SYSTEM

Adjustments

FRONT DISC BRAKES

Disc brakes are not adjustable. They are, in effect, self adjusting.

ADJUSTMENT OF REAR BRAKES

1. Using a punch, knock out lanced area in brake backing plate. If this is done with the drum installed on the vehicle, the drum must be removed and all metal cleaned out of the brake compartment. Be sure to obtain a new hole cover and install it in the backing plate after adjustment to prevent dirt and water from getting into the brakes. Use J-6166 to turn brake adjusting screw; expand brake shoes at each wheel until the wheel can just be turned by hand. The drag should be equal at all wheels.

2. Back off brake adjusting screw at each wheel 30 notches. If shoes still drag lightly on drum, back off adjusting screw one or two additional notches. Brakes should be free of drag when screw has been backed off approximately 12 notches. Heavy drag at this point indicates tight parking brake cables.

3. Install adjusting hole cover in brake backing plate.

4. Check parking brake adjustment.

STOP LIGHT SWITCH ADJUSTMENT

With pedal in fully released position, the stop light switch plunger should be fully depressed against the pedal shank. Adjust switch by moving in or out as necessary.

1. Make certain that the tubular clip is in brake pedal mounting bracket.

2. With brake pedal depressed, insert switch into tubular clip until switch body seats on clip. Audible clicks can be heard as the threaded portion of the switch is pushed through the clip toward the brake pedal.

3. Pull brake pedal fully rearward against pedal stop until audible clicking sounds can no longer be heard. Switch will be moved in tubular clip providing adjustment.

4. Release brake pedal and then repeat Step 3, to assure that no audible clicking sounds remain.

Brake Line

REMOVAL AND INSTALLATION

CAUTION: *Never use copper tubing because copper is subject to fatigue cracking and corrosion which could result in brake failure. Use double walled steel tubing.*

1. Obtain the recommended tubing and steel fitting nuts of the correct size. (Outside diameter of tubing is used to specify size.)

2. Cut tubing to length. Correct length may be determined by measuring old pipe using a cord and adding ⅛ in. for each double flare.

3. Make sure fittings are installed before starting flare. Double flare tubing ends using a suitable flaring tool. Follow instructions included in tool set. Double flaring tool must be used as single flaring tools cannot produce a flare strong enough to hold the necessary pressure.

4. Bend pipe assembly to match old pipe using a tubing bender. Clearance of at least 19mm (¾ in.) must be maintained to all moving parts or 13mm (½ in.) clearance to any vibrating parts.

Brake Hose

INSPECTION

The flexible hydraulic brake hose which transmits hydraulic pressure from the steel brake line on the body to the rear axle and to the calipers, should be inspected at least twice a year. The brake hose assembly should be checked for road hazard damage, for cracks and chafing of the outer cover, and for leaks and blisters. A light and mirror may be needed for an adequate inspection. If any of the above conditions are observed on the brake hose, it will be necessary to replace it.

FRONT BRAKE HOSE REPLACEMENT

1. Clean dirt and foreign material from both hose end fittings.

2. Disconnect brake pipe from hose fitting using a back-up wrench on fitting. Be careful not to bend frame bracket or brake pipe. It may be necessary to soak the connections with penetrating oil.

3. Remove hose from bracket.

4. Remove bolt from caliper end of hose. Remove hose from caliper, and discard the two copper gaskets on either side of fitting block.

5. Use a new copper gasket on each side of fitting block. Lubricate bolt threads with brake fluid, then with fitting flange engaged with the caliper orientation ledge, fasten hose to caliper, and tighten. Top and bottom gaskets to the front brake hose fitting block must not be switched. They will not interchange.

6. With weight of vehicle on suspension, install female fitting through frame bracket or cross member. The fitting fits the bracket in only one position and should be installed with the least amount of twist in the hose. There should be no kinks in hose.

7. Attach brake pipe to hose fitting using a backup wrench on the hose fitting.

8. Inspect to see that hose does not make contact with any part of suspension. Check in extreme right and extreme left turn conditions. If hose makes any contact, remove and correct.

9. Fill and maintain brake fluid level in reservoirs. Bleed brake system.

REAR BRAKE HOSE REPLACEMENT

1. Remove all three brake pipes from hose, two at junction block and, with the use of a back-up wrench, on the female fitting at bracket. Be careful not to bend bracket or pipes, use penetrating oil if necessary.

2. Remove fitting from the bracket.

3. Observe position at which junction block is mounted to the axle. When installing new hose, be sure the junction block is in the same position as before removal.

4. Remove bolt attaching junction block to axle.

5. Thread both rear brake pipes into junction block.

6. Bolt junction block to axle and torque rear pipes.

7. Install female end of hose through frame bracket. Female fitting will fit bracket in only one position, without twisting hose position female end in bracket.

8. Install nut.

9. Attach pipe to female fitting using a backup wrench on hose tighten fitting being careful not to bend or loosen frame bracket or pipe. Torque bracket if necessary.

10. Fill and maintain brake fluid level in reservoirs. Bleed system.

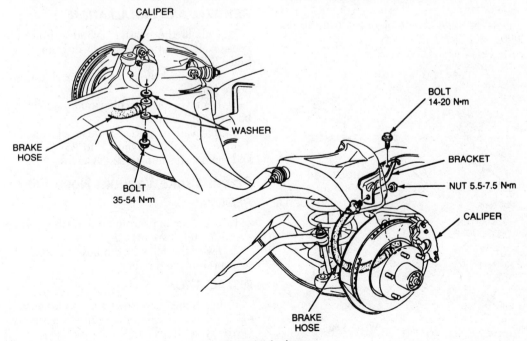

Front brake hose

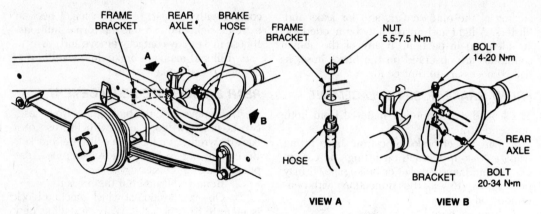

Rear brake hose

Master Cylinder

REMOVAL AND INSTALLATION

1. Disconnect the brake lines at the master cylinder. Cap the lines.

2. Remove the two master cylinder attaching nuts.

3. Remove the master cylinder.

4. Installation is the reverse of removal. Torque the mounting nuts to 25–30 ft. lbs.

OVERHAUL

1. Remove the master cylinder.

2. Remove the cover and empty the reservoir.

3. Check the cover and diaphragm for cracks or other damage.

4. Depress the primary piston and remove the lock ring.

5. Use compressed air to remove the pistons.

6. Clamp the master cylinder in a vise using the mounting flange, not the body.

7. Use a small pry bar to separate the reservoir from the body.

8. Do not remove the quick-take up valve from the cylinder body, as this is not serviceable.

9. Remove and discard the reservoir grommets.

10. Check the cylinder bore for pitting or corrosion. GM does not recommend that the bore be honed. They recommend replacement of the cylinder body if such damage is observed.

11. Assembly is the reverse of disassembly. Lubricate all parts, including the reservoir grommets, with clean silicone brake fluid.

Power Booster

REMOVAL AND INSTALLATION

1. Unbolt the master cylinder from the booster. It is not necessary to disconnect the brake lines.

2. Disconnect the booster pushrod from the brake pedal.

3. Remove the attaching nuts and lift the booster out.

4. Installation is the reverse of removal. Torque the master cylinder to 25–30 ft. lbs. and the booster nuts to 22–33 ft. lbs.

Power Brake Vacuum Hose Filter

REMOVAL

1. Use a pair of pliers to move the hose clamp approximately two inches.

2. Twist the filter in the hose to break the seal and remove the filter.

INSTALLATION

1. Install the filter. Be sure the vacuum check valve on the power brake unit is positioned vertically.

2. Position hose clamps to retain filter.

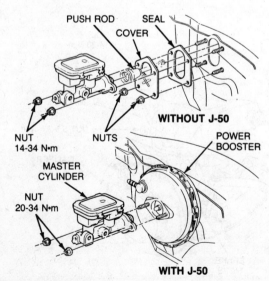

Master cylinder attachment

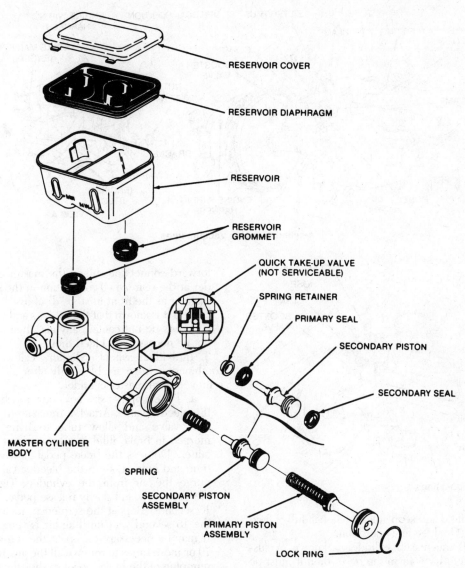

RESERVOIR COVER

RESERVOIR DIAPHRAGM

RESERVOIR

RESERVOIR GROMMET

QUICK TAKE-UP VALVE (NOT SERVICEABLE)

SPRING RETAINER

PRIMARY SEAL

SECONDARY PISTON

SECONDARY SEAL

MASTER CYLINDER BODY

SPRING

SECONDARY PISTON ASSEMBLY

PRIMARY PISTON ASSEMBLY

LOCK RING

Master cylinder exploded view

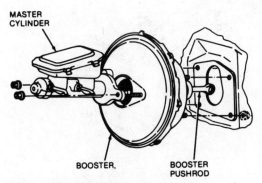

MASTER CYLINDER

BOOSTER,

BOOSTER PUSHROD

Power brake booster attachment

Pedal Travel

At reasonably frequent intervals, the brakes should be inspected for pedal travel, which is the distance the pedal moves toward the floor from a fully-released position. Inspection should be made with the brake pedal firmly depressed approximately 50 lbs. on manual systems or 100 lbs. on power systems while the brakes are cold.

On power brake-equipped vehicles, pump the pedal a minimum of 3 times with the engine off before making pedal travel checks. This exhausts all vacuum from the power brake unit.

Bleeding the System

If the vehicle is equipped with power brakes, remove the vacuum reserve by applying the brakes several times with the engine off.

1. Fill the master cylinder reservoirs with

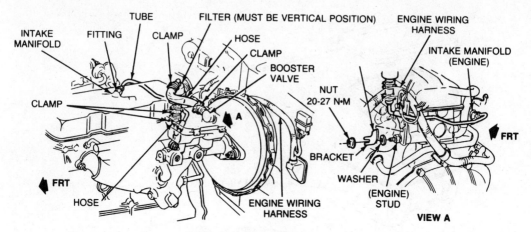

4-cylinder engine vacuum lines

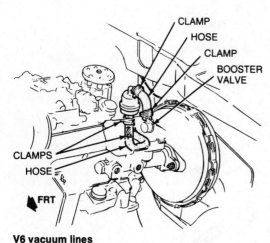

V6 vacuum lines

brake fluid and keep at least one-half full of fluid during the bleeding operation.

2. If the master cylinder is known or suspected to have air in the bore, then it must be bled before any wheel cylinder or caliper in the following manner:

a. Disconnect the forward (blind end) brake pipe connection at the master cylinder.

b. Allow brake fluid to fill the master cylinder bore until it begins to flow from the forward pipe connector port.

c. Connect the forward brake pipe to the master cylinder and tighten.

d. Depress the brake pedal slowly one time and hold. Loosen the forward brake pipe connection at the master cylinder to purge air from the bore. Tighten the connection and then release the brake pedal slowly. Wait 15 seconds. Repeat the sequence, including the 15 second wait, until all air is removed from the bore. Care must be taken to prevent brake fluid from contacting any painted surface.

e. After all air has been removed at the forward connection, bleed the master cylinder at the rear (cowl) connection in the same manner as the front in step "d" above.

f. If it is known that the calipers and wheel cylinders do not contain any air, then it will not be necessary to bleed them.

3. Individual wheel cylinder, calipers or combination valve are bled only after all air is removed from master cylinder.

a. Place a proper size box end wrench over the bleeder valve. Attach a transparent tube over valve and allow tube to hang submerged in brake fluid in a transparent container. Depress the brake pedal slowly one time and hold. Loosen the bleeder valve to purge the air from the cylinder. Tighten bleeder screw and slowly release pedal. Wait 15 seconds. Repeat the sequence, including the 15 second wait until all air is removed. It may be necessary to repeat the sequence 10 or more times to remove all the air. Rapid pumping of the brake pedal pushes the mas-

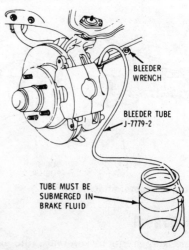

Brake bleeding

ter cylinder secondary piston down the bore in a manner that makes it difficult to bleed the rear side of the system.

4. If it is necessary to bleed all of the wheel cylinders and calipers, the following sequence should be followed: 1) Combination valve; 2) Right rear wheel cylinder; 3) Left rear wheel cylinder; 4) Right front caliper; 5) Left front caliper.

5. Check the brake pedal for "sponginess" and the brake warning light for indication of unbalanced pressure. Repeat entire bleeding procedure to correct either of these two conditions.

Combination Valve
REPLACEMENT

The combination valve is not repairable and must be serviced as a complete assembly.

When removing the electrical wire connector from the pressure differential switch, it is recommended that you squeeze the eliptical shaped plastic locking ring and then pull. This will move the locking tangs away from the switch. A pair of pliers can be used to aid in the removal of the connector.

1. Disconnect hydraulic lines at combination valve. Plug lines to prevent loss of fluid and entrance of dirt. Disconnect warning switch wiring harness from valve switch terminal.

2. Remove combination valve.

3. Install combination valve by reversing removal steps.

4. Bleed entire brake system. Do not move vehicle until a firm brake pedal is obtained.

FRONT DISC BRAKES

Disc Brake Pads
INSPECTION

Check both ends of the outer shoe by looking in at each end of the caliper. Check the lining thickness on the inner shoe by looking down through the inspection hole in the top of the caliper housing. Whenever the lining is worn to the approximate thickness of the shoe, the shoe and lining should be removed. After removal, measure the lining thickness. The shoe and lining should be replaced at any time when the lining is worn to within $\frac{1}{32}$ inch of a rivet or $\frac{1}{32}$ inch of the shoe at any point.

All front disc brakes have a wear indicator that makes a noise when the linings wear to a degree where replacement is required. The spring clip is an integral part of the inboard shoe and lining. When the lining is worn, the clip contacts the rotor and produces a warning noise.

Check flatness of brake pads. Place inboard and outboard pad surfaces together and check for gap between pad surfaces. If more than 0.13mm (.005 in.) gap is measured at middle of pad (midway between attaching lugs), pad must not be used. This applies to new or used brake pads.

CAUTION: *When servicing wheel brake*

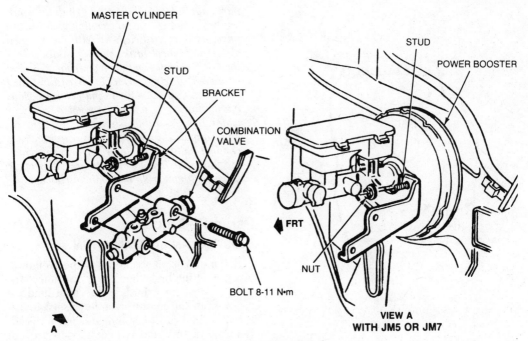

Combination valve

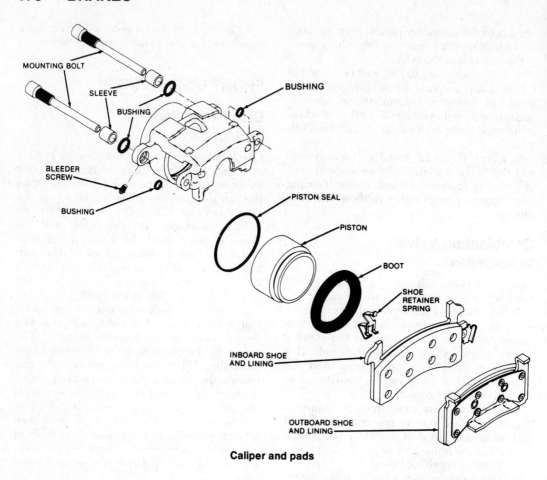

Caliper and pads

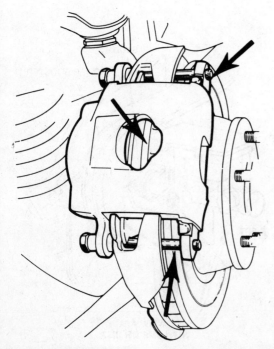

Inspecting the front pads

parts, do not create dust by grinding, sanding brake linings, or by cleaning wheel brake parts with a dry brush or with compressed air. Many wheel brake parts contain asbestos fibers which can become airborne if dust is created during servicing. Breathing dust containing asbestos fibers may cause serious bodily harm. A water dampened cloth or water based solution should be used to remove any dust on brake parts. Equipment is commercially available to perform the washing function. These wet methods will prevent asbestos fibers from becoming airborne.

Pad and Caliper

REMOVAL AND INSTALLATION

Pad removal is the same as caliper removal, except that the brake line is not disconnected.

1. Remove two thirds of the total fluid capacity from the master cylinder reservoir that supplies fluid to the system(s) being serviced. Removal of the fluid is necessary to prevent reservoir overflow when the caliper piston is

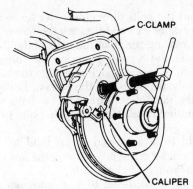

Using a C-clamp to bottom the piston

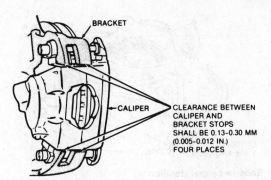

Checking caliper-to-bracket stop clearance

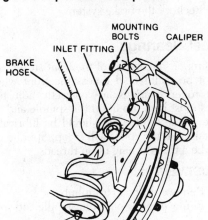

Caliper mounting

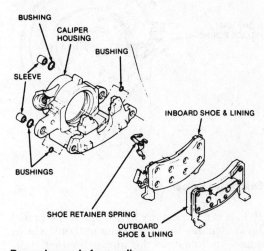

Removing pads from caliper

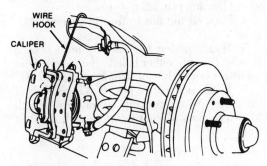

Suspending the caliper out of the way

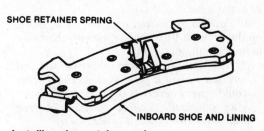

Installing shoe retainer spring

pushed back in its bore to remove the caliper. Discard the brake fluid removed.

2. Raise the vehicle on a hoist and remove the wheel covers and wheel assemblies. Position a 7 in. C-clamp on the caliper so that solid side of the clamp rests against the metal part of the outboard shoe. Tighten the C-clamp until the caliper moves away from the vehicle far enough to push the piston to the bottom of the piston bore. This will allow the shoes to back off from the rotor surfaces. Remove the C-clamp.

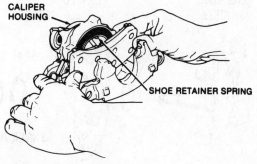

Installing pads in caliper

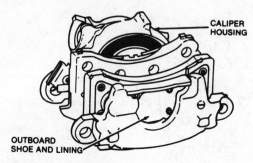

Shoe-in-caliper positioning

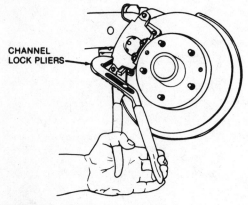

Seating the caliper

3. It is not necessary to disconnect the brake lines. Remove the two mounting bolts which attach the caliper to the support bracket. Lift caliper off the rotor. Support caliper with rope or wire. Do Not allow the caliper to hang by its brake hose.

4. Position the caliper over the rotor, lining up the holes in the caliper ears with the holes in the mounting bracket.

NOTE: *When reinstalling caliper be sure you have not turned it over, end over end. This would cause a severe twist in the brake hose. After positioning caliper on disc, observe brake hose being sure it is not twisted.*

5. Start the bolts through the sleeves in the inboard caliper ears and through the mounting bracket, making sure that the ends of the bolts pass under the retaining ears on the inboard shoe. Push bolts on through to engage the holes in the outboard shoes and the outboard caliper ears at the same time, threading the bolts into the mounting bracket. Torque the bolts to 35 ft. lbs.

6. Add fresh approved brake fluid to the master cylinder reservoirs to bring the level up to within 3mm (⅛ in.) of the top.

7. Pump brake pedal to seat lining against rotor.

8. Recheck the brake system.

Wheel Bearings

The proper functioning of the front suspension cannot be maintained unless the front wheel taper roller bearings are correctly adjusted. Cones must be a slip fit on the spindle and the inside diameter of cones should be lubricated to insure that the cones will creep. Spindle nut must be a free-running fit on threads.

ADJUSTMENT

1. Remove dust cap from hub.

2. Remove cotter pin from spindle and spindle nut.

3. Tighten the spindle nut to 12 ft. lbs. while turning the wheel assembly forward by hand to fully seat the bearings. This will remove any grease or burrs which could cause excessive wheel bearing play later.

4. Back off the nut to the "just loose" position.

5. Hand tighten the spindle nut. Loosen spindle nut until either hole in the spindle lines up with a slot in the nut. Not more than ½ flat.

6. Install new cotter pin. Bend the ends of the cotter pin against nut, cut off extra length to ensure ends will not interfere with the dust cap.

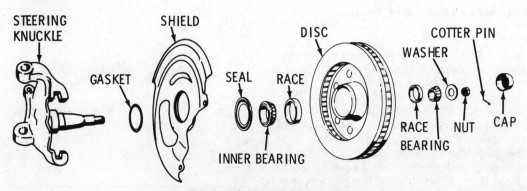

Front rotor and wheel bearings

7. Measure the looseness in the hub assembly. There will be from .03 to .13mm (.001 to .005 inches) end play when properly adjusted.

8. Install dust cap on hub.

Rotor, Hub and Wheel Bearing

REMOVAL AND INSTALLATION, AND BEARING PACKING

1. Remove caliper as outlined earlier.
2. Remove dust cap from hub.
3. Remove cotter pin, nut and washer from spindle.
4. Carefully pull hub assembly from spindle.
5. Remove the outer roller bearing assem-

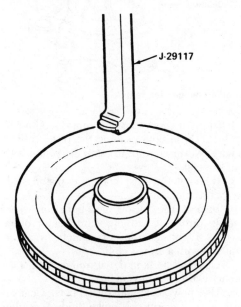

Front wheel bearing removal

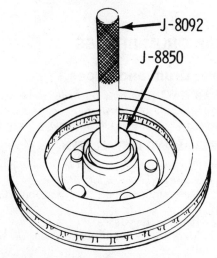

Installing inner bearing race

bly from hub. The inner bearing assembly will remain in the hub and may be removed after prying out the inner bearing lip seal. Discard seal.

6. Drive out old races from hub with tool J-29117 inserted behind races.

7. Wash all parts in clean solvent and air dry.

8. Check bearings for cracked cage and worn or pitted rollers.

9. Check bearing races for cracks, scores or a brinelled condition. Refer to front wheel bearing diagnosis.

10. If the outer races were removed, drive or press the races into the hub.

11. Clean off any grease in the hub and spindle and thoroughly clean out any grease in the bearings. Use clean solvent. Use of a small brush with no loose bristles will be helpful to clean out all old grease. Do not spin the bearing with compressed air while drying it or the bearing may be damaged.

12. Use an approved high temperature front wheel bearing grease. Do not mix greases as mixing may change the grease properties and result in poor performance.

13. Apply a thin film of grease to the spindle at the outer bearing seat and at the inner bearing seat, shoulder, and seal seat.

14. Put a small quantity of grease inboard of each bearing cup in the hub. This can be applied with your finger, forming a dam to provide extra grease availability to the bearing and to keep thinned grease from flowing out of the bearing.

15. Fill the bearing cone and roller assemblies full of grease. A preferred method for doing this is with a cone type grease machine that forces grease into the bearing. If a cone greaser is not available, the bearings can be packed by hand. If hand packing is used, it is extremely important to work the grease thoroughly into the bearings between the rollers, cone, and the cage. Failure to do this could result in premature bearing failure.

16. Place the inner bearing cone and roller assembly in the hub. Then using your finger, put an additional quantity of grease outboard of the bearing.

17. Install a new grease seal using a flat plate until the seal is flush with the hub. Lubricate the seal lip with a thin layer of grease.

18. Carefully install the hub and rotor assembly. Place the outer bearing cone and roller assembly in the outer bearing cup. Install the washer and nut and initially tighten the nut to 12 ft. lbs. while turning the wheel assembly forward by hand. Put an additional quantity of grease outboard the bearing. This provides extra grease availability to the bearing.

19. Final wheel bearing adjustment should be performed. Refer to Wheel Bearing Adjustment.

Caliper

OVERHAUL

1. Remove the caliper.
2. Remove the pads.
3. Place a thick shop rag in front of the piston.

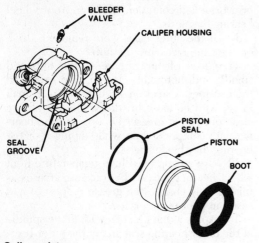

Caliper piston

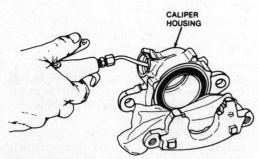

Place a clean rag as shown to catch the caliper piston when using compressed air burst to remove it from the caliper bore

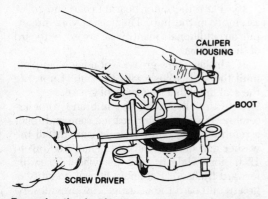

Removing the dust boot

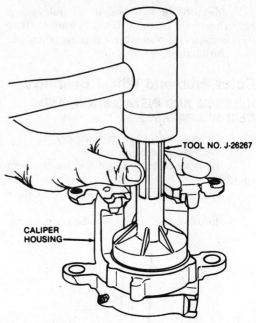

Installing the caliper seal

4. Apply a short burst of compressed air to the brake hose hole to force the piston out of its bore. Never attempt to catch the piston with your fingers!

5. Remove the dust boot and piston seal. Never use metal tools.

6. Inspect the piston and bore for wear, scoring, pitting, corrosion, scratches or other damage. Light corrosion or scratches may be removed with a crocus cloth.

7. Clean all parts in denatured alcohol. Dry all parts with compressed air.

8. Use new seals and dust boots. Coat all parts with clean silicone brake fluid. Assembly is the reverse of disassembly. Bleed the system.

REAR DRUM BRAKES

Brake Drum and Shoes

WARNING: *The dust on brake parts contains asbestos which is a cancer causing agent. Never use compressed air to remove the dust!*

REMOVAL AND INSTALLATION

NOTE: *Brake tools, available in most parts stores, make this job a lot easier.*

1. Raise and support the rear on jackstands.
2. Remove the wheels.
3. Mark the position of the drum on the axle hub.
4. Remove the drum.

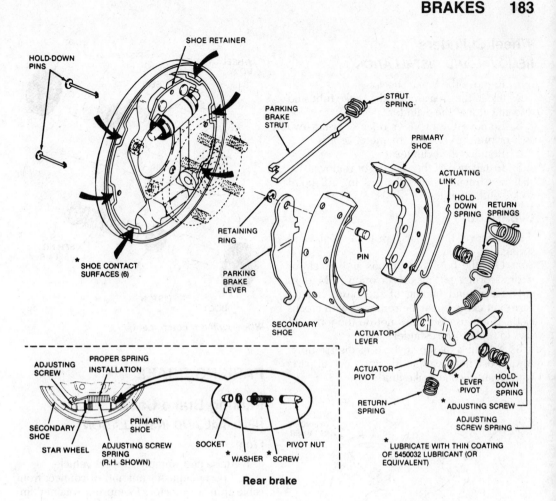

Rear brake

* LUBRICATE WITH THIN COATING
OF 5450032 LUBRICANT (OR
EQUIVALENT)

5. Remove the brake return springs with a tool meant for that purpose.

6. Remove the hold down springs.

7. Remove the actuator lever pivot and lever.

8. Spread the shoes apart and remove the parking brake lever.

9. Disconnect the parking brake cable.

10. Spread the shoes enough to clear the hub and remove them, along with the spring and adjusting wheel.

NOTE: *On low mileage trucks, the brake springs can be reused. On High mileage trucks, or if the condition of any part is in doubt, replace the springs.*

11. Installation is the reverse of removal. Prior to installing the shoes, spread a thin coat of lithium based grease on the flat pad surfaces on which the shoes rest. Check the brake drum for cracks or discoloration. If any damage is shown, have the drum turned at a machine shop. The maximum diameter of the drum is stamped on the drum outer surface.

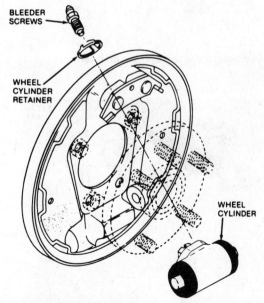

Wheel cylinder attachment

Wheel Cylinders
REMOVAL AND INSTALLATION

1. Remove the brake shoes.
2. Clean the area around the brake tube and disconnect it at the cylinder.
3. Remove the cylinder retainer using two awls or punches of ⅛ in. diameter or less.
4. Remove the cylinder.
5. Installation is the reverse of removal. Install new retainers using a 1⅛ in., 12 point socket and extension.

OVERHAUL

1. Remove the boots, pistons, seals and spring.
2. Dry the bore and pistons and check for wear, scoring, pitting or corrosion. GM does not recommend honing of the bore. If light corrosion exists it may be removed with crocus cloth. If crocus cloth does not do the job, GM says to replace the cylinder.
3. Assembly is the reverse of disassembly. Always use new seals and boots. Coat all parts with clean silicone brake fluid.

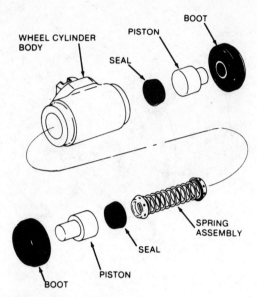

Wheel cylinder components

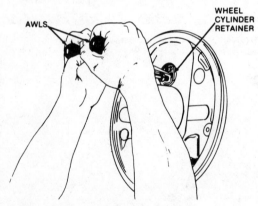

Removing the wheel cylinder retainer

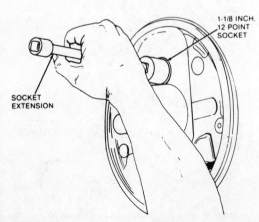

Installing the wheel cylinder retainer

PARKING BRAKE

Parking Brake Cable
REMOVAL AND INSTALLATION
Front

1. Raise and suitably support vehicle.
2. Loosen adjuster nut and disconnect front cable from connector. Compress retainer fingers and loosen at frame.
3. Remove supports and lower vehicle.
4. Remove windshield washer bottle.
5. Disconnect cable from parking brake pedal assembly, compress retainer fingers and remove cable.
6. Install cable by reversing removal procedure. Make sure cable is routed properly and securely retained.
7. Adjust parking brake cable.

Left And/Or Right Rear

1. Raise and suitably support vehicle.
2. Mark relationship of tire and wheel assembly to axle flange and remove.
3. Remove brake drum.
4. Loosen equalizer and disconnect cable at center retainer.
5. Compress plastic retainer fingers and remove retainer from frame bracket.
6. Remove rear brake shoe and disconnect cable.
7. Remove cable at frame and from brake backing plate.
8. Install cable by reversing procedure. Make sure cable is routed properly and securely retained.

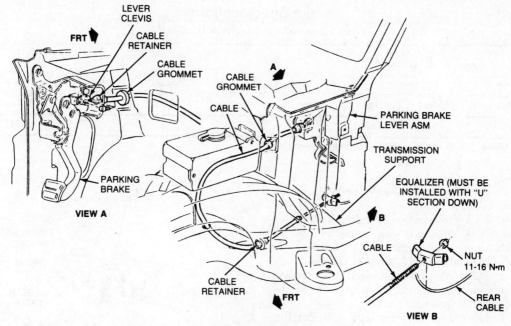

Front parking brake cable

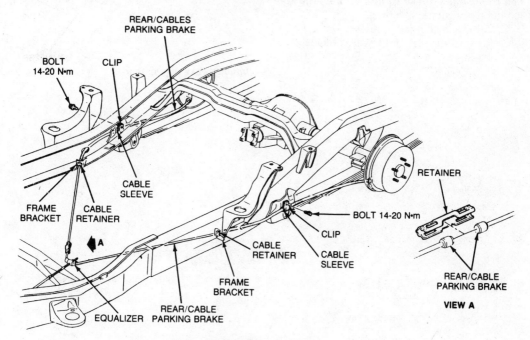

Intermediate rear cable

9. Adjust parking brake cable and lower vehicle.

Center

1. Raise and suitably support vehicle.
2. Remove adjuster nut at equalizer and pull cable from equalizer.
3. Disconnect cable at retainers.

4. Install cable by reversing procedure and adjust parking brake.

PARKING BRAKE ADJUSTMENT

Adjustment of parking brake cable is necessary whenever the rear brake cables have been disconnected. Brake is properly adjusted when

Brake Specifications

(All measurements are given in inches)

Master Cylinder Bore	Wheel Cylinder or Caliper or Caliper Bore		Brake Rotor or Drum Diameter		Minimum Lining Thickness	Brake Disc	
	Front	Rear	Front	Rear		Minimum Thickness	Maximum Run-out
.945	N.A.	.874	10.0	9.559 ①	¹⁄₃₂	.978	.004

① Brake drum must be replaced if diameter exceeds 9.60 in.

limiter wrench breaks at 8 to 12 notches (clicks) of pedal travel.

1. Lock parking brake pedal to mounting bracket by pinning through indicator hole (at 10 notches of pedal travel.)

2. Raise and suitably support vehicle.

3. Place a properly calibrated cable tension gauge on the left rear cable as close to the equalizer as practical.

4. Drive adjusting nut until 220–225 lbs. tension is indicated on gauge. It is very important that parking brake cables are not adjusted too tightly causing brake drag.

5. Remove lock pin and release brake.

6. Remove support and lower vehicle.

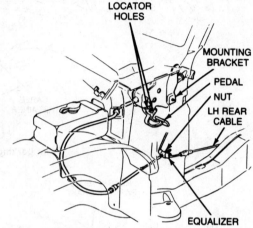

LOCATOR HOLES
MOUNTING BRACKET
PEDAL
NUT
LH REAR CABLE
EQUALIZER

Parking brake adjustment

Troubleshooting

10

This section is designed to aid in the quick, accurate diagnosis of automotive problems. While automotive repairs can be made by many people, accurate troubleshooting is a rare skill for the amateur and professional alike.

In its simplest state, troubleshooting is an exercise in logic. It is essential to realize that an automobile is really composed of a series of systems. Some of these systems are interrelated; others are not. Automobiles operate within a framework of logical rules and physical laws, and the key to troubleshooting is a good understanding of all the automotive systems.

This section breaks the car or truck down into its component systems, allowing the problem to be isolated. The charts and diagnostic road maps list the most common problems and the most probable causes of trouble. Obviously it would be impossible to list every possible problem that could happen along with every possible cause, but it will locate MOST problems and eliminate a lot of unnecessary guesswork. The systematic format will locate problems within a given system, but, because many automotive systems are interrelated, the solution to your particular problem may be found in a number of systems on the car or truck.

USING THE TROUBLESHOOTING CHARTS

This book contains all of the specific information that the average do-it-yourself mechanic needs to repair and maintain his or her car or truck. The troubleshooting charts are designed to be used in conjunction with the specific procedures and information in the text. For instance, troubleshooting a point-type ignition system is fairly standard for all models, but you may be directed to the text to find procedures for troubleshooting an individual type of electronic ignition. You will also have to refer to the specification charts throughout the book for specifications applicable to your car or truck.

TOOLS AND EQUIPMENT

The tools illustrated in Chapter 1 (plus two more diagnostic pieces) will be adequate to troubleshoot most problems. The two other tools needed are a voltmeter and an ohmmeter. These can be purchased separately or in combination, known as a VOM meter.

In the event that other tools are required, they will be noted in the procedures.

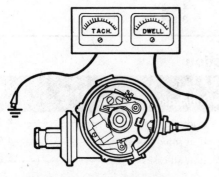

Tach-dwell hooked-up to distributor

Troubleshooting Engine Problems
See Chapters 2, 3, 4 for more information and service procedures.

Index to Systems

System	To Test	Group
Battery	Engine need not be running	1
Starting system	Engine need not be running	2
Primary electrical system	Engine need not be running	3
Secondary electrical system	Engine need not be running	4
Fuel system	Engine need not be running	5
Engine compression	Engine need not be running	6
Engine vacuum	Engine must be running	7
Secondary electrical system	Engine must be running	8
Valve train	Engine must be running	9
Exhaust system	Engine must be running	10
Cooling system	Engine must be running	11
Engine lubrication	Engine must be running	12

Index to Problems

Problem: Symptom	Begin at Specific Diagnosis, Number ____
Engine Won't Start:	
Starter doesn't turn	1.1, 2.1
Starter turns, engine doesn't	2.1
Starter turns engine very slowly	1.1, 2.4
Starter turns engine normally	3.1, 4.1
Starter turns engine very quickly	6.1
Engine fires intermittently	4.1
Engine fires consistently	5.1, 6.1
Engine Runs Poorly:	
Hard starting	3.1, 4.1, 5.1, 8.1
Rough idle	4.1, 5.1, 8.1
Stalling	3.1, 4.1, 5.1, 8.1
Engine dies at high speeds	4.1, 5.1
Hesitation (on acceleration from standing stop)	5.1, 8.1
Poor pickup	4.1, 5.1, 8.1
Lack of power	3.1, 4.1, 5.1, 8.1
Backfire through the carburetor	4.1, 8.1, 9.1
Backfire through the exhaust	4.1, 8.1, 9.1
Blue exhaust gases	6.1, 7.1
Black exhaust gases	5.1
Running on (after the ignition is shut off)	3.1, 8.1
Susceptible to moisture	4.1
Engine misfires under load	4.1, 7.1, 8.4, 9.1
Engine misfires at speed	4.1, 8.4
Engine misfires at idle	3.1, 4.1, 5.1, 7.1, 8.4

Sample Section

Test and Procedure	Results and Indications	Proceed to
4.1—Check for spark: Hold each spark plug wire approximately ¼" from ground with gloves or a heavy, dry rag. Crank the engine and observe the spark.	→ If no spark is evident:	→4.2
	→ If spark is good in some cases:	→4.3
	→ If spark is good in all cases:	→4.6

Specific Diagnosis

This section is arranged so that following each test, instructions are given to proceed to another, until a problem is diagnosed.

Section 1—Battery

Test and Procedure	Results and Indications	Proceed to
1.1—Inspect the battery visually for case condition (corrosion, cracks) and water level.	If case is cracked, replace battery:	**1.4**
	If the case is intact, remove corrosion with a solution of baking soda and water (**CAUTION:** *do not get the solution into the battery*), and fill with water:	**1.2**

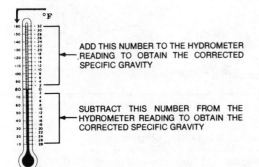

DIRT ON TOP OF BATTERY — PLUGGED VENT
CORROSION
LOOSE CABLE OR POSTS
CRACKS
LOW WATER LEVEL

Inspect the battery case

Test and Procedure	Results and Indications	Proceed to
1.2—Check the battery cable connections: Insert a screwdriver between the battery post and the cable clamp. Turn the headlights on high beam, and observe them as the screwdriver is gently twisted to ensure good metal to metal contact.	If the lights brighten, remove and clean the clamp and post; coat the post with petroleum jelly, install and tighten the clamp:	**1.4**
	If no improvement is noted:	**1.3**

TESTING BATTERY CABLE CONNECTIONS USING A SCREWDRIVER

Test and Procedure	Results and Indications	Proceed to
1.3—Test the state of charge of the battery using an individual cell tester or hydrometer.	If indicated, charge the battery. **NOTE:** *If no obvious reason exists for the low state of charge (i.e., battery age, prolonged storage), proceed to:*	**1.4**

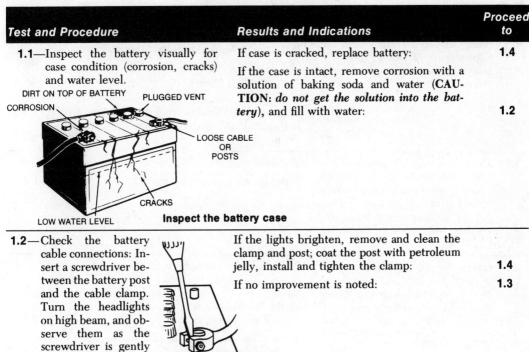

°F

ADD THIS NUMBER TO THE HYDROMETER READING TO OBTAIN THE CORRECTED SPECIFIC GRAVITY

SUBTRACT THIS NUMBER FROM THE HYDROMETER READING TO OBTAIN THE CORRECTED SPECIFIC GRAVITY

Specific Gravity (@ 80° F.)

Minimum	Battery Charge
1.260	100% Charged
1.230	75% Charged
1.200	50% Charged
1.170	25% Charged
1.140	Very Little Power Left
1.110	Completely Discharged

The effects of temperature on battery specific gravity (left) and amount of battery charge in relation to specific gravity (right)

Test and Procedure	Results and Indications	Proceed to
1.4—Visually inspect battery cables for cracking, bad connection to ground, or bad connection to starter.	If necessary, tighten connections or replace the cables:	**2.1**

Section 2—Starting System
See Chapter 3 for service procedures

Test and Procedure	Results and Indications	Proceed to
Note: Tests in Group 2 are performed with coil high tension lead disconnected to prevent accidental starting.		
2.1—Test the starter motor and solenoid: Connect a jumper from the battery post of the solenoid (or relay) to the starter post of the solenoid (or relay).	If starter turns the engine normally:	**2.2**
	If the starter buzzes, or turns the engine very slowly:	**2.4**
	If no response, replace the solenoid (or relay).	**3.1**
	If the starter turns, but the engine doesn't, ensure that the flywheel ring gear is intact. If the gear is undamaged, replace the starter drive.	**3.1**
2.2—Determine whether ignition override switches are functioning properly (clutch start switch, neutral safety switch), by connecting a jumper across the switch(es), and turning the ignition switch to "start".	If starter operates, adjust or replace switch:	**3.1**
	If the starter doesn't operate:	**2.3**
2.3—Check the ignition switch "start" position: Connect a 12V test lamp or voltmeter between the starter post of the solenoid (or relay) and ground. Turn the ignition switch to the "start" position, and jiggle the key.	If the lamp doesn't light or the meter needle doesn't move when the switch is turned, check the ignition switch for loose connections, cracked insulation, or broken wires. Repair or replace as necessary:	**3.1**
	If the lamp flickers or needle moves when the key is jiggled, replace the ignition switch.	**3.3**

Checking the ignition switch "start" position

STARTER RELAY (IF EQUIPPED)

2.4—Remove and bench test the starter, according to specifications in the engine electrical section.	If the starter does not meet specifications, repair or replace as needed:	**3.1**
	If the starter is operating properly:	**2.5**
2.5—Determine whether the engine can turn freely: Remove the spark plugs, and check for water in the cylinders. Check for water on the dipstick, or oil in the radiator. Attempt to turn the engine using an 18″ flex drive and socket on the crankshaft pulley nut or bolt.	If the engine will turn freely only with the spark plugs out, and hydrostatic lock (water in the cylinders) is ruled out, check valve timing:	**9.2**
	If engine will not turn freely, and it is known that the clutch and transmission are free, the engine must be disassembled for further evaluation:	**Chapter 3**

Section 3—Primary Electrical System

Test and Procedure	Results and Indications	Proceed to
3.1—Check the ignition switch "on" position: Connect a jumper wire between the distributor side of the coil and ground, and a 12V test lamp between the switch side of the coil and ground. Remove the high tension lead from the coil. Turn the ignition switch on and jiggle the key.	If the lamp lights:	**3.2**
	If the lamp flickers when the key is jiggled, replace the ignition switch:	**3.3**
	If the lamp doesn't light, check for loose or open connections. If none are found, remove the ignition switch and check for continuity. If the switch is faulty, replace it:	**3.3**

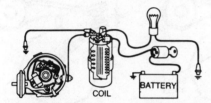

Checking the ignition switch "on" position

3.2—Check the ballast resistor or resistance wire for an open circuit, using an ohmmeter. See Chapter 3 for specific tests.	Replace the resistor or resistance wire if the resistance is zero. **NOTE:** *Some ignition systems have no ballast resistor.*	**3.3**

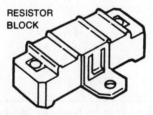

Two types of resistors

3.3—On point-type ignition systems, visually inspect the breaker points for burning, pitting or excessive wear. Gray coloring of the point contact surfaces is normal. Rotate the crankshaft until the contact heel rests on a high point of the distributor cam and adjust the point gap to specifications. On electronic ignition models, remove the distributor cap and visually inspect the armature. Ensure that the armature pin is in place, and that the armature is on tight and rotates when the engine is cranked. Make sure there are no cracks, chips or rounded edges on the armature.	If the breaker points are intact, clean the contact surfaces with fine emery cloth, and adjust the point gap to specifications. If the points are worn, replace them. On electronic systems, replace any parts which appear defective. If condition persists:	**3.4**

Test and Procedure	Results and Indications	Proceed to
3.4—On point-type ignition systems, connect a dwell-meter between the distributor primary lead and ground. Crank the engine and observe the point dwell angle. On electronic ignition systems, conduct a stator (magnetic pickup assembly) test. See Chapter 3.	On point-type systems, adjust the dwell angle if necessary. **NOTE:** *Increasing the point gap decreases the dwell angle and vice-versa.*	**3.6**
	If the dwell meter shows little or no reading;	**3.5**
	On electronic ignition systems, if the stator is bad, replace the stator. If the stator is good, proceed to the other tests in Chapter 3.	

CLOSE   OPEN

NORMAL DWELL

WIDE GAP

SMALL DWELL

INSUFFICIENT DWELL

NARROW GAP

LARGE DWELL

EXCESSIVE DWELL

Dwell is a function of point gap

| **3.5**—On the point-type ignition systems, check the condenser for short: connect an ohmeter across the condenser body and the pigtail lead. | If any reading other than infinite is noted, replace the condenser | **3.6** |

OHMMETER

Checking the condenser for short

| **3.6**—Test the coil primary resistance: On point-type ignition systems, connect an ohmmeter across the coil primary terminals, and read the resistance on the low scale. Note whether an external ballast resistor or resistance wire is used. On electronic ignition systems, test the coil primary resistance as in Chapter 3. | Point-type ignition coils utilizing ballast resistors or resistance wires should have approximately 1.0 ohms resistance. Coils with internal resistors should have approximately 4.0 ohms resistance. If values far from the above are noted, replace the coil. | **4.1** |

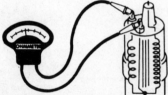

Check the coil primary resistance

Section 4—Secondary Electrical System
See Chapters 2–3 for service procedures

Test and Procedure	Results and Indications	Proceed to
4.1—Check for spark: Hold each spark plug wire approximately ¼″ from ground with gloves or a heavy, dry rag. Crank the engine, and observe the spark.	If no spark is evident:	**4.2**
	If spark is good in some cylinders:	**4.3**
	If spark is good in all cylinders:	**4.6**

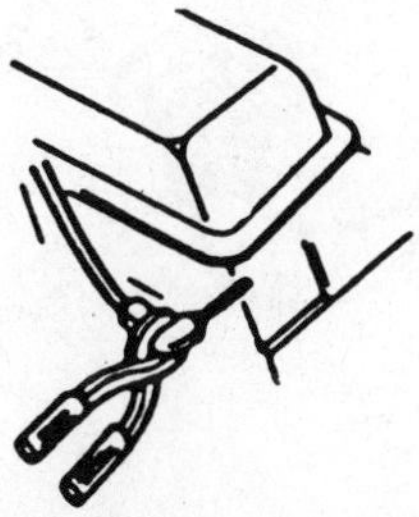

Check for spark at the plugs

4.2—Check for spark at the coil high tension lead: Remove the coil high tension lead from the distributor and position it approximately ¼″ from ground. Crank the engine and observe spark. **CAUTION: This test should not be performed on engines equipped with electronic ignition.**	If the spark is good and consistent:	**4.3**
	If the spark is good but intermittent, test the primary electrical system starting at 3.3:	**3.3**
	If the spark is weak or non-existent, replace the coil high tension lead, clean and tighten all connections and retest. If no improvement is noted:	**4.4**
4.3—Visually inspect the distributor cap and rotor for burned or corroded contacts, cracks, carbon tracks, or moisture. Also check the fit of the rotor on the distributor shaft (where applicable).	If moisture is present, dry thoroughly, and retest per 4.1:	**4.1**
	If burned or excessively corroded contacts, cracks, or carbon tracks are noted, replace the defective part(s) and retest per 4.1:	**4.1**
	If the rotor and cap appear intact, or are only slightly corroded, clean the contacts thoroughly (including the cap towers and spark plug wire ends) and retest per 4.1:	
	If the spark is good in all cases:	**4.6**
	If the spark is poor in all cases:	**4.5**

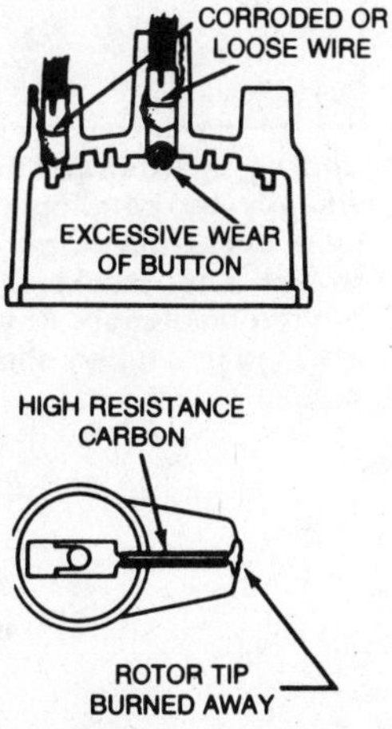

CORRODED OR LOOSE WIRE

EXCESSIVE WEAR OF BUTTON

HIGH RESISTANCE CARBON

ROTOR TIP BURNED AWAY

Inspect the distributor cap and rotor

Test and Procedure	*Results and Indications*	*Proceed to*
4.4—Check the coil secondary resistance: On point-type systems connect an ohmmeter across the distributor side of the coil and the coil tower. Read the resistance on the high scale of the ohmmeter. On electronic ignition systems, see Chapter 3 for specific tests.	The resistance of a satisfactory coil should be between 4,000 and 10,000 ohms. If resistance is considerably higher (i.e., 40,000 ohms) replace the coil and retest per 4.1. **NOTE:** *This does not apply to high performance coils.*	

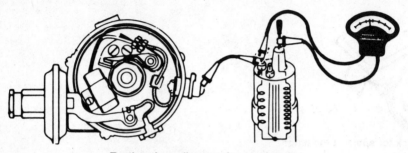

Testing the coil secondary resistance

4.5—Visually inspect the spark plug wires for cracking or brittleness. Ensure that no two wires are positioned so as to cause induction firing (adjacent and parallel). Remove each wire, one by one, and check resistance with an ohmmeter.	Replace any cracked or brittle wires. If any of the wires are defective, replace the entire set. Replace any wires with excessive resistance (over $8000\,\Omega$ per foot for suppression wire), and separate any wires that might cause induction firing.	**4.6**

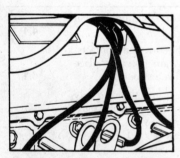

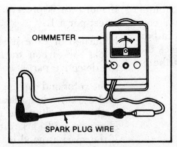

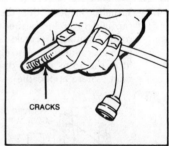

Misfiring can be the result of spark plug leads to adjacent, consecutively firing cylinders running parallel and too close together

On point-type ignition systems, check the spark plug wires as shown. On electronic ignitions, do not remove the wire from the distributor cap terminal; instead, test through the cap

Spark plug wires can be checked visually by bending them in a loop over your finger. This will reveal any cracks, burned or broken insulation. Any wire with cracked insulation should be replaced

4.6—Remove the spark plugs, noting the cylinders from which they were removed, and evaluate according to the color photos in the middle of this book.	See following.	**See following.**

Test and Procedure	Results and Indications	Proceed to
4.7—Examine the location of all the plugs.	The following diagrams illustrate some of the conditions that the location of plugs will reveal.	4.8

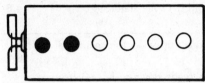

Two adjacent plugs are fouled in a 6-cylinder engine, 4-cylinder engine or either bank of a V-8. This is probably due to a blown head gasket between the two cylinders

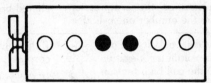

The two center plugs in a 6-cylinder engine are fouled. Raw fuel may be "boiled" out of the carburetor into the intake manifold after the engine is shut-off. Stop-start driving can also foul the center plugs, due to overly rich mixture. Proper float level, a new float needle and seat or use of an insulating spacer may help this problem

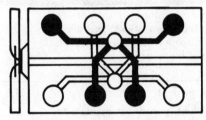

An unbalanced carburetor is indicated. Following the fuel flow on this particular design shows that the cylinders fed by the right-hand barrel are fouled from overly rich mixture, while the cylinders fed by the left-hand barrel are normal

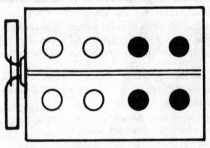

If the four rear plugs are overheated, a cooling system problem is suggested. A thorough cleaning of the cooling system may restore coolant circulation and cure the problem

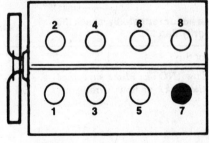

Finding one plug overheated may indicate an intake manifold leak near the affected cylinder. If the overheated plug is the second of two adjacent, consecutively firing plugs, it could be the result of ignition cross-firing. Separating the leads to these two plugs will eliminate cross-fire

Occasionally, the two rear plugs in large, lightly used V-8's will become oil fouled. High oil consumption and smoky exhaust may also be noticed. It is probably due to plugged oil drain holes in the rear of the cylinder head, causing oil to be sucked in around the valve stems. This usually occurs in the rear cylinders first, because the engine slants that way

Test and Procedure	Results and Indications	Proceed to
4.8—Determine the static ignition timing. Using the crankshaft pulley timing marks as a guide, locate top dead center on the compression stroke of the number one cylinder.	The rotor should be pointing toward the No. 1 tower in the distributor cap, and, on electronic ignitions, the armature spoke for that cylinder should be lined up with the stator.	**4.8**
4.9—Check coil polarity: Connect a voltmeter negative lead to the coil high tension lead, and the positive lead to ground (**NOTE:** *Reverse the hook-up for positive ground systems*). Crank the engine momentarily.	If the voltmeter reads up-scale, the polarity is correct:	**5.1**
	If the voltmeter reads down-scale, reverse the coil polarity (switch the primary leads):	**5.1**

Checking coil polarity

Section 5—Fuel System
See Chapter 4 for service procedures

Test and Procedure	Results and Indications	Proceed to
5.1—Determine that the air filter is functioning efficiently: Hold paper elements up to a strong light, and attempt to see light through the filter.	Clean permanent air filters in solvent (or manufacturer's recommendation), and allow to dry. Replace paper elements through which light cannot be seen:	**5.2**
5.2—Determine whether a flooding condition exists: Flooding is identified by a strong gasoline odor, and excessive gasoline present in the throttle bore(s) of the carburetor.	If flooding is not evident:	**5.3**
	If flooding is evident, permit the gasoline to dry for a few moments and restart.	
	If flooding doesn't recur:	**5.7**
	If flooding is persistent:	**5.5**

If the engine floods repeatedly, check the choke butterfly flap

Test and Procedure	Results and Indications	Proceed to
5.3—Check that fuel is reaching the carburetor: Detach the fuel line at the carburetor inlet. Hold the end of the line in a cup (not styrofoam), and crank the engine.	If fuel flows smoothly:	**5.7**
	If fuel doesn't flow (**NOTE:** *Make sure that there is fuel in the tank*), or flows erratically:	**5.4**

Check the fuel pump by disconnecting the output line (fuel pump-to-carburetor) at the carburetor and operating the starter briefly

CHILTON'S
AUTO BODY REPAIR TIPS

Tools and Materials • Step-by-Step Illustrated Procedures
How To Repair Dents, Scratches and Rust Holes
Spray Painting and Refinishing Tips

With a little practice, basic body repair procedures can be mastered by any do-it-yourself mechanic. The step-by-step repairs shown here can be applied to almost any type of auto body repair.

TOOLS & MATERIALS

You may already have basic tools, such as hammers and electric drills. Other tools unique to body repair — body hammers, grinding attachments, sanding blocks, dent puller, half-round plastic file and plastic spreaders — are relatively inexpensive and can be obtained wherever auto parts or auto body repair parts are sold. Portable air compressors and paint spray guns can be purchased or rented.

Auto Body Repair Kits

The best and most often used products are available to the do-it-yourselfer in kit form, from major manufacturers of auto body repair products. The same manufacturers also merchandise the individual products for use by pros.

Kits are available to make a wide variety of repairs, including holes, dents and scratches and fiberglass, and offer the advantage of buying the materials you'll need for the job. There is little waste or chance of materials going bad from not being used. Many kits may also contain basic body-working tools such as body files, sanding blocks and spreaders. Check the contents of the kit before buying your tools.

BODY REPAIR TIPS

Safety

Many of the products associated with auto body repair and refinishing contain toxic chemicals. Read all labels before opening containers and store them in a safe place and manner.

• Wear eye protection (safety goggles) when using power tools or when performing any operation that involves the removal of any type of material.

• Wear lung protection (disposable mask or respirator) when grinding, sanding or painting.

Sanding

1 Sand off paint before using a dent puller. When using a non-adhesive sanding disc, cover the back of the disc with an overlapping layer or two of masking tape and trim the edges. The disc will last considerably longer.

2 Use the circular motion of the sanding disc to grind *into* the edge of the repair. Grinding or sanding away from the jagged edge will only tear the sandpaper.

3 Use the palm of your hand flat on the panel to detect high and low spots. Do not use your fingertips. Slide your hand slowly back and forth.

WORKING WITH BODY FILLER

Mixing The Filler

Cleanliness and proper mixing and application are extremely important. Use a clean piece of plastic or glass or a disposable artist's palette to mix body filler.

1 Allow plenty of time and follow directions. No useful purpose will be served by adding more hardener to make it cure (set-up) faster. Less hardener means more curing time, but the mixture dries harder; more hardener means less curing time but a softer mixture.

2 Both the hardener and the filler should be thoroughly kneaded or stirred before mixing. Hardener should be a solid paste and dispense like thin toothpaste. Body filler should be smooth, and free of lumps or thick spots.

Getting the proper amount of hardener in the filler is the trickiest part of preparing the filler. Use the same amount of hardener in cold or warm weather. For contour filler (thick coats), a bead of hardener twice the diameter of the filler is about right. There's about a 15% margin on either side, but, if in doubt use less hardener.

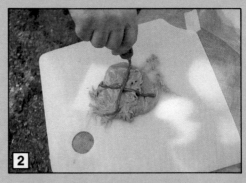

3 Mix the body filler and hardener by wiping across the mixing surface, picking the mixture up and wiping it again. Colder weather requires longer mixing times. Do not mix in a circular motion; this will trap air bubbles which will become holes in the cured filler.

Applying The Filler

1 For best results, filler should not be applied over ¼" thick.

Apply the filler in several coats. Build it up to above the level of the repair surface so that it can be sanded or grated down.

The first coat of filler must be pressed on with a firm wiping motion.

Apply the filler in one direction only. Working the filler back and forth will either pull it off the metal or trap air bubbles.

REPAIRING DENTS

Before you start, take a few minutes to study the damaged area. Try to visualize the shape of the panel before it was damaged. If the damage is on the left fender, look at the right fender and use it as a guide. If there is access to the panel from behind, you can reshape it with a body hammer. If not, you'll have to use a dent puller. Go slowly and work the metal a little at a time. Get the panel as straight as possible before applying filler.

1 This dent is typical of one that can be pulled out or hammered out from behind. Remove the headlight cover, headlight assembly and turn signal housing.

2 Drill a series of holes ½ the size of the end of the dent puller along the stress line. Make some trial pulls and assess the results. If necessary, drill more holes and try again. Do not hurry.

3 If possible, use a body hammer and block to shape the metal back to its original contours. Get the metal back as close to its original shape as possible. Don't depend on body filler to fill dents.

4 Using an 80-grit grinding disc on an electric drill, grind the paint from the surrounding area down to bare metal. Use a new grinding pad to prevent heat buildup that will warp metal.

5 The area should look like this when you're finished grinding. Knock the drill holes in and tape over small openings to keep plastic filler out.

6 Mix the body filler (see Body Repair Tips). Spread the body filler evenly over the entire area (see Body Repair Tips). Be sure to cover the area completely.

7 Let the body filler dry until the surface can just be scratched with your fingernail. Knock the high spots from the body filler with a body file ("Cheesegrater"). Check frequently with the palm of your hand for high and low spots.

8 Check to be sure that trim pieces that will be installed later will fit exactly. Sand the area with 40-grit paper.

9 If you wind up with low spots, you may have to apply another layer of filler.

10 Knock the high spots off with 40-grit paper. When you are satisfied with the contours of the repair, apply a thin coat of filler to cover pin holes and scratches.

11 Block sand the area with 40-grit paper to a smooth finish. Pay particular attention to body lines and ridges that must be well-defined.

12 Sand the area with 400 paper and then finish with a scuff pad. The finished repair is ready for priming and painting (see Painting Tips).

Materials and photos courtesy of Ritt Jones Auto Body, Prospect Park, PA.

REPAIRING RUST HOLES

There are many ways to repair rust holes. The fiberglass cloth kit shown here is one of the most cost efficient for the owner because it provides a strong repair that resists cracking and moisture and is relatively easy to use. It can be used on large and small holes (with or without backing) and can be applied over contoured areas. Remember, however, that short of replacing an entire panel, no repair is a guarantee that the rust will not return.

1 Remove any trim that will be in the way. Clean away all loose debris. Cut away all the rusted metal. But be sure to leave enough metal to retain the contour or body shape.

2 Grind away all traces of rust with a 24-grit grinding disc. Be sure to grind back 3-4 inches from the edge of the hole down to bare metal and be sure all traces of paint, primer and rust are removed.

3 Block sand the area with 80 or 100 grit sandpaper to get a clear, shiny surface and feathered paint edge. Tap the edges of the hole inward with a ball peen hammer.

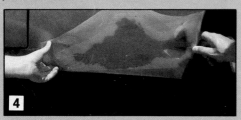

4 If you are going to use release film, cut a piece about 2-3″ larger than the area you have sanded. Place the film over the repair and mark the sanded area on the film. Avoid any unnecessary wrinkling of the film.

5 Cut 2 pieces of fiberglass matte to match the shape of the repair. One piece should be about 1″ smaller than the sanded area and the second piece should be 1″ smaller than the first. Mix enough filler and hardener to saturate the fiberglass material (see Body Repair Tips).

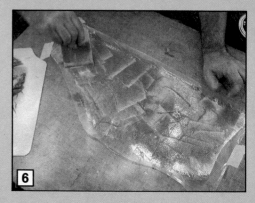

6 Lay the release sheet on a flat surface and spread an even layer of filler, large enough to cover the repair. Lay the smaller piece of fiberglass cloth in the center of the sheet and spread another layer of filler over the fiberglass cloth. Repeat the operation for the larger piece of cloth.

7 Place the repair material over the repair area, with the release film facing outward. Use a spreader and work from the center outward to smooth the material, following the body contours. Be sure to remove all air bubbles.

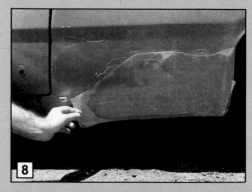

8 Wait until the repair has dried tack-free and peel off the release sheet. The ideal working temperature is 60°-90° F. Cooler or warmer temperatures or high humidity may require additional curing time. Wait longer, if in doubt.

9 Sand and feather-edge the entire area. The initial sanding can be done with a sanding disc on an electric drill if care is used. Finish the sanding with a block sander. Low spots can be filled with body filler; this may require several applications.

10 When the filler can just be scratched with a fingernail, knock the high spots down with a body file and smooth the entire area with 80-grit. Feather the filled areas into the surrounding areas.

11 When the area is sanded smooth, mix some topcoat and hardener and apply it directly with a spreader. This will give a smooth finish and prevent the glass matte from showing through the paint.

12 Block sand the topcoat smooth with finishing sandpaper (200 grit), and 400 grit. The repair is ready for masking, priming and painting (see Painting Tips).

Materials and photos courtesy Marson Corporation, Chelsea, Massachusetts

PAINTING TIPS

Preparation

1 SANDING — Use a 400 or 600 grit wet or dry sandpaper. Wet-sand the area with a 1/4 sheet of sandpaper soaked in clean water. Keep the paper wet while sanding. Sand the area until the repaired area tapers into the original finish.

2 CLEANING — Wash the area to be painted thoroughly with water and a clean rag. Rinse it thoroughly and wipe the surface dry until you're sure it's completely free of dirt, dust, fingerprints, wax, detergent or other foreign matter.

3 MASKING — Protect any areas you don't want to overspray by covering them with masking tape and newspaper. Be careful not get fingerprints on the area to be painted.

4 PRIMING — All exposed metal should be primed before painting. Primer protects the metal and provides an excellent surface for paint adhesion. When the primer is dry, wet-sand the area again with 600 grit wet-sandpaper. Clean the area again after sanding.

Painting Techniques

P aint applied from either a spray gun or a spray can (for small areas) will provide good results. Experiment on an old piece of metal to get the right combination before you begin painting.

SPRAYING VISCOSITY (SPRAY GUN ONLY) — Paint should be thinned to spraying viscosity according to the directions on the can. Use only the recommended thinner or reducer and the same amount of reduction regardless of temperature.

AIR PRESSURE (SPRAY GUN ONLY) — This is extremely important. Be sure you are using the proper recommended pressure.

TEMPERATURE — The surface to be painted should be approximately the same temperature as the surrounding air. Applying warm paint to a cold surface, or vice versa, will completely upset the paint characteristics.

THICKNESS — Spray with smooth strokes. In general, the thicker the coat of paint, the longer the drying time. Apply several thin coats about 30 seconds apart. The paint should remain wet long enough to flow out and no longer; heavier coats will only produce sags or wrinkles. Spray a light (fog) coat, followed by heavier color coats.

DISTANCE — The ideal spraying distance is 8″-12″ from the gun or can to the surface. Shorter distances will produce ripples, while greater distances will result in orange peel, dry film and poor color match and loss of material due to overspray.

OVERLAPPING — The gun or can should be kept at right angles to the surface at all times. Work to a wet edge at an even speed, using a 50% overlap and direct the center of the spray at the lower or nearest edge of the previous stroke.

RUBBING OUT (BLENDING) FRESH PAINT — Let the paint dry thoroughly. Runs or imperfections can be sanded out, primed and repainted.

Don't be in too big a hurry to remove the masking. This only produces paint ridges. When the finish has dried for at least a week, apply a small amount of fine grade rubbing compound with a clean, wet cloth. Use lots of water and blend the new paint with the surrounding area.

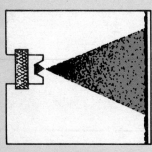

WRONG

Thin coat. Stroke too fast, not enough overlap, gun too far away.

CORRECT

Medium coat. Proper distance, good stroke, proper overlap.

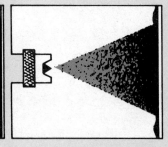

WRONG

Heavy coat. Stroke too slow, too much overlap, gun too close.

Test and Procedure	Results and Indications	Proceed to
5.4—Test the fuel pump: Disconnect all fuel lines from the fuel pump. Hold a finger over the input fitting, crank the engine (with electric pump, turn the ignition or pump on); and feel for suction.	If suction is evident, blow out the fuel line to the tank with low pressure compressed air until bubbling is heard from the fuel filler neck. Also blow out the carburetor fuel line (both ends disconnected):	**5.7**
	If no suction is evident, replace or repair the fuel pump: NOTE: *Repeated oil fouling of the spark plugs, or a no-start condition, could be the result of a ruptured vacuum booster pump diaphragm, through which oil or gasoline is being drawn into the intake manifold (where applicable).*	**5.7**
5.5—Occasionally, small specks of dirt will clog the small jets and orifices in the carburetor. With the engine cold, hold a flat piece of wood or similar material over the carburetor, where possible, and crank the engine.	If the engine starts, but runs roughly the engine is probably not run enough. If the engine won't start:	**5.9**
5.6—Check the needle and seat: Tap the carburetor in the area of the needle and seat.	If flooding stops, a gasoline additive (e.g., Gumout) will often cure the problem:	**5.7**
	If flooding continues, check the fuel pump for excessive pressure at the carburetor (according to specifications). If the pressure is normal, the needle and seat must be removed and checked, and/or the float level adjusted:	**5.7**
5.7—Test the accelerator pump by looking into the throttle bores while operating the throttle. **Check for gas at the carburetor by looking down the carburetor throat while someone moves the accelerator**	If the accelerator pump appears to be operating normally:	**5.8**
	If the accelerator pump is not operating, the pump must be reconditioned. Where possible, service the pump with the carburetor(s) installed on the engine. If necessary, remove the carburetor. Prior to removal:	**5.8**
5.8—Determine whether the carburetor main fuel system is functioning: Spray a commercial starting fluid into the carburetor while attempting to start the engine.	If the engine starts, runs for a few seconds, and dies:	**5.9**
	If the engine doesn't start:	**6.1**

Test and Procedure	Results and Indications	Proceed to
5.9—Uncommon fuel system malfunctions: See below:	If the problem is solved: If the problem remains, remove and recondition the carburetor.	**6.1**

Condition	Indication	Test	Prevailing Weather Conditions	Remedy
Vapor lock	Engine will not restart shortly after running.	Cool the components of the fuel system until the engine starts. Vapor lock can be cured faster by draping a wet cloth over a mechanical fuel pump.	Hot to very hot	Ensure that the exhaust manifold heat control valve is operating. Check with the vehicle manufacturer for the recommended solution to vapor lock on the model in question.
Carburetor icing	Engine will not idle, stalls at low speeds.	Visually inspect the throttle plate area of the throttle bores for frost.	High humidity, 32–40° F.	Ensure that the exhaust manifold heat control valve is operating, and that the intake manifold heat riser is not blocked.
Water in the fuel	Engine sputters and stalls; may not start.	Pump a small amount of fuel into a glass jar. Allow to stand, and inspect for droplets or a layer of water.	High humidity, extreme temperature changes.	For droplets, use one or two cans of commercial gas line anti-freeze. For a layer of water, the tank must be drained, and the fuel lines blown out with compressed air.

Section 6—Engine Compression

See Chapter 3 for service procedures

6.1—Test engine compression: Remove all spark plugs. Block the throttle wide open. Insert a compression gauge into a spark plug port, crank the engine to obtain the maximum reading, and record.	If compression is within limits on all cylinders:	**7.1**
	If gauge reading is extremely low on all cylinders:	**6.2**
	If gauge reading is low on one or two cylinders: (If gauge readings are identical and low on two or more adjacent cylinders, the head gasket must be replaced.)	**6.2**

Checking compression

6.2—Test engine compression (wet): Squirt approximately 30 cc. of engine oil into each cylinder, and retest per 6.1.	If the readings improve, worn or cracked rings or broken pistons are indicated:	**See Chapter 3**
	If the readings do not improve, burned or excessively carboned valves or a jumped timing chain are indicated: NOTE: *A jumped timing chain is often indicated by difficult cranking.*	**7.1**

Section 7—Engine Vacuum
See Chapter 3 for service procedures

Test and Procedure	Results and Indications	Proceed to
7.1—Attach a vacuum gauge to the intake manifold beyond the throttle plate. Start the engine, and observe the action of the needle over the range of engine speeds.	See below.	**See below**

INDICATION: normal engine in good condition

Proceed to: 8.1

Normal engine
Gauge reading: steady, from 17–22 in./Hg.

INDICATION: sticking valves or ignition miss

Proceed to: 9.1, 8.3

Sticking valves
Gauge reading: intermittent fluctuation at idle

INDICATION: late ignition or valve timing, low compression, stuck throttle valve, leaking carburetor or manifold gasket

Proceed to: 6.1

Incorrect valve timing
Gauge reading: low (10–15 in./Hg) but steady

INDICATION: improper carburetor adjustment or minor intake leak.

Proceed to: 7.2

Carburetor requires adjustment
Gauge reading: drifting needle

INDICATION: ignition miss, blown cylinder head gasket, leaking valve or weak valve spring

Proceed to: 8.3, 6.1

Blown head gasket
Gauge reading: needle fluctuates as engine speed increases

INDICATION: burnt valve or faulty valve clearance. Needle will fall when defective valve operates

Proceed to: 9.1

Burnt or leaking valves
Gauge reading: steady needle, but drops regularly

INDICATION: choked muffler, excessive back pressure in system

Proceed to: 10.1

Clogged exhaust system
Gauge reading: gradual drop in reading at idle

INDICATION: worn valve guides

Proceed to: 9.1

Worn valve guides
Gauge reading: needle vibrates excessively at idle, but steadies as engine speed increases

---

White pointer = steady gauge hand

Black pointer = fluctuating gauge hand

Test and Procedure	Results and Indications	Proceed to
7.2—Attach a vacuum gauge per 7.1, and test for an intake manifold leak. Squirt a small amount of oil around the intake manifold gaskets, carburetor gaskets, plugs and fittings. Observe the action of the vacuum gauge.	If the reading improves, replace the indicated gasket, or seal the indicated fitting or plug:	**8.1**
	If the reading remains low:	**7.3**
7.3—Test all vacuum hoses and accessories for leaks as described in 7.2. Also check the carburetor body (dashpots, automatic choke mechanism, throttle shafts) for leaks in the same manner.	If the reading improves, service or replace the offending part(s):	**8.1**
	If the reading remains low:	**6.1**

Section 8—Secondary Electrical System
See Chapter 2 for service procedures

Test and Procedure	Results and Indications	Proceed to
8.1—Remove the distributor cap and check to make sure that the rotor turns when the engine is cranked. Visually inspect the distributor components.	Clean, tighten or replace any components which appear defective.	**8.2**
8.2—Connect a timing light (per manufacturer's recommendation) and check the dynamic ignition timing. Disconnect and plug the vacuum hose(s) to the distributor if specified, start the engine, and observe the timing marks at the specified engine speed.	If the timing is not correct, adjust to specifications by rotating the distributor in the engine: (Advance timing by rotating distributor opposite normal direction of rotor rotation, retard timing by rotating distributor in same direction as rotor rotation.)	**8.3**
8.3—Check the operation of the distributor advance mechanism(s): To test the mechanical advance, disconnect the vacuum lines from the distributor advance unit and observe the timing marks with a timing light as the engine speed is increased from idle. If the mark moves smoothly, without hesitation, it may be assumed that the mechanical advance is functioning properly. To test vacuum advance and/or retard systems, alternately crimp and release the vacuum line, and observe the timing mark for movement. If movement is noted, the system is operating.	If the systems are functioning:	**8.4**
	If the systems are not functioning, remove the distributor, and test on a distributor tester:	**8.4**
8.4—Locate an ignition miss: With the engine running, remove each spark plug wire, one at a time, until one is found that doesn't cause the engine to roughen and slow down.	When the missing cylinder is identified:	**4.1**

Section 9—Valve Train

See Chapter 3 for service procedures

Test and Procedure	Results and Indications	Proceed to
9.1—Evaluate the valve train: Remove the valve cover, and ensure that the valves are adjusted to specifications. A mechanic's stethoscope may be used to aid in the diagnosis of the valve train. By pushing the probe on or near push rods or rockers, valve noise often can be isolated. A timing light also may be used to diagnose valve problems. Connect the light according to manufacturer's recommendations, and start the engine. Vary the firing moment of the light by increasing the engine speed (and therefore the ignition advance), and moving the trigger from cylinder to cylinder. Observe the movement of each valve.	Sticking valves or erratic valve train motion can be observed with the timing light. The cylinder head must be disassembled for repairs.	**See Chapter 3**
9.2—Check the valve timing: Locate top dead center of the No. 1 piston, and install a degree wheel or tape on the crankshaft pulley or damper with zero corresponding to an index mark on the engine. Rotate the crankshaft in its direction of rotation, and observe the opening of the No. 1 cylinder intake valve. The opening should correspond with the correct mark on the degree wheel according to specifications.	If the timing is not correct, the timing cover must be removed for further investigation.	**See Chapter 3**

Section 10—Exhaust System

Test and Procedure	Results and Indications	Proceed to
10.1—Determine whether the exhaust manifold heat control valve is operating: Operate the valve by hand to determine whether it is free to move. If the valve is free, run the engine to operating temperature and observe the action of the valve, to ensure that it is opening.	If the valve sticks, spray it with a suitable solvent, open and close the valve to free it, and retest. If the valve functions properly: If the valve does not free, or does not operate, replace the valve:	 10.2 10.2
10.2—Ensure that there are no exhaust restrictions: Visually inspect the exhaust system for kinks, dents, or crushing. Also note that gases are flowing freely from the tailpipe at all engine speeds, indicating no restriction in the muffler or resonator.	Replace any damaged portion of the system:	11.1

Section 11—Cooling System
See Chapter 3 for service procedures

Test and Procedure	Results and Indications	Proceed to
11.1—Visually inspect the fan belt for glazing, cracks, and fraying, and replace if necessary. Tighten the belt so that the longest span has approximately ½″ play at its midpoint under thumb pressure (see Chapter 1).	Replace or tighten the fan belt as necessary:	**11.2**

Checking belt tension

Test and Procedure	Results and Indications	Proceed to
11.2—Check the fluid level of the cooling system.	If full or slightly low, fill as necessary: If extremely low:	**11.5** **11.3**
11.3—Visually inspect the external portions of the cooling system (radiator, radiator hoses, thermostat elbow, water pump seals, heater hoses, etc.) for leaks. If none are found, pressurize the cooling system to 14–15 psi.	If cooling system holds the pressure: If cooling system loses pressure rapidly, reinspect external parts of the system for leaks under pressure. If none are found, check dipstick for coolant in crankcase. If no coolant is present, but pressure loss continues: If coolant is evident in crankcase, remove cylinder head(s), and check gasket(s). If gaskets are intact, block and cylinder head(s) should be checked for cracks or holes. If the gasket(s) is blown, replace, and purge the crankcase of coolant: NOTE: *Occasionally, due to atmospheric and driving conditions, condensation of water can occur in the crankcase. This causes the oil to appear milky white. To remedy, run the engine until hot, and change the oil and oil filter.*	**11.5** **11.4** **12.6**
11.4—Check for combustion leaks into the cooling system: Pressurize the cooling system as above. Start the engine, and observe the pressure gauge. If the needle fluctuates, remove each spark plug wire, one at a time, noting which cylinder(s) reduce or eliminate the fluctuation.	Cylinders which reduce or eliminate the fluctuation, when the spark plug wire is removed, are leaking into the cooling system. Replace the head gasket on the affected cylinder bank(s).	

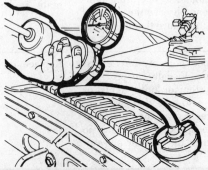

Pressurizing the cooling system

Test and Procedure	Results and Indications	Proceed to
11.5—Check the radiator pressure cap: Attach a radiator pressure tester to the radiator cap (wet the seal prior to installation). Quickly pump up the pressure, noting the point at which the cap releases.	If the cap releases within ± 1 psi of the specified rating, it is operating properly:	**11.6**
	If the cap releases at more than ± 1 psi of the specified rating, it should be replaced:	**11.6**

Checking radiator pressure cap

Test and Procedure	Results and Indications	Proceed to
11.6—Test the thermostat: Start the engine cold, remove the radiator cap, and insert a thermometer into the radiator. Allow the engine to idle. After a short while, there will be a sudden, rapid increase in coolant temperature. The temperature at which this sharp rise stops is the thermostat opening temperature.	If the thermostat opens at or about the specified temperature:	**11.7**
	If the temperature doesn't increase: (If the temperature increases slowly and gradually, replace the thermostat.)	**11.7**
11.7—Check the water pump: Remove the thermostat elbow and the thermostat, disconnect the coil high tension lead (to prevent starting), and crank the engine momentarily.	If coolant flows, replace the thermostat and retest per 11.6:	**11.6**
	If coolant doesn't flow, reverse flush the cooling system to alleviate any blockage that might exist. If system is not blocked, and coolant will not flow, replace the water pump.	

Section 12—Lubrication
See Chapter 3 for service procedures

Test and Procedure	Results and Indications	Proceed to
12.1—Check the oil pressure gauge or warning light: If the gauge shows low pressure, or the light is on for no obvious reason, remove the oil pressure sender. Install an accurate oil pressure gauge and run the engine momentarily.	If oil pressure builds normally, run engine for a few moments to determine that it is functioning normally, and replace the sender.	—
	If the pressure remains low:	**12.2**
	If the pressure surges:	**12.3**
	If the oil pressure is zero:	**12.3**
12.2—Visually inspect the oil: If the oil is watery or very thin, milky, or foamy, replace the oil and oil filter.	If the oil is normal:	**12.3**
	If after replacing oil the pressure remains low:	**12.3**
	If after replacing oil the pressure becomes normal:	—

Test and Procedure	Results and Indications	Proceed to
12.3—Inspect the oil pressure relief valve and spring, to ensure that it is not sticking or stuck. Remove and thoroughly clean the valve, spring, and the valve body.	If the oil pressure improves: If no improvement is noted:	— **12.4**
12.4—Check to ensure that the oil pump is not cavitating (sucking air instead of oil): See that the crankcase is neither over nor underfull, and that the pickup in the sump is in the proper position and free from sludge.	Fill or drain the crankcase to the proper capacity, and clean the pickup screen in solvent if necessary. If no improvement is noted:	**12.5**
12.5—Inspect the oil pump drive and the oil pump:	If the pump drive or the oil pump appear to be defective, service as necessary and retest per 12.1:	**12.1**
	If the pump drive and pump appear to be operating normally, the engine should be disassembled to determine where blockage exists:	**See Chapter 3**
12.6—Purge the engine of ethylene glycol coolant: Completely drain the crankcase and the oil filter. Obtain a commercial butyl cellosolve base solvent, designated for this purpose, and follow the instructions precisely. Following this, install a new oil filter and refill the crankcase with the proper weight oil. The next oil and filter change should follow shortly thereafter (1000 miles).		

TROUBLESHOOTING EMISSION CONTROL SYSTEMS

See Chapter 4 for procedures applicable to individual emission control systems used on specific combinations of engine/transmission/model.

TROUBLESHOOTING THE CARBURETOR
See Chapter 4 for service procedures

Carburetor problems cannot be effectively isolated unless all other engine systems (particularly ignition and emission) are functioning properly and the engine is properly tuned.

Condition	Possible Cause
Engine cranks, but does not start	1. Improper starting procedure 2. No fuel in tank 3. Clogged fuel line or filter 4. Defective fuel pump 5. Choke valve not closing properly 6. Engine flooded 7. Choke valve not unloading 8. Throttle linkage not making full travel 9. Stuck needle or float 10. Leaking float needle or seat 11. Improper float adjustment
Engine stalls	1. Improperly adjusted idle speed or mixture **Engine hot** 2. Improperly adjusted dashpot 3. Defective or improperly adjusted solenoid 4. Incorrect fuel level in fuel bowl 5. Fuel pump pressure too high 6. Leaking float needle seat 7. Secondary throttle valve stuck open 8. Air or fuel leaks 9. Idle air bleeds plugged or missing 10. Idle passages plugged **Engine Cold** 11. Incorrectly adjusted choke 12. Improperly adjusted fast idle speed 13. Air leaks 14. Plugged idle or idle air passages 15. Stuck choke valve or binding linkage 16. Stuck secondary throttle valves 17. Engine flooding—high fuel level 18. Leaking or misaligned float
Engine hesitates on acceleration	1. Clogged fuel filter 2. Leaking fuel pump diaphragm 3. Low fuel pump pressure 4. Secondary throttle valves stuck, bent or misadjusted 5. Sticking or binding air valve 6. Defective accelerator pump 7. Vacuum leaks 8. Clogged air filter 9. Incorrect choke adjustment (engine cold)
Engine feels sluggish or flat on acceleration	1. Improperly adjusted idle speed or mixture 2. Clogged fuel filter 3. Defective accelerator pump 4. Dirty, plugged or incorrect main metering jets 5. Bent or sticking main metering rods 6. Sticking throttle valves 7. Stuck heat riser 8. Binding or stuck air valve 9. Dirty, plugged or incorrect secondary jets 10. Bent or sticking secondary metering rods. 11. Throttle body or manifold heat passages plugged 12. Improperly adjusted choke or choke vacuum break.
Carburetor floods	1. Defective fuel pump. Pressure too high. 2. Stuck choke valve 3. Dirty, worn or damaged float or needle valve/seat 4. Incorrect float/fuel level 5. Leaking float bowl

Condition	Possible Cause
Engine idles roughly and stalls	1. Incorrect idle speed 2. Clogged fuel filter 3. Dirt in fuel system or carburetor 4. Loose carburetor screws or attaching bolts 5. Broken carburetor gaskets 6. Air leaks 7. Dirty carburetor 8. Worn idle mixture needles 9. Throttle valves stuck open 10. Incorrectly adjusted float or fuel level 11. Clogged air filter
Engine runs unevenly or surges	1. Defective fuel pump 2. Dirty or clogged fuel filter 3. Plugged, loose or incorrect main metering jets or rods 4. Air leaks 5. Bent or sticking main metering rods 6. Stuck power piston 7. Incorrect float adjustment 8. Incorrect idle speed or mixture 9. Dirty or plugged idle system passages 10. Hard, brittle or broken gaskets 11. Loose attaching or mounting screws 12. Stuck or misaligned secondary throttle valves
Poor fuel economy	1. Poor driving habits 2. Stuck choke valve 3. Binding choke linkage 4. Stuck heat riser 5. Incorrect idle mixture 6. Defective accelerator pump 7. Air leaks 8. Plugged, loose or incorrect main metering jets 9. Improperly adjusted float or fuel level 10. Bent, misaligned or fuel-clogged float 11. Leaking float needle seat 12. Fuel leak 13. Accelerator pump discharge ball not seating properly 14. Incorrect main jets
Engine lacks high speed performance or power	1. Incorrect throttle linkage adjustment 2. Stuck or binding power piston 3. Defective accelerator pump 4. Air leaks 5. Incorrect float setting or fuel level 6. Dirty, plugged, worn or incorrect main metering jets or rods 7. Binding or sticking air valve 8. Brittle or cracked gaskets 9. Bent, incorrect or improperly adjusted secondary metering rods 10. Clogged fuel filter 11. Clogged air filter 12. Defective fuel pump

TROUBLESHOOTING FUEL INJECTION PROBLEMS

Each fuel injection system has its own unique components and test procedures, for which it is impossible to generalize. Refer to Chapter 4 of this Repair & Tune-Up Guide for specific test and repair procedures, if the vehicle is equipped with fuel injection.

TROUBLESHOOTING ELECTRICAL PROBLEMS

See Chapter 5 for service procedures

For any electrical system to operate, it must make a complete circuit. This simply means that the power flow from the battery must make a complete circle. When an electrical component is operating, power flows from the battery to the component, passes through the component causing it to perform its function (lighting a light bulb), and then returns to the battery through the ground of the circuit. This ground is usually (but not always) the metal part of the car or truck on which the electrical component is mounted.

Perhaps the easiest way to visualize this is to think of connecting a light bulb with two wires attached to it to the battery. If one of the two wires attached to the light bulb were attached to the negative post of the battery and the other were attached to the positive post of the battery, you would have a complete circuit. Current from the battery would flow to the light bulb, causing it to light, and return to the negative post of the battery.

The normal automotive circuit differs from this simple example in two ways. First, instead of having a return wire from the bulb to the battery, the light bulb returns the current to the battery through the chassis of the vehicle. Since the negative battery cable is attached to the chassis and the chassis is made of electrically conductive metal, the chassis of the vehicle can serve as a ground wire to complete the circuit. Secondly, most automotive circuits contain switches to turn components on and off as required.

Every complete circuit from a power source must include a component which is using the power from the power source. If you were to disconnect the light bulb from the wires and touch the two wires together (don't do this) the power supply wire to the component would be grounded before the normal ground connection for the circuit.

Because grounding a wire from a power source makes a complete circuit—less the required component to use the power—this phenomenon is called a short circuit. Common causes are: broken insulation (exposing the metal wire to a metal part of the car or truck), or a shorted switch.

Some electrical components which require a large amount of current to operate also have a relay in their circuit. Since these circuits carry a large amount of current, the thickness of the wire in the circuit (gauge size) is also greater. If this large wire were connected from the component to the control switch on the instrument panel, and then back to the component, a voltage drop would occur in the circuit. To prevent this potential drop in voltage, an electromagnetic switch (relay) is used. The large wires in the circuit are connected from the battery to one side of the relay, and from the opposite side of the relay to the component. The relay is normally open, preventing current from passing through the circuit. An additional, smaller, wire is connected from the relay to the control switch for the circuit. When the control switch is turned on, it grounds the smaller wire from the relay and completes the circuit. This closes the relay and allows current to flow from the battery to the component. The horn, headlight, and starter circuits are three which use relays.

It is possible for larger surges of current to pass through the electrical system of your car or truck. If this surge of current were to reach an electrical component, it could burn it out. To prevent this, fuses, circuit breakers or fusible links are connected into the current supply wires of most of the major electrical systems. When an electrical current of excessive power passes through the component's fuse, the fuse blows out and breaks the circuit, saving the component from destruction.

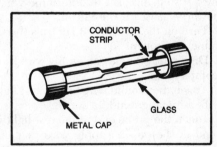

Typical automotive fuse

A circuit breaker is basically a self-repairing fuse. The circuit breaker opens the circuit the same way a fuse does. However, when either the short is removed from the circuit or the surge subsides, the circuit breaker resets itself and does not have to be replaced as a fuse does.

A fuse link is a wire that acts as a fuse. It is normally connected between the starter relay and the main wiring harness. This connection is usually under the hood. The fuse link (if installed) protects all the

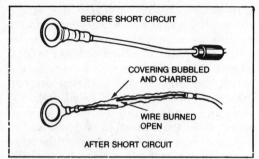

Most fusible links show a charred, melted insulation when they burn out

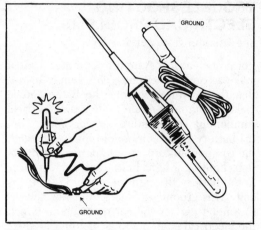

The test light will show the presence of current when touched to a hot wire and grounded at the other end

chassis electrical components, and is the probable cause of trouble when none of the electrical components function, unless the battery is disconnected or dead.

Electrical problems generally fall into one of three areas:

1. The component that is not functioning is not receiving current.

2. The component itself is not functioning.

3. The component is not properly grounded.

The electrical system can be checked with a test light and a jumper wire. A test light is a device that looks like a pointed screwdriver with a wire attached to it and has a light bulb in its handle. A jumper wire is a piece of insulated wire with an alligator clip attached to each end.

If a component is not working, you must follow a systematic plan to determine which of the three causes is the villain.

1. Turn on the switch that controls the inoperable component.

2. Disconnect the power supply wire from the component.

3. Attach the ground wire on the test light to a good metal ground.

4. Touch the probe end of the test light to the end of the power supply wire that was disconnected from the component. If the component is receiving current, the test light will go on.

NOTE: *Some components work only when the ignition switch is turned on.*

If the test light does not go on, then the problem is in the circuit between the battery and the component. This includes all the switches, fuses, and relays in the system. Follow the wire that runs back to the battery. The problem is an open circuit between the

battery and the component. If the fuse is blown and, when replaced, immediately blows again, there is a short circuit in the system which must be located and repaired. If there is a switch in the system, bypass it with a jumper wire. This is done by connecting one end of the jumper wire to the power supply wire into the switch and the other end of the jumper wire to the wire coming out of the switch. If the test light lights with the jumper wire installed, the switch or whatever was bypassed is defective.

NOTE: *Never substitute the jumper wire for the component, since it is required to use the power from the power source.*

5. If the bulb in the test light goes on, then the current is getting to the component that is not working. This eliminates the first of the three possible causes. Connect the power supply wire and connect a jumper wire from the component to a good metal ground. Do this with the switch which controls the component turned on, and also the ignition switch turned on if it is required for the component to work. If the component works with the jumper wire installed, then it has a bad ground. This is usually caused by the metal area on which the component mounts to the chassis being coated with some type of foreign matter.

6. If neither test located the source of the trouble, then the component itself is defective. Remember that for any electrical system to work, all connections must be clean and tight.

Troubleshooting Basic Turn Signal and Flasher Problems
See Chapter 5 for service procedures

Most problems in the turn signals or flasher system can be reduced to defective flashers or bulbs, which are easily replaced. Occasionally, the turn signal switch will prove defective.

F = Front   R = Rear   ● = Lights off   O = Lights on

Condition		Possible Cause
Turn signals light, but do not flash	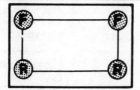	Defective flasher
No turn signals light on either side	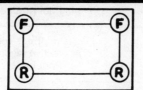	Blown fuse. Replace if defective. Defective flasher. Check by substitution. Open circuit, short circuit or poor ground.
Both turn signals on one side don't work	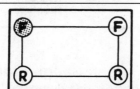	Bad bulbs. Bad ground in both (or either) housings.
One turn signal light on one side doesn't work	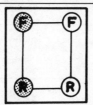	Defective bulb. Corrosion in socket. Clean contacts. Poor ground at socket.
Turn signal flashes too fast or too slowly		Check any bulb on the side flashing too fast. A heavy-duty bulb is probably installed in place of a regular bulb. Check the bulb flashing too slowly. A standard bulb was probably installed in place of a heavy-duty bulb. Loose connections or corrosion at the bulb socket.
Indicator lights don't work in either direction	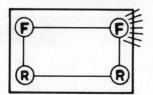	Check if the turn signals are working. Check the dash indicator lights. Check the flasher by substitution.
One indicator light doesn't light		On systems with one dash indicator: See if the lights work on the same side. Often the filaments have been reversed in systems combining stoplights with tail-lights and turn signals. Check the flasher by substitution. On systems with two indicators: Check the bulbs on the same side. Check the indicator light bulb. Check the flasher by substitution.

Troubleshooting Lighting Problems
See Chapter 5 for service procedures

Condition	Possible Cause
One or more lights don't work, but others do	1. Defective bulb(s) 2. Blown fuse(s) 3. Dirty fuse clips or light sockets 4. Poor ground circuit
Lights burn out quickly	1. Incorrect voltage regulator setting or defective regulator 2. Poor battery/alternator connections
Lights go dim	1. Low/discharged battery 2. Alternator not charging 3. Corroded sockets or connections 4. Low voltage output
Lights flicker	1. Loose connection 2. Poor ground. (Run ground wire from light housing to frame) 3. Circuit breaker operating (short circuit)
Lights "flare"—Some flare is normal on acceleration—If excessive, see "Lights Burn Out Quickly"	High voltage setting
Lights glare—approaching drivers are blinded	1. Lights adjusted too high 2. Rear springs or shocks sagging 3. Rear tires soft

Troubleshooting Dash Gauge Problems
Most problems can be traced to a defective sending unit or faulty wiring. Occasionally, the gauge itself is at fault. See Chapter 5 for service procedures.

Condition	Possible Cause
COOLANT TEMPERATURE GAUGE	
Gauge reads erratically or not at all	1. Loose or dirty connections 2. Defective sending unit. 3. Defective gauge. To test a bi-metal gauge, remove the wire from the sending unit. Ground the wire for an instant. If the gauge registers, replace the sending unit. To test a magnetic gauge, disconnect the wire at the sending unit. With ignition ON gauge should register COLD. Ground the wire; gauge should register HOT.
AMMETER GAUGE—TURN HEADLIGHTS ON (DO NOT START ENGINE). NOTE REACTION	
Ammeter shows charge Ammeter shows discharge Ammeter does not move	1. Connections reversed on gauge 2. Ammeter is OK 3. Loose connections or faulty wiring 4. Defective gauge

Condition	Possible Cause

OIL PRESSURE GAUGE

Condition	Possible Cause
Gauge does not register or is inaccurate	1. On mechanical gauge, Bourdon tube may be bent or kinked. 2. Low oil pressure. Remove sending unit. Idle the engine briefly. If no oil flows from sending unit hole, problem is in engine. 3. Defective gauge. Remove the wire from the sending unit and ground it for an instant with the ignition ON. A good gauge will go to the top of the scale. 4. Defective wiring. Check the wiring to the gauge. If it's OK and the gauge doesn't register when grounded, replace the gauge. 5. Defective sending unit.

ALL GAUGES

Condition	Possible Cause
All gauges do not operate All gauges read low or erratically All gauges pegged	1. Blown fuse 2. Defective instrument regulator 3. Defective or dirty instrument voltage regulator 4. Loss of ground between instrument voltage regulator and frame 5. Defective instrument regulator

WARNING LIGHTS

Condition	Possible Cause
Light(s) do not come on when ignition is ON, but engine is not started Light comes on with engine running	1. Defective bulb 2. Defective wire 3. Defective sending unit. Disconnect the wire from the sending unit and ground it. Replace the sending unit if the light comes on with the ignition ON. 4. Problem in individual system 5. Defective sending unit

Troubleshooting Clutch Problems

It is false economy to replace individual clutch components. The pressure plate, clutch plate and throwout bearing should be replaced as a set, and the flywheel face inspected, whenever the clutch is overhauled. See Chapter 6 for service procedures.

Condition	Possible Cause
Clutch chatter	1. Grease on driven plate (disc) facing 2. Binding clutch linkage or cable 3. Loose, damaged facings on driven plate (disc) 4. Engine mounts loose 5. Incorrect height adjustment of pressure plate release levers 6. Clutch housing or housing to transmission adapter misalignment 7. Loose driven plate hub
Clutch grabbing	1. Oil, grease on driven plate (disc) facing 2. Broken pressure plate 3. Warped or binding driven plate. Driven plate binding on clutch shaft
Clutch slips	1. Lack of lubrication in clutch linkage or cable (linkage or cable binds, causes incomplete engagement) 2. Incorrect pedal, or linkage adjustment 3. Broken pressure plate springs 4. Weak pressure plate springs 5. Grease on driven plate facings (disc)

Troubleshooting Clutch Problems (cont.)

Condition	Possible Cause
Incomplete clutch release	1. Incorrect pedal or linkage adjustment or linkage or cable binding 2. Incorrect height adjustment on pressure plate release levers 3. Loose, broken facings on driven plate (disc) 4. Bent, dished, warped driven plate caused by overheating
Grinding, whirring grating noise when pedal is depressed	1. Worn or defective throwout bearing 2. Starter drive teeth contacting flywheel ring gear teeth. Look for milled or polished teeth on ring gear.
Squeal, howl, trumpeting noise when pedal is being released (occurs during first inch to inch and one-half of pedal travel)	Pilot bushing worn or lack of lubricant. If bushing appears OK, polish bushing with emery cloth, soak lube wick in oil, lube bushing with oil, apply film of chassis grease to clutch shaft pilot hub, reassemble. NOTE: Bushing wear may be due to misalignment of clutch housing or housing to transmission adapter
Vibration or clutch pedal pulsation with clutch disengaged (pedal fully depressed)	1. Worn or defective engine transmission mounts 2. Flywheel run out. (Flywheel run out at face not to exceed 0.005") 3. Damaged or defective clutch components

Troubleshooting Manual Transmission Problems
See Chapter 6 for service procedures

Condition	Possible Cause
Transmission jumps out of gear	1. Misalignment of transmission case or clutch housing. 2. Worn pilot bearing in crankshaft. 3. Bent transmission shaft. 4. Worn high speed sliding gear. 5. Worn teeth or end-play in clutch shaft. 6. Insufficient spring tension on shifter rail plunger. 7. Bent or loose shifter fork. 8. Gears not engaging completely. 9. Loose or worn bearings on clutch shaft or mainshaft. 10. Worn gear teeth. 11. Worn or damaged detent balls.
Transmission sticks in gear	1. Clutch not releasing fully. 2. Burred or battered teeth on clutch shaft, or sliding sleeve. 3. Burred or battered transmission mainshaft. 4. Frozen synchronizing clutch. 5. Stuck shifter rail plunger. 6. Gearshift lever twisting and binding shifter rail. 7. Battered teeth on high speed sliding gear or on sleeve. 8. Improper lubrication, or lack of lubrication. 9. Corroded transmission parts. 10. Defective mainshaft pilot bearing. 11. Locked gear bearings will give same effect as stuck in gear.
Transmission gears will not synchronize	1. Binding pilot bearing on mainshaft, will synchronize in high gear only. 2. Clutch not releasing fully. 3. Detent spring weak or broken. 4. Weak or broken springs under balls in sliding gear sleeve. 5. Binding bearing on clutch shaft, or binding countershaft. 6. Binding pilot bearing in crankshaft. 7. Badly worn gear teeth. 8. Improper lubrication. 9. Constant mesh gear not turning freely on transmission mainshaft. Will synchronize in that gear only.

Condition	Possible Cause
Gears spinning when shifting into gear from neutral	1. Clutch not releasing fully. 2. In some cases an extremely light lubricant in transmission will cause gears to continue to spin for a short time after clutch is released. 3. Binding pilot bearing in crankshaft.
Transmission noisy in all gears	1. Insufficient lubricant, or improper lubricant. 2. Worn countergear bearings. 3. Worn or damaged main drive gear or countergear. 4. Damaged main drive gear or mainshaft bearings. 5. Worn or damaged countergear anti-lash plate.
Transmission noisy in neutral only	1. Damaged main drive gear bearing. 2. Damaged or loose mainshaft pilot bearing. 3. Worn or damaged countergear anti-lash plate. 4. Worn countergear bearings.
Transmission noisy in one gear only	1. Damaged or worn constant mesh gears. 2. Worn or damaged countergear bearings. 3. Damaged or worn synchronizer.
Transmission noisy in reverse only	1. Worn or damaged reverse idler gear or idler bushing. 2. Worn or damaged mainshaft reverse gear. 3. Worn or damaged reverse countergear. 4. Damaged shift mechanism.

TROUBLESHOOTING AUTOMATIC TRANSMISSION PROBLEMS

Keeping alert to changes in the operating characteristics of the transmission (changing shift points, noises, etc.) can prevent small problems from becoming large ones. If the problem cannot be traced to loose bolts, fluid level, misadjusted linkage, clogged filters or similar problems, you should probably seek professional service.

Transmission Fluid Indications

The appearance and odor of the transmission fluid can give valuable clues to the overall condition of the transmission. Always note the appearance of the fluid when you check the fluid level or change the fluid. Rub a small amount of fluid between your fingers to feel for grit and smell the fluid on the dipstick.

If the fluid appears:	It indicates:
Clear and red colored	Normal operation
Discolored (extremely dark red or brownish) or smells burned	Band or clutch pack failure, usually caused by an overheated transmission. Hauling very heavy loads with insufficient power or failure to change the fluid often result in overheating. Do not confuse this appearance with newer fluids that have a darker red color and a strong odor (though not a burned odor).
Foamy or aerated (light in color and full of bubbles)	1. The level is too high (gear train is churning oil) 2. An internal air leak (air is mixing with the fluid). Have the transmission checked professionally.
Solid residue in the fluid	Defective bands, clutch pack or bearings. Bits of band material or metal abrasives are clinging to the dipstick. Have the transmission checked professionally.
Varnish coating on the dipstick	The transmission fluid is overheating

TROUBLESHOOTING DRIVE AXLE PROBLEMS

First, determine when the noise is most noticeable.

Drive Noise: Produced under vehicle acceleration.

Coast Noise: Produced while coasting with a closed throttle.

Float Noise: Occurs while maintaining constant speed (just enough to keep speed constant) on a level road.

External Noise Elimination

It is advisable to make a thorough road test to determine whether the noise originates in the rear axle or whether it originates from the tires, engine, transmission, wheel bearings or road surface. Noise originating from other places cannot be corrected by servicing the rear axle.

ROAD NOISE

Brick or rough surfaced concrete roads produce noises that seem to come from the rear axle. Road noise is usually identical in Drive or Coast and driving on a different type of road will tell whether the road is the problem.

TIRE NOISE

Tire noise can be mistaken as rear axle noise, even though the tires on the front are at fault. Snow tread and mud tread tires or tires worn unevenly will frequently cause vibrations which seem to originate elsewhere; *temporarily, and for test purposes only,* inflate the tires to 40–50 lbs. This will significantly alter the noise produced by the tires, but will not alter noise from the rear axle. Noises from the rear axle will normally cease at speeds below 30 mph on coast, while tire noise will continue at lower tone as speed is decreased. The rear axle noise will usually change from drive conditions to coast conditions, while tire noise will not. Do not forget to lower the tire pressure to normal after the test is complete.

ENGINE/TRANSMISSION NOISE

Determine at what speed the noise is most pronounced, then stop in a quiet place. With the transmission in Neutral, run the engine through speeds corresponding to road speeds where the noise was noticed. Noises produced with the vehicle standing still are coming from the engine or transmission.

FRONT WHEEL BEARINGS

Front wheel bearing noises, sometimes confused with rear axle noises, will not change when comparing drive and coast conditions. While holding the speed steady, lightly apply the footbrake. This will often cause wheel bearing noise to lessen, as some of the weight is taken off the bearing. Front wheel bearings are easily checked by jacking up the wheels and spinning the wheels. Shaking the wheels will also determine if the wheel bearings are excessively loose.

REAR AXLE NOISES

Eliminating other possible sources can narrow the cause to the rear axle, which normally produces noise from worn gears or bearings. Gear noises tend to peak in a narrow speed range, while bearing noises will usually vary in pitch with engine speeds.

Noise Diagnosis

The Noise Is:	Most Probably Produced By:
1. Identical under Drive or Coast	Road surface, tires or front wheel bearings
2. Different depending on road surface	Road surface or tires
3. Lower as speed is lowered	Tires
4. Similar when standing or moving	Engine or transmission
5. A vibration	Unbalanced tires, rear wheel bearing, unbalanced driveshaft or worn U-joint
6. A knock or click about every two tire revolutions	Rear wheel bearing
7. Most pronounced on turns	Damaged differential gears
8. A steady low-pitched whirring or scraping, starting at low speeds	Damaged or worn pinion bearing
9. A chattering vibration on turns	Wrong differential lubricant or worn clutch plates (limited slip rear axle)
10. Noticed only in Drive, Coast or Float conditions	Worn ring gear and/or pinion gear

Troubleshooting Steering & Suspension Problems

Condition	Possible Cause
Hard steering (wheel is hard to turn)	1. Improper tire pressure 2. Loose or glazed pump drive belt 3. Low or incorrect fluid 4. Loose, bent or poorly lubricated front end parts 5. Improper front end alignment (excessive caster) 6. Bind in steering column or linkage 7. Kinked hydraulic hose 8. Air in hydraulic system 9. Low pump output or leaks in system 10. Obstruction in lines 11. Pump valves sticking or out of adjustment 12. Incorrect wheel alignment
Loose steering (too much play in steering wheel)	1. Loose wheel bearings 2. Faulty shocks 3. Worn linkage or suspension components 4. Loose steering gear mounting or linkage points 5. Steering mechanism worn or improperly adjusted 6. Valve spool improperly adjusted 7. Worn ball joints, tie-rod ends, etc.
Veers or wanders (pulls to one side with hands off steering wheel)	1. Improper tire pressure 2. Improper front end alignment 3. Dragging or improperly adjusted brakes 4. Bent frame 5. Improper rear end alignment 6. Faulty shocks or springs 7. Loose or bent front end components 8. Play in Pitman arm 9. Steering gear mountings loose 10. Loose wheel bearings 11. Binding Pitman arm 12. Spool valve sticking or improperly adjusted 13. Worn ball joints
Wheel oscillation or vibration transmitted through steering wheel	1. Low or uneven tire pressure 2. Loose wheel bearings 3. Improper front end alignment 4. Bent spindle 5. Worn, bent or broken front end components 6. Tires out of round or out of balance 7. Excessive lateral runout in disc brake rotor 8. Loose or bent shock absorber or strut
Noises (see also "Troubleshooting Drive Axle Problems")	1. Loose belts 2. Low fluid, air in system 3. Foreign matter in system 4. Improper lubrication 5. Interference or chafing in linkage 6. Steering gear mountings loose 7. Incorrect adjustment or wear in gear box 8. Faulty valves or wear in pump 9. Kinked hydraulic lines 10. Worn wheel bearings
Poor return of steering	1. Over-inflated tires 2. Improperly aligned front end (excessive caster) 3. Binding in steering column 4. No lubrication in front end 5. Steering gear adjusted too tight
Uneven tire wear (see "How To Read Tire Wear")	1. Incorrect tire pressure 2. Improperly aligned front end 3. Tires out-of-balance 4. Bent or worn suspension parts

HOW TO READ TIRE WEAR

The way your tires wear is a good indicator of other parts of the suspension. Abnormal wear patterns are often caused by the need for simple tire maintenance, or for front end alignment.

Excessive wear at the center of the tread indicates that the air pressure in the tire is consistently too high. The tire is riding on the center of the tread and wearing it prematurely. Occasionally, this wear pattern can result from outrageously wide tires on narrow rims. The cure for this is to replace either the tires or the wheels.

This type of wear usually results from consistent under-inflation. When a tire is under-inflated, there is too much contact with the road by the outer treads, which wear prematurely. When this type of wear occurs, and the tire pressure is known to be consistently correct, a bent or worn steering component or the need for wheel alignment could be indicated.

Feathering is a condition when the edge of each tread rib develops a slightly rounded edge on one side and a sharp edge on the other. By running your hand over the tire, you can usually feel the sharper edges before you'll be able to see them. The most common causes of feathering are incorrect toe-in setting or deteriorated bushings in the front suspension.

When an inner or outer rib wears faster than the rest of the tire, the need for wheel alignment is indicated. There is excessive camber in the front suspension, causing the wheel to lean too much putting excessive load on one side of the tire. Misalignment could also be due to sagging springs, worn ball joints, or worn control arm bushings. Be sure the vehicle is loaded the way it's normally driven when you have the wheels aligned.

Cups or scalloped dips appearing around the edge of the tread almost always indicate worn (sometimes bent) suspension parts. Adjustment of wheel alignment alone will seldom cure the problem. Any worn component that connects the wheel to the suspension can cause this type of wear. Occasionally, wheels that are out of balance will wear like this, but wheel imbalance usually shows up as bald spots between the outside edges and center of the tread.

Second-rib wear is usually found only in radial tires, and appears where the steel belts end in relation to the tread. It can be kept to a minimum by paying careful attention to tire pressure and frequently rotating the tires. This is often considered normal wear but excessive amounts indicate that the tires are too wide for the wheels.

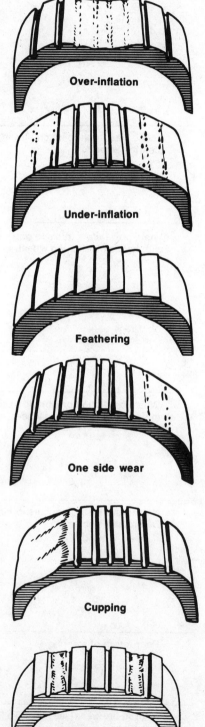

Over-inflation

Under-inflation

Feathering

One side wear

Cupping

Second-rib wear

Troubleshooting Disc Brake Problems

Condition	Possible Cause
Noise—groan—brake noise emanating when slowly releasing brakes (creep-groan)	Not detrimental to function of disc brakes—no corrective action required. (This noise may be eliminated by slightly increasing or decreasing brake pedal efforts.)
Rattle—brake noise or rattle emanating at low speeds on rough roads, (front wheels only).	1. Shoe anti-rattle spring missing or not properly positioned. 2. Excessive clearance between shoe and caliper. 3. Soft or broken caliper seals. 4. Deformed or misaligned disc. 5. Loose caliper.
Scraping	1. Mounting bolts too long. 2. Loose wheel bearings. 3. Bent, loose, or misaligned splash shield.
Front brakes heat up during driving and fail to release	1. Operator riding brake pedal. 2. Stop light switch improperly adjusted. 3. Sticking pedal linkage. 4. Frozen or seized piston. 5. Residual pressure valve in master cylinder. 6. Power brake malfunction. 7. Proportioning valve malfunction.
Leaky brake caliper	1. Damaged or worn caliper piston seal. 2. Scores or corrosion on surface of cylinder bore.
Grabbing or uneven brake action—Brakes pull to one side	1. Causes listed under "Brakes Pull" 2. Power brake malfunction. 3. Low fluid level in master cylinder. 4. Air in hydraulic system. 5. Brake fluid, oil or grease on linings. 6. Unmatched linings. 7. Distorted brake pads. 8. Frozen or seized pistons. 9. Incorrect tire pressure. 10. Front end out of alignment. 11. Broken rear spring. 12. Brake caliper pistons sticking. 13. Restricted hose or line. 14. Caliper not in proper alignment to braking disc. 15. Stuck or malfunctioning metering valve. 16. Soft or broken caliper seals. 17. Loose caliper.
Brake pedal can be depressed without braking effect	1. Air in hydraulic system or improper bleeding procedure. 2. Leak past primary cup in master cylinder. 3. Leak in system. 4. Rear brakes out of adjustment. 5. Bleeder screw open.
Excessive pedal travel	1. Air, leak, or insufficient fluid in system or caliper. 2. Warped or excessively tapered shoe and lining assembly. 3. Excessive disc runout. 4. Rear brake adjustment required. 5. Loose wheel bearing adjustment. 6. Damaged caliper piston seal. 7. Improper brake fluid (boil). 8. Power brake malfunction. 9. Weak or soft hoses.

Troubleshooting Disc Brake Problems (cont.)

Condition	Possible Cause
Brake roughness or chatter (pedal pumping)	1. Excessive thickness variation of braking disc. 2. Excessive lateral runout of braking disc. 3. Rear brake drums out-of-round. 4. Excessive front bearing clearance.
Excessive pedal effort	1. Brake fluid, oil or grease on linings. 2. Incorrect lining. 3. Frozen or seized pistons. 4. Power brake malfunction. 5. Kinked or collapsed hose or line. 6. Stuck metering valve. 7. Scored caliper or master cylinder bore. 8. Seized caliper pistons.
Brake pedal fades (pedal travel increases with foot on brake)	1. Rough master cylinder or caliper bore. 2. Loose or broken hydraulic lines/connections. 3. Air in hydraulic system. 4. Fluid level low. 5. Weak or soft hoses. 6. Inferior quality brake shoes or fluid. 7. Worn master cylinder piston cups or seals.

Troubleshooting Drum Brakes

Condition	Possible Cause
Pedal goes to floor	1. Fluid low in reservoir. 2. Air in hydraulic system. 3. Improperly adjusted brake. 4. Leaking wheel cylinders. 5. Loose or broken brake lines. 6. Leaking or worn master cylinder. 7. Excessively worn brake lining.
Spongy brake pedal	1. Air in hydraulic system. 2. Improper brake fluid (low boiling point). 3. Excessively worn or cracked brake drums. 4. Broken pedal pivot bushing.
Brakes pulling	1. Contaminated lining. 2. Front end out of alignment. 3. Incorrect brake adjustment. 4. Unmatched brake lining. 5. Brake drums out of round. 6. Brake shoes distorted. 7. Restricted brake hose or line. 8. Broken rear spring. 9. Worn brake linings. 10. Uneven lining wear. 11. Glazed brake lining. 12. Excessive brake lining dust. 13. Heat spotted brake drums. 14. Weak brake return springs. 15. Faulty automatic adjusters. 16. Low or incorrect tire pressure.

Condition	Possible Cause
Squealing brakes	1. Glazed brake lining. 2. Saturated brake lining. 3. Weak or broken brake shoe retaining spring. 4. Broken or weak brake shoe return spring. 5. Incorrect brake lining. 6. Distorted brake shoes. 7. Bent support plate. 8. Dust in brakes or scored brake drums. 9. Linings worn below limit. 10. Uneven brake lining wear. 11. Heat spotted brake drums.
Chirping brakes	1. Out of round drum or eccentric axle flange pilot.
Dragging brakes	1. Incorrect wheel or parking brake adjustment. 2. Parking brakes engaged or improperly adjusted. 3. Weak or broken brake shoe return spring. 4. Brake pedal binding. 5. Master cylinder cup sticking. 6. Obstructed master cylinder relief port. 7. Saturated brake lining. 8. Bent or out of round brake drum. 9. Contaminated or improper brake fluid. 10. Sticking wheel cylinder pistons. 11. Driver riding brake pedal. 12. Defective proportioning valve. 13. Insufficient brake shoe lubricant.
Hard pedal	1. Brake booster inoperative. 2. Incorrect brake lining. 3. Restricted brake line or hose. 4. Frozen brake pedal linkage. 5. Stuck wheel cylinder. 6. Binding pedal linkage. 7. Faulty proportioning valve.
Wheel locks	1. Contaminated brake lining. 2. Loose or torn brake lining. 3. Wheel cylinder cups sticking. 4. Incorrect wheel bearing adjustment. 5. Faulty proportioning valve.
Brakes fade (high speed)	1. Incorrect lining. 2. Overheated brake drums. 3. Incorrect brake fluid (low boiling temperature). 4. Saturated brake lining. 5. Leak in hydraulic system. 6. Faulty automatic adjusters.
Pedal pulsates	1. Bent or out of round brake drum.
Brake chatter and shoe knock	1. Out of round brake drum. 2. Loose support plate. 3. Bent support plate. 4. Distorted brake shoes. 5. Machine grooves in contact face of brake drum (Shoe Knock). 6. Contaminated brake lining. 7. Missing or loose components. 8. Incorrect lining material. 9. Out-of-round brake drums. 10. Heat spotted or scored brake drums. 11. Out-of-balance wheels.

Troubleshooting Drum Brakes (cont.)

Condition	Possible Cause
Brakes do not self adjust	1. Adjuster screw frozen in thread. 2. Adjuster screw corroded at thrust washer. 3. Adjuster lever does not engage star wheel. 4. Adjuster installed on wrong wheel.
Brake light glows	1. Leak in the hydraulic system. 2. Air in the system. 3. Improperly adjusted master cylinder pushrod. 4. Uneven lining wear. 5. Failure to center combination valve or proportioning valve.

Mechanic's Data

General Conversion Table

Multiply By	To Convert	To	
	LENGTH		
2.54	Inches	Centimeters	.3937
25.4	Inches	Millimeters	.03937
30.48	Feet	Centimeters	.0328
.304	Feet	Meters	3.28
.914	Yards	Meters	1.094
1.609	Miles	Kilometers	.621
	VOLUME		
.473	Pints	Liters	2.11
.946	Quarts	Liters	1.06
3.785	Gallons	Liters	.264
.016	Cubic inches	Liters	61.02
16.39	Cubic inches	Cubic cms.	.061
28.3	Cubic feet	Liters	.0353
	MASS (Weight)		
28.35	Ounces	Grams	.035
.4536	Pounds	Kilograms	2.20
—	To obtain	From	Multiply by

Multiply By	To Convert	To	
	AREA		
.645	Square inches	Square cms.	.155
.836	Square yds.	Square meters	1.196
	FORCE		
4.448	Pounds	Newtons	.225
.138	Ft./lbs.	Kilogram/meters	7.23
1.36	Ft./lbs.	Newton-meters	.737
.112	In./lbs.	Newton-meters	8.844
	PRESSURE		
.068	Psi	Atmospheres	14.7
6.89	Psi	Kilopascals	.145
	OTHER		
1.104	Horsepower (DIN)	Horsepower (SAE)	.9861
.746	Horsepower (SAE)	Kilowatts (KW)	1.34
1.60	Mph	Km/h	.625
.425	Mpg	Km/1	2.35
—	To obtain	From	Multiply by

Tap Drill Sizes

National Coarse or U.S.S.

Screw & Tap Size	Threads Per Inch	Use Drill Number
No. 5	40	.39
No. 6	32	.36
No. 8	32	.29
No. 10	24	.25
No. 12	24	.17
1/4	20	8
5/16	18	F
3/8	16	5/16
7/16	14	U
1/2	13	27/64
9/16	12	31/64
5/8	11	17/32
3/4	10	21/32
7/8	9	49/64

National Coarse or U.S.S.

Screw & Tap Size	Threads Per Inch	Use Drill Number
1	8	7/8
1 1/8	7	63/64
1 1/4	7	1 7/64
1 1/2	6	1 11/32

National Fine or S.A.E.

Screw & Tap Size	Threads Per Inch	Use Drill Number
No. 5	44	.37
No. 6	40	.33
No. 8	36	.29
No. 10	32	.21

National Fine or S.A.E.

Screw & Tap Size	Threads Per Inch	Use Drill Number
No. 12	28	.15
1/4	28	3
6/16	24	1
3/8	24	Q
7/16	20	W
1/2	20	29/64
9/16	18	33/64
5/8	18	37/64
3/4	16	11/16
7/8	14	13/16
1 1/8	12	1 3/64
1 1/4	12	1 11/64
1 1/2	12	1 27/64

Drill Sizes In Decimal Equivalents

Inch	Decimal	Wire	mm
1/64	.0156		.39
	.0157		.4
	.0160	78	
	.0165		.42
	.0173		.44
	.0177		.45
	.0180	77	
	.0181		.46
	.0189		.48
	.0197		.5
	.0200	76	
	.0210	75	
	.0217		.55
	.0225	74	
	.0236		.6
	.0240	73	
	.0250	72	
	.0256		.65
	.0260	71	
	.0276		.7
	.0280	70	
	.0292	69	
	.0295		.75
	.0310	68	
1/32	.0312		.79
	.0315		.8
	.0320	67	
	.0330	66	
	.0335		.85
	.0350	65	
	.0354		.9
	.0360	64	
	.0370	63	
	.0374		.95
	.0380	62	
	.0390	61	
	.0394		1.0
	.0400	60	
	.0410	59	
	.0413		1.05
	.0420	58	
	.0430	57	
	.0433		1.1
	.0453		1.15
3/64	.0465	56	
	.0469		1.19
	.0472		1.2
	.0492		1.25
	.0512		1.3
	.0520	55	
	.0531		1.35
	.0550	54	
	.0551		1.4
	.0571		1.45
	.0591		1.5
	.0595	53	
	.0610		1.55
1/16	.0625		1.59
	.0630		1.6
	.0635	52	
	.0650		1.65
	.0669		1.7
	.0670	51	
	.0689		1.75
	.0700	50	
	.0709		1.8
	.0728		1.85

Inch	Decimal	Wire	mm
	.0730	49	
	.0748		1.9
	.0760	48	
5/64	.0768		1.95
	.0781		1.98
	.0785	47	
	.0787		2.0
	.0807		2.05
	.0810	46	
	.0820	45	
	.0827		2.1
	.0846		2.15
	.0860	44	
	.0866		2.2
	.0886		2.25
	.0890	43	
	.0906		2.3
	.0925		2.35
3/32	.0935	42	
	.0938		2.38
	.0945		2.4
	.0960	41	
	.0965		2.45
	.0980	40	
	.0981		2.5
	.0995	39	
	.1015	38	
	.1024		2.6
	.1040	37	
	.1063		2.7
	.1065	36	
	.1083		2.75
7/64	.1094		2.77
	.1100	35	
	.1102		2.8
	.1110	34	
	.1130	33	
	.1142		2.9
	.1160	32	
	.1181		3.0
	.1200	31	
	.1220		3.1
1/8	.1250		3.17
	.1260		3.2
	.1280		3.25
	.1285	30	
	.1299		3.3
	.1339		3.4
	.1360	29	
	.1378		3.5
	.1405	28	
9/64	.1406		3.57
	.1417		3.6
	.1440	27	
	.1457		3.7
	.1470	26	
	.1476		3.75
	.1495	25	
	.1496		3.8
	.1520	24	
	.1535		3.9
	.1540	23	
5/32	.1562		3.96
	.1570	22	
	.1575		4.0
	.1590	21	
	.1610	20	

Inch	Decimal	Wire & Letter	mm
	.1614		4.1
	.1654		4.2
	.1660	19	
	.1673		4.25
	.1693		4.3
	.1695	18	
11/64	.1719		4.36
	.1730	17	
	.1732		4.4
	.1770	16	
	.1772		4.5
	.1800	15	
	.1811		4.6
	.1820	14	
	.1850	13	
	.1850		4.7
	.1870		4.75
3/16	.1875		4.76
	.1890		4.8
	.1890	12	
	.1910	11	
	.1929		4.9
	.1935	10	
	.1960	9	
	.1969		5.0
	.1990	8	
	.2008		5.1
	.2010	7	
13/64	.2031		5.16
	.2040	6	
	.2047		5.2
	.2055	5	
	.2067		5.25
	.2087		5.3
	.2090	4	
	.2126		5.4
	.2130	3	
	.2165		5.5
7/32	2188		5.55
	.2205		5.6
	.2210	2	
	.2244		5.7
	.2264		5.75
	.2280	1	
	.2283		5.8
	.2323		5.9
	.2340	A	
15/64	.2344		5.95
	.2362		6.0
	.2380	B	
	.2402		6.1
	.2420	C	
	.2441		6.2
	.2460	D	
	.2461		6.25
	.2480		6.3
1/4	.2500	E	
	.2520		6.
	.2559		6.5
	.2570	F	
	.2598		6.6
	.2610	G	
	.2638		6.7
17/64	.2656		6.74
	.2657		6.75
	.2660	H	
	.2677		6.8

Inch	Decimal	Letter	mm
	.2717		6.9
	.2720	I	
	.2756		7.0
	.2770	J	
	.2795		7.1
	.2810	K	
9/32	.2812		7.14
	.2835		7.2
	.2854		7.25
	.2874		7.3
	.2900	L	
	.2913		7.4
	.2950	M	
	.2953		7.5
19/64	.2969		7.54
	.2992		7.6
	.3020	N	
	.3031		7.7
	.3051		7.75
	.3071		7.8
	.3110		7.9
5/16	.3125		7.93
	.3150		8.0
	.3160	O	
	.3189		8.1
	.3228		8.2
	.3230	P	
	.3248		8.25
	.3268		8.3
21/64	.3281		8.33
	.3307		8.4
	.3320	Q	
	.3346		8.5
	.3386		8.6
	.3390	R	
	.3425		8.7
11/32	.3438		8.73
	.3445		8.75
	.3465		8.8
	.3480	S	
	.3504		8.9
	.3543		9.0
	.3580	T	
	.3583		9.1
23/64	.3594		9.12
	.3622		9.2
	.3642		9.25
	.3661		9.3
	.3680	U	
	.3701		9.4
	.3740		9.5
3/8	.3750		9.52
	.3770	V	
	.3780		9.6
	.3819		9.7
	.3839		9.75
	.3858		9.8
	.3860	W	
	.3898		9.9
25/64	.3906		9.92
	.3937		10.0
	.3970	X	
	.4040	Y	
13/32	.4062		10.31
	.4130	Z	
	.4134		10.5
27/64	.4219		10.71

Inch	Decimal	mm
7/16	.4331	11.0
	.4375	11.11
	.4528	11.5
29/64	.4531	11.51
15/32	.4688	11.90
	.4724	12.0
31/64	.4844	12.30
	.4921	12.5
1/2	.5000	12.70
	.5118	13.0
33/64	.5156	13.09
17/32	.5312	13.49
	.5315	13.5
35/64	.5469	13.89
	.5512	14.0
9/16	.5625	14.28
	.5709	14.5
37/64	.5781	14.68
	.5906	15.0
19/32	.5938	15.08
39/64	.6094	15.47
	.6102	15.5
5/8	.6250	15.87
	.6299	16.0
41/64	.6406	16.27
	.6496	16.5
21/32	.6562	16.66
	.6693	17.0
43/64	.6719	17.06
11/16	.6875	17.46
	.6890	17.5
45/64	.7031	17.85
	.7087	18.0
23/32	.7188	18.25
	.7283	18.5
47/64	.7344	18.65
	.7480	19.0
3/4	.7500	19.05
49/64	.7656	19.44
	.7677	19.5
25/32	.7812	19.84
	.7874	20.0
51/64	.7969	20.24
	.8071	20.5
13/16	.8125	20.63
	.8268	21.0
53/64	.8281	21.03
27/32	.8438	21.43
	.8465	21.5
55/64	.8594	21.82
	.8661	22.0
7/8	.8750	22.22
	.8858	22.5
57/64	.8906	22.62
	.9055	23.0
29/32	.9062	23.01
59/64	.9219	23.41
	.9252	23.5
15/16	.9375	23.81
	.9449	24.0
61/64	.9531	24.2
	.9646	24.5
31/64	.9688	24.6
	.9843	25.0
63/64	.9844	25.0
1	1.0000	25.4

Index

Chilton's Repair & Tune-Up Guides

The Complete line covers domestic cars, imports, trucks, vans, RV's and 4-wheel drive vehicles.

———— IMPORTANT ————

- **All vehicles are listed alphabetically by individual model names rather than by manufacturer.**
- **Numerical model names follow the alphabetical model name listing.**

Model Name	RTUG Title	Part No.
Accord	Honda 1973–84	6980
Alliance	Renault 1975–85	7165
AMX	AMC 1975–82	7199
Aries 1981–82	Chrysler K-Car 1981–82	7163
Arrow	Champ/Arrow/Sapporo 1978–83	7041
Arrow Pick-Ups	D-50/Arrow Pick-Up 1979–82	7032
Aspen 1976–80	Aspen/Volare 1976–80	6637
Astre 1975–77	GM Subcompact 1971–80	6935
Barracuda 1965–72	Barracuda/Challenger 1965–72	5807
Bavaria	BMW 1970–82	6844
Bel Air 1968–75	Chevrolet 1968–83	7135
Belvedere 1968–70	Roadrunner/Satellite/Belvedere/GTX 1968–73	5821
Biscayne 1968–71	Chevrolet 1968–83	7135
Blazer 1969–82	Blazer/Jimmy 1969–82	6931
Bobcat 1975–80	Pinto/Bobcat 1971–80	7027
Bonneville 1975–83	Buick/Olds/Pontiac 1975–83	7308
BRAT	Subaru 1970–84	6982
Bronco 1966–83	Ford Bronco 1966–83	7140
Bronco II 1984	Ford Bronco II 1984	7408
Brookwood 1968–72	Chevrolet 1968–83	7135
Brougham 1974–75	Valiant/Duster 1968–76	6326
B-210 1974–78	Datsun 1200, etc. 1973–84	7197
Caballero 1964–82	Chevrolet Mid-Size 1964–84	6840
Camaro 1967–81	Camaro 1967–81	6735
Camaro 1982–83	Camaro 1982–83	7317
Camry 1983–84	Toyota Corona, etc. 1970–84	7004
Capri 1970–77	Capri 1970–77	6695
Capri 1979–83	Mustang/Capri 1979–83	6963
Caprice 1975–83	Chevrolet 1968–83	7135
Caravan 1984–85	Caravan/Voyager 1984–85	7482
Carina 1972–73	Toyota Corolla, etc. 1970–84	7036
Catalina 1975–83	Buick/Olds/Pontiac 1975–83	7308
Cavalier 1982	GM J-Car 1982	7059
Celebrity 1982–83	GM A-Body 1982–83	7309
Celica 1971–83	Toyota Celica/Supra 1971–83	7043
Century, front wheel drive 1982–83	GM A-Body 1982–83	7309
Century, rear wheel drive 1975–83	Century/Regal 1975–83	7307
Challenger 1965–72	Barracuda/Challenger 1965–72	5807
Challenger 1977–83	Colt/Challenger/Vista 1971–83	7037
Champ	Champ/Arrow/Sapporo 1978–83	7041
Charger 2.2 1982–84	Omni/Horizon 1978–84	6845
Cherokee 1974–84	Jeep Wagoneer, etc. 1962–84	6739
Chevelle 1964–77	Chevrolet Mid-Size 1964–84	6840
Chevette 1976–84	Chevette/T-1000 1976–84	6836
Chevy Pick-Ups 1970–84	Chevrolet/GMC Pick-Ups/Suburban 1970–84	6936
Chevy Vans 1967–84	Chevy/GMC Vans 1967–84	6930
Chevy II 1962–68	Chevy II/Nova 1962–79	6841
Cimarron 1982	GM J-Car 1982	7059
Citation 1980–83	GM X-Body 1980–83	7049
Civic	Honda 1973–84	6980
Colt	Colt/Challenger/Vista 1971–83	7037
Comet 1971–77	Maverick/Comet 1971–77	6634
Commando 1971–73	Jeep Wagoneer, Commando, Cherokee, Truck 1962–84	6739
Concord	AMC 1975–82	7199
Continental 1982–85	Ford/Mercury Mid-Size 1971–85	6696
Corolla 1966–70	Toyota 1966–70	5795
Corolla 1970–84	Toyota Corolla, etc. 1970–84	7036
Corona 1966–70	Toyota 1966–70	5795
Corona 1970–81	Toyota Corona, etc. 1970–84	7004
Corsa	Corvair 1960–69	6691
Corvair 1960–69	Corvair 1960–69	6691
Corvette 1953–62	Corvette 1953–62	6576
Corvette 1963–84	Corvette 1963–84	6843
Cosmo	Mazda 1971–84	6981
Cougar 1967–71	Mustang/Cougar 1965–73	6542
Cougar 1972–85	Ford/Mercury Mid-Size 1971–85	6696
Country Sedan 1968–81	Ford/Mercury/Lincoln 1968–85	6842
Country Squire 1968–83	Ford/Mercury/Lincoln 1968–85	6842
Courier 1972–82	Ford Courier 1972–82	6983
Cressida 1978–84	Toyota Corona, etc. 1970–84	7004
Crown 1966–70	Toyota 1966–70	5795
Crown 1970–72	Toyota Corona, etc. 1970–84	7004
Crown Victoria 1981–85	Ford/Mercury/Lincoln 1968–85	6842
Cutlass 1970–82	Cutlass 1970–82 .	6933
Cutlass Ciera 1982–83	GM A-Body 1982–83	7309
Dart 1968–76	Dart/Demon 1968–76	6324
Dasher	VW Front Drive 1974–83	6962
Datsun Pick-Ups 1961–72	Datsun 1961–72	5790
Datsun Pick-Ups 1970–83	Datsun Pick-Ups 1970–83	6816
Demon 1971–76	Dart/Demon 1968–76	6324
deVille 1967–84	Cadillac 1967–84	7462
Dodge Pick-Ups 1967–84	Dodge/Plymouth Trucks 1967–84	7459
Dodge Vans	Dodge/Plymouth Vans 1967–84	6934
Duster 1970–76	Valiant/Duster 1968–76	6326
D-50 Pick-Up 1979–81	D-50/Arrow Pick-Ups 1979–81	7032
Eagle	AMC 1975–82	7199
El Camino 1964–82	Chevrolet Mid-Size 1964–84	6840
Eldorado 1967–84	Cadillac 1967–84	7462
Electra 1975–84	Buick/Olds/Pontiac 1975–85	7308
Elite 1974–76	Ford/Mercury Mid-Size 1971–85	6696
Encore	Renault 1975–85	7165
Escort, EXP 1981–85	Ford/Mercury Front Wheel Drive 1981–85	7055
Fairlane 1962–70	Fairlane/Torino 1962–75	6320
Fairmont 1978–83	Fairmont/Zephyr 1978–83	6965
FF-1	Subaru 1970–84	6982
Fiat, all models	Fiat 1969–81	7042
Fiesta	Fiesta 1978–80	6846
Firebird 1967–81	Firebird 1967–81	5996
Firebird 1982–83	Firebird 1982–83	7345
Firenza 1982	GM J-Car 1982	7059
Fleetwood 1967–84	Cadillac 1967–84	7462
Ford Pick-Ups 1965–84	Ford Pick-ups 1965–84	6913
Ford Vans	Ford Vans 1961–84	6849
Fuego	Renau!t 1975–85	7165
Fury 1968–76	Plymouth 1968–76	6552
F-10 1977–78	Datsun F-10, etc. 1977–82	7196
F-85 1970–72	Cutlass 1970–82	6933
Galaxie 1968–81	Ford/Mercury/Lincoln 1968–85	6842
GLC	Mazda 1971–84	6981
GMC Pick-Ups 1970–84	Chevrolet/GMC Pick-Ups/Suburban 1970–84	6936
GMC Vans	Chevrolet/GMC Vans 1967–84	6930
Gordini	Renault 1975–85	7165
Granada 1975–82	Granada/Monarch 1975–82	6937
Grand Coupe, Gran Fury, Gran Sedan	Plymouth 1968–76	6552
Grand Am 1974–80	Pontiac Mid-Size 1974–83	7346
Grand Prix 1974–83	Pontiac Mid-Size 1974–83	7346
Grand Safari 1975–85	Buick/Olds/Pontiac 1975–85	7308
Grand Ville 1975–83	Buick/Olds/Pontiac 1975–83	7308
Greenbriar	Corvair 1960–69	6691
Gremlin	AMC 1975–82	7199
GTO 1968–73	Tempest/GTO/LeMans 1968–73	5905
GTO 1974	Pontiac Mid-Size 1974–83	7346
GTX 1968–71	Roadrunner/Satellite/Belvedere/GTX 1968–73	5821
GT6	Triumph 1969–73	5910
G.T.350, G.T.500	Mustang/Cougar 1965–73	6542
Horizon 1978–84	Omni/Horizon 1978–84	6845
Hornet	AMC 1975–82	7199
Impala 1968–78	Chevrolet 1968–83	7135
Jeep CJ	Jeep CJ 1945–84	6817
Jeep Pick-Ups	Jeep Wagoneer, Commando, Cherokee, Truck 1962–84	6739
Jeepster 1966–70	Jeep Wagoneer, Commando, Cherokee, Truck 1962–84	6739
Jetta	VW Front Wheel Drive 1974–83	6962
Jimmy 1970–82	Blazer/Jimmy 1969–82	6931
Kingswood 1968–81	Chevrolet 1968–83	7135
Lakewood	Corvair 1960–69	6691
Lancer	Champ/Arrow/Sapporo 1977–83	7041
Land Cruiser 1966–70	Toyota 1966–70	5795
Land Cruiser 1970–83	Toyota Trucks 1970–83	7035
LeBaron 1982	Chrysler K-Car 1981–82	7163
LeCar	Renault 1975–85	7165
LeMans 1968–73	Tempest/GTO/LeMans 1968–73	5905
LeMans, Grand LeMans 1974–83	Pontiac Mid-Size 1974–83	7346
LeSabre 1975–85	Buick/Olds/Pontiac 1975–85	7308
Lincoln 1968–85	Ford/Mercury/Lincoln 1968–85	6842
LTD 1968–81	Ford/Mercury/Lincoln 1968–85	6842
LTD II 1977–79	Ford/Mercury Mid-Size 1971–85	6696
LUV 1972–81	Chevrolet LUV 1972–81	6815
Lynx, LN-7 1981–85	Ford/Mercury Front Wheel Drive 1981–85	7055
Mach I 1968–73	Mustang/Cougar 1965–73	6542
Malibu	Chevrolet Mid-Size 1964–84	6840
Matador	AMC 1975–82	7199
Maverick 1970–77	Maverick/Comet 1970–77	6634
Maxima 1980–84	Datsun 200SX, etc. 1973–84	7170
Mercury (Full-Size) 1968–85	Ford/Mercury/Lincoln 1968–85	6842
MG	MG 1961–81	6780
Mk.II 1969–70	Toyota 1966–70	5795
Mk.II 1970–76	Toyota Corona, etc. 1970–84	7004
Monaco 1968–77	Dodge 1968–77	6554
Monarch 1975–80	Granada/Monarch 1975–82	6937
Monte Carlo 1970–84	Chevrolet Mid-Size 1964–84	6840
Montego 1971–78	Ford/Mercury Mid-Size 1971–85	6696
Monza 1960–69	Corvair 1960–69	6691
Monza 1975–80	GM Subcompact 1971–80	6935
Mustang 1965–73	Mustang/Cougar 1965–73	6542
Mustang 1979–83	Mustang/Capri 1979–83	6963
Mustang II 1974–78	Mustang II 1974–78	6812
Nova	Chevy II/Nova 1962–79	6841
Omega 1980–81	GM X-Body 1980–83	7049
Omni 1978–84	Omni/Horizon 1978–84	6845
Opel	Opel 1964–70	5792
	Opel 1971–75	6575
Pacer	AMC 1975–82	7199
Patrol 1961–69	Datsun 1961–72	5790
Peugeot	Peugeot 1970–74	5982
Phoenix 1980–83	GM X-Body 1980–83	7049
Pinto 1971–80	Pinto/Bobcat 1971–80	7027

continued on next page

Model Name	RTUG Title	Part No.	Model Name	RTUG Title	Part No.
Plymouth Vans 1974–84	Dodge/Plymouth Vans 1967–84	6934	Z-28 1982–83	Camaro 1982–83	7317
Polara 1968–77	Dodge 1968–77	6554	4-4-2 1970–80	Cutlass 1970–82	6933
Prelude	Honda 1973–84	6980	024 1978–84	Omni/Horizon 1978–84	6845
PV-444, 544	Volvo 1956–69	6529	3.0S, 3.0Si, 3.0CS	BMW 1970–82	6844
P-1800	Volvo 1956–69	6529	6.9 1978–79	Mercedes-Benz 1974–84	6809
Quantum 1974–84	VW Front Wheel Drive 1974–84	6962	88, 98	Buick/Olds/Pontiac 1975–83	7308
Rabbit	VW Front Wheel Drive 1974–84	6962	99 1969–75	SAAB 99 1969–75	5988
Ramcharger	Dodge/Plymouth Trucks 1967–84	7459	100 LS, 100GL	Audi 1970–73	5902
Ranchero 1967–70	Fairlane/Torino 1962–70	6320	122, 122S	Volvo 1956–69	6529
Ranchero 1971–78	Ford/Mercury Mid-Size 1971–85	6696	142, 144, 145, 164	Volvo 1956–69	6529
Ranch Wagon	Ford/Mercury/Lincoln 1968–85	6842		Volvo 1970–84	7040
Ranger Pick-Up 1983–84	Ford Ranger 1983–84	7338	190E, 190D 1984	Mercedes-Benz 1974–84	6809
Regal 1975–85	Century/Regal 1975–85	7307	190C, 190DC 1961–66	Mercedes-Benz 1959–70	6065
Reliant 1981–85	Chrysler K-Car 1981–85	7163	200, 200D	Mercedes-Benz 1959–70	6065
Roadrunner 1968–73	Roadrunner/Satellite/Belvedere/GTX 1968–73	5821	200SX 1977–84	Datsun 200SX, etc. 1973–84	7170
			210 1979–81	Datsun 1200, etc. 1971–84	7197
RX-2, RX-3, RX-4	Mazda 1971–84	6981	220D, 220B, 220Sb, 220SEb	Mercedes-Benz 1959–70	6065
RX-7	RX-7 1979–81	7031			
R-12, 15, 17, 18, 18i	Renault 1975–85	7165	220/8 1968–73	Mercedes-Benz 1968–73	5907
Sapporo 1977–83	Champ/Arrow/Saporro 1978–83	7041	230 1974–78	Mercedes-Benz 1974–84	6809
Satellite 1968–73	Roadrunner/Satellite/Belvedere/GTX 1968–73	5821	230S, 230SL	Mercedes-Benz 1959–70	6065
			230/8 1968–69	Mercedes-Benz 1968–73	5907
Scamp 1971–76	Valiant/Duster 1968–76	6326	240D 1974–79	Mercedes-Benz 1974–84	6809
Scamp 1982	Omni/Horizon 1978–84	6845	240Z, 260Z, 280Z, 280ZX, 300ZX	Datsun Z & ZX 1970–84	6932
Scirocco	VW Front Wheel Drive 1974–83	6962			
Scout 1967–73	International Scout 1967–73	5912	242, 244, 245, 262, 264, 265	Volvo 1970–84	7040
Scrambler 1981–84	Jeep CJ 1981–84	6817			
Sentra 1982–84	Datsun 1200, etc. 1973–84	7197	250C, 250/8	Mercedes-Benz 1968–73	5907
Seville 1967–84	Cadillac 1967–84	7462	250S, 250SE, 250SL	Mercedes-Benz 1959–70	6065
Skyhawk 1975–80	GM Subcompact 1971–80	6935	280, 280C, 280S/8, 280SE, 280SE/8, 280SEL, 280SEL/8 280SL	Mercedes-Benz 1968–73	5907
Skyhawk 1982	GM J-Car 1982	7059			
Skylark 1980–83	GM X-Body 1980–83	7049			
Spirit	AMC 1975–82	7199			
Sport Wagon	Renault 1975–85	7165	280, 280C, 280CE, 280E, 280S, 280SE, 300CD, 300D, 300SD	Mercedes-Benz 1974–84	6809
Stanza	Datsun F-10, etc. 1977–82	7196			
Starfire 1975–80	GM Subcompact 1971–80	6935			
Starlet 1981–84	Toyota Corolla, etc. 1970–84	7036	300SE, 1961–63	Mercedes-Benz 1959–70	6065
Suburban 1968–76	Plymouth 1968–76	6552	300SEL, 3.5, 4.5, 6.3, 300SEL/8	Mercedes-Benz 1968–73	5907
Suburban 1970–84	Chevy/GMC Pick-Ups/Suburban 1970–84	6936			
			300TD 1979	Mercedes-Benz 1974–84	6809
Sunbird 1975–80	GM Subcompact 1971–80	6935	304	Peugeot 1970–74	5982
Super 90	Audi 1970–73	5902	310, 311 1962–69	Datsun 1961–72	5790
Supra 1979–84	Toyota Celica/Supra 1971–84	7043	310 1979–82	Datsun F-10, etc. 1977–82	7196
SX-4	AMC 1975–82	7199	320i	BMW 1970–82	6844
S-10 Blazer, S-15 Jimmy 1982–85	Chevy S-10 Blazer/GMC S-15 Jimmy 1982–85	7383	350SL 1972	Mercedes-Benz 1968–73	5907
S-10, S-15 Pick-Ups 1982–85	Chevy S-10/GMC S-15 Pick-Ups 1982–85	7310	380SEC, 380SL, 380SLC, 380SEL	Mercedes-Benz 1974–84	6809
TC-3 1978–82	Omni/Horizon/Rampage 1978–84	6845	400 1982	Chrysler K-Car 1981–82	7163
Tempest 1968–73	Tempest/GTO/LeMans 1968–73	5905	410, 411, 1963–68	Datsun 1961–72	5790
Tempo 1984–85	Ford/Mercury Front Wheel Drive 1981–85	7055	411, 412	VW 1970–81	7081
			450SLC 1973	Mercedes-Benz 1968–73	5907
Tercel 1980–84	Toyota Corolla, etc. 1970–84	7036	450SE, 450SEL, 450SEL 6.9, 450SL, 450SLC	Mercedes-Benz 1974–84	6809
Thunderbird 1977–83	Ford/Mercury Mid-Size 1971–83	6696			
Topaz 1983–85	Ford/Mercury Front Wheel Drive 1981–85	7055	500SEC, 500SEL	Mercedes-Benz 1974–84	6809
			504	Peugeot 1970–74	5982
Torino 1968–71	Fairlane/Torino 1962–75	6320	510 1968–71	Datsun 1961–72	5790
Torino, Gran Torino 1971–76	Ford/Mercury Mid-Size 1971–83	6696	510 1973, 1978–80	Datsun 200SX, etc. 1973–84	7170
			528i, 530i	BMW 1970–82	6844
Townsman 1968–72	Chevrolet 1968–83	7135	600	Honda 1973–84	6980
Toyota Pick-Ups 1966–70	Toyota 1966–70	5795	610 1973–76	Datsun 200SX, etc. 1973–84	7170
Toyota Pick-Ups 1970–83	Toyota Trucks 1970–83	7035	626	Mazda 1971–84	6981
Toyota Van 1984	Toyota Corona, etc. 1970–84	7004	630 CSi, 633 CSi	BMW 1970–82	6844
Trail Duster 1974–84	Dodge/Plymouth Trucks 1967–84	7459	710 1974–77	Datsun 200SX, etc. 1973–84	7170
Triumph, all models	Triumph 1969–73	5910	733i	BMW 1970–82	6844
Turismo 1982–84	Omni/Horizon 1978–84	6845	760, 760GLE	Volvo 1970–84	7040
T-37 1971	Tempest/GTO/LeMans 1968–73	5905	808 (1300, 1600)	Mazda 1971–84	6981
Vega 1971–77	GM Subcompact 1971–80	6935	810 1977–80	Datsun 200SX, etc. 1973–84	7170
Ventura 1974–79	Pontiac Mid-Size 1974–83	7346	900, 900 Turbo 1976–85	SAAB 900 1976–85	7572
Versailles 1978–80	Ford/Mercury Mid-Size 1971–83	6696	911, 914	Porsche 1969–73	5822
VIP 1969–74	Plymouth 1968–76	6552	924, 928	Porsce 924/928 1976–81	7048
Vista Cruiser 1970–72	Cutlass 1970–82	6933	1000 1981–84	Chevette/1000 1976–84	6836
Volare 1976–80	Aspen/Volare 1976–80	6637	1200 1500, 1600, 2000	Datsun 1961–72	5790
Voyager 1984	Caravan/Voyager 1984	7482	1200 1973	Datsun 1200, etc. 1973–84	7197
VW All models 1949–71	VW 1949–71	5796	1400, 1600, 1800 GL/DL/GF	Subaru 1970–84	6982
VW Types 1, 2, 3	VW 1970–81	6837			
Wagoneer 1962–84	Jeep Wagoneer, Commando, Cherokee, Truck 1962–84	6739	1500, 1600, 1600–2, 1800	BMW 1970–82	6844
			1800, 1800S	Volvo 1956–69	6529
XL 1968–75	Ford/Mercury/Lincoln 1968–83	6842	2000, 2002, 2002Ti, 2002Tii, 2500, 2800	BMW 1970–82	6844
XR-7 1977–83	Ford/Mercury Mid-Size 1971–83	6696			
Zephyr 1978–80	Fairmont/Zephyr 1978–83	6965	2000 1982	GM J-Car 1982	7059
Z-28 1967–81	Camaro 1967–81	6735	4000, 5000	Audi 4000/5000 1978–81	7028
			6000 1982–83	GM A-Body 1982–83	7309

Spanish Language Repair & Tune-Up Guides

Chevrolet/GMC Pick-ups 1970–82		Part No. 7468
Ford Pick-ups 1965–82		Part No. 7469
Toyota 1970–79		Part No. 7467
Chevrolet 1968–79		Part No. 7082
Datsun 1973–80		Part No. 7083
Ford 1968–79		Part No. 7084
Rabbit/Scirocco 1975–78		Part No. 7089
Volkswagen 1970–79		Part No. 7081

Chilton's Repair & Tune-Up Guides are available at your local retailer or by mailing a check or money order for **$12.50** plus **$2.25** to cover postage and handling to:

Chilton Book Company
Dept. DM
Radnor, PA 19089

NOTE: When ordering be sure to include your name & address, book part No. & title.